THE INTERNATIONAL POLITICS OF AGRICULTURAL TRADE

This book is the first major examination of Canadian-American agricultural trading relations from the perspective of international politics. Both Canada and the United States reap substantial benefits from agricultural trade across the border. But more important are the effects of their export promotion practices with third countries, including international pricing arrangements, surplus disposal measures, agricultural export credit, and export subsidies.

Relying extensively on primary documents and interviews, Theodore H. Cohn traces historical developments from the 1950s to the 1980s and assesses the relative importance of a number of variables in shaping the agricultural trade relations between the two states. Strictly bilateral issues such as trade barriers and the free trade agreement are discussed, but it is within the context of the international system that the significance of the interrelationship is most evident. Detailed case studies show the importance of relative economic size, interdependence, political/security objectives, the U.S. balance of payments, supply in the world market, and the weakness of the agricultural trade regime.

Cohn's conclusions point not only to increased conflict in the agricultural trade area but also to expanded efforts to negotiate solutions. As Canada and the United States found it increasingly difficult to achieve their trade objectives, they adopted a wider variety of strategies in pursuing them. The book shows that the controversial nature of the agricultural provisions in the Canada-U.S. Free Trade Agreement and difficulty in resolving issues at the Uruguay Round of GATT negotiations are the results of resistance to agricultural reform in the major trading nations and the complexity of the problems involved.

The International Politics of Agricultural Trade will be of interest to students of international politics and foreign policy, agricultural economics, and Canada-U.S. relations as well as to officials in government and international organizations.

THEODORE H. COHN is an associate professor of political science at Simon Fraser University. He has written extensively on global food and agricultural topics, Canadian food aid and trade policy, and World Bank and foreign debt issues.

CANADA AND INTERNATIONAL RELATIONS

The International Politics of Agricultural Trade: Canadian-American Relations in a Global Agricultural Context

Theodore H. Cohn

University of British Columbia Press

Vancouver 1990

ISBN 0-7748-0342-8
ISSN 0847-0510

∞

Printed on acid-free paper

Canadian Cataloguing in Publication Data

Cohn, Theodore H., 1940-
    The international politics of agricultural trade

    (Canada and international relations, ISSN 0847-0510; 3)
    Includes bibliographical references.
    ISBN 0-7748-0342-8

    1. Produce trade – Canada. 2. Canada – Foreign
economic relations – United States. 3. United States
– Foreign economic relations – Canada. I. Title.
II. Series.
HD9014.C22C64 1990   382′.41′0971   C89-091577-6

UBC Press
6344 Memorial Rd
Vancouver, B.C. V6T 1W5

HD
9014
C3
C634
1990

This book has been published with the help of a grant from the Social Science
Federation of Canada, using funds provided by the Social Sciences and Humanities
Research Council of Canada.

To my mother, Ethel Cohn Schatz,
and the memory of my father, Dr. Daniel E. Cohn

Contents

TABLES

Contents

Preface and Acknowledgments

This book results from my long-term interests in food aid, agricultural trade policy, and Canadian foreign policy. In my research and teaching, I have found that the voluminous literature on Canadian-American relations rarely mentions agricultural trade issues. On the other hand, most of the international relations literature on food and agriculture devotes little attention to U.S.-Canadian interactions. Agricultural economists have analysed American and Canadian policies in some detail, but their studies tend to be highly technical and less concerned with political factors.

There are many reasons why international relations scholars have devoted so little attention to Canadian-American agricultural trade relations, and they are outlined in the first chapter of this book. One of the most important reasons is that the United States and Canada send their principal food exports—grains and oilseeds—primarily to third countries. Most studies of U.S.-Canadian relations have focused on issues that can be examined in a more exclusively bilateral context, including foreign investment, energy, cultural sovereignty, and trade in manufactures. Nevertheless, when the linkages between Canadian-American relations and the international system are clearly recognized, the importance of agricultural trade issues becomes more evident. While this book discusses strictly bilateral issues such as Canada-U.S. trade barriers and the Canada-U.S. free trade agreement, the main emphasis is placed on third-country issues: surplus disposal, export subsidies, export credits, and international pricing.

My analytical framework relies on several approaches because no single theoretical approach seems adequate. References are made to Realist and Interdependence theories in international relations and to some of the literature in agricultural economics. More specifically, I examine a number of independent and dependent variables that are helpful in understanding Canadian-American agricultural trade relations.

The preparation of this book was funded in part by grants from the Donner Canadian Foundation for research projects at the University of British Columbia Institute of International Relations. I also received research support from the Dean of Arts Research Fund at Simon Fraser University.

I am especially grateful to those individuals who granted me access to a large number of documents which provided information on Canadian-American interactions in a variety of multilateral and bilateral organizations and groupings. In addition, interviews were conducted with individuals in the Canadian Departments of Agriculture, External Affairs, and (the now-absorbed) Industry, Trade and Commerce; in the Canadian International Development Agency; in the United States Department of Agriculture; and in the Food and Agriculture Organization's Consultative Subcommittee on Surplus Disposal. I am very grateful to all those individuals who provided their time and information.

I particularly want to thank Dr. Mark Zacher, director of the University of British Columbia Institute of International Relations, who read parts of the manuscript on several occasions and provided many helpful suggestions. Professor T. K. Warley at the University of Guelph sent me insightful papers that he wrote on agricultural trade issues, and these were useful in developing my ideas. I also wish to thank Inge Bailey, a knowledgeable researcher who provided assistance with certain aspects of the book and with whom I had many discussions. In addition, the comments of readers for the Social Science Federation of Canada and the University of British Columbia Press were extremely helpful in revising the manuscript. In 1985 some of my ideas were formulated when I was an adviser and participant at a conference on "Canadian Agriculture in a Global Context" at the University of Waterloo. Thanks are due to the conference organizers, Irene Sage Knell and Professor John English, and to Professors Andrew Cooper and Toivo Miljan (Wilfrid Laurier University). I also benefited from suggestions of a colleague in the Simon Fraser University Political Science Department, Professor Maureen Covell. My wife Shirley provided assistance with the footnotes and bibliography. Most importantly, she was an invaluable source of support and encouragement, and my children Daniel and Frank learned the real meaning of patience.

The International Politics
of Agricultural Trade

1

Introduction

A Special Joint Committee of the Canadian Senate and House of Commons was established in June 1985 to make recommendations "concerning the objectives and conduct of Canada's international relations." In its final report, the committee noted that "the dominant fact of Canada's international relations" is how it "relates to the United States."[1] This preoccupation with the United States is reflected in the many studies on U.S.-Canadian ties, but surprisingly little attention has been given to interactions between the two countries in the agricultural trade area. Agricultural economists have analysed American and Canadian trade policies in some detail, but they are usually less concerned with political factors.[2] As a result, the issue of Canadian-American agricultural trade relations has not been systematically examined through the broader lens of the international relations specialist.[3] A major reason for this lack of attention is that both states send their principal food exports (grains and oilseeds) primarily to third countries. Most studies of U.S.-Canadian relations focus on issues that can be examined in a more exclusively bilateral context, such as foreign investment, energy, cultural sovereignty, and trade in manufactures.

In recent years, some specialists have recognized that a serious shortcoming "of contemporary foreign policy analysis is its frequent depiction of Canada and the United States as a dyad, a pair separable and separated from the rest of the international system."[4] These authors have devoted more attention to third-country issues, but they generally have not focused on agricultural trade.[5] This book is designed to remedy these deficiencies by examining Canadian-U.S. agricultural trade relations from the perspective of international politics. Third-country issues involving surplus disposal, export credits, export subsidies, and pricing policies are given the most emphasis; but strictly bilateral

3

issues are also discussed. While agricultural trade across the U.S.-Canadian border is often rather routine and problem-free, bilateral disputes do arise, and they are sometimes quite serious. For example, Canada repeatedly protested against U.S. agricultural import quotas in the 1950s and 1960s, and the two countries had bitter conflicts over beef, pork, and corn trade in the 1970s and 1980s. Agriculture was also one of the most difficult issues confronting negotiators of the Canada-U.S. free trade agreement, which was signed by President Ronald Reagan and Prime Minister Brian Mulroney in January 1988.

This book focuses primarily on wheat because it is an important U.S. and Canadian export and a principal commodity in international trade. North American surplus problems have often centred on wheat and, consequently, so have export credits, export subsidies, concessional sales, and other surplus disposal efforts. The two states have also regularly held discussions and co-ordinated their policies on wheat issues. However, Chapter 7 deals with U.S.-Canadian bilateral trade barriers, and concentrates on a number of commodities traded across the common border.

In this introductory chapter, I discuss the importance of Canadian-American agricultural trade relations and the reasons why the issue has been neglected by international relation scholars. Some essential background on the basic characteristics of U.S.-Canadian relations in agriculture is also provided. The final part of the chapter focuses on the purposes and organization of the study.

THE IMPORTANCE OF CANADIAN-U.S. AGRICULTURAL TRADE RELATIONS

The importance of Canadian-American agricultural trade relations stems from a variety of factors, including *the centrality of North America in the global food regime; the interdependent nature of food and agricultural issues; the interdependence of the United States and Canada in this area; and the dependence of both countries on agricultural exports*.

A major reason for studying U.S.-Canadian agricultural trade relations is that *North America has a central role in the global food regime*. In this study, I use the term "North America" to refer to the United States and Canada, even though Mexico is also a North American state.[6] International regimes can be defined as "sets of implicit or explicit principles, norms, rules, and decision-making procedures around which actors' expectations converge in a given area of international relations."[7] There is disagreement about whether or not global food issues constitute a regime, particularly since the principles and rules for regulating agricultural trade are so inadequate. For example, the authors of one book opted for a regional approach to food politics, warning that "the analyst can fall into the trap of discussing a 'world food regime' that has yet to materialize."[8] However, a number of writers have examined the international relations of food as a regime, and I use the regime terminology in this book.[9]

North American centrality is mainly the result of the role of the United States, which is a far more important actor than Canada in agricultural markets. Although Canada is the world's second largest country in area, only 8 per cent of its land is suitable for crops and another 3 per cent for rough grazing; in contrast, 29 per cent of U.S. land is suitable for crops and a further 20 per cent for pasture and rangeland. The United States has the second largest amount of arable land in the world and the third largest amount of total agricultural land (including grazing land), while Canada ranks only sixth in arable land acreage and twelfth in total agricultural acreage. Both countries are more important as traders than producers of many agricultural commodities. For example, in 1984–85 the United States produced only 13.7 per cent of the world's wheat and 29.3 per cent of the world's coarse grain; but it accounted for 36.6 per cent of global wheat exports and for 55.5 per cent of coarse grain exports. Canada produced only 4.1 per cent of the world's wheat and 5.9 per cent of the world's barley; but it accounted for 16.8 per cent of global wheat exports and for 15.3 per cent of barley exports.[10]

Table 1.1 shows that the United States is the world's largest food exporter but that its share of total exports declined from 19.2 per cent in 1973 to 11.4 per cent in 1986. Canada was the fifth largest food exporter in 1973 and the sixth largest in 1986, with its share falling from 4.2 to 3.4 per cent. Most of the top ten food exporters in 1986 were also the largest importers, except for two leading exporters (Brazil and Denmark) and two major importers (Japan and the Soviet Union). The United States was the largest single food importer in some years and the second largest in others, with its share of global imports rising slightly from about 11 to 12 per cent between 1973 and 1985. Canada was the tenth largest food importer in both 1973 and 1985, but its share declined from 2.5 to 2 per cent.[11]

The United States ranks well above Canada as a food trader not only because of its greater productive capacity but also because of its greater overall balance of crops. Wheat is the only major-traded agricultural commodity in which Canada has a large share of world trade, and it clearly dominates the country's crop production. Canada is a significant exporter of barley and canola (an improved form of rapeseed) as well as wheat, but its share of production and trade in all grains and all fats and oils is relatively small. In contrast, American exports of corn and soybeans as well as wheat can have a significant impact on international markets for grains and oilseeds.[12] The greater importance of U.S. coarse grain and oilseed exports is evident from the figures in Table 1-2.

TABLE I–I

THE TEN LEADING FOOD EXPORTERS:

PERCENTAGE OF WORLD FOOD EXPORTS

(by dollar value)

	1973	1979	1985	1986
U.S.	19.2	16.9	13.9	11.4
France	7.9	7.5	8.0	8.6
Netherlands	6.5	6.8	6.6	7.3
F. R. Germany	3.5	4.4	4.8	5.5
Britain	2.5	3.3	3.4	3.7
Canada	4.2	3.2	4.0	3.4
Brazil	4.4	3.7	4.6	3.3
Belg.-Lux.	2.5	2.7	2.8	3.1
Italy	2.2	2.9	3.0	2.9
Australia	3.5	3.2	2.7	na*

*Not applicable. In 1986, Denmark replaced Australia as the tenth largest food exporter (with 2.8 per cent of exports).
Source: Derived from GATT, International Trade 1985-86 (Geneva, 1986), p. 38; GATT, International Trade 1986-87 (Geneva, 1987), p. 32.

TABLE I–2

U.S. AND CANADIAN CROP EXPORTS, 1986–87

(million tonnes)*

Commodity	United States	Canada
Wheat	27.3	20.8
Corn	38.2	0.1
Barley	3.0	6.7
Major oilseed	20.7	2.0

*Tonnes are metric tons.
Source: Mary Anne Normile and Carol A. Goodloe, U.S.-Canadian Agricultural Trade Issues: Implications for the Bilateral Trade Agreement (Washington, D.C.: U.S. Department of Agriculture, Economic Research, Agriculture and Trade Analysis Division, March 1988), p. 5.

Although Canada is not a major actor in the global food regime, it does contribute to North America's centrality in some respects. With a population of only about twenty-five million, Canada's agricultural production greatly exceeds its domestic requirements. As a result, in most years Canada has been the second largest single food aid donor and the second largest wheat exporter after the United States (see Table 1-3). It is no accident that Canadians have held prominent positions in international food organizations. For example, a Canadian wheat board commissioner became executive director of the World Food Program from 1977 to 1981; a Canadian agriculture minister became president of the World Food Council from 1983 to 1985; a Department of External Affairs official was elected as chairman of the International Wheat Council for 1985-86; a senior assistant deputy agriculture minister became executive director of the World Food Council in 1986; and a Canadian farm leader was elected president of the International Federation of Agricultural Producers in 1986.[13]

TABLE 1-3

PERCENTAGES OF GLOBAL WHEAT AND WHEAT FLOUR EXPORTS

| | Crop Years | | | | | |
	1960–61	1970–71	1975–76	1980–81	1985–86	1986–87*
U.S.	42.0	36.7	47.4	45.0	29.6	33.2
Canada	22.0	21.5	18.4	17.5	20.9	24.3
Australia	11.7	17.3	12.1	11.9	19.0	17.5
EC**	6.0	5.7	11.6	13.6	17.1	17.8
Argentina	4.6	3.1	4.6	4.2	7.3	5.1

*Preliminary **Data are for ten member states
Source: Canadian Wheat Board, Annual Reports (Winnipeg).

In view of the centrality of North America in the global food regime, U.S.-Canadian agricultural trade relations sometimes have a significant effect on the regime; and regime changes can in turn affect the bilateral relationship. For example, wheat prices consistently fell within the ranges established by the international wheat agreements from 1949 to 1967, largely because the United States and Canada maintained substantial reserves and met quarterly to agree on price levels. Australia and Argentina sometimes participated in the Canada-U.S. discussions, and the system functioned effectively because these four countries accounted for a predominant share of global wheat exports.[14] However, in the 1980s the predominance of North America was eroded while the European Community emerged as a formidable competitor, and co-operation among the major wheat exporters seriously declined. Canada (along with other smaller countries) watched rather helplessly as the U.S. and the EC became embroiled in an export subsidy war. Nevertheless, as the only country in both the Cairns Group of "fair traders" and the Group of Seven, Canada raised the issue of agricultural subsidies with the other six Western industrial states at the Venice Summit in June 1987.[15] With the current instability in international agricultural trading arrangements, pressures for change in Canadian-American relations are inevitable. In any case, there are close linkages between changes in U.S.-Canadian agricultural trade relations and alterations in the global food regime.

A second reason for studying U.S.-Canadian agricultural trade relations is that *food and agriculture are interdependence issues*. By interdependence, we mean "mutual dependence," in which "there are reciprocal (although not necessarily symmetrical) costly effects of transactions." Interdependence involves both "sensitivity" or mutual effects and "vulnerability" or the opportunity costs of altering a relationship; the greater the costs of disrupting a relationship, the greater is the vulnerability of a state.[16] The interdependent nature of food and agricultural matters is particularly evident during periods of worldwide food shortages. For example, before the end of World War II, President Franklin D. Roosevelt invited all United and Associated Nations to attend a conference at Hot Springs, Virginia, to discuss the possibilities of increasing world food supplies. One outcome of this conference was the establishment of the Food and Agriculture Organization (FAO) at a meeting in Quebec City in 1945. It is significant that the FAO was the first of the United Nations specialized agencies to be established.[17]

International relations scholars have often discussed food and agriculture in studies on interdependence.[18] Indeed, James Rosenau identified four "central features" of interdependence issues, and in each case he cited examples in the food and agricultural areas:[19]

(1) Interdependence issues involve highly complex and technical phenomena. (To increase food production, one must "acquire mastery over physical and biological processes that involve an extraordinary range of subprocesses.")

(2) Interdependence issues tend to encompass a great number of nongovernmental actors who are important to issue management. ("The actions of innumerable farmers . . . are central to the problem of increased food production.")

(3) Interdependence issues are considered through a highly fragmented decision-making process. Governmental agencies responsible for the relevant clientele have an unusual amount of authority and influence. ("In the American case . . . bureaus within the Agriculture Department tend to monopolize decision making on questions pertaining to the production and distribution of various foodstuffs.")

(4) Multilateral co-operation is essential for the management of interdepen-

dence issues. (Many of these issues "spring from conflicts over . . . the natural environment . . . the land (e.g., food productivity) . . . which do not conform to political boundaries and which most governments can thus neither dismiss nor handle on their own.").

A related characteristic of interdependence issues is that they are "intermestic," since they "involve both international and domestic aspects."[20] Nevertheless, governments have often been unwilling to recognize the interdependent nature of agricultural issues and to expose their domestic policies in this area to strong international influence. This attitude stems from the special characteristics of agriculture, including the unpredictable fluctuations in supply and demand; the chronic problem of food surpluses in relation to effective demand; the threat of serious social problems resulting from structural change in rural areas; the political influence of farmer, agribusiness, and other rural groups; and the importance countries attach to food self-sufficiency.[21]

There have been inexorable pressures on governments, however, to acknowledge the fact that food and agriculture are interdependence issues. During the 1970s agricultural trade expanded at the unprecedented rate of about 15 per cent annually, and almost all exporting countries shared in this growth. American agricultural exports had increased by about $415 million per year (in 1983 dollars) from 1940 to 1972, but from 1973 to 1981 they rose at about four times that rate. Domestic pressure on food markets also grew in the 1970s, and it became essential that the United States co-ordinate its domestic and international policies. For example, the U.S. imposed export restrictions on soybeans in 1973 and on grain to the USSR and Poland in 1975 to stem a rise in domestic prices. However, these decisions were highly controversial because of the growing U.S. dependence on agricultural exports and the fear that the country's reputation as a reliable supplier would suffer. The importance of international considerations became even more apparent when American agricultural exports drastically declined after 1981 because of the global recession, the relative strength of the U.S. dollar, and the competitive practices of other exporters.[22]

Foreign policy considerations also gained prominence because of the declining power of U.S. farm groups in relation to groups representing international interests. The number of American farmers steadily decreased from about 26 per cent of the population in 1933 to 3.6 per cent in 1978, and there were growing divisions within the farm community. It was therefore inevitable that the U.S. Department of Agriculture (USDA) "would have to share food policymaking to a greater extent, and that power would shift to some degree to economic and foreign policy institutions."[23] However, farm groups continue to affect policies in the United States, Canada, the EC, and Japan, and these countries are still reluctant to subject their domestic agricultural policies to international negotiation. A former U.S. Department of Agriculture official noted with irony that it could be "political suicide" for such countries to open their food policies to outside negotiation but that "it is the domestic agricultural policies of these trading partners that are the root cause of the agricultural trade problems that threaten to erupt into a major trade war."[24]

The interdependent nature of food and agricultural issues and the blurring of the distinction between foreign and domestic food issues have inevitably affected Canadian-American relations. Agriculture is included to a limited extent in their free trade agreement, and the two countries are jointly insisting that the GATT enlarge its jurisdiction over agriculture at the Uruguay Round. However, there have also been Canadian-U.S. differences over which issues are strictly domestic and which are subject to international negotiation. For example, many Canadians argue that their farm marketing boards and agricultural stabilization programs are domestic matters, but many Americans disagree. On the other hand, Canadians often reject the American view that U.S. price supports and irrigation subsidies are strictly domestic concerns.

A third, and closely related, reason for examining U.S.-Canadian agricultural trade relations is that *the two countries are highly interdependent in this area*. Robert Keohane and Joseph Nye found that "a third of the postwar Canadian-American agenda . . . involved relationships with third countries," and the two countries' interdependence in the agricultural trade area is significantly based on third-country issues.[25] This interdependence is highly asymmetrical, with Canada far more vulnerable to American export promotion activities in third-country markets than the U.S. is to Canadian activities.

Interdependence also stems from agricultural trade across the Canadian-American border, but the significance of this trade is often underestimated because of the types of commodities exchanged. For example, in 1986 about 28 per cent of Canada's agricultural exports to the United States (by value) were red meats and live animals, while 41 per cent of U.S. sales to Canada were fruits and vegetables. Commodities of this nature have a lower profile than grains and oilseeds, which account for about 75 per cent of Canadian and 65 per cent of American farm exports. Wheat and wheat flour alone accounted for 43.5 per cent of Canadian agricultural exports in 1985, and about one-half of this wheat was sent to the Soviet Union and China.[26]

However, Canadian-U.S. interdependence is evident when trade in *all* agricultural commodities is considered. The United States has been the largest supplier of Canadian farm imports every year in the postwar period. In addition, the U.S. was the largest single country market for Canadian exports in 1950–52, 1968–73, and 1983–87. Table 1–4 shows that the United States accounted for 32.1 per cent of Canada's agricultural exports and for 57.5 per cent of its imports in 1987. Table 1–5 shows that the interdependence is highly asymmetrical since Canada ranked fourth among U.S. markets after the European Community (EC), Japan, and the Republic of Korea in 1987, and took only 6.3 per cent of U.S. agricultural exports. However, Canada's importance as a U.S. agricultural market is more evident if the EC countries are considered individually. In 1987, the Netherlands was the only EC member that imported more U.S. agricultural products than Canada. Table 1–5 also shows that Canada ranked second in farm exports to the United States in 1987, supplying 10.9 per cent of the total. If the EC countries are viewed individually, Canada was the largest single country agricultural exporter to the United States in 1987.

TABLE 1–4

CANADA'S MAJOR AGRICULTURAL TRADING PARTNERS, 1987

Major Importers	Per cent	Major Exporters	Per cent
United States	32.1	United States	57.5
Japan	12.7	EC-12*	11.4
EC-12*	10.1	Australia	3.6
China	8.3	Brazil	3.6
USSR	7.9	New Zealand	2.5

*Includes Greece, Spain, and Portugal
Source: D. L. Aubé, *Canada's Trade in Agricultural Products 1985, 1986 and 1987* (Ottawa: Agriculture Canada 1988), pp. 28-29.

TABLE 1–5

UNITED STATES' MAJOR AGRICULTURAL TRADING PARTNERS, 1987

Major Importers	Per cent	Major Exporters	Per cent
EC-12	23.9	EC-12	20.4
Japan	19.9	Canada	10.9
Rep. of Korea	6.4	Mexico	9.2
Canada	6.3	Brazil	9.0
Taiwan	4.5	Australia	4.9

Source: USDA, Economic Research Service, *Foreign Agricultural Trade of the United States (FATUS), Calendar Year 1987 Supplement*, pp. 24-27, 256-58.

Although the volume of U.S.-Canadian agricultural trade is substantial, it comprises only a small percentage of their total bilateral trade. Table 1–6 shows that farm products constitute a far more important part of trade with other countries. Only 3.2 per cent of American exports to Canada in 1987 were agricultural, compared with 11.8 per cent for the European Community, 20.8 per cent for Japan, 8.5 per cent for Mexico, and 23.2 per cent for South Korea. On the other hand, only 3.1 per cent of Canadian exports to the United States were agricultural, compared with 9.9 per cent for the EC, 16.0 per cent for Japan, 88.5 per cent for the USSR, and 51.8 per cent for China. However, the agricultural percentage is smaller in the Canada-U.S. case partly because of the large volume of total trade between the two states. Indeed, they have the largest trading relationship of any two countries in the world.

TABLE 1–6

U.S. AND CANADIAN AGRICULTURAL EXPORTS AS A PERCENTAGE OF TOTAL
EXPORTS TO MAJOR MARKETS, 1987

Major U.S. Markets	Ag. Exports (per cent)	Major Cdn. Markets	Ag. Exports (per cent)
EC-12	11.8	U.S.	3.1
Canada	3.2	EC-12	9.9
Japan	20.8	Japan	16.0
Mexico	8.5	USSR	88.5
Rep. of Korea	23.2	China	51.8
All countries	11.7	all countries	7.3

Source: FATUS, 1987 Supplement, pp. 24-27; Canada's Trade in Agricultural Products 1985, 86 and 87, pp. 65-66.

The macro-statistics also do not reveal the degree to which Canada and the United States depend on each other for trade in particular commodities. About 81 per cent of Canada's live animal and red meat exports are shipped to the U.S., while 77 per cent of Canada's fresh vegetable imports and 55 per cent of its fresh fruit imports come from the United States. On the other hand, 75 per cent of American fresh vegetable and 30 per cent of fresh fruit exports are shipped to Canada; and Canada supplies 60 per cent of U.S. cattle imports, 90 per cent of its oilcake and meal imports, 70 per cent of its fresh pork imports, and almost all of its swine imports. Since Canada and the United States export some agricultural products almost exclusively to each other, this trade helps to maintain the vitality of particular geographic regions and farm commodity groups. Thus, a 1979 report prepared for the U.S. Senate Finance Committee noted that "among the developed nations of the world, Canada occupies a unique position in the U.S. agricultural trade picture."[27]

Despite the importance of cross-border agricultural trade, it is often considered to be routine and problem-free. Much of this trade results from geographic factors since it is sometimes more economically efficient to move commodities across the long border than within each nation. There is also a division of labour based on comparative advantage, such as the U.S. climatic advantages in fruit and vegetable exports. Fluctuations in trade result from cyclical factors and other variables such as climatic and health conditions. For example, Canada's oilseed exports increased in 1983 because of severe drought conditions in the United States, and U.S. corn exports rose in 1984 because of reduced Canadian supplies. Although bilateral trade is often routine, the intensity of recent disputes indicates that this is certainly not always the case. Agricultural producers in both countries are experiencing severe economic problems, and there have been growing political pressures for protectionism. Tensions have also increased over third-country issues, such as U.S. export subsidies, which pose a threat to Canadian exports.

While competition and conflict have increased, so has the search for co-operative solutions. Thus, the two governments decided to include agriculture in their bilateral free trade agreement, and agriculture is a major agenda item at the Uruguay Round of GATT negotiations. There are formidable obstacles to progress, but these efforts will no doubt continue for it is an indisputable fact that there is a considerable amount of U.S.-Canadian and global interdependence in agricultural trade.

A fourth reason for studying U.S.-Canadian agricultural trade relations is that *agricultural exports are very important to the economies of both countries*. American and Canadian officials generally give priority to manufactured and high-technology exports and devote less attention to agricultural trade since it is largely based on raw and semi-processed products. Indeed, in 1981 67.9 per cent of U.S. agricultural exports were unprocessed, 21.7 per cent were semi-processed, and only 10.4 per cent were fully processed; and the value-added component is considerably less for Canadian exports.[28] Agricultural exports also receive less attention because they account for a declining share of total exports. Between 1955 and 1987, Canada's agricultural exports as a share of the total fell from 18.7 to 7.3 per cent, while the U.S. agricultural percentage decreased from 20.7 to 11.3 per cent.

However, if agriculture is viewed in a wider context, its importance to the American and Canadian economies becomes more evident. Farm exports help to maintain vitality and employment in the various phases of each country's food system from the purchasing of agricultural inputs such as machinery and fertilizer to the production, processing, and distribution of foodstuffs. By 1980 only about 3.4 and 4.6 per cent of the American and Canadian labour forces were involved in the production of agricultural commodities; but approximately 25 per cent were employed in their respective food systems.[29] Agricultural trade also has broader effects on the national economies of both countries, and in 1980 a U.S. presidental advisory committee concluded that "every dollar that is returned to the farm sector from exports has more than doubled in the economy."[30] In more specific terms, agricultural exports are vital as an outlet for the production of particular commodities. From 30 to 35 per cent of Canada's national agricultural output is exported, including about 77 per cent of its wheat, 59 per cent of its canola (rapeseed), and 36 per cent of its barley. American agricultural exports increased from 13 per cent of total farm income in the 1960s to well over 25 per cent in the 1980s, and the U.S. usually exports about 60 per cent of its wheat and rice, 50 per cent of its cotton and soybeans, and 40 per cent of its coarse grains.

Furthermore, both countries have benefited from positive agricultural trade balances. Canada's agricultural balance from 1957 to 1987 was positive every year except one (1969), and it exceeded $4 billion annually from 1982 to 1984. Its non-agricultural balance by contrast was negative in fifteen years, and its total trade balance was negative in nine. The American agricultural trade balance from 1957 to 1987 was negative in only two years (1958–59), while its non-agricultural balance was negative in eighteen years, and its total trade balance was negative in fifteen. Farm exports helped to decrease the overall U.S. trade deficit in the 1970s, and as this deficit climbed in the 1980s, agriculture was one of the few areas where the U.S. balance continued to be positive. Tables 1–7 and 1–8 demonstrate the contribution of agriculture to the trade balances of the two countries.

TABLE 1–7

U.S. AGRICULTURAL, NON-AGRICULTURAL, AND TOTAL TRADE BALANCES

1983-1987

(U.S.$ billion)

Trade Balance	1983	1984	1985	1986	1987
Agricultural	+18.0	+16.2	+7.0	+3.1	+6.0
Non-Agricultural	−82.2	−138.6	−140.1	−159.2	−177.2
Total	−64.2	−122.4	−133.1	−156.1	−171.2

Source: USDA, FATUS, Calendar Year 1987 Supplement, p. 4.

TABLE 1–8

CANADIAN AGRICULTURAL, NON-AGRICULTURAL, AND TOTAL TRADE
BALANCES 1983-1987
(Cdn$ billion)

Trade Balance	1983	1984	1985	1986	1987
Agricultural	+4.3	+4.2	+2.9	+1.8	+2.1
Non-Agricultural	+8.6	+9.5	+8.3	+2.1	+3.3
Total	+12.9	+13.7	+11.2	+3.9	+5.4

Source: Agriculture Canada, Canada's Trade in Agricultural Products, 1983 to 1987 issues.

Despite the positive contribution of agriculture, both the United States and Canada have felt the effects of declining markets in recent years. Tables 1–7 and 1–8 show that the U.S. agricultural balance fell from +18.0 billion in 1983 to +6.0 billion in 1987, and the Canadian agricultural balance declined from +4.3 billion dollars in 1983 to +2.1 billion in 1987. It is one of the ironies of the global food system that surplus production is a chronic problem in North America and Western Europe, while many less-developed countries (LDCs) suffer from food shortages. LDCs were seriously affected by the world economic recession that began in the early 1980s, and massive debts, high interest rates, and currency depreciation placed severe constraints on their ability to pay for food imports.

The decline in export markets also resulted from dramatic production increases in the EC, China, and India, which account for almost half of the world's population. High EC price supports and export subsidies encourage surplus production, and the EC increased its share of the world wheat market from less than 8 per cent in the early 1970s to over 16 per cent in 1984–85. The United States suffered greater market losses than Canada in the early to mid-1980s, largely because of the strength of the American dollar. From 1982–83 to 1985–86, the U.S. share of global wheat exports fell from 41.4 to 28.9 per cent, while the Canadian share declined only slightly, from 20.9 to 19.7 per cent. The two countries have also felt the effects of wide price fluctuations in recent years. In summary, agricultural exports are of critical importance to both the United States and Canada.

Agricultural trade is thus certainly a central issue in Canadian-American relations. Both countries reap substantial benefits from food exports, and food and agriculture are interdependence issues. Agricultural trade across the U.S.-Canadian border is substantial, and it is affected by competing pressures for protectionism and free trade. Most importantly, the United States and Canada are often affected by each other's export promotion practices with third countries. The significance of Canadian-American agricultural trade relations is therefore obvious when their interactions are viewed within the context of the international system.

PURPOSES AND ORGANIZATION OF THE STUDY

This book examines Canadian-U.S. agricultural trade issues with a view to expanding our knowledge of the bilateral relationship. Since bilateral relations in this area are largely based on third-country issues, considerable attention is also given to the global food and agricultural system. No single theoretical approach is adequate by itself, and my analytical framework therefore relies upon several approaches. References will be made to Realist and Interdependence theorists in international relations and to some of the literature in agricultural economics. More specifically, I focus on four dependent variables which are also aspects of U.S.-Canadian relations: *the level of conflict in the bilateral relationship*; *the amount of co-operation in the bilateral relationship*; *the choice of strategies to achieve agricultural trade objectives*; *and the ability of each country to achieve its agricultural trade objectives*. These dependent variables are affected by the independent variables in Table 1–9. Interactions among the independent variables and among the dependent variables are also of interest.

A striking characteristic of the first two dependent variables, *conflict and co-operation*, is their tendency to co-exist in international relations:[31]

> Just as conflict is characteristic of international relations, so too is collaboration. Indeed, these two forms of interaction—conflict and cooperation, strife and harmony, war and peace—do not occur in isolation from one another, but are intimately related. . . . Allies who join together to pursue shared objectives often disagree, sometimes quite strenuously, over appropriate strategies, a fair division of labor, and an equitable sharing of burdens.

The co-existence of conflict and co-operation is particularly evident in issue areas and relationships (such as agricultural issues and Canadian-American relations) that are highly interdependent. Thus, Raymond Hopkins and Donald Puchala offered the following comments in response to an article by Helge Ole Bergesen on interdependence in the global food regime:[32]

> Underlying much of our analysis is an assumption about the effects of

interdependence—namely, that significant interdependence, especially when accompanied by disrupting events, forces government and corporate elites to deal with problems arising from such worldwide interconnections. The greater the interdependence, the greater the compulsion for elites to take action. Such action can be defensive or conflictual, as well as collaborative or cooperative.... In the current global food regime, and particularly over the last decade . . . *Bergesen is correct to observe an increase in conflict. We are equally correct to note in the same period an increase in collaboration and in cooperation.* (emphasis added)

Conflict and co-operation also co-exist in Canadian-American relations because of the asymmetrical nature of their interdependence, with Canada often having ambivalent attitudes towards its much larger neighbour. There are numerous examples of this ambivalence in the agricultural trade area: in the Cairns Group Canada joined with fellow members in criticizing U.S. and European Community policies, while in other fora Canada strongly endorsed American statements that singled out the EC for special criticism; Canada often expressed disapproval of the American Export Enhancement Program and yet lavishly praised the U.S. proposal to GATT for an end to trade-distorting agricultural subsidies; and the various regions and political parties in Canada were rent by divisions on the bilateral free trade agreement.

In this book, I hypothesize that during periods of conflict the United States and Canada often seek new means of consultation and co-operation to resolve their differences. Conflict regarding agricultural trade is included as an independent variable (as well as a dependent variable) in Table 1–9 because of this linkage between heightened conflict and subsequent efforts to upgrade co-operative efforts. The linkage between the two variables helps to explain Hopkins and Puchala's reference to the increase in *both* conflict and co-operation in the global food regime.[33]

A significant interstate conflict is deemed to exist in this study when there is

an interstate request that cannot be easily or costlessly complied with by the recipient government. The request need not take a particular diplomatic form, but there must be communication of a mutually understood preference for (or against) a particular course of action.[34]

Canadian-American co-operation exists when the two countries work together towards a common end or purpose, which can include a resolution of their differences. The expression of common views on contentious issues involving third parties is often an important indication of co-operation.

The third and fourth dependent variables are both concerned with agricultural trade objectives. Of particular interest here are four objectives that are directly related to agricultural trade: to restore, maintain, or increase market share; to export products at remunerative prices; to maintain or achieve a more favourable agricultural trade balance; and to limit imports of "supplementary" agricultural products. The first two of these objectives are concerned with export promotion; the fourth objective relates to import barriers, and the third objective may involve both the promotion of exports and import barriers. The objective of limiting imports commonly applies to "supplementary" agricultural commodities. These are "similar to or the same as commodities produced commercially in the importing country," and they compete directly with the importing country's products.[35] However, a state may also have a more generalized goal of limiting all agricultural imports to maintain or improve its agricultural trade balance. The United States and Canada may attach different priorities to the various agricultural trade objectives, and each country's priorities may change over time. There are also differences in the agricultural trade objectives of various producer groups within each country, and this issue is discussed in Chapter 7.

In addition to the four objectives mentioned above, the United States and to a lesser extent Canada sometimes adopt policies that limit their agricultural exports. However, export limitations are imposed in relation to specific countries and/or products, and the *overriding* agricultural export objectives of both the U.S. and Canada continue to involve the *promotion* of their exports (in terms of market share and price). For example, on various occasions the United States refused to export to certain Communist countries for political-security reasons. However, the U.S. sought to compensate for this policy (or to recoup its losses) by exporting elsewhere. Since "political-security objectives" can affect Canadian-American agricultural trade relations, they are included as an independent variable in Table 1-9. In June 1973, the United States imposed a temporary embargo on soybean exports to control rapidly increasing domestic prices and a threatened shortage of the commodity. This embargo was not imposed as "a deliberate Washington attempt to employ the food weapon for foreign policy reasons," but it was an extremely rare occurrence.[36] Indeed, I. M. Destler notes that "this was, according to press reports, the first time the U.S. had imposed such an embargo except in war or threat of war."[37] In retrospect, it seemed that the embargo was unnecessary, and it had an extremely adverse effect on the U.S. reputation as a reliable supplier of farm products. Since events such as the U.S. soybean embargo and the Canadian controls on red meat exports (see Chapter 7) have been so rare, they have had little effect on U.S.-

Canadian relations. The agricultural export objectives of interest in this study therefore relate to the two countries' promotion of their exports.

TABLE 1–9

INDEPENDENT VARIABLES AFFECTING U.S.-CANADIAN AGRICULTURAL
TRADE RELATIONS

Environmental Variables
U.S. balance of payments
Political/security objectives
Relative economic size
Interdependence between the two states

Agricultural-Specific Variables
Supply in world market
Relative size of the two countries' agricultural economies
Conflict regarding agricultural trade
Competition in agricultural trade
Strength of the agricultural trade regime/

With regard to imports, countries often import commodities to meet requirements that cannot be fulfilled with domestic production. While this is an additional agricultural trade objective, it rarely becomes an "issue" in Canadian-American relations. Both the United States and Canada are normally more than willing to meet each other's agricultural import requirements. But agricultural imports often become a contentious issue when the two countries impose import limitations, and these are the import objectives that are of interest in this study.

The third dependent variable is *the choice of strategies to achieve agricultural trade objectives*. The United States and Canada may resort to unilateral, bilateral, plurilateral, and/or multilateral strategies on particular issues. A plurilateral approach involves more countries than a bilateral approach, but fewer countries than a multilateral approach. Countries pursue a multilateral strategy by acting through "universal-membership" international organizations. These organizations do not limit their membership according to geographical areas, cultural groups, or economic/political criteria. As discussed in Chapter 3, the GATT and the Food and Agricultural Organization are "universal-membership" international organizations that deal with agricultural trade. Examples of a plurilateral strategy would include the attempt to promote co-operation among the major wheat exporters or within limited-membership organizations such as the Organization of Economic Co-operation and Development.[38]

Of particular interest in this study is the relative propensity of the United States and Canada to adopt unilateral strategies and the tendency of the other country to respond by requesting redress or a change in policy. I will test Keohane and Nye's finding that the smaller country (Canada)

> made the first request most frequently on socio-economic issues. These were precisely the issues on which the United States most often took the first governmental action. Thus the typical conflict pattern on these issues was for the United States (frequently the Congress) to take a unilateral, often "domestic" action to which the smaller partners tended to respond by demanding redress through diplomatic channels.[39]

The United States and Canada both often opt for multilateral or plurilateral over bilateral strategies because of the asymmetry in their relationship. As the smaller country, Canada may prefer strategies where it can ally with others and/or express its grievances against the U.S. in a group setting. As the larger country, the United States may prefer strategies that are globally rather than regionally oriented. However, there are particular circumstances under which both countries opt for bilateralism.

The fourth dependent variable is *the ability of each country to attain its agricultural trade objectives*. A particular problem for both countries is the fact that the four objectives mentioned above are not always compatible. For example, in 1985 the United States enacted its Export Enhancement Program to regain what it viewed as its fair market share for grain exports. This program contributed to a general lowering of prices and thus made it more difficult (for both Canada and the United States) to achieve the second agricultural export objective. Furthermore, each country sometimes imposes import barriers to limit competition and/or improve its trade balance. Such actions often lead to retaliation by the other side, and therefore they can interfere with both countries' agricultural export objectives.

Since the United States and Canada have both competitive and co-operative interests in promoting grain exports, each country's success in exporting sometimes depends on its ability to gain acceptance of its preferred policies in bargaining. This situation is especially true for the smaller country (Canada) in its negotiations with the larger (the U.S.). Chapters 4 to 7 of this book refer to some interstate conflicts where the United States and/or Canada expressed a "preference for or against a particular course of action."[40] I examine the conditions under which each country was able to further its export objectives by gaining acceptance of its preferred policies.

Table 1–9 shows that the independent variables in this study consist of four environmental and five agricultural-specific variables.[41] The first environmental variable, the *U.S. balance of payments*, "registers the changes in the country's financial claims and obligations vis-à-vis all other countries," usually over a year-long period. It is a measure of a country's "ability to earn enough for the goods and services it needs, and thus pay its way in the world."[42] The balance of payments consists of two types of transactions, the current account and the capital account. The capital account includes such items as direct investment and long and short-term capital flows. The current account includes the exports and imports of merchandise (the balance of trade) and of invisible services such as transportation, tourism, and interest and dividend payments. Of particular relevance to this study are the overall balance of payments and the balance of trade.

In the late 1940s, the United States had huge balance of trade surpluses and immense reserves that were continuing to grow. As a result, it deliberately ran a balance of payments deficit from 1947–58 that provided liquidity for the international economy. The U.S. continued to export more goods than it imported, but it regularly spent more each year than it earned through trade— primarily for military and economic assistance, maintaining bases abroad, and direct foreign investment. By 1958, however, the United States no longer sought a balance of payments deficit since its gold reserves were declining, and Europe and Japan were recovering from the war. The U.S. therefore adopted various measures to improve its payments balance, including restraints on foreign investment, tying of foreign aid, and programs to promote exports. The costs of domestic programs and the Vietnam conflict nevertheless contributed to a worsening of the U.S. payments position, and deficits seemed to be chronic by the end of the 1960s.[43]

The United States had a disastrous balance of payments deficit in 1971. Compared with the modest deficits of $1.9 billion to $3.8 billion over the previous five years, the 1971 deficit jumped to $10.6 billion. Most disturbing was the balance of trade in 1971 when U.S. imports exceeded exports for the first time since 1893. With the exceptions of 1973 and 1975, the United States now had a persistent and growing merchandise-trade deficit. This situation raised serious doubts about the vitality and strength of the American economy. Thus, various analysts maintained that "this shift in the United States' trading position gradually undermined its ability and willingness to lead the system" and that "nowhere is America's hegemonic decline more evident than in changing trade patterns."[44]

There is considerable evidence that the growing U.S. payments and (from 1971) trade deficits led to a more assertive U.S. foreign trade policy which contributed to tensions and conflict with Canada. For example, President Nixon's imposition of a 10 per cent import surcharge in August 1971 had a profound psychological effect on Canadians (see discussion below). Furthermore, in the late 1970s and 1980s Canadian exports to the United States and third countries were threatened by a greater American "use of aggressive reciprocity and by the use of trade measures to force access in foreign markets."[45] Canada was sometimes singled out for criticism because of its overall merchandise trade surplus and its surplus with the U.S. in most years after 1971.[46] As Table 1-7 shows, agriculture was one of the few areas where the United States continued to have a positive trade balance in the 1970s and 1980s. The United States therefore viewed its farm exports as one means of redressing its unfavourable balances elsewhere. It is hypothesized in this book that U.S. balance of payments and trade problems had an adverse effect on Canadian-American agricultural trade relations and on Canada's ability to achieve its agricultural export objectives.

The second environmental variable in Table 1-9, *political-security objectives*, is used here as a Realist concept. Realists typically contrast these objectives, which "include high-political concerns of assuring state survival—security matters" with "the more mundane or low-political objectives in such fields as trade, finance, monetary exchange, and health." In other words, when a state gives priority to political-security objectives, "military and security issues dominate the agenda."[47] An exporting country that emphasizes political-security objectives might formulate trade policy in an effort to affect the outcome of events on East-West issues, to exert influence on the policies of importers, to "punish" a country for following particular policies, or simply to express approval or disapproval. In this book, American and Canadian political-security objectives primarily relate to East-West issues and to attitudes toward trading with the Soviet bloc countries and the People's Republic of China. Of interest here are the willingness to trade with these countries and the terms of trade (such as export credits and export subsidies) that the United States and Canada are prepared to offer. Earlier studies on food aid have shown that Canada, as a smaller power, has had very different objectives in aid-giving than the United States. While Canadian objectives were mainly economic, the United States was more inclined (and more able) to seek political-security objectives.[48] In this study, I examine the effects of these objectives on Canadian-American agricultural trade relations.

The third environmental variable is *relative economic size*. An important indicator of this dimension is the gross national product (GNP), which has been described as "the best overall measure of economic performance."[49] The GNP is the monetary value of a nation's total output of goods and services, usually over a one-year period. In 1986, the American GNP was US$3,182.90 billion, about ten times the size of the Canadian GNP, which was Cdn$344.93 billion.[50] The U.S. population size in 1986 (241.6 million) was also about ten times the size of the Canadian (25.6 million). Canada therefore has a much smaller domestic market and it is far more dependent on exporting its production at remunerative prices. In 1986, Canadian exports of goods and nonfactor services accounted for 27.3 per cent of its gross domestic product (GDP), while the comparable figure for the United States was only 6.7 per cent.[51]

In view of the disparate size of the two economies, the United States can employ more resources for a variety of purposes, such as bolstering the agricultural trade regime, supporting American farmers, and promoting U.S. agricultural exports. However, Keohane and Nye have pointed out (in their issue structure model) that "economic capabilities relevant to one area may not be relevant to another."[52] While the United States is a far more important actor than Canada in the global food regime, the latter's capabilities and influence on some agricultural issues should not be discounted. This book examines the effect of the disparity of U.S. and Canadian economic size on the dependent variables.

The last environmental variable is *the interdependence between the United States and Canada*. The Canadian-American relationship has frequently been cited as a prime example of interdependence. In a historical study of relations among industrial states, Richard Rosecrance and his co-authors maintained that for the 1930–32 period "the U.S.-Canadian tie was still the primary interdependent bond in world politics"; and Robert Keohane and Joseph Nye described the Canadian-American relationship as "most likely to fit" their "three ideal conditions of complex interdependence."[53] Those writing about Canadian-American interdependence often refer to the multiplicity of channels and the intensity of contact between the two states—in such areas as trade, foreign investment, travel, and communications.

Interdependence is viewed as an environmental variable here because the two countries' relations in agricultural trade form only a part of their overall interdependent relationship. For example, the United States and Canada are each other's largest trading partners overall, and Table 1-10 shows their relative importance as export markets. Most writers feel that economic interdependence between the two countries has been increasing, and Table 1-11 shows that the U.S. and Canada gradually became more important markets for each other's exports from the 1920s to the 1970s. Statistics on foreign investment, on travel, and on the media (television, magazines, and so forth) demonstrate a similar growth in U.S.-Canadian societal connections since 1920.[54] Authors also often refer to the asymmetry of this interdependent relationship, and Tables 1–10 and 1–11 demonstrate that Canada is far more dependent on the American market than the U.S. is on the Canadian. While 74.9 per cent of Canada's total exports were directed to the United States in 1986, the U.S. sent only 20.9 per cent of its exports to Canada. The United States and Canada are also interdependent in agricultural trade specifically, and this interdependence is significantly based on third-country issues. In addition, as Tables 1–4 and 1–5 show, the United States and Canada are major agricultural trading partners.

TABLE 1–10

U.S. AND CANADIAN EXPORT MARKETS, 1986

(per cent of total exports)

Major Cdn. Markets	Per cent	Major U.S. Markets	Per cent
United States	74.9	Canada	20.9
Japan	4.7	Japan	12.4
Britain	2.1	Mexico	5.7
F. R. Germany	1.0	Britain	5.3
Soviet Union	0.9	F. R. Germany	4.9

Source: Derived from International Monetary Fund, Direction of Trade Statistics— Yearbook 1987, pp. 125-26, 404-5.

TABLE 1–11

CANADIAN EXPORTS TO THE U.S. AND U.S. EXPORTS TO CANADA

(per cent of total exports)

Year	Canadian % to U.S.	U.S. % to Canada
1920	45	12
1938	33	15
1953	59	19
1962	57	22
1971	66	21

Source: Robert O. Keohane and Joseph S. Nye, Power and Interdependence (Boston: Little Brown, 1977), p. 168.

Keohane and Nye postulate that interdependence has a variety of effects on the nature of interstate relations. However, they were not focusing on agricultural trade relations, and some of their hypotheses and findings are beyond the scope of this study. For example, these authors examined the effect of transnational corporations (TNCs) on the outcomes of Canadian-American conflicts, but none of the TNC cases they considered involved agricultural issues.[55] This fact is not surprising since TNCs play a more central role in non-agricultural areas of U.S.-Canadian relations. I also do not do a detailed examination of Keohane and Nye's hypothesis regarding the greater "intensity and coherence of the smaller state's bargaining position" since this would require an in-depth study of domestic politics in agriculture. There is evidence that domestic agricultural issues are more complex and involve a larger number of actors than domestic issues in many other areas. For example, American agricultural policy was influenced by a wide array of single-interest commodity groups from an early stage. This contrasts with "most other economic sectors," where "large coalitions of interests (labor, business) remained reasonably effective until the early to middle 1970s."[56] Commodity groups have also been extremely important in Canadian agriculture and, in addition, "the distribution of powers between federal and provincial governments and regional characteristics of agriculture has rendered difficult the process of policy harmonization."[57] In the concluding chapter, I offer some preliminary observations with regard to the Keohane-Nye hypothesis concerning "the intensity and coherence of bargaining positions" and some suggestions for further research in this area.

When interdependence increases, countries become more vulnerable to "disrupting events" in the interdependent relationship, and some sort of response becomes necessary. This response can be defensive and conflictual as well as co-operative.[58] In the Canadian-American relationship, the high degree of asymmetry further contributes to the dual effects of interdependence from the perspective of the smaller state. Thus, Maureen Appel Molot has noted that

> Canada's relations with its southern neighbor can be characterized as the politics of attraction and distance. . . . On some occasions Canada has sought to handle dyadic dependence by intensifying or expanding its ties with the United States, in the expectation that these closer ties would result in economic gains . . . whereas on others Canada has sought to reduce linkages, with a view to reducing its dependence on, or vulnerability to, actions of the superordinate actor.[59]

The effort to reduce linkages, which is often associated with the rise in nationalism in the smaller state, can contribute to conflict in the bilateral relationship.[60]

"The politics of distance" has always been a factor to consider in Canadian-

American relations, but from the 1950s to the 1980s restraint and co-operation *usually* prevailed (an important exception to this generalization is discussed below). Of particular interest here is the concept of vulnerability interdependence, which induces countries to engage in a form of "damage-control" to avoid serious disruption of their relationship.[61] Thus, the United States and Canada have often exercised restraint with each other in the use of their capabilities. As Keohane and Nye have noted, "the United States was constrained . . . by the regime that developed between the two countries after the war, which limited opportunities for linkage among issues and emphasized the virtues of responsiveness and conciliation."[62] The constraints on the United States have been especially important to Canada because of the greater U.S. economic capabilities and the asymmetrical nature of the two countries' interdependence.

I have also hypothesized that U.S.-Canadian conflict frequently provides the incentive for the two countries to devise new forms of consultation and co-operation. In view of the asymmetry between the two countries, this co-operation has often taken the form of "exemptionalism." Thus, Canada became accustomed to seeking, and receiving, exemptions from potentially injurious American economic policies that were applied to its allies. In the 1960s, for example, Canada had serious balance of payments problems, and it sought exemptions on three occasions from American measures designed to limit foreign access to U.S. capital. The United States granted the exemptions in all three cases, but it expected concessions from Canada in return (for example, Canada agreed to accept certain limitations on its monetary policy). Largely because of this exemptionalism, a number of writers have referred to U.S.-Canadian ties as a "special relationship." To the United States, the "special relationship" was a bargain involving "the extension [to Canada] of certain trade and financial concessions plus strategic security, on the one hand, in return for a relatively open investment and trading situation, on the other."[63]

However, while U.S.-Canadian conflict *normally* resulted in co-operative efforts to resolve the differences, there was one period during the last four decades when this was not the case. In the early years of the 1970s and a few years in the early 1980s, there was "an abrupt break in the tone and pattern of Canada-U.S. relations," and it is necessary to explain why this period was different.[64] A crucial turning point was the "Nixon shock" of August 1971, when the United States placed a 10 per cent surcharge on all dutiable imports. The U.S. also adopted several other contentious measures in this period, such as its DISC (Domestic International Sales Corporation) policies, to increase American competitiveness and the amount of manufacturing done in the United States. These measures resulted largely from general U.S. balance of payment and trade problems, and they were not aimed primarily at Canada.

However, when Canada sought an exemption from the import surcharge, the United States refused. While the economic effects of the temporary surcharge on Canada were not significant, the psychological effect of the changed U.S. attitude was great. It indicated to many Canadians "that the 'special relationship' no longer conferred exemption from general United States policy actions that might be harmful to Canada."[65]

Canada had adopted some policies to limit American influence on its economy in the 1960s, but the Nixon shock provoked a more broad-ranging response. In October 1972, the Department of External Affairs issued its *Options for the Future* paper.[66] Of the three "options" discussed, the first (that Canada should "maintain its present relationship" with the United States) and the second (that Canada should "move deliberately towards closer integration" with the United States) were rejected. The "Third Option," which involved efforts to diversify Canada's relations "to reduce the present Canadian vulnerability to American actions," was endorsed. In diversifying relations, special efforts would be made to upgrade ties with the European Community and Japan, Canada's second and third largest trading partners.

The Third Option policy was never formally approved by the full Canadian cabinet, and the rhetoric sometimes seemed to be more important than the actions taken. However, several policy initiatives can be attributed to the Third Option, including the creation of the Foreign Investment Review Agency (FIRA), the establishment of state-owned enterprises such as Petro-Canada and the Canada Development Corporation, some undertakings to encourage development of the Canadian media, and the signing of "contractual link" agreements with the European Community and Japan. In the late 1970s tensions between the United States and Canada receded, first under Prime Minister Pierre Trudeau and then under the short-lived Conservative government of Joe Clark. However, when the Trudeau Liberals returned to power in October 1980, tensions with the United States reached new heights.[67]

The most contentious issues in the early 1980s related to the establishment of the National Energy Program (NEP) to increase Canadian ownership in the oil and gas industry and the reports that Canada was planning to broaden FIRA's mandate. However, the Reagan administration reacted harshly to these initiatives, and Canada eventually adopted a less nationalistic stance. Thus, the U.S. government was given assurances that Canada would not upgrade FIRA and that the Canadianization provisions in the NEP would not be extended to other sectors of the Canadian economy. It was also becoming evident at this time that the Third Option policy was not succeeding. Canada's exports to the European Community and Japan continued to be more heavily concentrated on natural resources than its exports to the United States. Furthermore, as Table

1–12 shows, there was a dramatic increase in Canadian exports to the U.S. and a large decrease to the EC despite the Third Option policy. With American protectionism increasing, the Trudeau government's External Affairs Department issued a trade document in 1983 stating that "in the case of the USA, we will need to give greater recognition to the fact that a positive and stable relationship is fundamental to achieving many of Canada's economic objectives."[68] To achieve such a relationship, the document recommended the establishment of sectoral free trade agreements with the United States.

TABLE 1–12

CANADIAN EXPORTS TO THE U.S., THE EC, AND JAPAN

(per cent of total exports)

Major Canadian Markets	Years		
	1971	1983	1985
United States	65.7	70.2	75.2
European Community	13.5	7.4	5.6
Japan	4.2	5.0	4.7

Source: Derived from International Monetary Fund, *Direction of Trade Statistics, Annual 1971-77*, pp. 93-94, and *Direction of Trade Statistics, Yearbook 1987*, pp. 125-26.

When the Conservative government of Brian Mulroney came to power, its strategy "centered on an investment-for-trade formula whereby the government would remove the underlying cause of American displeasure with Canada (namely, the . . . NEP and . . . FIRA) and the United States would cooperate with Canada on trade issues."[69] Canada was increasingly alarmed by U.S. trade protectionism, and these fears contributed to the development of new forms of co-operation (the bilateral free trade agreement) and to a revival of interest in "exemptionalism." The Mulroney government wanted assured access to the U.S. market and thus a form of exemption from U.S. trade relief laws. While this (rather unrealistic) goal was not achieved in the free trade agreement, the Canadian government feels that the establishment of joint rules for using trade relief laws—over a five to seven year period—will give Canada more assured access (see Chapter 7). This rather lengthy introduction has been necessary because of the complexities of Canadian-American interdependence and because an understanding of major changes in bilateral relations in general is essential for discussion of the agricultural trade issue.

The agricultural variables in Table 1-9 have been taken from the literature on international relations and agricultural economics. The first of these is *supply in the world market*. Susan Strange examines the problem of "surplus capacity" in various processing and manufacturing industries, but she notes that this problem "has long existed in agricultural trade."[70] Surplus capacity exists when "for a sustained period of time and a large percentage of all producers, demand is not sufficient to absorb enough output for prices to sustain substantial employment and adequate returns on investment in a sector."[71]

It is one of the ironies of the global food system that surplus capacity has been a major problem confronting North American agriculture while many peoples in less-developed countries (LDCs) have suffered from periodic shortages. In the 1950s and 1960s, the United States (and to a lesser extent Canada) provided large amounts of food aid. However, with the worsening of U.S. balance of payments and trade problems, greater priority was given to exporting agricultural goods to those with "effective" demand, or demand backed by purchasing power. The poorer peoples in LDCs, while often in need of foodstuffs, are also those most lacking in effective demand.[72]

The editors of a book on surplus capacity note that "whatever the sector, the appearance of surplus capacity has produced conflicts of economic interest between states."[73] However, all of the case studies in the book deal with industrial and manufacturing sectors. In this study, I examine the effects of surplus capacity on the nature of Canadian-American agricultural trade relations. While grain surpluses have been far more common than shortages in North America, a major shortage period developed in the 1970s, and surplus/shortage cycles have existed for various agricultural commodities on a short-term basis. Furthermore, the amount of surpluses overhanging the market has varied over different periods. It is therefore possible to examine the effects of changing supply conditions on the U.S.-Canadian relationship.

The second agricultural-specific variable is *the relative size of the two countries' agricultural economies*. Earlier in this chapter, I discussed the fact that the United States is far more important than Canada in terms of its food production, productive potential, exports, and imports (see Tables 1-1, 1-2, and 1-3). It is hypothesized that Canadian agricultural exports to third-country markets are often highly vulnerable to U.S. policy decisions because of the much larger size of the American agricultural economy. In bilateral trade, it is expected that during surplus periods the Canadian market will sometimes be inundated with U.S. agricultural commodities. While Canada may also export its surpluses to the United States, Canadian producers often have much more to fear than their American counterparts from being overwhelmed by cross-border imports.

The third agricultural-specific variable is *conflict regarding agricultural trade*. Here conflict is examined as an independent as well as a dependent variable. In view of the high degree of interdependence between the United States and Canada, I hypothesize that heightened conflict often fosters new forms of co-operation between them, while a lessening of conflict makes such innovative forms of co-operation less necessary. These co-operative efforts may be aimed at managing conflict at both the bilateral and multilateral levels. The effect of conflict on the ability of the U.S. and Canada to achieve their agricultural export objectives and the strategies they employ will also be examined.

The fourth agricultural variable is *competition in agricultural trade*. Competition can be defined as "a striving, or vying with another . . . for profit, prize, position, or the necessities of life."[74] The level and nature of competition can obviously vary, with some competitive situations being "friendly" and others being closely associated with conflict. In periods of intense U.S.-Canadian competition, it is assumed that bilateral conflict is more likely and that both countries find it more difficult to achieve their agricultural export objectives. However, I also hypothesize that competition (like conflict) can encourage new forms of Canadian-American co-operation to manage the bilateral relationship.

Competition involving third countries is also of interest. In this context, the most important change has been the enhanced role of the European Community countries as agricultural exporters. One study comparing the 1961–65 and 1978–80 periods found that "West European exports of agricultural products appear to have increased faster than for any other region of the world—they increased by more than 50 per cent from the early 1960s to 1969–71 and then by another 77 per cent to 1978–80."[75] Table 1–1 also demonstrates the striking increase in the EC countries' percentage of global food exports. While the American and Canadian shares declined from 1973 to 1986, all of the EC exporters increased their shares during this period. Seven of the ten leading food exporters in 1986 were EC members, with Denmark replacing Australia as the tenth largest exporter (and Britain overtaking Canada) in 1986. Table 1–13 combines the shares of the EC countries from Table 1–1. It shows that the EC share of world food exports increased by 8.8 per cent from 1973 to 1986. In contrast, the U.S. and Canadian shares decreased by 7.8 and 0.9 per cent during the same period.

With regard to wheat exports in particular, Western Europe changed from being a net importer of about 12 million tons annually in the early 1950s to a net exporter of 8.6 million tons in 1982.[76] Table 1–3 shows that the EC's share of global wheat and wheat flour exports increased markedly, from 6.0 per cent in 1960–61 to 17.8 per cent in 1986–87. Thus, Robert Paarlberg has stated that between 1965 and 1983, the EC (nine nations at the time) transformed itself from a region with 20 million tons of net cereals *imports*, and a good customer for U.S. grain producers, into a region with 10 million tons of net cereals *exports*, and a menacing U.S. farm trade competitor. Relatively efficient grain producers in the United States, Canada, and Australia, who were unable to compete against lavish EC subsidies, were forced to give up valuable foreign market shares.[77]

TABLE I-13

THE TEN LEADING FOOD EXPORTERS, 1973 AND 1986:

PERCENTAGE OF WORLD FOOD EXPORTS

(by dollar value)

The Ten Leading Exporters	1973	1986	Change in %
EC countries*	25.1	33.9	+8.8
United States	19.2	11.4	-7.8
Canada	4.2	3.4	-0.9
Brazil	4.4	3.3	-1.1
Australia	3.5	n.a.**	n.a.**

*Six EC countries were among the top ten food exporters in 1973, and seven were among the top ten in 1986.
**Not applicable. In 1986, Denmark replaced Australia as the tenth largest food exporter.
Source: Derived from GATT, *International Trade 1985-86* (Geneva, 1986), p. 38; GATT, *International Trade 1986-87* (Geneva, 1987), p. 32.

In this book, I examine the effect of increased competition from the European Community on Canadian-American agricultural trade relations.

The last agricultural variable is *the strength of the agricultural trade regime*.[78] Chapter 3 on the international organizational setting shows that the principles and rules for regulating agricultural trade are unusually weak. From an early date, the GATT treated agriculture as an "exception" to many of its regulations. While other multilateral organizations and some plurilateral and bilateral groupings sought to supplement the GATT's efforts, these alternative bodies also proved to be inadequate over the long term. It is hypothesized that the weak agricultural trade regime has had a major effect on the nature of U.S.-Canadian relations in this area.

It should be noted that the variables in Table 1-9 deal primarily with systemic characteristics rather than with domestic agricultural politics. While domestic agricultural issues are discussed when necessary, it would be impossible to examine the wide range of actors involved with agricultural policy-making in this study.[79] General farm organizations in the United States (such as the American Farm Bureau Federation and the National Farmers' Union) gradually lost influence relative to narrower interest groups that developed around the U.S. commodity price support programs established in 1933. By the early 1950s, these commodity groups had become far more important than the general farm organizations.[80] A similar process occurred in Canada, where the Canadian Federation of Agriculture and the National Farmers' Union were replaced to some extent by groups with more focused interests.[81] Along with the numerous commodity groups in both countries, many other domestic actors have an influence on agricultural policy-making. In the United States, these include Cabinet departments and agencies; the Executive Office/White House; the House of Representatives and Senate Congressional committees and sub-committees; interest groups involving agribusiness, labour, consumers and others; export organizations; and the media. In Canada, the relevant actors include agencies of Agriculture Canada and other federal government departments; the ten provincial governments; interest groups, which include marketing boards that engage in lobbying activities; and a number of boards and commissions (such as the Canadian Wheat Board and the Canadian Dairy Commission) that sometimes become involved in the policy process. In view of the wide range of domestic actors involved with agricultural policy-making, it is beyond the scope of this study to examine domestic political issues systematically as independent variables. Nevertheless, some preliminary findings and suggestions for further research on the interface between systemic and domestic variables are discussed in the concluding chapter.[82]

The variables outlined are not all relevant to every chapter on the various issue areas. Each variable will be examined when applicable, and a discussion of all the variables together must await the concluding chapter. As background for this study, Chapter 2 provides an overview of Canadian-American agricultural trade relations from the 1950s to the present; and Chapter 3 examines the organizational setting, particularly the multilateral and bilateral fora in which the two states have interacted. Chapters 4 to 7 focus on specific agricultural trade issues that are relevant to the bilateral relationship: international pricing arrangements, U.S. surplus disposal policies, agricultural export credits, and trade barriers. These are the four substantive chapters on which the conclusions in Chapter 8 are based.

2

An Overview of Canadian-American Agricultural Trade Relations

This chapter provides a brief historical overview of Canadian-American agricultural trade relations from the 1950s to the late 1980s. Third-country issues are given primary emphasis here, while the strictly bilateral issues are discussed in more detail in Chapter 7. The organization of this chapter is based on one of the agricultural variables—supply in the world market. Five general phases in the evolution of U.S.-Canadian agricultural trade relations can be identified: the build-up of surpluses in the 1950s; the continuance of surpluses in the 1960s; the development of foodgrain shortages in the early 1970s; the re-emergence of surpluses in the late 1970s; and the persistence of surpluses in the 1980s. Although fluctuations in supply and demand may occur over much shorter time periods, this general trend approach is useful when examining Canadian-American relations.[1] Some preliminary observations are made in this chapter regarding several of the independent and dependent variables, and these are examined further in Chapters 4 to 7.

THE BUILD-UP OF SURPLUSES: THE 1950S

Global demand for wheat imports declined sharply with the end of the Korean War in 1953 and the gradual adjustment to peacetime conditions. At the same time, wheat production and stocks in the major exporting countries were increasing to record levels as a result of technological advances in agriculture, U.S. price support policies, and West European protectionism. The surplus conditions contributed to tensions and conflict in Canadian-American relations, largely because of differences in the economic size and capabilities of the two countries. The United States could devote far more funds than Canada to supporting its farmers and disposing of its agricultural surpluses, and Canada often protested against the huge American expenditures in this area.

The U.S. government moved to support domestic agricultural prices in the 1930s through "nonrecourse loans" to producers and the removal of agricultural goods from the market.[2] American farmers had little interest in world market values for their products since their prices were being artificially maintained, and they rapidly increased production. Efforts to control agricultural output through acreage allotments (beginning with the 1938 crop) and marketing quotas (starting with the 1941 crop) met with only limited success at prevailing support prices, and large stocks accumulated in the 1950s. As a result, there were intense political pressures to dispose of American surpluses through concessional and commercial exports.[3] The United States relied partly on export subsidies, which permitted traders to sell wheat at international prices and be reimbursed for the difference between the higher domestic prices and their export receipts. However, the Agricultural Trade Development and Assistance Act (Public Law 480) was the most important means of disposing of surpluses. Title I of PL 480 authorized the sale of U.S. agricultural goods for foreign (or local) currencies; Title II supplied foodstuffs on a grant basis for famines or other emergencies; Title III provided food to private voluntary organizations and bartered food for strategic materials; and Title IV (which was added in 1959) authorized the sale of surpluses for dollars on long-term credit.

Unlike the United States, Canada could not contemplate adopting costly price support and surplus disposal measures to assist its wheat producers. With a smaller domestic market and economic base, Canada was far more dependent on exporting wheat at satisfactory prices. Furthermore, coarse grains and oilseeds rivalled wheat as major U.S. crops, whereas wheat was Canada's most important agricultural commodity. It would be incorrect to assume that Canadian agriculture was completely unsupported in this period. Indeed, price support legislation was introduced in 1944 to protect dairy, hog, and egg farmers from postwar price decreases such as those experienced after World War I. Furthermore, the Agricultural Stabilization Act (ASA) of 1958 was designed to maintain the prices of nine commodities at 80 per cent of the previous ten-year average market price. Government intervention was, nevertheless, far more limited than in the United States, and Canadian wheat production in the Prairie provinces did not qualify for price supports. The Canadian Wheat Board (CWB) is a crown corporation that controls the foreign marketing of wheat and barley grown in Manitoba, Saskatchewan, Alberta and the Peace River region of British Columbia.[4] Producer returns depend on the CWB's success in moving wheat at remunerative prices, and market forces therefore played a much greater role in bringing about agricultural adjustments in Canada.[5]

Canada often criticized American price support and surplus disposal policies and felt especially threatened by practices such as tied sales and barter (see Chapter 5). For example, the Canadian trade and commerce minister maintained that "there is no doubt that by their [U.S.] disposal policies they have displaced our products in certain markets."[6] Canadian officials also argued that U.S. "hard" concessional transactions were really an unfair form of price-cutting. Although the United States was less concerned about competition, it did occasionally criticize Canada's export practices. For example, a 1956 U.S. Department of Agriculture (USDA) publication maintained that "Canada carries out an aggressive sales campaign for its surplus commodities . . . and it excludes U.S. products from competition with Canadian surpluses."[7]

Despite Canadian hostility towards American surplus disposal activities, conflict was limited because of U.S. restraint and responsiveness to competitors' complaints. The United States was willing to alter some of its more objectionable surplus disposal measures and to discontinue the use of others. For example, PL 480 as enacted in 1954 had specified that the president should take precautions to safeguard the usual marketings of the *United States*. However, other exporters were included in a 1957 addition to the law, which stated that PL 480 sales should "not disrupt world prices of agricultural commodities or normal patterns of commercial trade with friendly countries."[8] This was also the period when the United States had huge financial reserves and balance of trade surpluses, and its surplus disposal policies were therefore strongly oriented towards food aid as well as trade. By directing surpluses through concessional channels, the U.S. PL 480 program "at times provided an 'umbrella' over commercial markets" of Canada and other agricultural exporters.[9] The consequences for Canada would have been far more serious if the United States had moved aggressively to increase its commercial sales.

The United States and Canada also engaged in co-operative efforts at this time to limit their competition and conflict and to help manage the agricultural trade regime. Indeed, as the largest wheat exporters, they had a shared interest in controlling agricultural surpluses and supporting commercial prices. They therefore agreed to hold substantial wheat reserves off the commercial market, and they endorsed a series of International Wheat Agreements with pricing provisions. This system was effective in promoting price stability and food security because the U.S. and Canada (along with Australia and Argentina) accounted for a predominant share of global wheat exports.

The existence of conflict during this period, and the co-operative efforts to resolve it, were clearly illustrated by Canada's dual reaction to President

Dwight D. Eisenhower's 1959 proposal for a Food for Peace Conference. The government of Prime Minister John Diefenbaker wanted assurances that the Eisenhower proposals would not legitimize subsidized overproduction and surplus disposal programs that interfered with commercial exports. In addition, a Canadian official suggested the conference should examine the decline in Canada's wheat exports at a time when American exports were rapidly increasing.[10] Despite the Canadian criticisms, however, the Diefenbaker government strongly supported the Eisenhower initiative as providing an opportunity for major wheat exporters to "review problems affecting products and trade in wheat and surplus disposal programs now in effect."[11]

While Canada benefited from American restraint in the 1950s, various U.S. groups (governmental as well as non-governmental) expressed growing dissatisfaction with the policies being followed. By the late 1950s, the United States was less eager to maintain a balance of payments deficit, and yet the costs for storing and disposing of agricultural surpluses continued to rise. An assistant secretary of agriculture (and later the first director of the Food for Peace Program) summarized the Eisenhower administration's problems as follows:[12]

> We sold what we could for cash. What we couldn't sell for cash we sold for credit. What we couldn't sell for dollars we sold for foreign currency. What we couldn't get money for we bartered. What we couldn't get anything for we gave away. What we couldn't export by any means we stored. And still the stocks increased.

The United States gradually altered its policies in the 1960s to confront the problem of growing surpluses. In some respects, the new American policies were to be far more injurious to Canada than the policies of the 1950s.

THE CONTINUANCE OF SURPLUSES: THE 1960S

Co-operation among wheat exporters seriously declined in the mid-1960s, largely because of U.S. dissatisfaction with its role as a residual supplier; that is, importing countries purchased American agricultural goods on commercial terms only after the supplies of other exporters were exhausted. This residual status resulted from an overvalued dollar and from the American price support system. The U.S. Commodity Credit Corporation (CCC) administers a nonrecourse loan program under which a farmer may obtain a loan at the price support level and use a commodity(ies) as collateral. The farmer may either repay the loan within a specified period and regain control of the commodity or default on the loan. If the farmer defaults, the CCC takes ownership of the commodity, and this takeover fully satisfies the loan obligation. Thus, the government acquires grain stocks to prevent surpluses from being exported at prices below the loan rate. Since the United States was the largest grain exporter, the U.S. price supports became guidelines to competitors in setting their own export prices. They could gain a competitive advantage by pricing their exports just below the U.S. support level because American farmers would forfeit their stocks to the CCC rather than export at the lower price.

In view of its role as a residual supplier, the United States had to rely more than others on concessional sales and export subsidies. For example, 73.2 per cent of Canadian wheat and flour exports were sold on normal commercial terms from 1961–62 to 1968–69, compared with only 35 per cent for the United States. A further 22.2 per cent of Canada's wheat was sold with government credit, and only 4.6 per cent was food aid. In contrast, about 65 per cent of American wheat exports were moving under PL 480 and other aid programs, and U.S. wheat export subsidies in 1962 averaged $0.54 per bushel.[13] By 1964, U.S. government costs for the wheat program amounted to two-thirds of the value of production, which contributed to the growing balance of payments deficit. During this time the United States became more critical of Canada's commercially oriented policies, and one analyst remarked that "Canada has been creating part of the North American wheat problem" by rapidly increasing production at a time when U.S. output was decreasing.[14]

It is not surprising that the United States enacted a series of measures in the 1960s to reduce agricultural expenditures and increase commercial exports. For example, the 1965 Food and Agriculture Act lowered price supports and replaced high loan rates with direct payments to farmers to maintain incomes. Since farmers had less incentive to increase production, mandatory acreage restrictions were no longer necessary.[15] Furthermore, the PL 480 law was amended in 1966 to decrease concessionality. Local currency sales were to be phased out and replaced by long-term dollar credit sales; 50 per cent of all food aid was to be carried in American ships; and middle-income developing countries were expected to "graduate" from the status of concessional to commercial importers. As a result, the portion of U.S. wheat exports moving under PL 480 fell from 77 per cent in 1964–65 to 33 per cent by 1970–71. It is interesting that the new U.S. policies were in fact similar to those traditionally followed by Canada:[16]

In shifting the objective of agricultural programs from income support to price stabilization, in embracing export market development as the key to agricultural development, in seeking to minimize public expenditures on agriculture, and in giving more rein to market forces . . . U.S. agricultural policy in the period 1961–72 gradually assumed more of the features that characterized farm policy in Canada throughout the postwar years.

However, Canada had more to fear from upgraded American efforts to increase its commercial exports than the United States did from Canadian efforts. The Canadian Agriculture Congress therefore expressed serious concerns that "Canada . . . is no longer in the protected position it held while the U.S. offered restrained competition in commercial wheat markets."[17]

The effects of the new American policies on Canada were moderated to some extent because of U.S. concern in the 1960s with political-security objectives. As a superpower preoccupied with the Cold War, the United States was limiting its trade with the major Communist countries for political reasons. The United States first sold grain to the Soviet Union in 1963, but this sale resulted from a large increase in Soviet import requirements and was not followed by further U.S. sales until 1972.[18] As a smaller country, Canada was more preoccupied with economic issues, and it benefited from the lack of American competition for the major Communist markets. While the share of Canadian farm exports to Britain, the European Community, the United States, and Japan fell from over 80 per cent in 1961 to 52 per cent in 1966, the portion to the centrally planned economies rose to 33 per cent. However, Canada's sales to China (the PRC) and the USSR did not fully compensate for its losses to the U.S. elsewhere, and the Canadian share of world wheat exports declined from 24 per cent in 1955–60 to 21 per cent in 1961–63. Canada was also fearful of large fluctuations in its sales to the Communist states, and these sales in fact plummeted when the Soviets entered the market with surplus wheat in 1968. Largely because of the decline in its wheat exports, 1969 was the only year in recent history that Canada was a net agricultural importer. In the late 1960s, the Canadian government therefore "began a manyfold expansion of its program for foreign market development, in order to regain lost wheat markets and to win new outlets for the expanded output of barley and rapeseed."[19]

The late 1960s was also a period of increasing competition with other exporters such as the European Community and Australia, and Chapter 4 discusses the breakdown of the 1967 International Grains Arrangement. Nevertheless, the United States and Canada continued to co-ordinate their policies (as they had in the 1950s) in an effort to limit their conflicts and to maintain international wheat prices. For example, the U.S., Canada, and Australia all developed plans for production cutbacks in a joint attempt to create a better balance between the supply and demand for wheat. Canada introduced a "Lower Inventory for Tomorrow" (LIFT) program in 1970, a one-year adjustment program that paid farmers to remove up to twenty-two million acres of prairie wheat land from production; and in 1972 the United States held out of production about sixty-two million acres.[20] While these measures were designed to stabilize the world wheat market, it is ironic that they were one factor contributing to the serious foodgrain shortages of the 1970s.

THE DEVELOPMENT OF SHORTAGES: THE EARLY 1970S

After the United States, Canada, and Australia initiated their cutback programs to decrease global food stocks, inclement weather and massive Soviet imports in 1972–73 pushed these stocks to their lowest levels in twenty years. The United States, however, did not anticipate the impending shortages or the magnitude of Soviet purchases when it provided export subsidies for grain sales to the USSR in 1972. Canada also lacked foresight, and some of its "most important export-promotion programs were launched only a few months ahead of the big and unexpected upswing in world agricultural trade which started in mid-1972."[21]

The shortage period of the 1970s was in general marked by a lower level of U.S.-Canadian conflict since both countries experienced strong commercial demand for their grain exports. However, the United States had its first negative trade balance in the twentieth century in 1971, and some of the resultant changes in American policies posed a potential threat to Canada. In an effort to improve its overall trade position, the United States began to promote its agricultural exports far more aggressively. Doing so generally involved an emphasis on greater market orientation, but the government became involved when necessary to push U.S. commercial advantages.

By 1973 foodgrain shortages rather than surpluses had become the major problem, and U.S. policy moves toward greater market orientation were therefore accelerated. With the 1973 Agricultural and Consumer Protection Act, market prices of wheat and feedgrains were supported only at market clearing levels; individual crops were free of controls; and land diversion, when needed, was not tied to specific commodities. Secretary of Agriculture Earl Butz described American food policy during this period as emphasizing "abundance, full production, freedom from government restraints, [and] encouragement by the government of full production of farm goods."[22] Senior management in the U.S. Department of Agriculture (USDA) continued to speak of a market-oriented economy between 1974 and 1976, and these views were prevalent until the end of Gerald Ford's presidency in January 1977.

However, it was easier to espouse free-market policies when farm incomes, prices, and exports were increasing to record levels, and some analysts argued that Secretary Butz "was speaking from the vantage point of circumstances rather than political philosophy."[23] It should also be noted that American policy during this period was not completely market-oriented. For example, the United States imposed restrictions on dairy and beef imports, and a temporary embargo on soybean exports in the 1970s. Of particular concern to Canada were the efforts of the U.S. government to increase its share of agricultural exports. Indeed, the Nixon-Butz period was notable for the concerted use of export credits, subsidies, and barter to promote sales on a commercial cash basis. It was also in the 1970s that the United States began to show more interest in trading with the Communist states. The American payments and trade problems clearly affected President Richard Nixon's attitude towards the Soviet Union and China, and the desire to export to these countries.

The huge Soviet grain purchases from the United States in 1972–73 were the first since 1963, and they were followed by a five-year long-term agreement (LTA) between the two countries signed in October 1975. The agreement committed the USSR to purchase six to eight million tonnes of grain per year and to hold consultations if further imports were required. In return, the U.S. agreed to provide up to eight million tonnes of grain to the Soviet Union, unless its crop fell below a certain level. The United States had pressured for this agreement to guarantee the stability of its food supplies and to protect its consumers from major shifts in foreign demand. However, the U.S. had also become more interested in long-term sales to the USSR, and an American official stated that priority "number two in 1975 was the desirability that they would take a certain quantity from us every year."[24]

Despite these examples of government intervention, the 1973 U.S. Agricultural and Consumer Protection Act was a significant step towards a free-market farm policy. The United States was highly successful in capturing a larger share of the world wheat market through a combination of "supply availability, assured delivery and aggressive selling by the U.S. private grain trade at a time when world prices were relatively high."[25] Furthermore, the downgrading of U.S. political-security objectives in the face of its balance of trade problems signalled new competition for Canada in the Communist markets. Table 2–1 shows that Canada lost market share while the American share of wheat exports was increasing dramatically.

In contrast to American policy directions, Canadian federal and provincial government involvement in agriculture increased significantly during the 1970s. Of particular importance were moves to strengthen price and income stabilization measures, since fluctuations in international grain markets were a growing threat to producers. The Western Grain Stabilization Act was passed in July 1975 to stabilize the net cash returns for six cereal crops in the area

TABLE 2–1

INTERNATIONAL WHEAT MARKET SHARES

(per cent)

Year	U.S.	Canada
1970-71	36.5	21.4
1971-72	32.2	26.1
1972-73	46.9	22.8
1973-74	49.3	18.5
1974-75	44.6	17.7
1975-76	47.4	18.2

Source: International Wheat Council, *World Wheat Statistics*, reprinted in Alex McCalla, Andrew Schmitz, and Gary Storey, "Australia, Canada, and the United States: Trade Partners or Competitors," *American Journal of Agricultural Economics*, 61 (December 1979): 1028.

under Wheat Board jurisdiction, and the Agricultural Stabilization Act was revised to allow rapidly changing prices and production costs to be reflected in deficiency payments to producers. Various provinces also introduced more commodity-specific income stabilization plans.[26] Canada emphasized stabilization in the 1970s in part to insulate itself, since it simply could not compete with the expansive policies of its much larger neighbour. Indeed, a noted American agricultural economist acknowledged that U.S. "legislative lurches and lunges and . . . administrative decisions have profound influence upon Canada; effects that are not considered in our farm policy determinations."[27]

Along with Canada's interest in price and income stabilization there were also pressures to adopt a more outward-looking approach, and the expansion of its market development program continued into the shortage period. The western grain-producing provinces were highly critical of federal policies that gave too little priority to export growth, and they pressured Ottawa to upgrade its agricultural export programs. The provinces also expanded their own promotional activities, and Alberta (which exports about two-thirds of its farm production) was in the forefront in this respect. To increase foreign trade, Alberta created a Marketing Division in its Agriculture Department and a Foreign Marketing Section in its Industry and Commerce Department in 1972; and the Alberta Export Agency was established in 1973 to provide export credit, export insurance, and other assistance to firms involved in expanding agricultural markets. These promotional efforts caused a U.S. Department of Agriculture publication to warn that "a strong Canadian drive to win a larger share of the world market is bound to have some impact on U.S. commercial interests . . . even if world demand for farm goods remains strong."[28]

The demand for foodgrains in fact continued to be strong for most of the 1970s because of growth in the global economy, the recycling of petrodollars, easy credit terms, and production shortfalls in major consuming countries. However, when surpluses began to reappear in the late 1970s, there were pressures for a change in policies, and the Organization for Economic Co-operation and Development correctly predicted that a softening of demand might "stimulate pleas from the [U.S.] agricultural sector to re-enact earlier programmes."[29]

THE RE-EMERGENCE OF SURPLUSES: THE LATE 1970S AND 1980S

When the 1973 U.S. Agricultural and Consumer Protection Act was about to expire, the Senate Agricultural Committee sought recommendations for developing the 1977 farm bill. Secretary Butz felt that his market-oriented policy should be continued since it had ended set-asides and government-held stocks, released sixty million acres of idle land for production, decreased farm program costs from $3.4 billion in 1966 to $278 million in 1975, and helped to pay for oil imports with increased farm exports. However, the Nixon-Butz policies had been implemented when commodity prices and farm incomes were at record high levels. By the time the 1977 Food and Agriculture Act was drafted, American farmers had produced sizable wheat, corn, and soybean harvests, and other major exporters were also increasing production. Furthermore, export markets were shrinking as a result of debt problems in developing countries and self-sufficiency drives in the European Community, India, and China.

In response to Congressional pressures for increased support, the 1977 farm bill marked a return to a more active governmental role. It contained higher support prices for major crops, larger payment limits for individual producers, incentives for farmers to hold stocks on their farms, and a set-aside program with acreage limitations.[30] However, many farmers felt that the price supports and other types of assistance in the 1977 Act were inadequate. The most dramatic reaction came from the American Agriculture Movement (AAM), the strongest farm protest movement in recent U.S. history. Many AAM supporters were younger, medium to large grain farmers who had invested heavily in land and equipment in the early 1970s when agricultural prices were high and faced financial hardship when surpluses re-emerged. They demanded that agricultural commodity prices be set at 100 per cent of parity and that restrictions be placed on imports, and they sometimes used strong pressure tactics to achieve their objectives. Canadians encountered the AAM directly when it blockaded beef imports at several western border points and in effect stopped livestock shipments to the United States for about one month.[31]

While it is not possible to draw direct linkages between the AAM and American policies, the movement probably sped up the adoption of some new programs.[32] After a sharp drop in U.S. government costs during the mid-1970s, outlays to support farm income quadrupled in two years to about $7.9 billion in fiscal year 1978. The president signed an Emergency Agricultural Act in May 1978, allowing the secretary of agriculture to increase target prices for wheat and feedgrains; and the 1978 Agricultural Trade Act was designed "to strengthen the economy . . . through increased sales abroad of United States agricultural commodities."[33] To promote exports, the Trade Act authorized the establishment of agricultural trade offices, raised agricultural attachés to the rank of counsellor in ten countries, increased minimum grain shipments under PL 480, and introduced an intermediate credit program.

Canadian farmers, like their American counterparts, were adversely affected by the re-emergence of surpluses and the high degree of market instability. Furthermore, export promotion provisions such as intermediate credit in the 1977 U.S. farm bill were considered to be a threat to Canada's commercial markets. However, other aspects of the bill were beneficial to Canada, such as the higher support prices which bolstered the world price for wheat and feed-grains and the set-aside program which provided some relief from surpluses. Canada also benefited from reduced competition in the Soviet market as U.S. strategic-security objectives re-emerged as a factor in its agricultural export policies. In October 1979, as a result of a poor harvest, the Soviet Union obtained U.S. government approval to purchase 25 million tonnes of grain during the 1980 agreement year of their long-term agreement. However, President Jimmy Carter responded to the December 1979 Soviet invasion of Afghanistan with a suspension of all grain deliveries in excess of the 8 million tonnes guaranteed under the long-term agreement (the embargo was not lifted until 24 April 1981). The United States received assurances from Canada, Australia, and the European Community that they would limit their 1980 grain sales to the USSR to "normal" levels; but a substantial increase could be defended as normal since exports to the Soviets fluctuate widely. Although Canada initially supported the embargo, it concluded an unprecedentedly large long-term agreement with the USSR in May 1981, and Canadian wheat sales to the Soviets rose from about 2.6 million tonnes in 1979–80 to 4.2 million in 1980–81, 5 million in 1981–82, and 9 million in 1982–83.[34]

However, Canada's success was not unblemished, and the United States scored gains in other markets. Even though Canada's sales to the Soviet bloc were substantial, it had lost many traditional markets in Western Europe and elsewhere. The American position on political-security issues had also changed from the 1950s and 1960s, and it did not hesitate in seeking to recoup its embargo losses by turning to the China market. Indeed, the United States and China signed their first long-term grain agreement in October 1980, which Canada viewed "as a blatant U.S. effort to undercut an important and growing Canadian market."[35] The Wheat Board responded with a statement of intent to sell more wheat to the Soviet Union, and a few weeks later Canada's participation in the embargo was formally ended.

The 1981 U.S. farm bill, which replaced the 1977 bill, reflected the traditional policy goals of supporting commodity prices and protecting farm income. However, the debate over the bill indicated less willingness by the executive branch and some congressmen to give farmers price and income protection. The administration wanted to limit annual costs by eliminating target prices and deficiency payments for grains and ending set-aside and disaster payment authority. These proposals were not adopted, but in the give-and-take with Congress, the administration did manage to prevent massive increases in price supports. Nevertheless, cost estimates at the time of the 1981 farm bill were unrealistic, and overruns developed because of grain and dairy surpluses. Most importantly, the 1981 legislation authorized the use of export subsidies if necessary to match foreign export subsidies. This authorization was followed by further legislation in 1982 that directed the USDA to use from $175 to $190 million for export subsidies, interest-rate "buy-downs" (reductions) on export credits, or direct government export credits. This legislation marked an escalation in competition between the United States and the European Community, and it was to have serious implications for Canada.[36]

THE PERSISTENCE OF SURPLUSES: THE 1980s

Long before the U.S. Congress began to consider seriously a 1985 farm bill to replace the expiring 1981 Act, there was "more interest . . . in that legislation than has attended any farm bill of recent memory."[37] The unusual amount of interest resulted from a combination of factors that had produced widespread discontent with American farm policies. Since the U.S. Export Enhancement Program and the Food Security Act of 1985 have had a major impact on Canadian-American relations, some space must be devoted to the factors leading to their enactment.

Global surpluses persisted in the 1980s because of a variety of factors. These included the economic recession during 1981–83, the serious foreign debt problems in many developing countries, the decisions of some major importing states to provide greater incentives to agricultural production, and the techno-logical advances in agriculture. Furthermore, the emergence of feedgrains and soybeans (which are used for livestock production) as major exports contrib-uted to growing instability in agricultural trade. These commodities are more sensitive to changes in global income than wheat and rice exports since con-sumers in many areas cut back on meat purchases during difficult periods.

All agricultural exporters were adversely affected by these developments, but the *relative* position of the United States also deteriorated. Although part of the U.S. export losses resulted from its sales embargo on the Soviet Union, the more significant costs were largely structural. It was increasingly evident that American farm legislation was unable to control the problems that were plagu-ing the agricultural economy. Until the late 1960s, commercial international markets were less significant for American agricultural production, and farm programs were primarily responsive to a domestically oriented clientele. How-ever, as dependence on exports increased, the U.S. agricultural sector became highly vulnerable to the unfavourable market conditions. This change led a Council on Foreign Relations fellow to state that "we have entered an era of permanent grain surpluses, of a buyer's market for grain exports where the United States can no longer set the rules."[38]

Under the umbrella of high American support prices, a strong U.S. dollar, and U.S. acreage reduction programs, competitors were able to increase their market shares. When the government set price support levels at all-time highs in the 1981 farm bill, it enabled competitors to undercut U.S. prices and induced them to increase production. The strong American dollar of the early 1980s further boosted the support level in relation to the currencies of other countries and made U.S. agricultural products even less competitive. Indeed, the dollar rose for the seventh consecutive year in 1985, and American grain prices in 1984–85 were at least 20 per cent higher than those of export competitors. Furthermore, the high price supports gave U.S. farmers an incentive to con-tinue or expand production even though the market was weakening. The result was the 1983 Payment-in-Kind (PIK) Program, which removed seventy-eight million acres from production and was the largest acreage and stock reduction program in U.S. history. However, export competitors simply took advantage of the U.S. production cutbacks by increasing their own agricultural output levels.[39]

In view of the factors cited above, American farm product exports dropped record amounts in 1985, and the U.S. agricultural trade surplus fell to its lowest level since 1972. The U.S. share of world grain exports fell from 55.4 per cent in 1980–81 to 36.4 per cent in 1985–86, the lowest level in fifteen years. American wheat exports in particular declined from 42.2 million tonnes in fiscal 1981 to 25.5 million in 1986, and U.S. corn exports fell from 59.4 million tonnes in fiscal 1981 to 31.1 million in 1986. The United States also was holding a larger percentage of the world's grain surplus, with its shares of total stocks increasing from 25 per cent in 1974 to 45 per cent in 1984. In addition, financial stress in the U.S. farm sector was becoming a critical issue. Farm income would have been negative during certain periods in the absence of federal subsidies, farm bankruptcies more than doubled from 1983 to 1984, and farm debt rose from $50 billion in 1970 to $216 billion in 1983. American policymakers were under tremendous pressure to rescue the farmer from the deepening crisis, but at the same time the justification for continuing costly programs was being increasingly questioned.[40]

American dissatisfaction with its competitors was aimed primarily at the European Community because it directly subsidizes its agricultural exports through export subsidies (known as export restitutions). However, Table 2-2 shows that the EC was certainly not the only competitor that increased its market shares at U.S. expense, and there were also criticisms of other competitors. American officials criticized Canada in particular for not adjusting its grain production and stocks to available world markets and for securing some Wheat Board sales at below market prices. Indeed, a 1985 GAO report claimed that "to gain market position, Canada has aggressively marketed its grain at competitive prices and with below-market credit terms."[41]

TABLE 2-2

WORLD TRADE IN WHEAT AND WHEAT FLOUR (JULY/JUNE)

Exporter	Market Shares (per cent)	
	1980-81	1985-86
Argentina	4.1	7.0
Australia	11.8	18.7
Canada	18.1	19.7
European Community	13.5	17.3
United States	44.8	29.0

Source: Derived from U.S., General Accounting Office, *Implementation of the Agricultural Export Enhancement Program* (Washington, D.C.: GAO/NSIAD-87-74BR, March 1987), p. 35.

The United States established the Export Enhancement Program (EEP) in May 1985 to regain what it viewed as its market share and to force the European Community to the bargaining table. The EEP authorizes the Commodity

Credit Corporation to offer government-owned commodities as bonuses to U.S. exporters to expand sales of agricultural products in targeted markets. The bonuses are a form of export subsidy since the exporters can sell commodities at prices well below those of the U.S. market. Since the EEP contributed to a drastic decline in agricultural export prices, it is discussed in detail in Chapter 4 (on pricing). However, some general background is provided here.

Before the announcement of the EEP, the U.S. Department of Agriculture was not seriously considering export subsidies as a policy option. The CCC had frequently used export subsidies in the 1950s and 1960s since government price supports had been far above international price levels. However, there was a strong negative reaction in the 1970s when sales to the Soviet Union were subsidized at the same time as world grain prices were increasing. The CCC's export subsidy programs were therefore discontinued in 1973 and did not re-emerge as a policy instrument until 1983. The USDA opposed export subsidies in principle and the Reagan administration tended to view subsidies as unfair trading practices. Nevertheless, pressure from the Senate leadership and the director of the Office of Management and Budget resulted in the establishment of the EEP. The United States repeatedly assured Canada, Argentina, and Australia that the EEP was aimed only at the European Community, but the three countries felt increasingly threatened as the program was expanded.[42]

The 1985 Food Security Act was "considered by many to represent a turning point in U.S. farm policy" since it was "the first time such legislation emphasized export expansion as a primary objective."[43] In addition to reducing loan rates for several agricultural products, the 1985 Act also directed the secretary of agriculture to use commodities valued at $2 billion (later changed to $1 – 1.5 billion) for the EEP over a three-year period. This program differed from the EEP as established in May 1985 since it was now to be broadened and made mandatory. A diverse coalition of countries (the "Cairns Group") that was formed to protest against the EEP and the U.S.-EC export subsidy war is discussed in Chapter 4. Canada was a founding member of the Cairns Group, but its criticisms of American policies at group conferences were relatively restrained. Indeed, the CWB minister repeatedly expressed the view that "what we see the U.S. doing is largely responding in frustration to what the Europeans are doing."[44] Furthermore, the United States and Canada supported similar policies on trade-distorting subsidies in the GATT Uruguay Round in efforts to confront the growing problems in this area. Agricultural trade across the U.S.- Canadian border was an additional source of dispute in the 1980s as pressures for protectionism increased. However, the two countries concluded a free trade agreement with some agricultural provisions to deal with bilateral differences and provide a stimulus for the resolution of multilateral conflicts.

CONCLUSIONS

Some preliminary conclusions can now be drawn regarding the independent and dependent variables. This chapter has clearly demonstrated that conflict is more likely in Canadian-American relations when large surpluses overhang the market. However, it is during these periods that the United States and Canada—in view of their interdependence—tend to seek new forms of co-operation to deal with (multilateral as well as bilateral) competition and conflict. For example, the two countries co-ordinated their stockholding policies in the 1950s and their production cutback programs in the late 1960s and 1970s. Furthermore, in the 1980s surplus period they concluded a bilateral free trade agreement with agricultural provisions, and they jointly pressured for greater coverage of agricultural trade issues in the Uruguay Round of GATT negotiations.

During the 1970s shortage period, there was generally less conflict between the two countries in agricultural trade. This relative harmony was especially notable since the Nixon import surcharge and Canada's Third Option policy contributed to fairly high levels of bilateral conflict in the 1970s in other areas. However, some fundamental economic changes were occurring at this time that eventually led to serious problems in agricultural trade relations. The growing U.S. balance of payments deficit contributed to more aggressive American trade policies, and the United States began to compete for Canada's Communist markets. During this period, the European Community's agricultural production and exports were also increasing, and the stage was set for a major confrontation between the EC and the United States. When surpluses re-emerged, the underlying sources of tension in the 1970s became full-blown conflicts in the 1980s.

This chapter also provides some preliminary findings regarding the strategies each country uses to achieve its agricultural export objectives. In view of its greater economic size and capabilities, the United States was often more inclined than Canada to adopt unilateral strategies, extending from the PL 480 program in the 1950s to the Export Enhancement Program in the 1980s. In Chapters 4 to 6, the issue of export strategies is examined in greater detail.

Finally, some preliminary statements can be offered regarding the ability of each country to achieve its agricultural export objectives. The nature of the agricultural trade regime, with the American price supports often serving as guidelines to competitors, at times permitted Canada (and other exporters) to undercut U.S. price levels. However, when the United States was determined to promote its agricultural exports, it could rely upon its greater economic size and capabilities. American agricultural trade policies in the 1950s and 1960s were restrained, and Canada fared reasonably well in achieving its agricultural export objectives (i.e., with regard to price and market share). The balance of payments was not a major problem for the U.S. during this period, and it was generally content to give priority to market share over pricing objectives (especially in the 1950s). Thus, a large percentage of American grain was exported on a concessional basis through the PL 480 program. While supply on the world market presented a problem for both countries, they co-operated to achieve their common objectives of controlling surpluses and stabilizing commercial prices.

As its balance of payment problems increased, however, the United States became more aggressive in promoting its commercial agricultural exports. This change posed a threat to Canada's export objectives, and the United States as well as Canada was threatened by the re-emergence of surpluses in the late 1970s and 1980s. However, the most marked change was the increase in competition with the European Community, and one analyst has stated that "no government policy has caused more change since 1960, in any area of the world economy than the CAP [the EC's Common Agricultural Policy]."[45] The resultant U.S.-EC export subsidy "war" interfered with the export objectives of many countries (including the main opponents) and exposed the weaknesses of the agricultural trade regime's norms and regulations as never before. While little attention has been given to the regime variable to this point, it is examined in detail in the next chapter, which focuses on the organizational setting for Canadian-American agricultural trade relations.

3

The Organizational Setting

This chapter examines some of the cross-national organizations and groups that have dealt with food and agriculture since Canadian-American relations have been shaped in part by this organizational setting. An examination of these intergovernmental bodies is of particular relevance to one of the agricultural-specific variables, "the strength of the agricultural trade regime." Since the late 1940s, the General Agreement on Tariffs and Trade (GATT) has been responsible for much of the normative, rule-creating and rule-supervisory activity in international trade. Examples of GATT norms include the precept that trade liberalization is a valuable objective; GATT rules include the obligation of members (or contracting parties) to grant most-favoured-nation (MFN) treatment to each other; and GATT supervisory functions include the rendering of decisions when member states formally register complaints against each other.[1]

Despite the GATT's pre-eminence among international organizations involved with trade, it has treated agriculture as an exception from an early date. As a result, the principles and rules for regulating agricultural trade are very rudimentary. Frustration with the GATT led to the use of other international organizations (such as the Food and Agriculture Organization) to deal with agricultural trade issues, but they are more consultative in nature than the GATT, and their jurisdiction is limited. In this and subsequent chapters, I outline some of the effects of the inadequacy of the agricultural trade regime on Canadian-American relations. For example, in the 1950s and 1960s, the two countries supplemented multilateral mechanisms for resolving agricultural trade disputes and promoting co-operation with a series of bilateral committees or groupings. These groupings ranged from formal committees—such as ministerial committees—to more informal contacts, such as bilateral working groups and consultations between agriculture ministers. Indeed, informal bilateral consultations and meetings have frequently been more important than formal organizations in Canadian-American relations.[2] In view of the large number of intergovernmental bodies involved with food and agriculture, it is necessary to be selective.[3] Some formal and informal groupings of lesser relevance to Canadian-American agricultural trade relations are not examined in this book, while others that are important are discussed only in other chapters. For example, a detailed discussion of the Canada-U.S. duopoly, the International Wheat Council, and the International Wheat Agreements is provided in Chapter 4.

MULTILATERAL ORGANIZATIONS

The General Agreement on Tariffs and Trade was created in 1947 as a temporary treaty to provide guidelines for postwar trade negotiations until a permanent International Trade Organization (ITO) assumed this responsibility. However, the U.S. Congress did not assent to membership in the more formal and elaborate ITO, and the GATT has therefore provided the organizational basis for the postwar trade regime. The GATT provides a forum for conducting international trade negotiations and for discussing and settling disputes. Its signatories include over ninety contracting parties (or member countries), including most major trading nations other than the Soviet Union, and many of its rules are accepted by outsiders. The GATT's importance stems from its ability to establish rules and obligations that are legally binding, but its effectiveness largely depends on the commitment of its members.

During the postwar negotiations, the United States insisted on special treatment for agricultural trade, largely because of its own policies to protect farm prices and incomes. Section 22 of the 1933 Agricultural Adjustment Act (AAA) had authorized the use of import quotas to prevent interference with U.S. price support programs, and these quotas were in effect legalized by special exceptions which were included in the General Agreement. Although GATT Article XI calls for the elimination of quantitative restrictions, such restrictions are permitted for agricultural products when they are needed for enforcing governmental measures that "restrict the quantities" or "remove a temporary surplus of the like domestic product." The United States also relied on export subsidies to market its agricultural goods competitively, and here too the GATT rules accorded with American policy requirements. While Section B of GATT Article XVI prohibited export subsidies, an exception was provided (largely at U.S. insistence) for agricultural and other primary products. Finally, the GATT's jurisdiction in regard to concessional agricultural exports was extremely limited. When the United States enacted its PL 480 program, Australia proposed that the GATT adopt measures such as mandatory prior consultations and compulsory arbitration to protect competing exporters. However, the United States was unwilling to accept a major GATT role in this area, and the issues of concessional food exports and surplus disposal were passed on to the much less demanding Food and Agriculture Organization.[4]

Canada and some other primary product exporters argued that the larger and richer states would benefit most from the GATT's lenient rules for agriculture. Nevertheless, many countries approved of the GATT exceptions or at least did not vigorously oppose them. Most West European states felt that their own support programs were thereby legitimized, and food-short developing countries welcomed the availability of American surpluses at subsidized prices. Within a few years, even the GATT exceptions did not satisfy the U.S. Congress, and it amended Section 22 of the Agricultural Adjustment Act to permit the imposition of farm import quotas regardless of any international agreement. The president then responded to Congressional pressures and imposed quantitative restrictions on a number of agricultural products. Since these restrictions violated the GATT requirement that concomitant domestic measures (such as supply management) must be adopted, the United States sought a special waiver from its obligations. The GATT granted it an unusually broad waiver in 1955 that has no time limit, applies to any programs subsequently introduced, and only requires submission of an annual report. Since the United States was the world's largest trading nation and a strong supporter of free trade, this waiver inevitably detracted from GATT's effectiveness in agriculture. Canada and many other agricultural exporters strongly opposed the waiver, and in later years it hindered American (and Canadian) efforts to challenge the restrictive policies of the European Community and Japan.[5]

Despite the early contribution of the United States to agricultural protectionism, it gradually became more concerned with the high costs and inefficiencies in agriculture as its balance of payments problems increased. As a result, the U.S. and Canada eventually joined in pressuring for trade liberalization in this area. The two countries were particularly concerned about the growing impact of the European Community's Common Agricultural Policy (CAP), and they insisted that agriculture should be included in the Kennedy and Tokyo Rounds of GATT negotiations. During the Kennedy Round (1964–67), they supported a decrease in EC agricultural protectionism, an increase in the minimum wheat price, and a greater sharing of responsibility for food aid. However, the American case for trade liberalization was weakened by its approval of import restrictions for beef, veal, and lamb while the Kennedy Round negotiations were at a critical stage.[6] In the end, the EC and Britain resisted demands for trade liberalization, and the results of the Kennedy Round in agriculture were disappointing. The GATT did endorse a grains agreement in principle, and the details of the 1967 International Grains Arrangement (IGA) were worked out at a conference under the auspices of the International Wheat Council and the United Nations Conference on Trade and Development. However, the IGA price floor for wheat was unrealistically high, and it was therefore ignored by most countries.

At the Tokyo Round (1973–79), the United States and Canada continued to seek greater market access for their agricultural goods, while their trading partners demanded that the U.S. and Canada relax their import controls on meat and dairy products. Despite American insistence that progress be made in agriculture, the Tokyo Round gains were in fact quite limited. Most participants in the Tokyo Round (as in the Kennedy Round) agreed to decrease and bind their tariffs and to enlarge their import quotas in the agricultural sector. However, the Tokyo Round could only be completed when the United States backed down on its demand that agriculture should be negotiated "identically with other products, which would have meant that trade restrictions on agriculture would be subjected to the same disciplines being negotiated in the nonagricultural area."[7] The European Community demanded that the agricultural negotiations be treated separately from negotiations on industrial products, and the Tokyo Round reached a generally "successful" conclusion only after the U.S. expressed a willingness to compromise with the EC on this issue. The price of this compromise was the agreement among the major trading nations to continue treating agriculture as an exception. Thus, industrial tariff cuts were instituted by a linear across-the-board technique in the Tokyo Round, while agricultural cuts were negotiated on an item-by-item basis, primarily between pairs of countries.[8] Furthermore, the GATT members failed to examine the effect of their domestic agricultural policies on international trade, the U.S. refused to relinquish its 1955 GATT waiver, and the European Community continued to maintain that its Common Agricultural Policy was not negotiable.

Some analysts argue that agricultural trade has diverged even further from GATT liberal principles in recent years with the greater use of long-term agreements and of central buying and selling agencies to trade agricultural commodities.[9] Furthermore, the U.S.-EC export subsidy conflict and the increasing pressures for protectionism in the U.S. Congress have posed an additional threat to liberal trading principles. There are, nevertheless, some encouraging signs that the increased competition and conflict in agricultural trade are forcing the major trading nations (in view of their interdependence) to consider seriously upgrading the role of GATT in this area. For example, major countries have held informal discussions on members' agricultural policies in the GATT and the Organization for Economic Co-operation and Development. Furthermore, GATT's dispute-settlement procedures have been used more frequently in recent years to challenge agricultural trade restrictions. In addition, a GATT ministerial meeting established a Committee on Trade in Agriculture (CTA) in November 1982 to do preparatory work for the Uruguay Round of trade negotiations. The Punta del Este Declaration launching the Uruguay Round in September 1986 stated that "negotiations shall aim to achieve greater liberalization of trade in agriculture" through reducing import barriers, increasing disciplines on the use of subsidies, and minimizing the adverse effects of sanitary regulations and barriers.[10]

As in the Kennedy and Tokyo Rounds, the United States and Canada have insisted that substantial progress must be made in agriculture during the Uruguay Round. Indeed, before the signing of the Punta del Este Declaration, the U.S. trade representative warned that the United States would only support new trade talks if agriculture and services were identified as "priority areas."[11] Furthermore, in July 1987 the Reagan administration introduced an ambitious and controversial proposal before GATT calling for "the elimination, over a ten-year period, of all export subsidies, all barriers to each other's markets . . . and all domestic subsidies that affect [agricultural] trade."[12] However, a major gap continues to exist between free trade rhetoric and the willingness of major countries to subject their agricultural policies to international negotiation. Thus, the United States indicated that the Reagan proposal would only be implemented on a reciprocal basis, and the U.S.-EC export subsidy contest is continuing in the interim (this issue is discussed in Chapter 4). Canada reacted favourably to the Reagan proposal, but it would also be reluctant to give up a number of its protectionist policies in agriculture. These problems are summarized in a U.S. government report, which concludes that GATT members "have usually placed domestic considerations . . . ahead of international trade impacts when developing agricultural policies" and that "this ordering of priorities . . . continues to inhibit efforts to strengthen GATT agricultural provisions."[13]

Frustration with the GATT led to the use of additional fora to deal with agricultural trade issues. Among these were the Organization for European Economic Co-operation (OEEC) and its successor, the Organization for Economic Co-operation and Development (OECD). The OEEC was established in 1948, with the West European countries as members and the United States and Canada having observer status. Its objectives included the promotion of economic stability and growth through European co-operation, and there was considerable concern about distortions in the agricultural policies of member countries. The OEEC at first adopted a GATT-like approach in attempting to prohibit quantitative restrictions on trade, but it later sought to expand trade through the identification of common interests and the co-ordination of national policies. This approach stemmed from recognition of the fact that domestic policies must be considered if agricultural trade problems are to be ameliorated, and a process of "confrontation" of national policies was developed. Each country's agricultural policies were examined by the other OEEC members, and there was an exchange of information, suggestions, and criticisms. It was felt that this confrontation process would induce national decision-makers to take greater account of each other's interests, but there is little evidence that national agricultural policies were altered as a result.

In September 1961 the OEEC was superseded by the OECD, which includes in its membership the non-Communist European countries (Yugoslavia is a special status country), Australia, Canada, Japan, New Zealand, Turkey, and the United States. The OECD publishes numerous analytical studies of issues that concern its members. In addition, it serves as a forum for discussing its members' economic policies, reviewing common problems, and sharing experiences and views. In many respects, the OECD and the GATT have represented complementary rather than competing mechanisms for dealing with problems. For example, the OECD Trade Committee has examined trade issues from a policy perspective, whereas the GATT has focused on the legal aspects of trade. OECD discussions on emerging issues have sometimes led to binding agreements in subsequent GATT negotiations. While preparations were underway for the GATT Uruguay Round, two OECD committees were conducting a Ministerial Trade Mandate (MTM) study requested by the OECD Ministerial Council. This study endeavours to show quantitatively the extent to which developed countries' agricultural sectors are distorted by income protection measures, and it sets an agenda for multilateral policy reform through national policy changes. When the preliminary report of the MTM work was released in May 1987, the OECD Council of Ministers issued a communiqué "committing" its members to reforming their domestic agricultural policies and to confronting agricultural trade problems in the GATT. However, the Uruguay Round will show whether the developed states are in fact willing to make the necessary policy changes.[14]

The OECD also has contributed to the development of some informal but organized commodity arrangements that have not required a negotiating conference or ratification by national legislatures. In 1963, for example, exporters established a gentlemen's agreement to sell whole milk at prices above an agreed minimum level.[15] However, the OECD continues to serve primarily as a forum for informal consultation and co-operation on trade issues. With its small membership and its confidential proceedings, it exerts influence on national policy decisions through dialogue rather than binding resolutions or commitments. It therefore could never substitute for the GATT in establishing and supervising norms and rules of conduct for agricultural trade.

Another multilateral body dealing with agricultural trade is the Food and Agriculture Organization's *Consultative Subcommittee on Surplus Disposal* (CSD). The creation of the CSD was directly related to the development of the U.S. Public Law 480 program. While PL 480 provided some countries with needed assistance, U.S. competitors feared that unregulated concessional sales would interfere with their commercial exports. Of particular concern was the American share of global wheat exports to less-developed countries, which increased from 36 per cent in fiscal years 1950–54 to 68 per cent in 1960–64. During the same period, Canada's share of global wheat exports to the LDCs decreased from 23 to 6 per cent, Australia's from 17 to 9 per cent, and Argentina's from 14 to 5 per cent. About 45 per cent of American wheat sales to LDCs in 1960–64 moved under the PL 480 program. The effects of PL 480 on U.S. competitors were already evident in 1954, and they wanted an international mechanism to regulate concessional transactions. GATT considered the issue in 1954–55, but largely because of U.S. opposition, it did not take action. As a result, the Food and Agriculture Organization (FAO) began to monitor the effects of concessional transactions on commercial sales.[16]

In 1954, the major trading nations adopted the FAO Principles of Surplus Disposal, which rely on the concept of "additionality" to ensure that surplus disposal programs such as PL 480 do not interfere with normal trading patterns. According to the additionality concept, agricultural commodities that are exported on concessional terms to a recipient country must be additional to (and therefore must not displace) normal commercial imports. The FAO Principles of Surplus Disposal "represent a commitment by signatory countries," but they "are not a binding instrument."[17] Since the legal status of the principles is unclear, their effectiveness depends on the willingness of members to accept the FAO's suggestions. To assist it in monitoring adherence to the principles, the FAO's Committee on Commodity Problems established the Consultative Subcommittee on Surplus Disposal (CSD). The subcommittee meets in Washington, D.C., on a monthly basis, and its membership is open to all FAO members. Governments are normally represented on the CSD by their agricultural or commercial counsellors or attachés based in Washington. About forty-six member states, the EC, nineteen observer states, and seven international organizations are represented. The CSD is served by a secretariat supplied by the FAO Liaison Office for North America in Washington and has backup support from the FAO in Rome. It has generally been dominated by the developed-country agricultural exporters, and the United States and Canada have been prominent members.

After developing a proposed food aid transaction, the donor country usually consults bilaterally with third countries that supply the same (or a related) commodity to the recipient. Following these bilateral consultations, the aid donor then consults multilaterally through the CSD, and all members may comment on the proposed transaction. To determine which transactions were within the CSD's purview, the FAO adopted a definition of surplus disposal as "an export operation (other than a sale covered by an international commodity agreement) arising from the existence or expectation of abnormal stocks, and made possible by the grant of special or concessional terms through government intervention."[18] The CSD generally does not deal with surplus disposal involving insignificant amounts of food aid, and its jurisdiction with regard to nonsurplus food aid is uncertain.[19] In 1970, the FAO tried to define the CSD role more precisely by compiling a list of transactions occurring in international trade. Thirteen of the twenty types listed were considered to be within the CSD's area of responsibility, and these were identified as the "Catalogue of Transactions."[20] Although CSD members must notify and consult with countries likely to be affected by transactions in the catalogue, they are not *required* to alter their policies in response to criticisms. The development of the catalogue has not ended debate over the CSD's role, and the most contentious issue concerns its competence—versus the GATT's—to deal with "grey area" transactions which have terms somewhere between concessional and commercial levels (see Chapters 5 and 6).

The major issues considered by the CSD gradually evolved along with changes in the global food system. In the early period of its operations, the subcommittee focused primarily on PL 480 since the United States was the only food aid donor of major significance. In the 1960s and 1970s, the CSD gradually broadened its focus and examined the policies of Canada, the European Community, and others as they joined the U.S. in providing substantial amounts of food aid. The CSD also became more concerned with LDC requirements, but it has continued to place primary emphasis on the interests and objectives of the developed-country agricultural exporters. It is difficult to assess the effectiveness of the FAO Principles of Surplus Disposal and the CSD. Although the principles are not binding, they have led to changes in the practices of food-exporting countries that were damaging to competitors' interests. Thus, the basic features of the principles were incorporated in the 1958 revision of PL 480 and in the Food Aid Convention of the 1967 International Grains Arrangement; and the World Food Program has also been guided by them. However, the scope of activities covered by the principles is limited. They do not apply to the use of export subsidies in commercial transactions, are less effective in regulating grey-area sales, and are not directly concerned with the domestic policies that lead to surpluses. They have been most effective in dealing with surplus disposal through food aid, but even in these transactions the additionality principle has not always been met, and third-country commercial exporters have suffered market losses.[21] Chapter 5 discusses the role of the FAO principles and the CSD in Canadian-American agricultural trade relations.

In summary, the GATT was ineffective during the period from the 1950s to the 1980s in establishing and upholding norms and rules to regulate agricultural trade transactions. While other international organizations (such as the OECD and the FAO's Consultative Subcommittee) performed some useful functions in this area, they were ill-equipped to take over the GATT's normative, rule-creating, and rule-supervisory roles. Canada often preferred to raise its concerns about American surplus disposal activities along with other countries in multilateral fora such as the CSD. However, in view of the limited mandates of the international organizations, Canada also felt the need to express its views more directly in bilateral fora with the United States. A number of bilateral groupings were therefore established in the 1950s and 1960s, often at Canada's initiative, which discussed food aid and agricultural trade issues. The next section of this chapter deals with some of these bilateral groups and committees.

BILATERAL GROUPINGS

A multitude of bilateral groups have dealt with agricultural trade issues, some of them focusing on food and agriculture only and others having broader mandates. These groupings were more prevalent in the 1950s and 1960s. Among the more general groups was the *Ministerial Committee on Trade and Economic Affairs* (or Trade Committee), which was established in November 1953. Canada had proposed that the Trade Committee be created in an effort to combat American protectionism under the Eisenhower administration. The committee's stated objectives were "to consider matters affecting the harmonious economic relations between the two countries" and to exchange views and information on issues that could adversely affect bilateral trade.[22] Like most Canadian-American committees, the Trade Committee provided an informal setting where priorities could be established, ministers could become better acquainted, and the way could be smoothed for more formal negotiations. The meetings were also designed to counteract "tunnel vision" or overspecialization by individual ministers. Although bilateral committees confer legal parity, there is no assurance of operational parity, and the disparity between American and Canadian influence was very apparent in the Trade Committee.[23]

In earlier years the Trade Committee provided an effective forum for discussion, and its achievements were quite creditable. However, the informal meetings were gradually replaced by a more structured format, in which considerable effort was spent on preparing communiqués for the press. The exploratory and frank consultations were lost because of the increased publicity, and the meetings tended to become a platform for predictable, standard speeches. The Trade Committee met only thirteen times, usually on Canada's initiative, and the meetings were suspended after November 1970 for a number of reasons: it had become almost impossible to bring American and Canadian ministers together every year (especially the Americans, who devoted less attention to Canada); the November 1970 meeting was a failure because of personality conflicts and inadequate preparation; the U.S. imposition of its 10 per cent import surcharge in August 1971 seemed to end the two countries' "special relationship"; and other forms of bilateral communication were used during the early 1970s, including summit meetings and conferences between individual ministers.

The Trade Committee's decline was especially detrimental to Canadian interests since it had "force[d] the American Government to think, at least once a year, about Canada on an orderly basis and within a set context."[24] Canada regularly raised the issue of agricultural protectionism at the meetings because the U.S. Congress had been agitating for additional import restrictions on frozen fish fillets, oats, and dairy products; on the other hand, the U.S. complained about Canadian restrictions on turkeys, peas, and other agricultural products. Canada also repeatedly expressed its concerns about U.S. surplus disposal policies, and a communiqué from the first Trade Committee meeting stated that the two governments "in disposing of agricultural surpluses abroad . . . [would] consult with interested countries and not . . . interfere with normal commercial marketing."[25] PL 480 operations were well established by the time of the second Trade Committee meeting in September 1955, and Canada strongly protested that the U.S. surplus disposal program was interfering with its commercial grain sales. Canadian ministers in fact won some important concessions at the meetings, including an agreement not to interfere with normal commercial marketings, a U.S. pledge not to follow objectionable barter policies, and a decision to establish agricultural trade and marketing committees. Partly because of these agreements, U.S. surplus disposal policies became a less important issue in Canadian-American relations. However, one should not overestimate the Trade Committee's effectiveness since the United States did not always adhere to the agreed principles.[26]

As mentioned, the Trade Committee decided (at Canada's behest) to set up agricultural trade and marketing committees or working groups. When Canada expressed concerns about U.S. surplus disposal practices at the September 1955 Trade Committee meeting, a Consultative Committee on Grain Marketing (or Consultative Committee) was formed to resolve the difficulties. In the Consultative Committee, Canada complained that American surplus disposal programs were contributing to a serious reduction of its commercial markets, and it specifically criticized U.S. barter, wheat and flour subsidies, and auction sales. On the other hand, the United States sought assurances that Canada would supply credit to Eastern Europe only on commercial terms, and it requested that Canada 'voluntarily" limit feed wheat, seed wheat, barley, and oat exports to the United States. Although it was established to deal with conflictual issues, the Consultative Committee also served as a forum for bilateral co-operation to resolve common American and Canadian problems. For example, mutual concerns were expressed regarding the European Community's agricultural practices, and the two countries co-ordinated their policies on an International Wheat Agreement.

Canadian officials acknowledged that the Consultative Committee discussions had some effect on U.S. wheat disposal policies, but "there was a feeling that the meetings were not constructive . . . and . . . a growing concern about the continual enlargement of American programmes." In contrast, American officials were far more positive, maintaining that the "exchange of views at these meetings were helpful" in keeping Canadian-American relations "on a friendly and co-operative basis."[27] The meetings in fact were beneficial in some respects, but the benefits were limited. While the United States dropped certain policies that threatened Canadian agricultural exports, they often replaced them with other practices that were equally objectionable.

In January 1959, the Ministerial Trade Committee established another working group, the Quarterly Meetings on Wheat and Related Matters. The Trade Committee issued a communiqué indicating that the "quarterly meetings of wheat experts from the two countries . . . [would] attempt to solve periodically any problems involving wheat and flour, including those arising from United States surplus disposal operations." The meetings also provided an opportunity to consult on Canadian shipments to Communist countries and less-developed countries (LDCs) and served as a forum for exchanging views and promoting co-operation on the GATT, World Food Program, European Community, and other issues. Canada considered the quarterly meetings to be extremely important since they contributed to U.S. acceptance of the additionality principle for its surplus disposal programs and to U.S. awareness of the adverse effects of its agricultural barter program on commercial transactions. The quarterly meetings were suspended after fourteen sessions had been held between January

1959 and May 1963, partly because of differences over Canada's pricing policies on wheat sales to the Soviet Union and China. American and Canadian officials met in April and June 1964 to review bilateral consultative procedures, and there were consultations in the Kennedy Round and regular diplomatic communications. However, the United States became more preoccupied with expanding its commercial sales (and less responsive to Canadian complaints), and it did not move immediately to reinstitute the quarterly meetings.[28]

In the June 1967 Ministerial Trade Committee meeting, the United States and Canada decided to establish the Technical Committee in Agricultural Marketing and Trade Problems (or the Technical Committee). However, this was not even mentioned in a press release. The Technical Committee consisted of senior American and Canadian officials and first met in November 1967, with further meetings planned for the spring and fall of each year. But, it never issued communiqués, and there was no public announcement of the Technical Committee's demise when the Ministerial Trade Committee at its November 1970 meeting opted instead for a less formal "agricultural consultation procedure." This consultative procedure could be invoked by either the United States or Canada to deal with bilateral agricultural trade disputes. Representatives meeting to resolve disputes normally included members of the U.S. Department of Agriculture and Canadian Department of Industry, Trade and Commerce. Others participating when necessary included the U.S. Department of State, the president's special trade representative, and Canada's Department of External Affairs. This consultative process was adopted for trade disputes involving eggs, fruits, vegetables, poultry, and other agricultural products.[29]

In recent years, consultations between the American secretary of agriculture and the Canadian agriculture minister have been held on a regular basis. For example, in May 1977 the agriculture minister and agriculture secretary began a series of discussions concerning developments in Canada-U.S. agriculture, cooperation in agricultural research, the International Wheat Agreement, and the multilateral trade negotiations. This relationship was regularized in October 1984 when the agriculture secretary, agriculture minister, and minister of state for the Canadian Wheat Board agreed to hold semi-annual ministerial-level meetings. The leaders emphasized the importance of these meetings in view of the growth of bilateral trade in agricultural products and the significant exports of both countries to third-country markets.[30]

In addition to the Ministerial Trade Committee and its working groups and the one-to-one meetings between ministers, the Canada-United States Interparliamentary Group (IP Group) has also devoted some attention to agricultural trade issues. Canadian parliamentarians had pressured for creation of a liaison group since World War II in efforts to increase the awareness and sensitivity of the U.S. Congress to Canada's concerns. There was considerable delay, however, in establishing such a group since American legislators did not feel that it was necessary. Only after bilateral relations deteriorated in the late 1950s (largely because of Canadian annoyance with Congressional actions) did legislators in both countries feel that an IP Group might help to alleviate conflicts. The hearings that led to the formation of the group revealed that U.S. surplus disposal policies were one of the major sources of tension. Indeed, a 1958 editorial in the Toronto *Globe and Mail* argued that the lack of liaison with the Congress "helps to explain why so much legislation directly affecting Canada—tariff changes, import quotas, statutes authorizing the dumping of U.S. surplus wheat abroad—is passed without any consideration of its effect on Canadian interests."[31]

The Interparliamentary Group was finally established in 1959 by joint resolutions of the U.S. Congress and Canadian Parliament, and it brings legislators from the two countries together about once a year to discuss mutual problems. It was agreed at the group's January 1959 organizational session that meetings would be off-the-record and closed to the press and that votes would not be taken. Aside from these regular meetings, the group would have no ongoing existence through an operating staff.

The IP Group has served primarily as a forum for exchanging information, discussing bilateral problems, and promoting mutual understanding. Before 1975, the leaders of the two national delegations had prepared a joint report for release at the end of each conference, but these reports were uninformative and gave the impression of greater unanimity than actually existed. Since 1975 each country has drafted its own reports, and they generally have been longer and more descriptive. The behaviour of the American and Canadian delegations has differed in some major respects, largely because of asymmetry of attention between the two countries. Since Canadian legislators usually have more griev-ances to express, they "have tended to coalesce 'to present a united front to the American delegates.'" In contrast, Canadian issues have attracted much less attention in the United States, and "American delegates have usually felt less need to present a common front."[32]

Agricultural trade has been regularly discussed in the IP Group, but the issues examined have obviously changed over time. In the 1950s and 1960s, Canadian parliamentarians criticized U.S. surplus disposal policies, and Ameri-can congressmen in turn conveyed their antagonism over Canada's trade with the Communist states (especially China and Cuba). To some extent the meet-ings have contributed to mutual understanding among legislators. For example, several Canadian delegates indicated that "we had to convince the Americans that we weren't ogres for selling to the Communists or even sympathetic to them, as many seemed to think—just because we were selling wheat."[33] In the early 1980s, the group occasionally held ad hoc meetings that focused on international wheat-marketing.[34] Most recently, the IP Group has served as a forum for the exchange of legislative views on contentious issues such as the U.S. Export Enhancement Program and the bilateral free trade agreement.[35]

The IP Group also has contributed to habits of co-operation that help to explain the meetings between American and Canadian senators from wheat-growing areas during the 1978–79 International Wheat Agreement negotiations (discussed in Chapter 4). These senators held major meetings in June and September 1978 to promote greater co-operation among the exporting states in maintaining wheat prices. However, while the IP Group has provided legislators with greater knowledge and understanding of each other, its overall record has been mixed. In 1975, the Canadian Senate Committee on Foreign Affairs concluded that the group "could become an important instrument for increasing Congressional awareness of Canada" but that it "has not come close to achieving its potential."[36]

Another relevant bilateral group is the *Canadian-American Committee*, which was created in 1957 "to study problems arising from growing interdependence between Canada and the United States."[37] The committee consists of business, labour, professional, and agricultural leaders, and it is sponsored by two nonprofit research organizations—the National Planning Association in the United States, and the C. D. Howe Institute in Canada.[38] Meetings are held twice a year (once in each country) and give members the opportunity to discuss a broad range of issues with government officials, scholars, and other individuals knowledgeable about Canada-U.S. relations. The committee's most important function is to sponsor research studies on the bilateral relationship, and policy statements are released on a number of subjects "to increase public understanding in Canada and the United States of the extent of interdependence between the two countries."[39] The committee's studies include valuable analyses of bilateral and international trade issues. In the 1950s and 1960s, a number of the studies and policy statements focused specifically on agricultural trade problems, but from the 1970s to early 1980s these problems received little attention. This situation paralleled the inattention to the agricultural aspect of Canadian-American relations in the scholarly literature. In subsequent chapters, frequent reference is made to the earlier committee studies.

CONCLUSIONS

Some concluding observations regarding the independent and dependent variables are now in order. First, the limited ability of the GATT and other international organizations to deal with agricultural trade issues is a reflection of the inadequate agricultural trade regime. Partly because of the limitations of these multilateral channels, Canada turned to bilateral strategies to achieve some of its agricultural export objectives. As a smaller country, Canada often pressured for the creation of bilateral groups with the United States for a variety of reasons: it had more grievances to express, it was concerned about the lack of U.S. attention to its complaints, and it needed American support on many third-country agricultural trade issues. Thus, Canada proposed that the Minis-terial Committee on Trade and Economic Affairs be created in efforts to combat U.S. protectionism; Canada's concerns regarding American surplus disposal policies were a major factor in the establishment of the Consultative Commit-tee on Grain Marketing and the Quarterly Meetings on Wheat and Related Matters; and Canadian parliamentarians had favoured a link with the U.S. Congress long before American legislators acknowledged the need.

A second observation is that the United States was often inclined to adopt unilateral strategies in the 1950s and 1960s. American unilateralism resulted partly from the country's economic size and importance and partly from its role as the largest agricultural exporter. Thus, the United States sought to prevent the GATT from establishing stringent norms and regulations for agricultural trade, and it also requested a broad-ranging waiver from its GATT obligations in 1955. Furthermore, the U.S. PL 480 program was a major unilateral initiative that had far-reaching consequences for export competitors. This chapter pro-vides some confirmation of Keohane and Nye's finding that the typical conflict on socio-economic issues "was for the United States . . . to take a unilateral . . . action to which the smaller partners tended to respond by demanding redress through diplomatic channels."[40]

This chapter also provides further support for the hypothesis that competi-tion and conflict can lead to new forms of co-operation between interdependent states. Canada sought to establish bilateral groupings in the 1950s and 1960s to voice its dissatisfaction with U.S. surplus disposal policies, and the United States often responded positively to this request. The United States and Canada obviously valued their "special relationship," which was partly based on Cana-dian efforts to seek exemptions from American actions. In other cases, groups were formed in response to a deterioration in bilateral relations (e.g., the Interparliamentary Group) or as a response to "problems arising from growing interdependence" (e.g., the Canadian-American Committee).[41] These groups provided fora, not only for the discussion of bilateral differences but also for the development of common American and Canadian positions with regard to the European Community, the GATT, the World Food Program, and the Interna-tional Wheat Agreements. In the early 1970s, the Ministerial Committee on

Trade and Economic Affairs was disbanded, and no new agricultural working groups were formed. While this partly resulted from the special circumstances of the period (see Chapter 1 on the Third Option policy), there was also little need for agricultural groupings to resolve differences during a time of food-grain shortages. With the re-emergence of surpluses in the late 1970s, the American and Canadian agriculture ministers began to hold meetings, and these meetings were regularized in 1984. Furthermore, agriculture (and the issue of dispute settlement) was included in the bilateral free trade agreement, in part because of the need to resolve serious conflicts in this area.

Finally, this chapter tells us more about the conditions under which American political-security objectives led to co-operation or conflict. Chapter 2 demonstrated that U.S. preoccupation with security issues contributed to a co-operative relationship with Canada in the 1950s and 1960s since the United States limited its trade with Canada's major Communist markets. However, this chapter shows that conflict sometimes developed when the United States tried to impose its political-security objectives on others. Thus, the Canada-U.S. quarterly meetings were suspended in part because the United States objected to Canadian pricing policies on wheat exports to the Soviet Union and China. In conclusion, when the United States limited *its own* activities with the Communist states, its actions normally contributed to co-operation with Canada. However, conflict sometimes occurred when the U.S. expected Canada to follow similar policies.

While this chapter has focused on the weakness of the international agricultural trade regime in general terms, Chapter 4 deals with the regime's failure in one specific area: pricing arrangements. "Pricing" was one of the four main agricultural trade objectives of the United States and Canada (see Chapter 1). Yet, the two countries could not depend on regime norms and rules in this area and therefore sought other means (such as a Canadian-American duopolistic arrangement) of achieving their pricing objectives.

4

International Pricing Arrangements

A major agricultural trade objective of both the United States and Canada is to export their commodities at remunerative prices. This common objective has led to close interactions between the two states, particularly in the case of the wheat trade. Indeed, changes in international wheat-pricing arrangements over time often have been closely linked with alterations in Canadian-American relations. For example, many scholars feel that duopolistic co-operation between the United States and Canada was largely responsible for the stability of international wheat prices in the 1950s and 1960s. The breakdown of this duopoly in the late 1960s eventually led to a situation of unstable and declining prices in the 1980s, with the U.S. and the European Community involved in an export subsidy war, and Canada critically watching from the sidelines. This chapter traces the gradual evolution of pricing arrangements, focusing on the period of duopolistic co-operation during the 1950s and 1960s; the breakdown of the duopoly in the late 1960s; the period of rapid price increases in the early to mid-1970s; the search for new pricing arrangements in the late 1970s; and the period of unstable and declining prices during the late 1970s and 1980s.

THE CANADIAN-AMERICAN DUOPOLY AND PRICE STABILITY

There is a long history of informal Canadian-American consultation on agricultural trade issues, and these co-operative habits are a function of the interdependence between the two states. Bilateral consultations on grain issues have been almost continuous from the time of the Depression, when the United States urged the Canadian government to join in efforts to control production and exports. The consultations continued during World War II, particularly when the U.S. had a shortage of feedgrains, and after the war when a new International Wheat Agreement was concluded.[1]

In the early postwar years, consultation was especially close between the two countries' export agencies, the Commodity Credit Corporation (CCC) and the Canadian Wheat Board (CWB). To co-ordinate the movement of Canadian grain to the United States during the war (in 1943), the chief commissioner of the Wheat Board had suggested that it should establish an office in Washington, D.C., for liaison purposes. The CWB was then invited to occupy an office in the U.S. Department of Agriculture (USDA) building. The American government and the CWB therefore maintained daily contact on such issues as the combined food board, the international emergency food council, the European Recovery Program, and the International Wheat Agreement negotiations. The heads of the two export agencies (the CCC and the CWB) met to discuss major issues, and consultations were also held at the ministerial level when necessary. After Dwight D. Eisenhower became president in 1953, the advantages of these close contacts became less evident to his administration. It requested that the Wheat Board move its office out of the USDA building, and this change marked a shift towards more formal negotiations between the two governments. Nevertheless, informal bilateral co-operation continued to exist in other forms.[2]

With the development of North American grain surpluses in the 1950s, it was inevitable that competition between the United States and Canada would increase. Canadian feedgrain, malting barley and rye exports to the U.S. were 'the first to suffer strain and curtailment under surplus conditions. Price competition also emerged in an attempt to maintain market shares in the shrinking overseas markets for wheat and flour.'[3] To limit their competition and to co-operate in expanding wheat markets and managing prices, the United States and Canada maintained the habits of consultation they had developed in earlier years. Many analysts have characterized their co-operative arrangements in the 1950s and 1960s as a "Canadian-American duopoly." Since the duopoly was closely linked with the maintenance of the International Wheat Agreements, it is first necessary to provide some information on these agreements.

International efforts to maintain stable wheat prices began after the build-up of surpluses in the late 1920s and the subsequent collapse of prices during the Depression. The first International Wheat Agreement (IWA) was established in 1933, and its stated objectives were "to adjust the supply of wheat to effective world demand and eliminate the abnormal surpluses which have been depressing the wheat market, and to bring about a rise and stabilization of prices."[4] The agreement proved to be ineffective in stabilizing prices, and it virtually broke down within a year. However, it initiated the important principle that both wheat-exporting and -importing countries should participate in such agreements and should have rights and obligations. A Wheat Advisory Committee set up to monitor the application of the 1933 IWA was superseded in August 1942 by the International Wheat Council (IWC), which is responsible for convening conferences and for overseeing the implementation of agreements. The IWC was at first located in Washington, D.C., but it was later moved to London. Its membership consists of about sixty countries, including the major exporting and importing states.

The second IWA in 1949 was far more successful than the 1933 agreement in achieving its objectives of assuring "supplies of wheat to importing countries and markets for wheat to exporting countries at equitable and stable prices," and the same was true of the IWAs in 1953, 1956, 1959, and 1962.[5] Maximum and minimum prices were established for wheat traded under the IWAs, and consuming countries agreed to import a specific quantity (the 1949 to 1956 IWAs) or percentage of their total requirements (the IWAs since 1959) from producing countries that were signatories to the agreements. The minimum and maximum prices were based on the price of a reference wheat, No. 1 Manitoba Northern (the highest quality Canadian wheat), delivered at Fort William/Port Arthur, Canada. The average export price for the reference wheat was unusually stable and remained within the IWA price range for most of the 1949–67 period.[6]

While the wheat agreements deserve some credit for this price stability, cooperation between the United States and Canada, whose representatives met quarterly to agree on price levels, was probably a more important factor. For example, prices of wheats other than the reference wheat were not specified in the IWAs, and price differentials were usually established through informal understandings between the U.S. and Canada.[7] Australia and Argentina sometimes participated in these discussions, but price stability was most likely maintained by a Canadian-American duopoly rather than an oligopoly for several reasons. First, the United States and Canada accounted for between 60 and 70 per cent of the world wheat trade during this period. Second, only these two countries had sufficient storage facilities to permit stockholding, and after a sharp rise in carryover stocks in 1953, they consistently held from 80 to 90 per cent of the total stocks of the five major exporting states. The United States and Canada were also willing to control domestic production and maintain stocks, and their actions played a crucial role in stabilizing prices. For example, when the Soviet Union purchased massive amounts of wheat in 1963–64, world trade reached record levels, and carryover stocks were reduced by almost nine million tonnes. Nevertheless, prices rose by only about 10 per cent and did not reach the maximum level set in the 1962 IWA. This successful containment of prices resulted from the existence of about fifty-five million tonnes of carryover stocks at the beginning of 1963–64, most of which were held by the United States and Canada.[8]

Although the United States and Canada both contributed to the successful operation of the duopoly, the asymmetry in their economic size and productive potential was markedly evident. Canada was the dominant price leader, but only because the United States was agreeable to having Canada lead. The U.S. was showing considerable restraint during this period by disposing of much of its surplus wheat through non-commercial channels (i.e., through PL 480), and it probably preferred not to dominate the commercial wheat market overtly as the price leader. However, when the United States became increasingly dissatisfied with the duopolistic arrangement, it switched from a bilateral to a unilateral strategy. As soon as the United States chose to do so, it was able to emerge as the "dominant force in world wheat pricing."[9]

THE BREAKDOWN OF THE DUOPOLY

Jon McLin has described the Canadian-American duopoly of the 1950s and 1960s as a "surrogate system" of world food security since it functioned in the absence of an international arrangement with explicit multilateral obligations and administrative responsibilities undertaken by an international secretariat. It is evident that the duopoly had some beneficial effects, but the decision to terminate it depended on only two states that became less supportive when co-operation in international wheat trade declined in the mid-1960s. Thus, surrogate international arrangements often lack political, legal, and institutional restraints against unilateral decision-making, and they are unreliable substitutes for a regime with formalized principles and regulations.[10]

American officials became increasingly dissatisfied with the duopolistic arrangement in the 1960s, largely because voluntary acreage restrictions and high support prices made the United States a residual supplier in the commercial wheat market. Growing American concerns about its balance of payments deficit merely added to the dissatisfaction with its role. Furthermore, the United States always priced its wheat above the IWA minimums (until its policy changed in 1965), but Canada and other exporters sometimes set prices at lower levels through their marketing boards to increase their market shares. Table 4–1 shows that the American portion of total wheat exports (including concessional sales) was often in the 40 per cent range but that its percentage of *commercial* wheat exports was considerably lower. On the other hand, a large share of Canadian wheat exports were moved on a commercial basis. In 1964–65, for example, Canada accounted for 34 per cent of the world's commercial wheat exports, while the U.S. share was only 12 per cent. It is not surprising that a USDA official questioned "whether or not it is in U.S. interests to continue to support world wheat prices at levels which hold a price umbrella over our competitors at a time when our own commercial wheat markets are increasingly found in dollar short developing countries."[11]

TABLE 4–1

U.S. AND CANADIAN SHARES OF WORLD WHEAT EXPORTS

(percentages)

	1953/4-1955/6	1959/60-1961/2	1962/3	1963/4	1964/5
Commercial Exports					
Canada	35	36	35	37	34
United States	10	21	12	22	12
Total Exports					
Canada	29	23	22	27	24
United States	29	45	43	42	39

Source: Jon McLin, "Surrogate International Organization and the Case of World Food Security, 1949-1969," *International Organization* 33-1 (Winter 1979): 52.

To strengthen its competitive position, the United States lowered its price supports for wheat and adopted more aggressive marketing techniques. Since American wheat was priced very competitively from early 1965, the U.S. share of international markets increased, from 7 to 22 per cent in Britain and from 53 to 79 per cent in Japan. Canada criticized this new price aggressiveness of the United States and maintained that its own ability to offer prices below the IWA-negotiated minimum was limited since the IWA reference wheat was a Canadian variety.

Despite the growing discord, the United States and Canada continued their co-operative efforts and joined with Australia and Argentina to propose that a new wheat agreement be negotiated. Representatives of these four countries met in Washington in September 1966 and adopted a common position, which they subsequently discussed with the major importers. The American delegates, however, sought to ensure that a new agreement would not be patterned on the old model. They proposed that market-sharing provisions should come into effect when world wheat prices fell below the agreed minimums. This would prevent other exporters from gaining markets at U.S. expense because of cut-throat pricing. The United States also tried to obtain assurances that exporters would "manage" domestic wheat supplies to decrease the pressure of surpluses. In addition, the U.S. used delaying tactics to pressure for the inclusion of coarse grains as well as wheat in a new agreement. This prompted the president of the Saskatchewan Wheat Pool to state that "Canadians do not want to see discussion about trade in these grains actually do damage to an agreement about trade in wheat."[12]

An International Grains Arrangement (IGA) was eventually approved in 1967, even though some major American demands (for example, with regard to coarse grains) had not been met. The IGA consisted of two separate instruments: a Wheat Trade Convention (WTC), which was a successor to the IWAs and only applied to trade in wheat; and a Food Aid Convention, which provided for foodgrain contributions from donor states to less-developed countries (LDCs). The WTC followed the same basic approach as the 1959 and 1962 IWAs, committing importing countries to purchase a minimum share of their wheat from exporting members and exporters to satisfy the importers' commercial requirements. Unlike previous agreements, however, minimum and maximum prices in the 1967 WTC were based on an American rather than a Canadian reference wheat, U.S. Hard Red Winter No. 2, delivered at U.S. gulf port positions. This change was simply an acknowledgement that the United States was a far more important agricultural exporter than Canada: American wheat now predominated in international trade; Canada's No. 1 Manitoba Northern wheat was not regularly traded throughout the year; and the U.S. gulf ports were the world's largest wheat shipping centres.[13]

The 1967 Wheat Trade Convention was in trouble from the time it was ratified for a number of reasons. The minimum agreed prices in the WTC were unrealistically high and did not accurately reflect changes in supply in the world market. This pricing problem was largely the result of the unusually long period (nearly a year) between the conclusion of the negotiating conference and the entry into force of the agreement. Thus, the production of abundant crops and a decline in world trade after 1965–66 caused export prices to fall dramatically even before the WTC came into force. Some traditional importers had increased grain yields because of favourable weather and technological advances, and purchases from the Soviet Union in particular declined. Wheat stocks rose by over nineteen million tonnes in 1968–69 alone and were in excess of sixty-two million tonnes by the end of that year. As a result, the executive secretariat for the International Wheat Council was forced to conclude that "the effect of the great weight of supplies available to the world market, including the substantial exportable surpluses of non-member countries and the contraction of import demand . . . made the price range negotiated in 1967 untenable."[14]

American discontent with the international pricing arrangements was also a major factor in the ineffectiveness of the WTC. The United States had pledged that it would agree to no industrial bargains at the GATT Kennedy Round without significant progress in the agricultural area. Since something had to be given to its farmers, the U.S. was willing to endorse the WTC with its promise of higher, artificially-pegged prices. However, the United States felt less committed to the WTC price levels because they were not backed by market-sharing or supply management agreements. It therefore disposed of 750 million bushels of grain in world markets in 1967–68, contributing to a decrease in prices below WTC levels even before the convention went into effect. The undersecretary of agriculture explained to a Senate subcommittee in March 1968 that the United States had to act unilaterally since market-sharing was not embodied in the wheat agreement. In contrast to the United States, Canada held wheat off the market during this period in attempts to strengthen the WTC pricing provisions. American farmers were less dependent on the WTC since they were insulated from world prices by domestic income and price support policies. However, Canadian farmers received only minor subsidies, and the WTC was therefore viewed as essential to maintaining their prices. Another factor in Canadian support for the WTC was the greater importance of wheat to the economy. Thus, the Saskatchewan Wheat Pool president remarked that "when Canada talks about grain production and exports we really talk about wheat," while the United States "sometimes gives more attention to the coarse grains and oilseed crops."[15]

It should be emphasized that the United States certainly was not alone in following policies that undermined the duopoly and the 1967 Wheat Trade Convention. The Australian policy of pricing to sell its entire wheat crop, combined with its production increases during the late 1950s and 1960s, also had a destabilizing effect on the duopoly. In addition, non-members of the WTC such as the Soviet Union had a destabilizing influence since they did not adhere to the minimum prices established. The most important countries other than the United States, however, were the members of the European Community. France "apparently took the lead in breaking down minimum prices established under the International Grains Arrangement," and the EC's protectionist Common Agricultural Policy (CAP) contributed to heightened competition and conflict among the major exporters.[16]

The fundamental elements of the CAP were announced in 1962, and it came into effect for grains in July 1967. A fully controlled market was established in which target prices were set for major crops. To insulate the market from world prices, the European Community adopted a variable levy system to boost the entry price of commodities so that Community products would always enjoy a competitive advantage over imports. In cases of surplus production, the EC provided subsidies for exports or diversion to lower use, such as animal feed. Receipts of agricultural tariffs and levies were put in a Guidance and Guarantee Fund to finance the subsidies. The United States and Canada argued that the CAP was contributing to mounting surpluses that were being foisted on the international market and that enormous export subsidies to dispose of French soft wheat surpluses were in fact interfering with some North American markets.

From the time the WTC came into effect, then, strong downward pressures were being exerted on the negotiated price level, and prices declined to well below the WTC minimums in the late summer and fall of 1968. The major exporters began high-level discussions and a long series of private consultations in September 1968 in efforts to reconcile their competing interests and prevent a further worsening of the price situation. A special meeting of the exporters was held in Washington, D.C., in July 1969 to discuss a U.S. proposal that the pricing provisions of the WTC be suspended for six months. Under threat of a price war, Australia indicated that it would co-operate in maintaining the market shares of the United States and Canada, and according to some analysts, the Canadian-American duopoly became a "triopoly" for about two years.[17] The quarterly meetings between U.S. and Canadian wheat authorities began to include Australia, and Australia became more willing (and able) to share the burden of stockholding to maintain prices. Table 4-2 shows that Australian carryover stocks increased sharply in 1968–69 and in 1969–70, but they continued to be far smaller than American and Canadian stocks.

TABLE 4-2

U.S., CANADIAN, AND AUSTRALIAN END-OF-SEASON CARRYOVER STOCKS

(1000 tonnes)

Season	U.S.	Canada	Australia
1963-64	24,532	12,504	552
1965-66	14,565	11,434	453
1967-68	14,657	18,112	1,402
1968-69	22,226	23,183	7,259
1969-70	24,086	27,452	7,217
1970-71	19,894	19,882	3,404

Source: International Wheat Council, *World Wheat Statistics*, in Chris M. Alaouze, A. S. Watson, and N. H. Sturgess, "Oligopoly Pricing in the World Wheat Market," *American Journal of Agricultural Economics* 60 (May 1978): 178.

The consultations among the major wheat exporters did result in some measures to stabilize prices, such as the American, Canadian, and Australian policies to bring production into better balance with demand. However, these efforts to promote stabilization occurred totally outside the domain of the 1967 WTC, and in the end orderly marketing was not maintained (as it had been, for example, in 1963-64). Furthermore, the duopoly—or triopoly—was weakening in the face of increased competition from the European Community, and there seemed to be no other comparable "surrogate system" to replace it.

THE PERIOD OF RAPID PRICE INCREASES

Despite the disappointing record of the 1967 WTC, major exporting and importing countries continued to seek international co-operation, and preparatory work for a new wheat agreement began in 1970. A 1971 Wheat Trade Convention was eventually ratified, but it differed markedly from previous agreements since price ranges were not included. The new agreement simply provided for the continuation of the International Wheat Council and its functions of monitoring world prices and collecting information on the wheat trade. The failure to include pricing provisions in the 1971 WTC stemmed partly from a variety of technical problems. For example, the United States objected to the fact that only the prices of its wheats had been firmly stated in the 1967 agreement, while the prices of most other wheats had been determined with less precision. However, no alternative recommendation for choosing a reference wheat for the 1971 WTC was agreed upon. There were also disagreements between the United States, on the one hand, and Canada and Australia on the other, regarding the price range to be established.

Even though they failed to decide upon an effective WTC with pricing provisions, the major wheat exporters continued to maintain co-operative habits through informal meetings. From September 1968, the United States, Canada, and Australia had been holding high-level meetings to prevent a worsening of the price situation, to bring production into better balance with demand, and to explore whether exporting states could be assured of equitable market shares. As a result of these meetings, the three major exporters developed programs to limit production. Canada introduced its "Lower Inventory for Tomorrow" (LIFT) program in 1970, a one-year adjustment program that provided farmers with financial payments to convert large amounts of wheat acreage into summerfallow and perennial forage land. The LIFT program marked the first time that Canada imposed direct limitations on acreage, and it caused a decrease from a predicted twenty-two million acres of wheat to an actual twelve million acres in 1970. While Canadian wheat stocks had been expanding prior to the LIFT program, they declined sharply thereafter. American production cutbacks were naturally of a much greater magnitude than Canada's. In 1972, the United States held out of production about sixty-two million acres of land, an amount that approached the total acreage of the principal crops planted in Canada that year.[18]

With the production cutbacks in the major exporting countries, the world was especially vulnerable to inclement weather, massive Soviet grain purchases, and other unexpected events, and carryover stocks in 1972–73 fell to their lowest levels in twenty years. International wheat prices increased by about 200 per cent since the United States and Canada were no longer holding large reserves and the 1971 WTC did not contain pricing provisions. This situation marked a sharp contrast to the 1963–64 period when carryover stocks were sufficient to absorb the shock of large and unexpected Soviet purchases. Furthermore, the change to a scarcity situation precluded the possibility of establishing a new agreement with price ranges since surplus rather than deficit conditions have usually provided the main motivation for concluding international wheat agreements.[19]

Beginning in 1972–73, then, the world wheat market was characterized by high, unstable prices and low carryover stocks. Instead of a duopoly or an oligopoly, the market was operating essentially on a competitive basis. The American policy shift towards a more market-oriented policy in 1973 simply added to the price instability. Furthermore, the U.S. balance of payments problems that had led President Nixon to end the convertibility of the dollar into gold in August 1971 was yet another destabilizing factor.[20]

> Unfortunately for U.S. agriculture, boom and bust global macroeconomic instability has been a fact of life since 1971 when the "Bretton Woods" system of fixed international currency exchange rates finally collapsed. World commodity markets—including farm markets—have borne much of the burden of this collapse.

Although American and Canadian farmers benefited from the increased demand for grains, they also faced uncertainty in view of the wider price fluctuations after 1972. Price instability poses an especially difficult problem for farmers since they must make production commitments long before their commodities can be marketed. Today, these commitments involve the purchase of expensive equipment and other inputs because modern agriculture has become so capital intensive. The renewal of surpluses, combined with the new forces of instability, would prove to be an excessively difficult combination for many North American farmers.

THE SEARCH FOR NEW PRICING ARRANGEMENTS

When grain surpluses re-emerged in the late 1970s, the major wheat exporters became more interested in replacing the 1971 Wheat Trade Convention (which had been extended) with an agreement to stabilize prices. The industrial, and LDC importing states were also interested in a new wheat agreement with pricing provisions for several reasons. The world food crisis of 1973–74 had demonstrated to many developing countries that they were extremely vulnerable when carryover stocks were depleted and prices rapidly increased. Although the richer countries were able to pay the higher prices for imports during the food crisis, they were affected by the inflation that resulted from the increased costs for basic foodstuffs. The World Food Council had recommended that a new wheat agreement should establish an international system of nationally held grain reserves to ensure food security, and with the re-emergence of surpluses it was possible to establish such reserves. As a result, the International Wheat Council in 1977 asked its Preparatory Group to prepare a draft wheat agreement as a negotiating text, and a United Nations Negotiating Conference was convened on 13 February 1978 during the Tokyo Round of multilateral trade negotiations.[21]

As in previous wheat trade negotiations, the 1978–79 conference was preceded by meetings between Canada and the United States to resolve their differences and establish common positions. The representatives at these meetings were the U.S. secretary of agriculture, the minister responsible for the Canadian Wheat Board, and the Canadian minister of agriculture. These bilateral meetings were followed by informal discussions with Australia and Argentina to establish solidarity among the four major exporters, and they continued to hold separate discussions throughout the negotiating period. As Canada's chief negotiator at the talks noted, the exporting countries worked "very closely together . . . [and] met regularly both when the Conference was sitting and when it was not."[22] The major exporters did not adopt a common position on *every* issue; for example, Australia and Argentina were less enthusiastic than the U.S. and Canada about establishing large wheat reserves. Nevertheless, the exporters did develop a united front for each session of the IWA talks. The situation had changed, however, since the days of the Canadian-American duopoly. International competition and conflict on wheat issues had increased, partly because of the growing influence of the European Community, Japan, and some LDCs; and the United States and Canada were less willing to hold substantial wheat reserves to stabilize prices if others did not contribute to the costs of stockholding. It was therefore evident from the start that a wheat agreement with price ranges would be difficult to negotiate.[23]

To promote price stability and food security, negotiators at the conference generally agreed that surpluses should trigger a build-up of wheat reserves, and shortages should result in a release of reserves. However, there were differences among the exporters, importers and LDCs in four major areas: the size of the reserves, the minimum and maximum prices that should trigger the accumulation or release of reserves, special treatment for LDC signatories, and limitations on the use of export subsidies.

The conference delegates generally felt that a substantial level of wheat stocks was necessary to achieve the pricing objectives of a new agreement. Nevertheless, there was a wide divergence of views on the volume of global reserve stocks required and the distribution of stocks among members. The exporters felt that large reserves (about twenty-five to thirty million tonnes) would protect the market against strong downward pressure on prices, and the LDCs considered large reserves necessary to provide security against global food shortages. However, major commercial importers such as the European Community and Japan wanted smaller reserves, in the range of twelve to fifteen million tonnes. They were unwilling to contribute to the cost of maintaining large reserves, primarily because their purchasing power insulates them from severe shortfalls when there is a scarcity of foodstuffs.

Delegates also differed over the minimum price that should trigger the build-up of reserves during surplus periods, and the maximum price that should trigger the release of reserves in shortage periods. The United States, Canada, Australia, and Argentina naturally wanted a higher minimum price for their exports, while Japan and the EC pressured for a lower one. The industrial countries eventually agreed on a price range because the European Community (which exports as well as imports wheat) wanted relatively higher prices than Japan and was willing to compromise on price levels. However, the LDCs accounted for about 54 per cent of world wheat imports in 1978–79, and they felt that the proposed prices would put too heavy a strain on their financial resources. They therefore argued for lower trigger prices or, alternatively, for a dual system with reduced prices for poorer countries.

The developing countries also felt that the industrial states should provide financial assistance to help them defray the costs of acquiring reserves, improving storage facilities, and maintaining adequate stocks. However, the major trading countries refused to provide such assistance as part of a new wheat agreement. They feared that such special provisions would weaken the commercial aspects of the agreement and encouraged the LDCs to obtain the necessary assistance through regular aid and development programs. This position disappointed the LDC representatives, who "felt that although they were attending the negotiations, they were being effectively excluded from the decision-making process."[24] When the major exporters and importers met privately during the negotiations, participants in fact were usually limited to the "group of six," which included mostly industrial countries (the United States, Canada, Australia, the European Community, and Japan) and only one LDC (Argentina).

Finally, the issue of agricultural export subsidies was another source of contention that remained unresolved when the conference adjourned. The United States, Canada, and Australia wanted a new wheat agreement to place limits on the use of export subsidies. However, the European Community strongly opposed such restrictions and steadfastly maintained that the export subsidies in the Common Agricultural Policy were not negotiable.

An interesting aspect of the 1978–79 wheat agreement negotiations was the extent to which various American and Canadian groups established common positions through transnational and transgovernmental linkages. "Transnational relations" are "interactions across the border in which at least one actor is nongovernmental," and "transgovernmental relations" are "direct interactions between agencies (governmental subunits) of different governments, where those agencies act relatively autonomously from central governmental control."[25] Robert Keohane and Joseph Nye consider transnational and transgovernmental linkages to be one of the major characteristics of their complex interdependence model. The main American and Canadian actors involved were certain farming groups and senators from some of the major agricultural states and provinces. Both the farming groups and senators viewed an agreement among the exporters alone (that is, without the consuming states) as an alternative strategy for achieving their pricing objectives.

"Producer advisers" representing farm groups on the delegations of the major exporting countries encouraged the exporters to harden their positions at the IWA negotiations and pressured for establishment of a pricing arrangement solely by exporters if the talks failed. The producer advisers from the United States, Canada, Australia, and Argentina maintained close and ongoing contacts during the negotiations. For example, they held their own unofficial and closed meeting in London in June 1978 after an unsuccessful session of the negotiations in Geneva. These advisers had considerable influence on the positions of exporter governments, and Canada's chief negotiator at the IWA talks acknowledged that "an agreement had to be seen as acceptable to the Canadian producing groups if it were to be accepted by the government."[26]

The producer advisers were generally less supportive of a wheat agreement with pricing provisions than they had been in earlier years for a variety of reasons. They had less confidence in the ability of such agreements to stabilize prices in view of the collapse of the 1967 Wheat Trade Convention; their income security was less dependent on international pricing arrangements since farm programs had developed more income support features; and stable wheat prices were considered to be insufficient because of the rapidly escalating costs for farm machinery and other inputs. Producer advisers therefore pressured the exporters to support higher trigger prices for wheat reserves and to reject LDC demands for assistance as part of a commercial wheat agreement. The producer advisers from the United States, Canada, Australia, and Argentina also emphasized the necessity for "increased cooperation between exporting countries, especially if there is no [IWA] agreement achieved."[27]

Some American and Canadian senators from wheat-growing areas who engaged in transgovernmental policy co-ordination were also proponents of exporter co-operation. When the chairman of the Canadian Senate's Committee on Agriculture visited Washington in April 1977 for informal discussions with U.S. congressmen, it was decided that the agriculture committees of the two senates should hold periodic meetings. The first major meeting, held in Winnipeg in June 1978, included American and Canadian senators, Canadian Wheat Board officials, and prominent farm leaders. Many delegates argued that the wheat-exporting states should establish their own pricing agreement as an alternative to an IWA because the major importers (notably Japan and the European Community) were unwilling to accept a reasonable minimum price. Movement towards establishing an exporters' agreement was also viewed as a useful tactic for persuading the importing countries to make concessions at the IWA negotiations.[28] Although Australia and Argentina were not represented at the meeting, the senators felt that they would endorse an exporters' agreement and would share responsibility for carrying reserve stocks. Indeed, Canada had been authorized to express Australia's willingness to join in a Canadian-American pricing agreement.

The influence of the senators, however, was limited because of major policy differences within the United States. The American senators, in fact, "carefully pointed out that the meeting did not have official status insofar as . . . [they] could not speak for the Carter administration." In contrast, the Canadian Wheat Board minister "indicated that he felt he was able to speak for the position of the Trudeau administration."[29] American domestic differences emerged over several issues at the meeting, including a CWB proposal that "our two countries, in the very near future and whether or not there is progress on the International Wheat Agreement, establish a small task force of senior marketing officials to identify the costs and benefits to each country of close exporter cooperation and to outline the means by which cooperation can be achieved."[30] The senators agreed to recommend creation of the task force but felt that the United States (as the largest wheat exporter) had to take the initiative. After returning to Washington, the U.S. senators wrote to President Carter requesting that the task force be established, but the Carter administration did not agree to the proposal.

The Canadian and American senators held a second meeting in Washington in September 1978, with some members of the House of Representatives and about one hundred leaders of U.S. farm organizations also attending. As in the first meeting, the Trudeau government was far more supportive than the Carter administration of the senators' efforts. The Canadian senators had been given assurances that their government would participate with the United States in an acceptable wheat-pricing arrangement and in fact wanted discussions to begin on the alternatives. In contrast, the American senators emphasized that the talks were merely exploratory, and a senior agricultural official expressed the Carter administration's disapproval of a pricing agreement that did not include the importing countries. The American government was less committed than the Canadian to an exporter pricing agreement for a variety of reasons: U.S. farm prices were less dependent on the maintenance of international prices because of the larger U.S. domestic market and the country's ability to provide income and price supports; wheat was relatively less important to the United States since it is also a major exporter of coarse grains and oilseed crops; the dominant role of the private sector in U.S. agricultural trade made a collusive government-to-government agreement less appealing; the administration felt that a wheat cartel supported by higher U.S. prices would permit other exporters to undercut these prices; and an exporters' wheat-pricing agreement would inevitably be compared with producer associations such as the Organization of Petroleum Exporting Countries (OPEC), which the U.S. opposed even more strongly than Canada.[31]

The senators were careful to distinguish their proposals from those of producer associations such as OPEC. Thus, they argued that their desire to establish a minimum wheat price at no less than the cost of production was considerably different from OPEC efforts to institute the highest possible oil prices. They also expected that importing states would be satisfied with the prices established, even though the importers would have to accept the professed intentions of the major exporters "on faith." Despite the efforts to distinguish an exporters' wheat agreement from a cartel such as OPEC, the United States seemed anxious to include the major importers. Thus, a Canadian senator attending the meetings concluded that "in view of the attitude of the American government . . . we will probably have to wait until all of the possibilities of a new international wheat agreement have been exhausted before we can find out whether further cooperation between these four big exporters is possible."[32]

In summary, both the American and Canadian senators and producer advisers pressured for a hardening of the exporters' position in the negotiations and/or for a plurilateral strategy involving only the major exporters. In the end, the differences among the major exporters, importers, and LDCs could not be resolved, and the IWA negotiations were suspended in February 1979 without agreement. The conference recommended that the International Wheat Council extend the 1971 Wheat Trade Convention (which has no economic provisions) and determine when the conditions existed for a resumption of negotiations. After establishing a special committee to examine the issue, the IWC concluded in November 1979 that there was little prospect in the foreseeable future of negotiating a new agreement with pricing provisions. The IWC prediction proved to be correct since little has happened since 1979. Although a new Wheat Trade Convention came into force in July 1986, it does not contain price ranges or a reserve buffer-stock mechanism. The 1986 WTC is simply designed to promote co-operation between exporters and importers through an exchange of views.

After the IWA negotiations were suspended in February 1979, the Canadian Wheat Board minister (as a follow-up to the approach of the producer advisers and senators) invited the major exporters to a ministerial meeting in Saskatchewan in May 1979 to discuss the possibility of concluding an exporters' agreement. The participants were the CWB minister, the U.S. and Argentinian secretaries of agriculture, and the Australian secretary of trade and resources. The ministers resisted pressures to establish a minimum price for wheat exports and opted instead for influencing prices through informal co-operation on production levels and other measures. To expedite this plan, they decided to hold regular officials' meetings to exchange ideas on production and marketing.[33] Successive Canadian Wheat Board ministers supported action by exporters to strengthen world prices, but the United States was reluctant to sanction the formation of any group that would appear to be like a cartel. After 1979, the next major meeting of responsible ministers from the exporting countries was held in June 1986 in Whistler, British Columbia. This was followed by yet another meeting in February 1987 in San Diego, California. However, some major changes had occurred since 1979. Most importantly, the European Community was now also represented, and the major issue had become the U.S.-EC export subsidy war rather than an exporters' pricing agreement.[34]

In retrospect, it is evident that an exporters' pricing agreement bypassing the consumer states would have been extremely risky. The degree of international market power that foodgrain exporters can exert is limited by a variety of factors. First, exporters cannot depend on scarcity as a reliable source of influence because foodgrain supplies fluctuate widely and surpluses commonly recur. Second, international trade in grains accounts for only a small percentage of global production and consumption; and third, foodgrain importers would increase their own production if the exporters adopted confrontational policies.[35]

Some agricultural economists even suggest that (except for periods of extreme shortage such as 1973–74) world wheat prices are essentially determined by the major importers rather than the exporters. They do not deny that a Canada-U.S. duopoly—or a triopoly with Australia—may have existed. However, they are sceptical that the holding of carryover stocks provided market power for the exporters, especially when the stocks were "excessive," as was frequently the case. They also argue that the effects of such exporter arrangements were minor relative to the buying power of the major importers. Thus, the European Community, China, the Soviet Union, and Japan accounted for 30 to 40 per cent of global wheat imports in the late 1970s, and these countries were able to directly influence prices by their policies. Finally, some economists reject both the oligopsony (buyer power) and oligopoly (seller power) models of price determination and argue that wheat prices are determined by the interaction between supply and demand.[36]

Even if it were possible to control wheat prices through an international cartel arrangement, the political obstacles to such an arrangement would be overwhelming. It would be necessary to limit the amount of wheat marketed in total and by each supplier, to enforce quantity and pricing restrictions among suppliers, and to ensure that suppliers held reserves during surplus periods. A higher degree of government market control would be necessary to implement these arrangements than exists in the United States, and "at present there is no evidence that imposing this much government control is either politically or philosophically acceptable."[37] In summary, the Canadian government was highly supportive of the senators who pressured for a pricing agreement only among exporters. However, the U.S. government was unwilling to go along with this proposal and opted instead for either a unilateral strategy or an agreement involving both exporting and importing countries.

A PERIOD OF UNSTABLE AND DECLINING PRICES

In the absence of co-operation among the major trading nations and an effective international wheat agreement, the world wheat market entered a period of unstable and declining prices. A major reason for this instability was the marked increase in the amount of wheat going to the centrally planned economies and the developing countries. Their share of world wheat imports rose from 60 per cent in 1960–61 to 85 per cent in 1979–80. The imports of these countries tend to fluctuate widely because of great variability in production, the unpredictability of government policies, and the indebtedness problems of some major LDCs. In addition, the United States and Canada had become more reluctant to employ stockholding to stabilize prices. This factor was especially true for Canada, where the ratio of ending stocks to production fell from 62 per cent in 1979–80 to 38 per cent in 1981–82.[38]

After the American share of world grain exports had grown from 41 per cent in 1970 to over 58 per cent by 1979, it fell sharply to less than 49 per cent from 1980 to 1984. A major part of this loss resulted from U.S. grain prices, which were at least 20 per cent higher than those of export competitors in 1984–85. The relatively high U.S. prices resulted from the rising value of the American dollar, high domestic support levels, and shrinking technological advantages. As discussed in Chapter 2, the loan value determined by Congress set a floor under American prices, allowing farmers to take crops off the market as world prices declined and creating an "umbrella" for U.S. competitors. The 1981 farm bill significantly increased both the loan value and target price supports for farmers, and the U.S. again became a residual supplier. In addition, the United States was the only grain producer to couple its domestic support system with reductions in output when supplies were excessive. American production controls lowered domestic surpluses to some extent, but they were not effective in raising prices because of the production policies of other countries. Indeed, most states continued to increase output during surplus periods, and they often erected import barriers that thrust an even greater amount of price adjustment on the exporting countries. Thus, the U.S. price support and stockholding policies (the farmer-owned reserve) worked to its disadvantage during surplus periods.

The United States established the Export Enhancement Program (EEP) in May 1985 in efforts to regain its lost market share, to dispose of its huge surpluses, and to force the European Community to negotiate away its export restitution program. The EEP was implemented following intensive lobbying by an informal group of agricultural trade organizations, and the program was subsequently modified by the 1985 Food Security Act and the 1986 Food Security Improvements Act. The EEP provides surplus agricultural commodities owned by the Commodity Credit Corporation as a bonus to U.S. exporters to expand sales of specified agricultural products in targeted markets. Most of the early EEP agreements were for wheat and wheat flour, but the eligible commodities after April 1986 also included eggs, dairy cattle, vegetable oil, poultry feed, and barley.

Many agricultural groups had wanted an across-the-board export subsidy program; but from the start the EEP was directed against the European Community, and the number of markets that could be targeted was therefore limited. The administration maintained that the EEP was targeted in order not to compete directly with sales of non-subsidizing states; for wheat and flour these states included Argentina, Australia, and Canada. Almost all countries subsidize their agriculture to some extent, and there were differences within the administration over the policy towards Canada because of its transportation subsidies. Nevertheless, the prime target was the European Community since it is considered to be the largest subsidizer of wheat and other agricultural exports.[39] The administration approved initiatives for markets in which non-subsidizing states as well as the EC had shares but only if the recipient countries gave assurances that they would continue to buy traditional amounts from the non-subsidizers.

A controversial targeting decision was the administration's exclusion of the Soviet Union and China from the EEP. The USSR was the largest traditional customer for American wheat, and the EC's share of the Soviet wheat market had risen from 5 per cent in the 1981 crop year to 22 per cent in 1985. The reason given for excluding the Soviet Union was that the United States did not wish to interfere with sales by Canada, Argentina, and Australia. However, an official of the U.S. General Accounting Office reported that this was simply "a convenient explanation for not allowing the Soviets to purchase subsidized wheat under the program for foreign policy reasons."[40]

The delay in extending the EEP to the Soviet Union and China was an indication that political-security objectives continued to play *some* role in American agricultural export policy. In the 1980 presidential election campaign, Ronald Reagan had promised to lift the embargo on the Soviet Union imposed by President Carter, and he fulfilled that promise on 24 April 1981. However, Alexander Haig has maintained that the debate about the embargo in fact continued after the election:

> During the campaign, Reagan had not criticized the grain embargo as such, but he said that it imposed an inequitable burden on farmers, and he had promised to lift it. Secretary of Agriculture Block reminded him of that promise . . . at the very first Cabinet meeting . . . [Edwin] Meese took the uncomplicated position that the President had made a campaign promise and must keep it. My attempts to persuade Block and Meese, and ultimately Reagan, that the embargo was a very important foreign policy issue did not succeed.[41]

While some officials still wished to draw linkages between grain exports and security issues, the change in the U.S. balance of payments and trade position, as well as the plight of the American farmer, made such a policy less feasible.

The United States simply could no longer permit its competitors to gain a commercial advantage. Thus, even Alexander Haig conceded that

> it was inevitable that we should end the embargo. Canada had already announced that it would not limit 1981 sales to the Soviets; Australia was wavering; President Valery Giscard d'Estaing of France . . . warned us, confidentially, that he would be obliged to sell 600,000 metric tons of grain to Moscow. All of this, added to ongoing Argentinian sales, created commercial anxieties.[42]

In similar fashion, the United States was losing commercial sales because of its failure to extend the Export Enhancement Program to the Soviet Union and China. American wheat and flour exports increased to certain markets targeted under the EEP, but exports to markets not targeted during 1985–86 decreased significantly. Indeed, the USSR did not even fulfil the minimum purchase requirement in its long-term agreement (LTA) with the United States. The Soviets may have felt discriminated against since they were ineligible for the EEP, but U.S. Agriculture and State Department officials believed that the Soviets were not buying simply because of lower prices elsewhere.[43] China made requests on several occasions to purchase subsidized U.S. wheat, but its requests were denied. As a result, the U.S. market share of Chinese wheat imports was less than 10 per cent during 1985 and 1986.[44]

In August 1986, the administration reluctantly changed its policy toward the Soviet Union and announced that it was eligible to purchase wheat under the EEP. The initial offer to the USSR did not provide for a sufficient subsidy to make U.S. wheat prices competitive, and the Soviets therefore did not accept it. Nevertheless, the decision to include the Soviets in the EEP was highly controversial. American State and Defense officials strongly opposed this decision, and the secretary of state criticized a system where "American taxpayers make it possible for a Soviet housewife to buy American-produced food at a price lower than an American housewife's."[45] However, USDA officials indicated that they wanted to remove the Soviet excuse for not fulfilling its minimum purchase requirements under the long-term agreement. The broadening of the program also resulted from congressional and farm group pressure based on continuing problems with U.S. export performance.

While the American decision to expand the EEP was applauded by many domestic groups, it was extremely disturbing to Canada. Prime Minister Brian Mulroney had contacted President Reagan twice to prevent the United States from extending wheat export subsidies to the Soviet Union, and Canada joined Australia and Argentina in reacting angrily to the policy change. The Canadian grain industry received yet another blow in January 1987, when the United States offered export subsidies to China for one million tonnes of wheat. However, when Canada protested over this further extension of the EEP, a senior USDA official stated that he did not "feel terribly, terribly sorry for our illustrious Canadian neighbours" when he looked "at the increase in grain yields in Canada in recent years."[46] In April 1987, the United States and Soviet Union resolved their price differences when the U.S. offered to sell four million tonnes of wheat at a price made competitive by an increased subsidy.[47]

The European Community's initial reaction to the EEP was restrained, but it later endeavoured to protect its markets by providing increased and country-specific restitutions. It also maintained that the EEP was an illegal subsidy program, since it was targeted and was undercutting world prices. A U.S. official appearing before a subcommittee of the House Committee on Agriculture stated that it is "difficult to determine whether the Community or the United States has been responsible for undercutting prices in particular cases" but that "the EEP clearly has had an impact on lowering commodity prices in certain targeted countries."[48] The non-subsidizing states also experienced increased competition from the EC as a result of the Community's sales being displaced by the EEP, and this competition further contributed to lower prices. Canada was generally more concerned with prices than with the volume of its exports, but its only option was to follow the prices downward to retain markets. It should be mentioned that export subsidies were not the only factors considered responsible for the decline in prices. For example, Dale Hathaway also attributed the price decline to the behaviour of centralized selling agencies such as the Canadian and Australian Wheat Boards and argued that the United States blamed "its current export problems on EC export subsidies without recognizing the immense effects of state buying and selling practices on the current situation."[49]

In response to the price declines, Canada joined in a diverse coalition of industrial, developing, and Communist countries to form the Cairns Group of so-called non-subsidizing nations in August 1986. The founding members were Argentina, Australia, Brazil, Canada, Chile, Colombia, Fiji, Hungary, Indonesia, Malaysia, New Zealand, The Philippines, Thailand, and Uruguay. The diverse interests of the Cairns Group were a source of weakness, but the members realized that separately they had little influence. At the first Cairns conference the member states pledged to exert effective political pressure to end the unfair subsidies of the United States and the European Community. While Canada joined with Australia in protesting the extension of the EEP to the Soviet Union, Canadian criticisms were relatively restrained. Canada was negotiating a free trade agreement with the United States at the time, and it looked to the U.S. to defend their common interests in the GATT. Thus, Canada tended to identify the EC rather than the U.S. as the main source of the export subsidy problem.

The United States defended itself against Cairns Group criticisms by claiming that the domestic policies of many countries were responsible for global agricultural trade problems and that the U.S. itself was a victim of EC export practices. To demonstrate its resolve for reform, the U.S. government in July 1987 called for the elimination over a ten-year period of all farm subsidies that directly or indirectly distort trade.[50] President Reagan described this initiative as "the most ambitious proposal for world agricultural trade reform ever offered."[51]

There was considerable opposition to the Reagan plan in the United States and Canada on the grounds that it was impractical, too extreme, and lacking in credibility. For example, John Kenneth Galbraith stated that "there is absolutely no chance of this kind of move being successful"; Dale Hathaway said that the plan was doomed because farmers everywhere knew they would be hurt if subsidies ended; and the Canadian Federation of Agriculture president called the Reagan plan "unrealistic and unacceptable."[52] In addition, some critics maintained that the United States was hypocritical in increasing its own use of export subsidies while advocating their elimination. The U.S. in fact emphasized that it would not reduce subsidies unilaterally but only as part of an international agreement. Nevertheless, the Canadian government was quite supportive of the American proposal. Prime Minister Mulroney described the plan as a "bold move," and Canada's Agriculture minister stated that "it is important that we do not undercut the U.S. position . . . because they are the driving force at the GATT and are leading the way in reforming the trade rules." Canada subsequently presented its own GATT proposal, which was closely aligned with the American plan. The Canadian proposal called for "the elimination of all subsidies which distort trade and of all access barriers, over a period to be negotiated."[53]

The most important opposition to the Reagan plan came from the European Community and Japan. These countries viewed the U.S. proposal as being extremely unrealistic since it went too far toward eliminating government influence in world agricultural trade. The EC also submitted its own proposal (in October 1987), calling for short-term emergency measures to reduce grain, dairy, and sugar surpluses and for a gradual decrease in agricultural support. The Cairns Group submitted a compromise proposal designed to address the short-term concerns of the EC and the long-term concerns of the United States.

The Cairns Group plan called for freezing production and export subsidies by the end of 1988, rolling them back, and then eliminating them by the end of the century.

In April 1989, the GATT Negotiating Group on Agriculture finally achieved a breakthrough when the U.S. and EC (and other GATT members) reached a compromise agreement. It involved an immediate freeze on government support for agriculture and a progressive reduction in such support over the long term. While this *appeared* to be the compromise agreement the Cairns Group was seeking, the accord was in fact loosely worded to fit the requirements of the U.S. and EC.[54] For example, it did not call for the elimination of farm subsidies since the EC would not accept such wording, and the U.S. Export Enhancement Program was largely unaffected. Thus, in the Spring of 1989 it was still uncertain that the Big Three (the U.S., EC, and Japan) would reach an eventual agreement on export subsidies—and on pricing—at the Uruguay Round.

CONCLUSIONS

From the 1950s to the 1980s there were close linkages between wheat-pricing arrangements and Canadian-American relations, and some further conclusions can be drawn regarding the independent and dependent variables. Since grain surpluses have been far more common than shortages in the major exporting states, international arrangements are needed to ensure that grain is exported at remunerative and stable prices. However, this chapter has shown that an agricultural trade regime with explicit multilateral principles and rules is lacking and that U.S. and Canadian pricing objectives could only be achieved through some sort of "surrogate" arrangement. The Canada-U.S. duopoly performed this function in the 1950s and 1960s, in part through its support for the international wheat agreements. Nevertheless, the duopoly required sacrifices on the part of the United States and Canada—such as stockholding—that they were increasingly unwilling (and unable) to make. When the duopoly broke down in the late 1960s, no other group or organization assumed its functions of controlling surpluses and stabilizing prices. In the late 1970s, a number of American and Canadian senators and producer advisers pressured for an exporters' pricing agreement, but there is evidence that it would have been unsuccessful even if the U.S. administration had approved it. Clearly, the lack of principles and regulations in the agricultural trade regime was detrimental to both U.S. and Canadian pricing objectives, and after the 1960s increased competition precluded the development of another surrogate arrangement such as the duopoly.

This chapter provides further information about export strategies as well as export objectives. The Canadian-American duopoly was a clear demonstration of the two countries' support for bilateralism/plurilateralism (when Australia and Argentina participated), which largely resulted from their interdependent relationship. The transnational and transgovernmental linkages between North American producer advisers and senators in the late 1970s was a further example of interdependence that was conducive to the adoption of bilateral/plurilateral strategies.

However, this chapter also shows (as do Chapters 2 and 3) that the United States was more willing than Canada to turn to unilateral strategies when they were deemed necessary. A major explanatory variable here was the relative size and diversity of the two countries' agricultural economies. While Canada's agricultural exports were more concentrated in wheat, the U.S. was also a major exporter of coarse grains and oilseeds, and it was less dependent than Canada on international wheat-pricing arrangements. Thus, Canada feared that a Wheat Trade Convention would not be concluded in 1967 because of U.S. delaying tactics over the inclusion of coarse grains; the Canadian-American duopoly was ended largely because of U.S. dissatisfaction with the arrangements and the Carter administration refused to endorse an exporters' pricing agreement in the late 1970s, even though the Trudeau administration supported such an arrangement. With its larger economy, the United States was also willing to pursue unilateral strategies such as the EEP to restore or maintain its market share, even at the cost of lowering grain prices. Canada, by contrast, has always been more dependent on remunerative prices for its exports, and it therefore endorsed the Cairns Group proposal condemning the price-depressing effects of the U.S.-EC export subsidy war.

Finally, this chapter provides additional information about co-operation and conflict. Keohane and Nye found that Canadian-American relations were far more interdependent than Australian-American relations,[55] and a comparison of the two countries' behaviour in the Cairns Group is consistent with this view. While Australian criticisms of U.S. export subsidies were strident, Canada had a moderating influence and tended to identify the European Community rather than the United States as the main offender. Although Canada was disturbed by the extension of the EEP to the Soviet Union, it also continued to look to American support for its pricing objectives. Thus, Article 701 of the bilateral free trade agreement states that

the Parties agree that their primary goal with respect to agricultural subsidies is to achieve, on a global basis, the elimination of all subsidies which distort agricultural trade, and the Parties agree to work together to achieve this goal, including through multilateral trade negotiations such as the Uruguay Round.[56]

Canada's ambivalent behaviour stemmed largely from its asymmetrical relationship with its much larger neighbour. Even when it was resentful of American actions, Canada was aware that the United States was the "dominant fact" of its international relations.[57] Chapter 5, on surplus disposal measures, examines the asymmetrical nature of Canadian-American interdependence in greater detail.

5

American Surplus Disposal Measures

Canada has often been critical of U.S. surplus disposal policies, and a 1959 Canadian-American Committee report warned that "pervasive and vigorous conflicts of interest [over surplus disposal] are potentially dangerous to many aspects of Canadian-American relations.[1] This chapter focuses on the two types of surplus disposal transactions that Canada criticized most vehemently, American tied sales and agricultural barter. Indeed, Canadian officials maintained that barter and tied sales "represented unorthodox and unfair competition, bringing inevitable encroachment on Canada's ordinary commercial markets."[2] An environmental variable that is of particular interest in this chapter is "relative economic size." American surplus disposal activities were most important in the period before the United States experienced serious balance of payments problems (that is, from the 1950s to the early 1970s). As a result, the United States was willing—and able—to engage in large-scale concessional sales to maintain its market share. Since Canada was more dependent than the United States on exporting wheat at satisfactory prices, it did not have the economic means to consider seriously the adoption of similar measures. Thus, the minister of trade and commerce indicated that he was "surprised—perhaps shocked is a better word—at the suggestions that . . . Canada should follow the very same policies of surplus disposal that we criticize when followed by our competitors."[3]

Since Canada could not emulate American surplus disposal practices, its main efforts were devoted to altering U.S. behaviour. Canadian criticisms were frequently voiced in multilateral fora such as the General Agreement on Tariffs and Trade since other exporting states were similarly disturbed by the dumping of American surpluses. For example, Canada's delegate to the twelfth session of the GATT Contracting Parties maintained that export subsidies, sales for local currencies, barter deals, and tied sales had contributed to an increase in U.S. wheat exports from 347 million bushels in 1955–56 to 547 million in 1956–57, while Canadian exports had fallen from 309 to 261 million bushels.[4] However, the GATT never established effective jurisdiction over American surplus disposal measures, and Canada therefore turned to the Food and Agriculture Organization's Consultative Subcommittee on Surplus Disposal (CSD). The CSD provided an important forum for the discussion of tied sales and (to a lesser extent) barter, but its mandate was limited, and some U.S. measures did not even fall under its usual notification and consultation procedures. Furthermore, the United States was willing to provide the CSD with only limited information on certain issues, especially in the case of barter transactions. As a result, Canada also sought bilateral discussions with the United States, particularly in the Canada-U.S. Ministerial Committee on Trade and Economic Affairs and in a series of agricultural working committees (see Chapter 3).

In view of the interdependence between the two countries, the United States often agreed to the creation of bilateral groupings where Canada could express its views on American policies. The U.S. also sometimes exercised restraint in the use of its surplus disposal measures. Nevertheless, American tied sales and barter continued to be a source of tension and conflict from the 1950s to the early 1970s.

AMERICAN TIED SALES

Canada was a persistent and harsh critic of American tied sales provisions in PL 480 agreements, maintaining that they interfered with the commercial trade of other exporters. The United States, on the other hand, felt that tied sales were an essential component of its food aid and trade policies. Before examining this issue in the context of Canadian-American relations, it is first necessary to describe the two types of tied sales commonly used by the United States: tied usual marketing requirements and tied offset purchasing requirements.

As discussed in Chapter 3, the FAO Principles of Surplus Disposal and the CSD seek to ensure that member countries adhere to the "additionality" principle. According to this principle, agricultural commodities which are exported on concessional terms to a recipient country should be additional to (and therefore should not displace) the country's normal commercial imports. The primary instrument for achieving additionality is a "usual marketing requirement" (UMR), which is negotiated between donor and recipient countries in food aid agreements. The UMR is a commitment by the recipient state to maintain its normal amount of commercial imports of a particular commodity in addition to its concessional imports of the same or a related commodity. The calculation of a UMR normally is based on the recipient's average annual commercial imports during the previous five years.[5] UMRs that are global or untied permit the recipient to purchase the commodity from any "friendly" country, while tied UMRs require that all or part of the commercial imports come from the food aid supplier.[6] The first American agreement containing a tied UMR was signed with Finland on 6 May 1955, and tied UMR provisions were subsequently included in a number of PL 480 agreements. Although the United States sometimes tied the entire UMR, partial tying was more common. With partial tying, a minimum percentage of the commercial imports were to be purchased from American sources.

In addition to establishing UMRs, the major exporters also stipulated that food aid is "intended for domestic consumption and not to enable the recipient country to increase its exports of the same or a like commodity."[7] Less-developed countries that re-exported commodities they received in PL 480 agreements or that increased their exports of the same (or related) commodities, had to "offset" these exports with additional commercial purchases. These additional purchases are referred to as "offset purchasing requirements" (or offsets). As with UMRs, offsets may be required on a global basis or may be tied to the food aid donor. In the 1950s and 1960s, a large percentage of the offset purchasing requirements in PL 480 agreements were tied to the United States.

Canada and some other exporters endorsed the establishment of *global* UMRs and offset purchasing requirements as a means of ensuring that concessional transactions did not interfere with commercial sales. However, they felt that UMRs and offsets tied to the United States directly infringed on their commercial markets. After discussing the American arguments in favour of tying and the Canadian counterarguments, I will examine the extent to which U.S. policies were altered in response to external and domestic pressures.

The United States repeatedly asserted that it used tied UMRs to protect its legitimate trading interests and not to invade the traditional markets of other suppliers. It maintained that the tied portion of its UMR was based on the recipient's historical share of commercial imports from the United States and that competing exporters therefore did not lose markets. The U.S. also used tied UMRs to prevent its food aid recipients from turning exclusively to other countries for their commercial purchases because of special linkages or bilateral understandings. Since the United States was providing most of the world's foreign assistance, tying at least assured it of something in return. Furthermore, competing exporters benefited from the fact that the American food aid removed some surpluses from commercial markets.

The United States used similar arguments to defend tied offset purchasing requirements, maintaining that its food aid was designed to meet the recipient country's domestic requirements and not to enable interference with American commercial sales. The American delegate to the CSD also discussed the reasons why the U.S. considered global offsets to be less acceptable than tied offsets:

> If the offset permitted the assisted country to purchase the required offset quantities from any source, then a situation could develop where the United States was exporting on concessional assistance terms; the assisted country was selling commercially, possibly in competition with the U.S.; and third countries were benefiting from additional commercial sales made possible by the original U.S. commodity aid transaction. In this situation all countries would have benefited at the expense of the U.S. because of concessional assistance financed by the U.S.[8]

Finally, the United States felt that it could not compete on an equal basis with countries that relied on state trading organizations such as the Canadian and Australian Wheat Boards, and it maintained that tied sales were justified under these circumstances.

Canada did not accept the American arguments in favour of tying, and it regularly criticized these practices in multilateral and bilateral fora during the 1950s and 1960s. For example, the Canadian delegate to the twelfth session of the GATT Contracting Parties emphatically stated that U.S. tied sales arrangements should be ended; a Canadian representative at the Canada-U.S. Ministerial Committee on Trade and Economic Affairs maintained that tied sales were directly opposed to multilateral trading principles; and Canadian delegates to the CSD often objected "to the use of tied sales in concessional agricultural transactions."[9]

In Canada's view, American tying in PL 480 agreements was contrary to the FAO Principles of Surplus Disposal. While global UMRs permitted all countries to compete for agricultural sales, tied UMRs were viewed as discriminatory since they provided the supplying country with a guaranteed market and excluded competition from other exporters. Furthermore, Canada doubted that tied sales were necessary to protect the United States' "historical share" of the commercial market. On the contrary, tied UMRs contributed to *increased* U.S. sales while limiting the opportunity of competitors to expand their exports. In addition, it was argued that tied sales reduced the benefits of food aid to recipients since higher costs were involved in the tied purchases.

Canada was equally opposed to American tied offset purchasing requirements. It was especially critical of the tied offsets in PL 480 *wheat* agreements, maintaining that they were inconsistent with the understanding established among the major wheat exporters. It urged the United States to include offset requirements only on a global basis since other wheat exporters would then be able to compete for the market opportunities. Finally, Canada resented the American position that tied sales were necessary because competing exporters relied on state trading organizations such as the Wheat Board. A Canadian official countered that the U.S. Commodity Credit Corporation was the world's largest government sales agency promoting surplus disposal and that it was better placed than others to undercut commercial sales.[10]

The United States undoubtedly altered some of its policies in response to the criticisms of Canada and other exporters. For example, after discussions between Canadian and American officials in 1957, "the tied sales requirement was relaxed, but not abandoned."[11] Furthermore, in 1959 the U.S. dropped its tied UMR requirements in PL 480 wheat agreements, even though it continued to use tied offsets for wheat and tied UMRs for most other commodities.[12] The official reason given for this policy change was that the International Wheat Agreements adequately protected American commercial trade, but persistent pressures from competing exporters also contributed to the untying of UMRs for wheat. For example, Canada and Australia strongly criticized U.S. wheat tying in a variety of fora, including the Wheat Utilization Committee (WUC). The major exporters established the WUC in 1959 to promote the increased consumption of surplus wheat and to ensure that non-commercial wheat exports were compatible with commercial objectives. Another forum for the discussion of U.S. wheat tying was the Canadian-American Committee, which emphasized that "countries receiving wheat under special surplus disposal arrangements [should] be guaranteed complete freedom when deciding the exporting country or countries from which any additional wheat is obtained on ordinary commercial terms."[13] After the United States ceased using tied UMRs for wheat, international agreements continued to proscribe the practice in later years. For example, the 1967 and 1971 International Wheat Agreements stipulated that members involved in concessional transactions "may provide that a specified level of commercial imports of wheat, agreed with the recipient country, be maintained on a *global* basis by that country" (emphasis added).[14]

Although tied UMRs for wheat were phased out, the United States continued to use tied offsets for wheat and tied UMRs for most other commodities. Canada usually joined with other exporters to pressure for changes in American policy, and the CSD in particular was encouraged to become more actively involved with the tied sales issue. In 1963, Canada and the Netherlands suggested that the CSD should attempt to reach a consensus on the legitimacy of tied sales. Despite American reservations, the CSD agreed that its secretariat and a small group of delegates should prepare a study summarizing the basic issues. A "Working Group on Tied Sales" appointed by the CSD in March 1966 to perform this function was composed of the delegates for Argentina, Australia, Canada, Denmark, the Netherlands, New Zealand, the United Kingdom, and the United States.[15]

As a result of the working group's deliberations, the CSD released its first "Report on Tied Sales" in July 1969. PL 480 sales were the main topic of discussion in the report because they were the most common type of tied sales and because U.S. statistics were made available. The report examined American tying practices during the 1963–67 period and noted that in 1966 about 10 per cent (by value) of the UMRs established for PL 480 commodities were tied—or 25 per cent when wheat and wheat flour were excluded. While the United States frequently used tied UMRs for cotton, tallow, tobacco, and vegetable oils, it only rarely used them for rice, meat, and dairy products. The CSD was unable to determine the amount of American trade conducted under tied offset purchasing requirements, because offsets usually relate to future possibilities rather than to firmly programmed transactions. Offset requirements under Title I of PL 480 involved the supply of wheat, edible oil, and cotton.[16]

After the first tied sales report was submitted to the CSD, Canada pressured for the creation of a second working group to continue monitoring the issue. However, the United States insisted that "differences are not going to be resolved by another study group whose terms of reference make it clear that the purpose is to condemn the U.S."[17] Since it did not seem possible to establish a new working group over American opposition, the Canadian representative proposed instead that the CSD secretariat monitor and report on trends in tied sales and the impact of these sales on world markets. This proposal was accepted, and the second CSD Report on Tied Sales was based upon discussions in the entire subcommittee (rather than in a working group). The second report indicated that there were eighty-nine instances of American tied UMRs from 1968 to 1972, a decrease of about 35 per cent from the preceding five-year period. Edible oils, tobacco, and cotton accounted for two-thirds of the tied UMRs in the earlier period and for three-fourths in the later period.

The working groups and reports on tied sales demonstrate that Canada and some other exporters were somewhat successful in directing the CSD's continuing attention to the issue. Even the United States reluctantly agreed to the CSD studies of tied sales and provided requested data and assistance to the secretariat. However, some important U.S. domestic actors, such as the General Accounting Office and the Congress, strongly favoured a continuance of tying. Since the CSD is located in Washington, D.C., and is dependent on American goodwill and staffing assistance, its criticisms of U.S. tying policies must have been muted as a result. Although the CSD considered the tied sales issue to be within its legislative competence, its views of tied sales were inconclusive. The subcommittee believed that tied sales should be avoided whenever possible since they "could result in harmful interference with . . . international trade." Nevertheless, it also recognized "the concern of the concessional exporting country to protect its commercial trade."[18] The first CSD Report on Tied Sales was in fact extremely guarded in its criticisms of American policies. The report acknowledged that "in some instances, the existence of a tied UMR may have prevented a shift of commercial imports from U.S. to non-U.S. sources that might otherwise have occurred for purely commercial reasons." Nevertheless, it also concluded that "in the small number of cases where available data permitted analysis, the tied UMRs enabled the United States to maintain its trade and did not appear to have the effect of displacing other suppliers."[19] In view of the ambivalent attitude of the FAO and CSD, an American official was able to state in September 1972 that U.S. tied sales policies had never been explicitly prohibited:[20]

> Nowhere in the FAO recommended Principles is there language that can be construed as prohibiting "tied sales" as practiced by the United States. The United States would never have agreed to such a provision. It has followed the practice of tying certain of its concessional sales programs since before these principles were established and made it quite clear during all the years that the FAO Principles were being elaborated that it was not committing itself to dropping this practice. Other signatories of these understandings have no grounds, then, for charging that the United States is not living up to its commitments.

The deliberations in the CSD provide considerable evidence that American policy was not in fact substantially altered as a result of the subcommittee's working group and reports. For example, when pressures were building to establish a second working group on tied sales, the United States indicated that its policy had not changed and that it had nothing new to add to another report. The United States also maintained that its domestic legislation would take priority over CSD decisions, and a U.S. official noted in March 1973 that tying of UMRs facilitated compliance with Section 103(n) of PL 480, as amended.[21] Furthermore, Canada informed the CSD in April 1973 that "while incidence of tied sales on certain commodities . . . has been decreasing over the past five years . . . with other commodities, such as oilseed products, [the] absolute and relative incidence of tied sales has substantially increased."[22]

Thus, the ability of Canada and some other exporters to influence U.S. policy-making in the tied sales area was clearly limited, even though they were able to focus the CSD's continued attention on the subject. American policy was altered in some areas, but major changes in U.S. policy eventually occurred for reasons other than the pressures exerted in the CSD. First, and most importantly, U.S. concessional sales declined, and tying became less relevant after the dramatic shift from foodgrain surpluses to shortages in the 1970s. Second, the United States may have become interested in regulating tied sales when the European Community began to use its own tying procedures. The drawbacks of unilateral strategies such as tied sales became more evident to the United States when similar practices were adopted by major competitors. Indeed, the U.S. and Canada occasionally joined in criticizing the EC for allegedly engaging in *unrestricted* tied sales. These are sales "where the supply of food aid is made contingent on a given commercial import not limited to the normal level of commercial imports from the supplying country and without provision for safeguarding the normal commercial trade of exporting countries."[23]

Criticisms of EC practices surfaced in the CSD in 1969 amidst reports that the Community was making food aid grants conditional on commercial wheat purchases. The United States and Canada expressed concerns that these were unrestricted tied sales, warned that unrestricted tying could convert food aid into discount selling for the donor's commercial benefit, and noted that such practices were completely at variance with the FAO Principles of Surplus Disposal. The United States maintained that it did not resort to *unrestricted* tying because its tied UMRs were based on the normal level of U.S. commercial exports to the recipient state.[24] The FAO did in fact reject unrestricted tying, even though it refused to explicitly prohibit "normal" tied sales of the U.S. variety. The Committee on Commodity Problems agreed that unrestricted tied sales were contrary to the FAO Principles since they could pre-empt markets and infringe on the commercial exports of third countries. Nevertheless, the difference between U.S. "normal" tied sales and EC "unrestricted" tied sales depended partly on "the eye of the beholder." Canada and others continued to question the U.S. assertion that its tied sales were based on its historical market share.

In summary, Canada showed a definite preference for multilateral strategies in its attempts to alter American policies on tied sales (and therefore to achieve its agricultural export objectives). Since other major exporters shared its concerns, Canada no doubt felt that the CSD offered the best opportunity for influencing the United States. The U.S. did alter its policies in some respects. For example, it virtually ended the use of tied UMRs for wheat; and the second CSD Report on Tied Sales indicated that American tied UMRs from 1968 to 1972 decreased by about 35 per cent from the previous five-year period. Nevertheless, Canada was more successful in focusing the CSD's attention on U.S. tying practices than it was in bringing about major changes in American policy. In the end, tied sales were phased out primarily because they were no longer necessary when serious foodgrain shortages developed. Despite Canada's criticisms of U.S. tied sales practices in the 1950s and 1960s, even in this area there were co-operative efforts to limit competition and conflict. For example, the United States was willing to provide the CSD with a considerable amount of information and data on its tied sales practices, even though it resented the subcommittee's involvement with the issue. Furthermore, the U.S. and Canada adopted common policies in criticizing what they considered to be unrestricted tying policies of the European Community.

AMERICAN AGRICULTURAL BARTER

American agricultural barter was another surplus disposal mechanism that Canada repeatedly expressed concerns about in the 1950s and 1960s. Barter has been defined as the straight exchange of goods of comparable value without any flow of cash taking place, but there are many variants that do not fully accord with this definition. Barter is considered to be a type of countertrade, which can be defined as "any contractual commitment imposed as a condition of purchase by the importer on the exporter . . . [that] generally involves the take back of goods and/or services."[25] Before examining agricultural barter in the context of U.S.-Canadian relations, it is first necessary to discuss the origins and evolution of the American program.

The U.S. agricultural barter program had political-security as well as agricultural export objectives. It initially had the dual purpose of reducing stocks of American agricultural commodities and of acquiring foreign-produced strategic metals and minerals. The Commodity Credit Corporation (CCC) Charter Act of 1949, which provided the general authority for barter, empowered the CCC to supply the agricultural goods and accept the strategic materials. These materials were stored in government stockpiles to prevent overdependence on foreign suppliers during national emergencies. The list of CCC-held commodities eligible for barter was periodically altered, but wheat, corn, grain sorghums, barley, flaxseed, oats, rye, tobacco, cottonseed oil, cotton, peanuts, dried skim milk, and rice were often included. In 1954, Congress provided a legislative mandate to expand barter activities with Title III, Section 303 of PL 480. Title III authorized the secretary of agriculture to barter CCC-owned agricultural commodities not only for strategic materials, but also for goods, materials, or equipment required for foreign assistance and offshore construction programs.[26]

American agricultural barter was anomalous since the government actually exchanged commodities with U.S. private traders rather than with foreign governments; this procedure permitted the United States to maintain its historical position against government-to-government barter agreements. Contracts were drawn with U.S. private firms to deliver to the CCC named strategic materials, and in return these firms took an equivalent value of CCC-owned agricultural commodities and exported them. The U.S. barter contractors often sold the agricultural products for dollars, which were then used to purchase the approved strategic materials. The barter or exchange, therefore, took place only between the CCC and the American contractors.

In earlier years, the CCC had immediately transferred the materials it acquired to the strategic stockpile or to other U.S. agencies. However, the strategic stockpile soon became overloaded, and a "supplemental stockpile" was created in the mid-1950s to store barter imports that were not urgently needed. The supplemental stockpile had no limit on quantities to be acquired, and it was simply one indication that the barter program was designed "not primarily to acquire additional materials for their national defense value but to facilitate the disposal of agricultural surpluses in foreign markets."[27] It was often desirable to exchange surplus agricultural goods for materials that were less perishable, bulky, and costly to store. By late 1961, materials acquired through the barter program were valued at about $223 million and $962 million in the strategic and supplemental stockpiles respectively. President Kennedy's reaction to these expanding inventories again demonstrated that the primary reason for barter was surplus disposal. In September 1962, he shifted the emphasis of agricultural barter from the acquisition of strategic materials to the procurement of supplies and services needed by overseas agencies, such as the Department of Defense and the Agency for International Development. Although this change was partly designed to reduce the outflow of dollars, it also facilitated the export of agricultural commodities.[28]

The primacy of surplus disposal was also evident from changes in the U.S. legislation, which at first limited barter to bilateral contracts. Since the countries that furnished strategic materials did not necessarily require an equivalent value of agricultural goods, bilateral barter was largely replaced by multilateral and then open-end contracts. With these contracts, American agricultural commodities could be exported to different countries than those providing the strategic materials. It was not until 1968 (when barter for strategic materials was largely displaced by barter for overseas procurement) that PL 480 was amended to again restrict barter to bilateral transactions.

The United States was flexible not only in its barter methods, but also in the geographical focus of its barter activities. The U.S. Department of Agriculture maintained that barter transactions were commercial. However, they were in fact not so easy to classify, and they were often used with importing countries that lacked effective demand (that is, demand backed by purchasing power).[29] Most barter agreements in the 1950s were concluded with West European countries and Japan, which were prohibiting the convertibility of their currencies and resorting to foreign exchange controls because of balance of payments problems. As purchasing power in Japan and Europe increased, American policy statements signalled a gradual reorientation of barter towards the Third World. For example, in 1961 the USDA maintained that barter for strategic materials provided "an additional market for the products of less developed countries"; in 1962, it was announced that emphasis would be given to barter "as an aid in assisting some of the lesser developed countries"; and in 1963, the USDA predicted that "future barters for those materials in stockpile surplus will be chiefly with under-developed countries."[30]

The data on barter confirm this shift toward the LDCs, but they also show that industrial states continued to account for a substantial portion of the transactions. Before 1958–59, well over 75 per cent of U.S. agricultural barter exports went to Japan and Europe. However, from 1969 to 1973, the portion of barter exports to these countries ranged from a low of 30.3 per cent (in 1970) to a high of 45.9 per cent (in 1972). The geographic distribution also varied according to the agricultural products exported. Of particular importance to Canada were U.S. barter wheat shipments for overseas procurement, and by the late 1960s these were directed almost entirely to the Third World. For example, in fiscal year 1969 51.2 per cent of U.S. barter wheat went to Latin American LDCs, 47.5 per cent to Asian LDCs, 1.4 per cent to African LDCs, and only 0.1 per cent to European countries.[31] Despite the shift toward the Third World, the primary motivation for barter continued to be American surplus disposal rather than LDC economic development. Thus, a Canadian-American Committee report stated that the U.S. barter program could provide some economic assistance to LDCs but that "its role in this connection . . . is likely to be sporadic and fortuitous in the sense that it is difficult to mesh barter transactions in an appropriate framework of economic aid to particular countries." The committee concluded that "other surplus disposal techniques will be more effective in achieving specific economic aid objectives."[32]

Tables 5–1 and 5–2 show that there was considerable fluctuation in the value of U.S. agricultural barter exports in the early years of the program. However, barter exports steadily increased from 1963 (when barter for offshore procurement was given more emphasis) to 1973. On 1 July 1973 agricultural barter was suspended for the same reason that it had been introduced in 1949: surplus disposal considerations. In the words of a former barter administrator, "relatively tight supplies of some major agricultural commodities resulted in the

TABLE 5–1

VALUE OF U.S. AGRICULTURAL BARTER EXPORTS

($million, fiscal years)

1950	8	1962	198
1951	9	1963	60
1952	43	1964	112
1953	14	1965	130
1954	34	1966	229
1955	125	1967	295
1956	298	1968	302
1957	400	1969	269
1958	100	1970	467
1959	132	1971	870
1960	149	1972	876
1961	144	1973	1088

Source: Willard W. Cochrane and Mary E. Ryan, *American Farm Policy, 1948-1973* (Minneapolis: University of Minnesota Press, 1976), tables 7-6 and 7-7.

TABLE 5–2

U.S. AGRICULTURAL BARTER EXPORTS AS A PERCENTAGE OF U.S.

AGRICULTURAL EXPORTS UNDER ALL FORMS OF GOVERNMENT ASSISTANCE

(fiscal years)

1950	0.4	1962	5.3
1951	0.7	1963	1.8
1952	4.8	1964	2.8
1953	1.2	1965	3.2
1954	2.8	1966	5.6
1955	9.6	1967	7.1
1956	14.9	1968	8.9
1957	12.9	1969	12.5
1958	3.8	1970	13.8
1959	6.2	1971	19.8
1960	5.7	1972	20.0
1961	5.0	1973	18.2

Source: Cochrane and Ryan, *American Farm Policy*, derived from tables 7-6 and 7-7.

suspension of the program."[33] The 1974 Foreign Assistance Act gave the president authority to barter goods and services for strategic materials, but this authority was not used.

However, the re-emergence of U.S. agricultural surpluses and strategic material shortages, as well as LDC balance of payment problems, led to pressures for a revival of agricultural barter. In 1981, a House of Representatives subcommittee asked the Department of Defense to help initiate a program to barter agricultural surpluses for needed stockpile materials. The Defense Department then established an ad hoc working group to identify countries interested in barter agreements. Furthermore, "of the hundred or so bills and resolutions dealing with agricultural trade ... introduced in the U.S. Congress during 1983 ... some twenty were concerned, in one way or another, with the encouragement of international barter."[34] As a result, under presidential directive, the USDA signed agreements with Jamaica in 1982–83 to barter dairy products for bauxite. These agreements were difficult to reach because of differences over suitable commodities, and as in the past U.S. surplus disposal took priority over economic development considerations. While Jamaica preferred to receive wheat and corn, American price restrictions made these products too expensive. The United States eventually persuaded Jamaica to take dried milk and butter oil instead because CCC inventories of dairy products as of July 1983 were valued at over $3.25 million.

There was some interest in negotiating other barter deals after the Jamaican agreements were concluded, and the 1985 Food Security Act states that barter can be an effective secondary method of reducing agricultural surpluses and adding materials to the National Defense Stockpile. In the 1985 Act, Congress also mandated the USDA to carry out two pilot barter programs and the CCC to barter commodities for petroleum products if the strategic petroleum reserve fell below a certain level.[35] The Omnibus Trade Bill of 1988 urged the U.S. secretary of agriculture to implement the pilot barter provisions of the 1985 Food Security Act and called for the creation of an interagency group on countertrade and an office of barter in the Department of Commerce. After the Jamaican agreements of 1982–83, the United States concluded a small number of countertrade agreements in which it exported grain to Brazil, Ghana, and Malawi. In view of the financial crisis in Mexico, the U.S. government also in effect bartered grain for Mexican oil, which was added to the strategic petroleum reserve.[36] Nevertheless, prospects for additional agricultural barter/countertrade agreements are uncertain because of restrictive U.S. legislative requirements, conflicting domestic interests, the protests of competing exporters, and the difficulty in finding countries willing to take U.S. agricultural surpluses in exchange for strategic materials.[37]

From the 1950s to the 1980s, Canada concluded countertrade agreements involving the export of grain to a limited number of countries, including Nigeria, the Balkan states, South Korea, the Soviet Union, Yugoslavia, and even the United States. Canadian grain was exchanged for a variety of products ranging from cars, generators, and furniture to corn and oil.[38] However, Canada was more dependent than the United States on exporting wheat at satisfactory prices, and it never seriously considered emulating the U.S. agricultural barter program. Furthermore, as a smaller power without wide-ranging military interests, Canada did not require the large stockpiles of strategic materials which served as the basis for many American barter agreements. Thus, in 1955 the minister of trade and commerce remarked that "some people would like us to go in . . . for barter" but that it is simply "a concealed form of 'give-away' or discount."[39]

As with the case of tied sales, Canada sought to express its views on American barter in multilateral fora such as the CSD. Insofar as barter was a form of surplus disposal, it was considered to be within the CSD's competence in the 1950s and 1960s. As discussed, the CSD seeks assurances that concessional exports are additional to commercial sales and do not displace them. The CSD has developed a two-tiered process by which aid-supplying countries are expected to notify and consult with competing exporters that may be adversely affected by their transactions. The aid supplier first consults bilaterally with third countries that normally export similar products to the recipient country, and then multilateral consultations are conducted through the CSD.

The U.S. barter program was frequently discussed in the CSD, and the subcommittee established a working group on barter (which included the American and Canadian representatives) in March 1960. Canada joined with other exporters in criticizing the U.S. program, and it supported formation of the CSD's barter working group. However, the United States refused to provide the CSD with detailed information regarding its barter transactions because it felt that this would place unacceptable constraints on the private barter contractors. Furthermore, the CSD working group members could not reach an agreement on the scope of their study or even on a definition of barter after holding eight meetings during 1960–61. In 1969, the Committee on Commodity Problems (CCP) stripped the CSD of its responsibilities in this area when it decided that barter transactions should no longer fall within the FAO's jurisdiction. The CCP felt that barter was directly related to commercial trade and therefore the responsibility of the GATT, even though it had some concessional characteristics.

The GATT's difficulties in dealing with agricultural trade issues, however, were evident in the case of barter. Indeed, the GATT never reached a decision regarding consultations, reporting obligations, or surveillance procedures for agricultural barter transactions. Since the CSD and the GATT proved to be inadequate fora, Canada sought regular bilateral consultations with the United States on barter issues. The Canada-U.S. Ministerial Committee on Trade and Economic Affairs was a major forum for discussion of surplus disposal practices such as barter, but its annual meetings were too infrequent for the adequate expression of Canadian concerns. Thus, Canada's negative reaction to revisions in the U.S. barter program was a primary reason for the joint committee's decision (at its fourth meeting in January 1959) to establish bilateral quarterly meetings on wheat and related matters.[40]

As Table 5-1 demonstrates, the American program had an erratic history, marked generally by increases in barter from 1950 to 1957, fluctuations at a lower level from 1958 to 1962, steady increases from 1963 to 1973, and an abrupt suspension of the program in 1973. The variable levels were a reflection of numerous policy reassessments and changes resulting from domestic political factors, external protests, and changes in supply-demand relationships for foodstuffs.

In the CSD and the quarterly meetings, Canada cited numerous examples to support its case that agricultural barter was an unfair and unorthodox form of price-cutting. It argued that U.S. barter contractors benefited from favourable interest rates and other incentives, enabling them to accept a lower dollar price on sales of CCC agricultural commodities; that the CCC commodities could be offered at cut-rate prices when strategic materials were readily available and in abundant supply; and that barter's association with foreign assistance programs was a strong indication of U.S. government involvement in promoting such transactions. Despite the linkage with PL 480, Canada noted that barter was not foreign aid and that a "barter differential" paid to American exporters to make them more competitive was simply a hidden form of export subsidy. As in the case of tied sales, Canada felt that barter transactions should be additional to the commercial sales of *all* major exporters and not only to American sales. Criticism in the 1950s was also directed at the barter program's focus on Europe and Japan. Canada maintained that its largest commercial market for wheat exports (in Western Europe) was being threatened and suggested that the United States should reorient barter transactions towards countries with less effective demand.[41]

  It is evident that the United States was sensitive to Canadian concerns from an early date and that Canada was able to exert some influence. For example, in an April 1954 meeting of the National Security Council, the secretary of state questioned whether the U.S. should dispose of surpluses and "help a good friend" by providing wheat to Brazil "in exchange for materials which we might not need very much." President Eisenhower replied that "if the transaction did not place obstacles in Canada's path it should be done by all means."[42] Canadian objections to the geographic focus of U.S. barter on Europe and Japan also contributed to the development of a classification system of country eligibility in the late 1950s. Canadian markets in Western Europe (including Britain, Belgium, Luxembourg, the Netherlands, Switzerland, and West Germany) were classified in an "X" category for some commodities, meaning that American barter exports would not be authorized. In a December 1962 listing these countries were not eligible to receive barter exports of wheat and wheat flour, rye, corn, grain sorghums, barley, and cotton; but barter exports of tobacco, non-fat dry milk, butter, and cheddar cheese were still permitted.

Although Canada's protests had some effect on the development of the U.S. barter program, the amount of influence it could exert should not be overestimated. For example, the decline in American barter exports to Europe and Japan resulted primarily from the increased purchasing power in these countries, and Canadian criticisms may have only accelerated the process. Furthermore, the United States continued to direct a substantial (although decreased) percentage of its barter exports to Europe and Japan. Some of the ineligible European countries were reclassified in subsequent revisions of the system, and Western Europe was eligible for U.S. barter for overseas procurement during the 1960s. American domestic politics were also more important than external pressure in determining the direction of the barter program. An examination of the American political process demonstrates that Canada was more successful in exerting influence on the barter issue when there was greater divergence among the attitudes and interests of domestic U.S. actors.

The Eisenhower administration took a cautious approach towards barter in the 1950s for a number of reasons. Barter transactions with Europe were replacing American dollar sales, unlimited barter could overstimulate U.S. agricultural production, and some strategic materials greatly exceeded domestic requirements. However, Congressional agricultural leaders (representing producer interests) emphasized the positive aspects of barter and even introduced legislation requiring the secretary of agriculture to conclude barter transactions. Some legislators were highly critical of the executive branch for its caution on the barter issue. For example, they charged that the State Department "is afraid of offending some foreign countries and therefore has not permitted the Department of Agriculture to freely carry out the intent of the Congress to dispose of this surplus."[43]

Canada benefited from these domestic U.S. differences since the United States was willing to alter some of its practices during this period. It was in the late 1950s that the United States first applied the additionality principle to barter, developed its country classification system, agreed to Canada's request for the quarterly meetings, and shifted the focus of barter toward LDCs. However, domestic frictions decreased with the election of President John F. Kennedy since his administration was willing to promote agricultural exports aggressively in accordance with the demands of the Democratic-controlled Congress. The barter program was reassessed with a view to increasing such transactions, and President Kennedy announced a reorientation of barter from the acquisition of strategic materials to offshore procurement of goods and services in late 1962. This change led to a steady increase in barter activity from 1963 to 1973 (see Tables 5-1 and 5-2). While Canada had lost sales in the 1950s because of U.S. barter in Europe and Japan, in the 1960s it was losing markets in the LDCs. For example, Table 5-3 shows that Canadian sales of wheat and flour to Costa Rica, Guatemala, Honduras, and Nicaragua virtually disappeared from 1964 to 1968 and that its sales to Ecuador were seriously eroded. Starting in 1965 an increasing percentage of U.S. wheat exports to Central America was bartered, and in 1967 *all* U.S. wheat shipments to Costa Rica, Guatemala, Honduras, and Nicaragua were barter transactions. In Ecuador, barter covered one-half of American wheat shipments in 1965 and all of American wheat shipments in 1966 and 1967. As in the case of tied sales, the U.S. barter program was suspended only when the shortages of the 1970s developed.

TABLE 5-3

CANADIAN AND U.S. EXPORTS OF WHEAT AND FLOUR*

(thousand tonnes)

	1964 Ca. U.S.		1965 Ca. U.S.		1966 Ca. U.S.		1967 Ca. U.S.		1968 Ca. U.S.	
Costa Rica	24	26	28	18	24	37	—	46	—	71
Guatemala	13	53	6	61	1	72	—	59	1	59
Honduras	3	25	3	30	2	30	—	27	**	39
Nicaragua	14	16	14	18	7	28	—	22	—	35
Ecuador	32	25	32	37	11	55	8	58	14	63

*Figures for Ecuador are only wheat.
**Less than one thousand tonnes.
Source: S. C. Hudson, *Future Market Outlets for Canadian Wheat and Other Grains*, prepared for the Economic Council of Canada, January 1970 (Ottawa: Queen's Printer, 1970), pp. 179, 183.

Despite the divergence of American and Canadian interests on the barter issue, it is important to note that even in this case the two countries had some common interests. Although Canadian officials consistently criticized the U.S. program, Canada actually received some benefits from the multilateral and open-end barter agreements. Indeed, Canada was the second largest source of strategic materials under the USDA barter program, supplying exports valued at U.S.$141,797,000.[44] When an American program reappraisal in 1957 threatened to reduce barter transactions drastically, the *Financial Post* (Toronto) discussed the possibility that this would have mixed effects on Canada. The *Post* noted that the United States had been stockpiling Canadian lead and zinc in exchange for surplus wheat and commented wryly that "the only reason we may be able to sell more wheat in the world market is because we will soon be selling a lot less lead and zinc."[45] The possible benefits to Canada notwithstanding, the official government position was to disapprove of agricultural barter. In 1961, for example, a Canadian company (Consolidated Mining and Smelting) had an interest in bartering lead and zinc for agricultural commodities. A Department of Trade and Commerce official nevertheless maintained that such opportunities to export strategic materials could not offset the detrimental effects of American barter on Canada's grain markets.[46]

It is widely felt that international trade in exchange for money is far more efficient and desirable than countertrade. However, countertrade is currently being used in international markets for various reasons. These include the LDC debt crisis, the highly competitive situation for the export of certain products, and the substantial government involvement in the economies of some countries. The American government generally views countertrade as being contrary to an open trading system, but it will not normally oppose participation by private U.S. companies. As a result, agricultural barter could at some point re-emerge as an issue in Canadian-American relations.

CONCLUSIONS

There were many similarities between the tied sales and barter issues. They were both unilateral strategies adopted by the United States to maintain (or increase) its market share of agricultural exports during a period of foodgrain surpluses. While agricultural barter also fulfilled the U.S. political-security objective of adding to its strategic stockpile, there is considerable evidence that surplus disposal was the main motivation. Since the United States was not yet experiencing balance of payment problems, it was willing to provide large amounts of foodstuffs on concessional terms, and both tied sales and barter had concessional aspects.

Tied sales and barter were also both considered to be extremely objectionable by Canada. Most importantly, they were viewed as "grey-area" transactions that were neither fully concessional nor fully commercial. Canada considered such transactions to be a disguised form of price-cutting that threatened its commercial markets and provided only questionable benefits to LDCs. Since Canada did not have the economic resources to engage in tied sales and agricultural barter, it simply could not compete with these surplus disposal measures. To protect its agricultural markets, Canada resorted to persistent and vociferous objections to the American practices. Canada first opted for multilateral strategies in both the tied sales and barter cases since other countries shared its objections. However, the CSD's effectiveness in establishing meaningful guidelines for both tied sales and barter was limited, which was yet another indication of the inadequate regime in agricultural trade. The United States was particularly unwilling to accept a CSD role in the case of barter because of the role of U.S. private traders in these transactions. Canada therefore supplemented its multilateral efforts with bilateral strategies when voicing its complaints on the barter issue.

The United States often defended tied sales and barter as defensive measures designed to preserve its market share and to contend with questionable trading practices (such as state trading) of competing exporters. Nevertheless, Canadian-American interdependence played a role in efforts by the two countries to seek co-operative means of resolving their differences. First, the United States was somewhat sensitive to the criticisms of Canada and other exporters, and in the case of tied sales it even provided the CSD (albeit reluctantly) with detailed information on its transactions. Some practices that were particularly objectionable to competing exporters were altered. For example, the U.S. dropped its tied UMR requirements in PL 480 wheat agreements and gradually reoriented its barter transactions from Europe and Japan toward the LDCs. Second, the United States and Canada created bilateral groupings such as the quarterly meetings, partly to deal with barter, and these groupings contributed to consultation and co-operation on a variety of issues. Third, the two countries had some common interests even on the barter and tied sales issues, which may have muted the differences between them. For example, Canada and the United States joined together in the CSD to criticize the European Community's use of unrestricted tied sales, and Canada was the second largest source of strategic materials for the USDA barter program.

Nevertheless, U.S.-Canadian interdependence is highly asymmetrical, and Canada's influence on the United States should not be overestimated. Thus, domestic political considerations and the international market situation seemed to be more important in molding American policy than the complaints of Canada and other exporters. In the 1950s congress pressured the Eisenhower administration to accelerate its surplus disposal activities, and in the 1960s it supported the more aggressive position of the Democratic administrations. The United States therefore continued to use tied sales and barter as surplus disposal mechanisms for about two decades until 1973. Tied sales and barter became "non-issues," not because of U.S. responsiveness to other exporters, but because of the dramatic turnaround from foodgrain surpluses to shortages in 1972–73. With the re-emergence of surpluses in the late 1970s and 1980s, calls for the use of barter and other methods to dispose of surpluses (such as export subsidies) were renewed. The failure of the United States to launch a major agricultural barter program in the 1980s related more to domestic divisions and the difficulty in implementing such a program than it did to opposition from Canada and other exporters.

American tied sales and barter were prime illustrations of the vast difference in U.S. and Canadian economic size and capabilities. Canada lacked the resources to emulate these practices, and—in the case of barter—it did not require and could not absorb massive stockpiles of strategic materials. Most of the bilateral conflict in this area therefore stemmed from this asymmetrical situation, where U.S. surplus disposal measures threatened Canadian markets, and Canada could do little in return. Chapter 6 on agricultural export credits deals with a very different type of issue, where Canada was often able to develop programs that were quite competitive with those of the United States.

6

Canadian and U.S. Agricultural Export Credits

The United States and Canada consider agricultural export credit to be an important market development tool, and credit transactions have given rise to frequent interactions between the two countries. Unlike the surplus disposal measures discussed in Chapter 5, the provision of credit normally does not require massive amounts of economic resources. Canada was therefore able to compete with the United States in the export credit area, and both countries at various times took the lead in adopting innovative practices. From the 1950s to the early 1970s, the two countries became progressively more dependent on export credits and credit guarantees to market their agricultural products. Credit became less important during the period of foodgrain shortages in the mid-1970s, but it again became crucial to sales when surpluses re-emerged. This chapter focuses on four major phases that were significant in the evolution of export credit practices: export credits to the Soviet Union and Eastern Europe in the 1950s; American credits to the less-developed countries (LDCs) and Canadian credits to the Communist states in the 1960s; special export deals and market development efforts in the late 1960s and 1970s; and aggressive and innovative U.S. practices in the late 1970s and 1980s. However, it is first necessary to provide a definition of export credit and to differentiate between commercial and concessional credits.

The various forms of export financing assistance are not clearly defined in the literature, and terms such as export credits, export subsidies, subsidized export credits, and export credit subsidies are often used interchangeably. However, it is generally agreed that official export credits are a type of export subsidy. Export subsidies can be defined as "government incentive programs that differentially favour export sales by comparison with domestic sales" or as fixed government payments per unit of a product exported.[1] Export credits are subsidies that specifically involve export financing; that is, the provision of money, goods, or services, with special payment terms available to the recipient. In addition to focusing on export credits, this chapter also examines closely related official activities such as credit guarantees and credit insurance. Export credit insurance "insures exports or guarantees creditors against commercial or political (sometimes called transfer or country) risks in international transactions."[2]

A special situation obtains with regard to Title I of the American PL 480 program. Title I transactions in the 1950s and 1960s involved the sale of agricultural products for local currencies, with repayment periods of up to forty years. Although these shipments were termed "local currency sales," they were in fact more comparable to grants or donations than to credit. However, they are discussed in this chapter because of their clearcut linkages with Canadian credit sales. When the United States relied heavily on local currency sales to move its surplus wheat, it had less need to resort to credit transactions. Canada, by contrast, could not afford to adopt highly concessional measures, and it responded to PL 480 with other practices such as commercial credit. In addition, some of Canada's export credit innovations—such as the move towards longer-term credits—were influenced by American experiences with PL 480. Thus, even though I do not consider local currency sales to be a type of export credit, their impact must be examined. In later years, PL 480 became directly relevant to the export credit issue when the United States instituted twenty-year dollar credits under Title IV.

Credit derives its commercial or concessional characteristics from a comparison of usual open market terms with terms obtainable under government support. More specifically, the most important criteria in determining whether credit is commercial or concessional are *the repayment period, the amount of government involvement, and the interest rate.* In the absence of a strong agricultural trade regime, the definitions of commercial and concessional gradually evolved in accordance with the changing practices of the United States, Canada, and other exporters. The most contentious export financing issues related to these changing definitions and to "grey area" transactions that could not be easily categorized. The FAO's Consultative Subcommittee on Surplus Disposal (CSD) sometimes provided a forum for these disputes, and it tried to minimize conflict by setting parameters for various types of credit transactions.

Government involvement in agricultural export financing has steadily increased, and it has been a crucial factor behind the softening of credit terms. American and Canadian policies contributed in a major way to this increased government involvement, and the actions and counteractions of the two countries clearly demonstrated their interdependence. The massive size of the PL 480 program conditioned countries to expect a greater governmental role in food trade as well as aid since private traders would never offer such generous repayment terms. In addition, the Canadian Wheat Board (CWB) assumed an exporter role from an early period, and the Canadian government participated in credit programs to socialist and LDC markets that emphasized state trading and buyer incentives. Once national governments had increased their role in the promotion of agricultural exports, international organizations became involved in delineating transactions as commercial or concessional. Insofar as a consensus has evolved regarding credit, it is largely the result of international cooperation in multilateral fora. Of particular relevance are the questions of what governments and international organizations agree to treat as commercial versus concessional credit and what they consider harmful to competing interests and in need of regulation. This government involvement represents a change in the international food system since the private trade has a diminished role in determining who receives imports and on what terms.

With regard to the *repayment period*, wheat sales with credit terms of over six months were generally viewed as concessional in the 1950s and 1960s. The International Wheat Agreement (IWA) categorized credit beyond the six-month limit as a "special" sale, and the CSD stipulated that an exporter wishing to extend such credit had to consult with its competitors beforehand. However, credits of up to three years gradually came to be more accepted as commercial transactions. Canada therefore maintained that its Export Credit Insurance Corporation credit facility was commercial, even though its terms began to stretch first to twelve months and eventually to three years. Canada also never conceded that its credit sales to Eastern Europe under twelve, eighteen and thirty-six month terms were anything but commercial. As for the United States, its 1956 Commodity Credit Corporation (CCC) credit sales program introduced a three-year term, which was similarly portrayed as commercial. Largely in response to these policy changes, the CSD excluded credit transactions of up to three years from its concerns.[3] This exclusion in effect sanctioned a definition of such transactions as commercial, even though the six-month period retained some significance (particularly for wheat). Beyond the three-year credit period lies a "grey area" of exports that are neither clearly commercial nor clearly concessional. The CSD coined the term to denote transactions in which its jurisdiction was uncertain and established a Grey Area Panel to discuss the growing problems with such deals. The grey-area term sometimes has been used in reference to additionality, usual marketing requirements, and pricing and it has never been clearly defined. In this chapter, however, it refers to transactions with credit periods of between three and ten years.[4]

The standard of comparison for commercial versus concessional *interest rates* was whether or not they approximated those offered by private sector financial institutions. Interest rates were usually not as contentious an issue in Canadian-American relations as credit duration and government involvement. When longer repayment periods were provided, it often followed that the interest rates were also more concessional. However, there were instances when interest rates attracted some attention. For example, Canada maintained that its 1961 credit sale to China was commercial despite the longer repayment terms because the interest rate and degree of government intervention were within commercial limits. The United States also maintained that its CCC interest rates were commercial, but Canada argued that they were sometimes concessional.[5]

The following discussion will demonstrate that Canadian-American interaction usually took its cue from policy innovations in the areas of credit duration and/or government involvement and that disagreements over grey-area transactions were particulary intense.

EARLY COMMERCIAL CREDIT SALES: THE 1950S

American and Canadian government agencies were authorized to provide agricultural export credits from an early date. In 1934 the U.S. government established the Export-Import Bank to assist in financing foreign purchases, and the Eximbank was a major source of credit for food transfers to Western Europe from 1948 to 1954. However, the Eximbank was eventually overshadowed by the Commodity Credit Corporation, which started to offer export financing in 1956 and became the principal government agency providing agricultural credit. In Canada, the Wheat Board had an export marketing mandate from an early period, and the government instituted the CWB Credit Grain Sales Program and the Export Credit Insurance Corporation (ECIC) in 1944. Credits to foreign buyers could either be insured by the ECIC or guaranteed by the Canadian government. Export credits became a source of competition and conflict in Canadian-American relations when major foodgrain surpluses developed after the Korean War. Canada used government-financed credits to develop new markets in the Communist countries, partly because it could not compete with U.S. concessional exports to traditional markets in Western Europe and the LDCs. American export financing activities in the 1950s included PL 480 transactions and more commercial CCC export credit sales.

The export credit issue demonstrates that Canada adopted unilateral strategies and innovations in areas where it could compete with the United States. Indeed, Canada played a major role from an early date in lengthening the repayment period for agricultural export credit. Canada first began to extend the length of credit sales when it sold 250,000 tonnes of wheat to Yugoslavia during 1952–54 under the CWB export credit program. Apart from small cash downpayments, ECIC insurance covered the full value of the sales, and a twelve-month payment period applied. These sales were significant because Canada had not previously extended one-year credit for wheat purchases. Indeed, the ECIC was not initially designed to provide insurance for wheat exports, and the minister responsible for the Wheat Board wanted to adhere to the principle of unassisted wheat sales. The Canadian government of the day described the sales as exceptional measures under short-term arrangements for a few countries that lacked purchasing power. In the Yugoslav case, there were the additional circumstances of its break with the Soviet Union and its resultant economic difficulties.[6]

However, Canada was also beginning to view export credits as an effective marketing tool for moving its growing surpluses and as a countermeasure to PL 480 financing. In 1959 a Canadian official reported that countries unable to meet full commercial terms could import wheat with ECIC coverage, and the U.S. Department of Agriculture (USDA) noted that the ECIC credit ceiling was increased from $100 million in 1944 to $200 million in 1958 "to further assist export sales of Canadian wheat."[7] While Canada was extending export credits to Yugoslavia, the United States was providing aid largely for ideological and security reasons. Yugoslavia was one of the first recipients of agricultural commodities under PL 480, and in 1954 total PL 480 aid to that country reached almost $100 million. The terms of this assistance were so concessional that the United States eventually "undertook to provide Yugoslavia's import needs."[8] Having been shut out of Yugoslavia, Canada sought to develop another socialist market in Poland.

Competition for the Polish market developed at an early stage, largely because it was a reluctant follower of the USSR and because its food import needs could not be fully met by Soviet supplies. Since U.S.-subsidized commodity exports were restricted to "friendly countries" (which did not include the Soviet bloc), a special case had to be made for Poland. While the United States was deliberating over Poland's eligibility, Canada began extending export credits. It refused Poland's first request for wheat on credit in 1954, but then approved credit sales in 1955–56 for almost 350,000 tonnes of wheat. The ECIC insurance for the sales approached $21 million, and there was a one-year credit term. The reversal of Canada's attitude regarding credit sales to Poland certainly owed something to anticipated U.S. policy changes. At the time Canada agreed to supply this credit, the PL 480 program was rapidly expanding, Poland was seeking a relaxation of American trade restrictions, and the USDA was predicting agricultural sales to the East bloc of well over two million tonnes.[9]

TABLE 6–1

CANADIAN CREDIT WHEAT EXPORTS TO POLAND*

Crop Year	Tonnes
1955-56	349,029
1956-57	259,188
1957-58	39,291
1958-59	51,469
1959-60	17,160

*In 1958-59 and 1959-60, Canada also exported 95,722 and 115,429 tonnes of barley on credit, respectively.
Source: Derived from Charles F. Wilson, *Grain Marketing in Canada* (Winnipeg: Canadian International Grains Institute, 1979), table 24-4.

Canada extended credit sales to Poland every year from 1955–56 to 1970–71, but Table 6–1 shows that its wheat shipments were much higher when the United States was debating over Poland's eligibility. The early Canadian sales certainly demonstrated the value of this market to the United States, and Canada provided information on its Polish and Yugoslav credit sales in the Canada-U.S. Consultative Committee on Grain Marketing. American policy was finally altered in January 1957, making Poland eligible for PL 480 assistance and CCC export credits. Title I loans were supplied for $46 million worth of wheat and corn (more than twice the Canadian sales) and $20 million worth of cotton, fats, and oils, and a $30 million Eximbank credit was also provided.[10] As Table 6–1 shows, the precipitous drop in Canada's wheat exports to Poland in 1957–58 coincided with these U.S. transactions. The Yugoslav and Polish cases indicate that American political-security objectives sometimes had a detrimental effect on Canada's agricultural export prospects, and the role of the political-security factor is discussed further at the end of this chapter.

Canada did not openly object to CCC credit sales to Poland, but American concessional sales were a different matter. At a January 1957 meeting of the Consultative Committee on Grain Marketing, Canadian officials protested that "PL 480 sales for Polish currency . . . would result in the extension of an indeterminate loan and would eliminate Canada from market." Canada also warned that it "might be forced to sign [long-term] bilateral agreements which would exclude United States imports . . . simply for our protection" if the U.S. surplus disposal program continued.[11] When Poland renewed its request for Canadian wheat in February 1957, it required generous credit terms because it already owed $11 million to Canada for earlier wheat purchases. Canada was therefore able to secure a three-year agreement with forward purchase commitments in exchange for extending Poland's debt repayment period and providing three-year credit terms. This agreement removed part of the Polish market from access to U.S. concessional sales. Most importantly, Canada's three-year "Polish credit terms" subsequently served as a model for its agreements with other East European countries.

While the lengthening of Canadian wheat credits to three years was quite remarkable, it did not arouse any major controversy. The Americans continued to limit their CCC wheat credits to a six-month period, but they were reluctant to criticize Canadian policy for several reasons. The CCC was authorized to extend three-year credits for agricultural products other than wheat, the 1957 U.S.-Polish agreement included PL 480 loans with five-year terms, the United States was not unduly concerned about Canadian competition during this period, and Poland required the credit because of its financial problems. There is considerable evidence, however, that market pre-emption was Canada's primary concern. For example, a former Canadian grain official stated that "the United States held the more powerful hand in the concessional terms it could offer through its PL 480 agreements" but that Canada could command "competitive weaponry . . . through the negotiation of trade treaties which assured the sale of Canadian wheat, and through its venture into the realm of credit sales."[12] Credit requests, usually coupled with requests for most-favoured nation (MFN) status, were granted in exchange for forward purchase commitments in three- or five-year long-term agreements. By 1963-64, Canada had concluded long-term credit agreements with Poland, Hungary, Czechoslovakia, East Germany, and Bulgaria.[13]

Canada's early credit initiatives also targeted non-Communist countries, but its success in these markets was rather limited. After Brazil received Canadian credit exports of over 200,000 tons of wheat in 1953-54, it became one of the first recipients of PL 480 Title I wheat shipments in 1954-55. The United States was able to meet Brazil's needs on vastly more generous terms and (like Argentina) with lower shipping costs. Although Canada was unable to re-enter the Brazilian market until 1970, it retained interest in that market and complained about American barter and local currency sales. Canada also negotiated relatively modest credit wheat sales (between 20,000 and 40,000 tons) with Israel in four of the five crop years from 1953 to 1957. The Canadian sales began before the PL 480 program was instituted, but they fell after the United States placed Israel on the Title I list in 1955. The last Canadian credit sale coincided with the 1957 introduction of expanded options for using Title I foreign currencies and with the U.S. designation of Israel as a "first priority" country. Canada complained about the concessional American exports, but it continued exporting some wheat to Israel without credit until well into the 1960s.[14]

In summary, Canada introduced several credit innovations in the 1950s (such as the three-year "Polish credit terms") and demonstrated its ability to compete with the United States in the export credit area. However, when the United States provided concessional PL 480 loans to Canada's credit markets, it was usually successful in pre-empting those markets. Since Canada lacked the resources to compete directly with PL 480, it had to rely instead on establishing long-term agreements that were linked with export credits.

American political-security objectives had mixed effects on Canadian credit markets during this period. While Canada's credit sales to Yugoslavia, Poland, and Israel were one factor that prompted U.S. interest in these markets, political reasons undoubtedly provided another major stimulus. Since the United States viewed these three countries as pivotal in a strategic-security sense, it considered them prime recipients for PL 480 aid, and Canada was therefore unable to compete.[15] On the other hand, the United States was shunning agricultural trade with most of the Soviet bloc, which enabled Canada to establish a foothold in many East European markets. The United States also felt little need to criticize Canada's initiatives, even though Canada often complained about American practices. Since the U.S. payments and trade positions were quite strong in the 1950s, it was often more concerned with political-security objectives than with economic objectives.[16]

It is significant that Canadian-American competition during this period contributed to changing perceptions of "commercial credit" in the global food system. Agricultural exporters initially required almost immediate payment for commercial sales, regardless of the recipient's financial capabilities. One-year credit was then introduced, and three-year financing subsequently shifted perceptions of the commercial market to a new level. Certainly with three-year credit, an element of assistance is incorporated in nominally commercial transactions. As a result, importers came to expect more financing concessions, and exporters proposed multi-year supply arrangements as a *quid pro quo*. Although U.S.-Canadian competition was a factor in the lengthening of credit terms, the two countries later co-operated in upholding the new perception of credit. For example, when wheat shortages developed in the early 1970s, Canada and the United States reduced the volume of credit exports but not the length of the credit period. Both countries by then considered credit terms of three years at about market-level interest rates to be acceptable, which led to the CSD's eventual sanctioning of these terms as commercial.

DIVERSIFICATION AND CONSOLIDATION: THE 1960S

The United States continued to direct its financing assistance to LDCs in the 1960s, while Canada maintained its interest in the Communist markets. However, there was greater potential for competition and conflict as the U.S. took actions to deal with its worsening balance of payments. For example, it introduced new financing arrangements such as long-term dollar credits aimed at hard currency rewards and market development. These new terms shifted American surplus disposal activities toward the more affluent LDCs, which were often prime targets for Canadian commercial exports. On the other hand, Canada's expansion into the Chinese and Cuban markets generated American criticism and even attempts at intervention. Nevertheless, the United States and Canada consulted frequently in bilateral and multilateral fora in the 1960s in an effort to manage these conflicts.

In 1959 the United States enacted Title IV of PL 480, which authorized the sale of American agricultural products for dollars with payment periods of up to twenty years. Proceeds from the resale of these commodities in recipient LDC markets were to be used for economic development projects. This long-term dollar credit program was designed to fill the gap between three-year CCC export credits and forty-year Title I local currency loans. It sought to maximize dollar sales and presaged the eventual phasing out of local currency agreements between 1969 and 1971. Canada could not match the concessional terms of Title IV, and it was rather critical of the program. Along with other exporters, it argued that U.S. long-term credit sales should be confined to LDCs with foreign exchange shortages and that they should be subject to the FAO procedures of consultation and additionality. The United States promised that it would adhere to the FAO safeguards and indicated that other exporters would benefit from Title IV's emphasis on economic development in LDCs.

Title IV was not in fact implemented during the Eisenhower presidency, largely because of domestic cleavages. For example, the State Department agreed with foreign competitors that the long-term contracts were actually concessional transactions. In addition, officials in the Departments of State and Agriculture were attuned to the concerns of commercial exporters (U.S. as well as foreign) that Title IV might displace their sales.[17] The new Kennedy administration, however, was more responsive to Congressional pressures, and it began to implement Title IV in 1962. Canadian complaints resulted in some delays, but the U.S. government eventually approved agreements over Canada's objections with El Salvador, Ecuador, and the Dominican Republic. While Canada's wheat exports to these three countries were not immediately affected, they did decline dramatically beginning in 1966.[18]

At first Title IV only authorized government-to-government agreements, but from 1962 the U.S. government was also permitted to conclude agreements with American and foreign private traders or "private trade entities" (PTEs). The PTE option was appealing to American officials since it signalled a greater emphasis on private company transactions and on hard currency repayments. However, export competitors warned that private sector involvement would make it difficult to secure U.S. adherence to the FAO principles.[19] Canada routinely complained about individual PTE agreements and opposed Title IV in principle as yet another U.S. concessional program that interfered with commercial markets. However, Canadian representatives usually took a moderate stance in CSD discussions for several reasons. They were reluctant to criticize Title IV's economic development goals, concerned that excessive complaints might induce the United States to take more notice of Canada's exports to the Communist markets, and aware that the impact of Title IV on Canadian exports was limited. Indeed, the program accounted for only 2.3 per cent of PL 480 expenditures from 1962 to mid-1965, and many early recipients of PTE agreements (such as Iran, Taiwan, and Spain) were not major importers of Canadian agricultural products.[20] Canada's moderate attitude in effect provided a degree of endorsement for the American policy changes, and from 1969 to 1971 PL 480 local currency loans were gradually phased out and replaced by long-term dollar credits.

In addition to Title IV, credit exports to the Communist states were another issue affecting Canadian-American relations during the 1960s. Canada had offered the Soviet Union credit as part of their three-year trade treaty in 1955, but the USSR paid cash for all of its wheat purchases. The Soviets also paid cash for Canadian wheat when their bilateral long-term agreement (LTA) was renewed in 1960, 1963, and 1966. However, it is of interest that Canada again offered the USSR credit for grain purchases in 1963 when negotiations were stalled over other items and that the Soviets again declined.[21] In the end, Canada sold the USSR an unprecedented five million tons of wheat and 575,000 tons of flour valued at $500 million in 1963. The United States exported much smaller amounts of wheat to the Soviets that year, but unlike Canada it did not offer credit. The Johnson Debt Default Act prohibited the provision of credit to the Soviet Union as long as its wartime lend-lease debts were not settled. The U.S. made no further wheat sales to the USSR until 1971-72, and Canadian credit to the Soviets re-emerged as an issue only in the late 1970s.

A far more contentious issue related to Canadian credit sales to China (PRC). Canada sold wheat to the PRC for cash in 1955, 1958, and 1960, and in April 1961 the two countries signed their first long-term agreement. As a result of this LTA, China became Canada's second-largest customer after Britain, and the Canadian share of the global wheat market rose from 30 to 35 per cent. The credit terms, which provided for a 25 per cent cash down payment and 270 days on the balance, were a compromise between China's request for the Polish terms (10 per cent cash down and thirty-six months) and Canada's desire for cash or six-month credit sales. The Canadian government assumed direct credit guarantees because the size of the agreement exceeded the ECIC's facilities, and this practice became fairly common thereafter.[22]

China had requested credit in early 1960, and a senior Canadian official noted that the government's "willingness to extend export credits to the PRC in the early days of our trading relationship and even before diplomatic recognition has no doubt contributed to our strong competitive position in that market."[23] These credit exports were at first a major source of controversy in U.S.-Canadian relations. For example, in October 1961 Canada reacted harshly to an American request for advance consultation concerning its sales to Communist countries and indicated that such issues should not require U.S. clearance. Furthermore, the American government interfered with Canada's purchase of necessary wheat-loading equipment in the United States, and with flour-milling and ship-bunkering in Canada for deliveries to China.[24] These actions were based on the Trading with the Enemy Act and Foreign Assets Control legislation, which sought to limit the trade of U.S. subsidiaries with certain Communist countries (including China, Cuba, North Vietnam, and North Korea). Canadian officials protested that this extraterritorial application of U.S. law was highly objectionable since the Wheat Board was a crown agency concluding sales that were beneficial to the Canadian economy.

After 1961, however, bilateral exchanges regarding China became more cordial. American disapproval shifted to enquiries and complaints rather than acts of interference, and Canada took note of these concerns without altering its basic policies. There were a number of reasons for the more moderate American attitude. U.S. extraterritoriality could have led to a serious confrontation because there was strong support in Canada for the China sales; it was difficult to single out Canada for criticism since other allies such as Australia and France were also selling to China; Canada's exports of surplus wheat to China reduced competition in other markets; The State Department prevailed over others that were less sensitive to Canadian concerns; and Canada provided extensive information on its China transactions and was responsive to the U.S. position against political recognition.[25]

American criticism also declined as Canada's credit terms acquired greater legitimacy. The China sales, like the credit sales of the 1950s, showed that more liberal financing practices could evolve into widely accepted norms through verbal assertions and repeated usage. Initially, the United States objected to "the easy credit the Canadian Wheat Board extended to the Chinese for their wheat purchases."[26] Canada had advised the U.S. of its efforts to obtain the 1961 long-term agreement on a cash or six-month credit basis, but it eventually agreed to China's demand for a nine-month period. In May 1961 Canadian officials acknowledged that the nine-month terms for such a massive credit sale were concessional, and they also reported the terms as special to the International Wheat Council. However, by July 1961 Canada was describing the China transaction as commercial, and the United States, though disagreeing, was not voicing major objections. By 1962, Canada was simply advising the U.S. *ex post facto* of further credit sales to China at regular commercial rates. By late 1963, the repayment period for the last two contracts under the LTA had stretched to twelve months, and it became eighteen months under the second LTA (1964–66). Although the Americans objected that long-term credits to China were a form of economic aid, Canada was able to extend the credit period without significant problems. In summary, bilateral conflict over credit sales to China was resolved because the United States softened its position and accepted Canadian representations as valid. However, co-operative Canadian behaviour was also a factor. Canada's credit terms to China (25 per cent cash down, eighteen months extension on the balance) were not liberalized further after 1963, and they remained within the limits widely accepted for transactions with other countries.[27]

The American CCC credit program, which was established in 1956, was yet another contentious issue during this period. Although the program experienced its greatest growth in the late 1970s, Canada's strongest criticisms were voiced during the early 1960s. Canada expected Congressional allocations for CCC export credits to increase at this time because of the new U.S. emphasis on hard currency transactions, and American attempts to reassure the Canadian government were unsuccessful. For example, the United States noted that CCC program used only about 20 per cent of its funding capacity in the early 1960s, but Canada nevertheless felt that CCC credit was eroding its cash markets. The U.S. also offered assurances that it would exercise restraint, limit wheat credit exports to six months or less, establish eligibility schemes for CCC credit, and respect Canada's fair share of markets. However, Canada deplored the absence of definite U.S. undertakings to implement these promises.[28]

In their discussions concerning the CCC program, Canada and the United States both perceived export credits in a way that would strengthen their competitive positions. The U.S. did not welcome CSD scrutiny of its CCC credit transactions, and it maintained that they were commercial. Canadian officials, on the other hand, felt the need for multilateral safeguards and insisted that CCC credit sales were concessional. In fact, the two countries were emphasizing different criteria in their definitions of a commercial transaction, and there were no clear international guidelines to settle the issue. While the United States noted that the CCC credit repayment period was relatively short, Canada focused instead on the level of government involvement. It argued that U.S. government involvement was high since the CCC was funded by Congressional allocations from a vast public purse, and the United States used credit to advance its political priorities. In countering these arguments, the United States emphasized the prominent role of the private grain trade in CCC sales and the absence of formal government-to-government agreements of the Canadian variety.

Canada may have used a double standard in judging American credit exports, particularly since three-year Canadian credit to Eastern Europe was being described as commercial. Nevertheless, the Canadian government was trying to establish safeguards because of the much greater U.S. economic resources. Canada feared that American inroads into its markets would lead to a credit race that the U.S. would inevitably win. Furthermore, the United States sometimes tied CCC credit to imports of surplus commodities under the PL 480 program. Finally, an enlarged CCC credit program threatened to unravel the implicit understanding that the United States would focus on cash-poor LDCs, while Canada would export to Communist countries and more affluent LDCs.

Although Canada often complained about the CCC program, it was careful not to be too critical. The inconsistencies of its own practices, the success of its credit sales to the Communist countries, and the interdependent nature of the bilateral relationship encouraged a moderate response. Thus, even while protesting against individual CCC transactions (in Italy, Norway, Guatemala, and Japan), Canada cautioned other exporters against overly harsh criticism of the United States. It also acknowledged that the U.S. was justified in seeking more hard currency sales and was fair (in certain cases) in taking Canadian interests into account. American officials reacted even more mildly to Canadian criticisms, and rarely mentioned Canada's own credit practices. This moderation largely resulted from the shared objectives of the two states (for example, in orderly marketing) and the desire to maintain bilateral harmony.

The market damage to Canada would undoubtedly have been greater if the United States had implemented its CCC program more vigorously. The American offer to freeze CCC wheat credits at six months, for example, was one indication that other exporters did have some influence. Canada's ability to alter

U.S. behaviour was, nevertheless, clearly limited. For example, Canada suggested that a multilateral working party on concessional wheat sales devise criteria and procedures for government credit transactions, but this suggestion proved futile. Furthermore, the United States continued to conclude CCC credit sales more or less as it saw fit. In view of the emerging consensus in the IWA and CSD that credits of the CCC variety were commercial, Canada eventually had to accept the program as being outside the CSD safeguard procedures.

To summarize, the potential for bilateral conflict increased for a variety of reasons in the 1960s. The United States responded to its balance of payment problems by placing more emphasis on long- and short-term dollar credit sales, and Canada often viewed these changes as a threat to its commercial markets. On the other hand, Canada extended export credits to China, which the U.S. considered a political challenge to its strong ideological stance against the PRC. However, both countries exercised restraint in the use of their credit programs, and they were somewhat responsive to each other's complaints. For example, the United States did not extend its CCC credit wheat exports beyond a six-month period, and Canada concurred with the strong American position against the political recognition of China. The two countries also provided each other with extensive information on their credit transactions in bilateral and multilateral fora.

The United States and Canada were, in addition, restrained in their criticisms of each other's programs, and Canadian representatives took a moderate stance on the PL 480 Title IV and the CCC credit programs in multilateral discussions. The United States eventually accepted Canada's broader definition of commercial credit exports to China, which contributed to the evolving consensus on the limits of commercial versus concessional transactions. Since the U.S. credit programs were limited in scope in the 1960s and the United States was not competing for Canada's China market, the two countries were able to limit their competition and conflict through a mixture of restraint and consultation in a variety of fora.

NEW PROGRAMS AND SPECIAL DEALS: THE LATE 1960S AND 1970S

Canada and the United States did not initiate export credit innovations during the mid-1960s because grain sales were generally satisfactory, stocks were manageable, and the U.S. was implementing production control measures. However, the potential for conflict increased in the late 1960s with the development of burdensome surpluses, the growing emphasis of U.S. farm policy on commercial exports, the decline in Canada's share of global wheat exports, and the emergence of the European Community as a major export competitor.

These changes engendered new export financing initiatives, including the expansion of American long- and short-term credit sales and the creation of Canada's Expanded Credit Program and Export Development Corporation.

The credit innovations of the late 1960s reflected the convergence of American and Canadian marketing methods and targets as the United States shifted toward more commercial exports. PL 480 local currency sales declined from $1.2 billion in 1964 to $540 million in 1968, and they were then phased out by legislation between 1968 and 1971. In contrast, long-term dollar credit sales accounted for over 50 per cent of all PL 480 shipments after 1970, marking a new stage in "transforming aid recipients into commercial customers."[29] The U.S. policy change was also evident from its pledges to the Food Aid Convention (FAC), a part of the International Grains Arrangement that committed signatories to contribute specified amounts of foodgrains (or their cash equivalent) as aid. When the FAC was renewed in 1971, the U.S. insisted that long-term dollar credit sales should count toward its contributions. The United States also shortened the repayment periods for its PL 480 credit sales and in 1969 stopped providing concessional financing for transportation costs arising out of its cargo preference legislation. Importers purchasing on long-term credit therefore had to absorb the costs for shipping at least 50 per cent of U.S. agricultural goods in more expensive American bottoms. Furthermore, the shorter-term CCC credit sales steadily increased in value from $111 million in 1968 to $913 million in 1973, and the percentage of wheat exports covered by CCC credit rose as well. One factor in establishing credit terms was the determination to make CCC credit "better than other credit available to the importers and attractive enough to meet the competition from other countries."[30] Some of the main CCC credit recipients were markets of great interest to Canada, such as South Korea, The Philippines, and Japan.

Along with its shift toward more commercial exports, the U.S. government also began to relax its trade restrictions with the Communist countries. As one element in the easing of restrictions, the United States offered CCC credit to China beginning in February 1972. This credit was not utilized for several years, but it was evident that the U.S. would become a major competitor for the China market. Indeed, China purchased U.S. grain for the first time in 1972, and in 1973 over 50 per cent of the PRC's wheat and corn imports were from the United States. Canadian apprehensions over American competition led the House of Commons Agriculture Committee to state that "the Trading with the Enemy Act has been of assistance to us in selling a lot more of our better grains to some of the Communist countries ... now ... will we be able to hang on to this business?"[31] As a result, Canada sought and obtained assurances from the PRC that it would remain the preferred supplier.

The Nixon administration also wanted to ease relations with the Soviet Union, and it became eligible for CCC credit in 1971. A U.S.-Soviet agreement announced in July 1972 included $750 million in credit for grain purchases over three years, $500 million dollars of which was to be in CCC credits. Maritime and commerce agreements and the settlement of the Soviet lend-lease debt followed in October and opened the way for further credit transactions. In subsequent sales, CCC credit was utilized at over $0.5 billion dollars, bringing the total program above the $1 billion mark for the first time. However, the provision of American credits and subsidies to the USSR proved to be a major policy blunder when prices rose rapidly thereafter. Congressional demands regarding issues such as Soviet immigration policy were an additional factor contributing to the nullification of the October 1972 commercial agreement in January 1975. Despite these continuing frictions, it was evident that CCC credit would play an important role in promoting U.S. exports in the Communist markets.[32]

In Canada, a 1969 Federal Task Force on Agriculture reacted to the greater U.S. emphasis on commercial exports with a warning that the country "has already lost a share of the world wheat market to the United States, and may lose even more unless our wheat exports remain fully competitive . . . in price and credit conditions."[33] At this time, Canada was developing a wide range of new institutions and programs to stimulate agricultural exports in a surplus situation of "crisis proportions."[34] The urgency in developing these programs was evident since 1969 was the only year in recent history that Canada was a net agricultural importer. The new Canadian programs were part of a trend developing in both North American states (although from opposite poles) to integrate market expansion and LDC economic development goals and to apply concessional means toward commercial ends.

In the credit area, Canada replaced the Export Credit Insurance Corporation with the Export Development Corporation (EDC) in 1969. The Task Force on Agriculture described the ECIC's policies as being "excessively conservative" since the interest rates it charged were higher than those of competing countries. In contrast, the EDC (which assumed all of the ECIC's functions) was designed to "expand operations and facilitate borrowing at lower interest rates," despite "the danger of substituting some non-commercial sales for commercial."[35] The most important Canadian initiative during this period was the Expanded Credit Program, which drew on American experience with concessional transactions and provided three- to ten-year loans to LDCs with below-market interest rates and cash downpayments as low as 5 per cent. About forty countries were eligible for the expanded credit, but contracts were negotiated on a case-by-case basis with the degree of concessionality determined by competitive requirements.

The Expanded Credit Program was generally viewed as an exceptional, short-term deviation from the Canadian principle of selling grain on a strictly commercial basis. For example, a 1985 government publication states that "financing subsidies have not been used on Canadian wheat sales since the early 1970s when sales were made . . . on terms of from five to ten years to meet U.S. competition in potential commercial markets."[36] Yet, sales under the Expanded Credit Program were made to at least six countries and initially created considerable controversy. While Canada felt that it had to lengthen the credit period to retain its market share, the United States viewed this policy change as unfair competition in markets developed by American aid. Thus, a USDA publication stated that the Expanded Credit Program led to a number of sales "to countries that had never bought Canadian wheat, or to countries that had been only occasional customers" and that all program recipients "have also been buyers of U.S. wheat."[37] This negative perception was reinforced when the Canadian Wheat Board assumed responsibility for Expanded Credit since the United States associates the CWB with state trading and government intervention.

The cases of Peru and Brazil, however, show that Canadian-American interactions regarding the Expanded Credit Program varied greatly in specific instances. The first Expanded Credit agreement was concluded with Peru. That country's main wheat suppliers had been the United States (under PL 480) and Argentina, with Canada in third place until the mid-1960s when Australia entered the market. Total wheat exports to Peru rose from about 400,000 to 600,000 tons per year during the 1960s, but Canada's share dwindled to less than 1,000 tons by 1968. Canadian markets were also disappearing in Central America, Ecuador, and The Philippines, mainly as a result of U.S. concessional and barter exports. To limit its declining export prospects, Canada concluded an Expanded Credit agreement with Peru in 1969, which provided for the sale of 200,000 tons of wheat with five-year credit terms at a subsidized interest rate of 5 per cent.[38] Peru welcomed this agreement since the United States was hardening its export terms, and Table 6-2 shows that there was a dramatic change in the ratio of Canadian to American exports beginning in 1969–70.

The United States strongly criticized the Canada-Peru agreement, arguing that CSD procedures for prior consultation and for estimating a usual marketing requirement (UMR) had been disregarded. American officials also described the agreement as a grey-area transaction that provided only minimal benefits to the recipient country. However, Peru took issue with the U.S. arguments, and Canada rejected most of the complaints as unfounded.

Exchanges in multilateral meetings left no doubt that Canada felt justified in countering U.S. surplus disposal methods such as barter with its new credit facility. Canada did apologize for giving belated notification under the CSD rules, but it was willing to stretch the procedures because it felt that they already permitted questionable U.S. practices.[39] In summary, the exchange underlines a basic difference in the Canadian and American approaches. To the United States, the Peruvian market was a discrete entity and the Canadian credit sale an unwarranted attempt to change the established rules. From Canada's perspective, its credit practices could not be judged in isolation since the United States could employ a much wider array of export promotion methods. Thus, there was a correlation between U.S. barter transactions here, PL 480 loans there, and Canadian credits elsewhere. In the longer term, Canada had to phase out its concessional credit offerings, and the United States utilized its greater capabilities to retrieve the Peruvian market from 1971-72 (see Table 6-2).

TABLE 6-2

WHEAT AND WHEAT FLOUR EXPORTS TO PERU (EXCLUDING DONATIONS)

(thousand bushels)

	Canada	United States
1967-68	23	9,089
1968-69	10	3,773
1969-70	6,120	5,758
1970-71	9,527	6,942
1971-72	6,064	16,476

Source: Omero Sabatini, Canada's Export Market Development for Agricultural Products (Washington, D.C.: USDA, 1975), p. 41.

Canada's success with Expanded Credit was more dramatic in Brazil than in Peru, yet the American reaction was more subdued. Except for the early 1950s, Canada had not been able to break into the Brazilian market, which was dominated by Argentina and the United States. American exports to Brazil in the late 1960s were Title I, barter, and long-term credit (Title IV) transactions, with dollar credits eventually replacing local currency sales. A 1970 assessment of future market outlets for Canadian grains concluded that "penetration of the Brazilian wheat market will require special concessional provisions competitive with those extended by the United States which is already firmly established in that market."[40] As a result, a Canadian-Brazilian agreement was concluded under the Expanded Credit Program in June 1970, with ten-year credit terms covering wheat shipments of over 400,000 tons in 1970–71 and over 350,000 tons in 1971–72. Table 6–3 shows that this contributed to Canada's emergence as an important supplier of wheat to Brazil.

TABLE 6–3

WHEAT AND WHEAT FLOUR EXPORTS TO BRAZIL (EXCLUDING DONATIONS)

(thousand bushels)

	Canada	United States
1967-68	0	47,464
1968-69	0	28,688
1969-70	0	33,184
1970-71	15,533	28,777
1971-72	13,588	16,334

Source: Omero Sabatini, *Canada's Export Market Development for Agricultural Products* (Washington, D.C.: USDA, 1975), p. 41.

Canada reported the sale as additional to Brazil's normal commercial imports and maintained that Expanded Credit was necessary in view of American attempts to pre-empt the Brazilian market. Brazil's total wheat import requirements were estimated at about 2.5 million tons per year, with a U.S.-set commercial UMR of 1.6 million tons for 1969. However, Canada maintained that other exporters could in fact compete for only 600,000 tons of the UMR since the balance was pre-empted by U.S. supplies which were "tied" to its concessional shipments. Moreover, Canada complained that even the 600,000 tons were primarily American barter transactions, which were not always completely commercial. Unlike the case of Peru, the United States did not react strongly to these charges and it did not voice major objections to Canada's incursion into the Brazilian market. A stronger reaction would have elicited little sympathy since Argentina was accusing the U.S. as well as Canada of shutting other exporters out of market growth in Brazil. Argentina maintained that the Canadian sale was particularly objectionable because concessional terms were being used to enter a commercial market and because there was little history of Canadian sales to Brazil. However, Canada rejected these arguments and did not withdraw from the market.[41] Credits were the main export promotion device that Canada could employ, whereas Argentina as an LDC could not compete with either Canadian or American buyer incentives. Canada also offered Expanded Credit to some other LDCs, and the impact of these sales is apparent from Table 6–4.

TABLE 6–4

WHEAT AND FLOUR EXPORTS TO COUNTRIES USING CANADA'S EXPANDED CREDIT

(thousand bushels)

	Egypt	Syria	Philippines	Algeria
1967-68				
U.S.	862	3,102	21,923	9,436
Canada	0	0	0	0
1968-69				
U.S.	0	0	18,360	8,538
Canada	164	2,030	0	0
1969-70				
U.S.	0	0	16,631	5,263
Canada	3,197	4,061	0	0
1970-71				
U.S.	0	3,369	16,565	8,183
Canada	12,862	10,477	6,022	11,765
1971-72				
U.S.	0	5,174	14,418	16,701
Canada	892	9,227	6,364	8,204

Source: Omero Sabatini, *Canada's Export Market Development for Agricultural Products* (Washington, D.C.: USDA, 1975), p. 41

The United States certainly did not lose interest in any of these markets or cede them to Canada. On the contrary, in an increasing number of countries American and Canadian export promotion activities began to converge and create disputes. Analysts generally agreed that Canada's market expansion initiatives were successful. For example, an Agriculture Canada official reported that "there were significant increases in Canadian agricultural exports in 1970 and 1971 reflecting in part the greater use of the credit facilities for sales to developing countries."[42] On a more negative note, a USDA study expressed concerns that "the new attitude for future export development programs is that whatever the product, Canada must anticipate, and where necessary create, as well as maintain, the demand for it."[43] However, the anticipated growth of Canada's special credit terms did not occur because of the emergence of food-grain shortages in 1972–73. Canada also could not compete with U.S. concessional export assistance over the longer term, and from a practical as well as a philosophical perspective Expanded Credit was out of character for it. Thus, Canada abandoned the program in 1972, and it later reacted negatively to the introduction of three- to ten-year credits by the United States (discussed in the next section).

In summary, American and Canadian export promotion activities in this period continued to converge from opposite directions. The United States began to offer stricter credit terms, with wider coverage to previously neglected markets—most notably the Soviet Union and China. Canada responded to the U.S. moves by offering credit on more generous terms and also directing its marketing efforts to a broader range of countries. The American and Canadian credit initiatives were a response not only to their bilateral competition but also to increased competition with other major grain producers such as the European Community. This was the period when the 1967 International Grains Arrangement broke down, an indication that competition and conflict would re-emerge in intensified form after the shortage period of the 1970s.

NEW PROGRAMS, OLD PROBLEMS: THE LATE 1970S AND 1980S

Export credits played a minor role in agricultural trade for much of the 1970s, largely because of the global food shortages. American long-term credit sales ceased, and the Eximbank ended its financing support for agricultural exports in 1976. The United States continued to provide CCC credit, but the program was sharply curtailed as a result of supply constraints, and wheat and feed-grains were temporarily declared ineligible commodities.[44] Canada and the United States both reserved their commercial credit for countries with serious financial problems, and bilateral conflict over credit issues was minimal. However, when grain surpluses returned in the late 1970s and 1980s, the U.S. established some new export financing programs to strengthen its competitive position. It first relied on innovative credit mechanisms (the Intermediate and Blended Credit Programs) and later emphasized export subsidies through the Export Enhancement Program discussed in Chapter 4. Canada vigorously complained that these initiatives were threatening its commercial markets, but it did not attempt to emulate the American policies.

The 1978 U.S. Agricultural Trade Act authorized the CCC to provide *intermediate credit* (IC) for three- to ten-year periods. This credit could be used to finance the export of breeding animals; to establish facilities in importing countries for handling, marketing, processing, storing, and distributing agricultural commodities; and to meet credit competition for agricultural exports. However, the act explicitly stated that "intermediate credit financing may not be used to encourage credit competition, or for the purpose of foreign aid or debt rescheduling."[45] This exclusion clause was used to substantiate the American position that intermediate credit was commercial and therefore not subject to CSD safeguards or to Cargo Preference legislation. Proponents of the IC program argued that it would not have competitive benefits if recipients were required to transport 50 per cent of the commodities in U.S. vessels.

The United States established the IC program for a number of reasons. Intermediate credit was designed to combat mounting surpluses and to offer LDCs with balance of payment problems financial incentives to purchase commodities; the U.S. wanted to remain competitive in one of the few areas (i.e., agriculture) where it had a positive trade balance, and the IC emphasis on developing long-term markets in middle-income LDCs was consistent with this objective; the techniques available for increasing exports were limited since the U.S. required more lucrative solutions than the surplus disposal policies of the 1950s; some genuine intent to help LDCs could not be discounted (even though the U.S. claimed that IC was strictly commercial); and some American political leaders—especially in Congress—felt that other countries provided more export financing and gained unfair advantages. The European Community was viewed as the principal culprit, but the perception also extended to others. For example, in 1978 a senior USDA official stated that "Canada has a ten-year program similar to the intermediate credit programs we offer."[46] The official neglected to mention, however, that Canada had not used such credits since the early 1970s.

Despite the sentiments in favour of intermediate credit, the program suffered from serious domestic divisions. Many congressmen and private business groups viewed it as necessary to promote agricultural exports, but the State Department opposed it. Although some of its officials supported the program, the Department of Agriculture took a cautious approach to implementation. As a result, regulations for breeding animals did not take effect until August 1978, and those for establishing facilities in importing countries were proposed a year later. After the CCC concluded one agreement with Spain for breeding cattle and one with Israel for grain-handling facilities, the IC program became inoperative owing to a lack of funding, and its initial three-year authority was not renewed.

Even though the impact of the IC program was limited, Canada felt extremely threatened by the program and gave it much critical attention. For example, Canada expressed concerns that the IC transaction for the sale of U.S. dairy breeding stock to Spain would have an adverse effect on its commercial exports. However, Canadian-American differences usually focused on general principles rather than specific transactions. The United States conceded that the credit period in its IC program was longer than normal, but it maintained that the program was commercial since interest rates were at commercial levels and the commodities involved required longer-term credit. As a result, American authorities insisted that the IC program was "not food aid and therefore would not be notified to the CSD."[47] Canada led the other exporters in rejecting the American view on this issue. Canadian officials argued that three- to ten-year credit had not been used since 1972 and that it would lead to a deterioration in the terms of trade for agricultural exporters. Since Canada viewed intermediate credit as concessional, it insisted that the program should be under CSD auspices, with provisions made "for the establishment of usual marketing requirements and for a re-export ban as safeguard for commercial markets."[48]

The United States responded to Canada's concerns with expressions of support for its FAO obligations, assurances that intermediate credit would not be used to encourage competition, and suggestions that the program would not be large scale. Nevertheless, it would not agree to apply CSD procedures, and instead it proposed several alternatives. At first the U.S. offered to adopt a voluntary advance information system, but Canada felt that the CSD procedures provided important safeguards. The United States then proposed that the Organization for Economic Cooperation and Development (OECD) rather than the CSD should oversee the IC program. The OECD had in fact already developed some consensual limitations on longer-term export credits, but they did not apply to agriculture.[49] However, Canada strongly criticized the U.S. proposal because the OECD had less demanding requirements than the CSD and had no procedure for establishing UMRs. The OECD proposal was supported by the USDA and Eximbank but not by the State Department, and Canada quietly sought support from the latter for its position. Above all, Canada felt that the CSD's authority should not be undermined.[50]

The CSD and OECD were both absolved from taking a clear stand on the IC program because of its short history. There were a number of reasons for phasing out the program. First, it suffered from significant divisions among domestic groups as well as concerted protests by other exporters. In addition, funding restraint was a factor since the CCC budget jumped to a record $1.7 billion in 1978. In an effort to limit financing outlays, the first ceiling was set on funding for CCC export credit sales in 1979, and there was a shift in emphasis from direct loans to credit guarantees. The substantial funds required to buy up American grain contracts affected by the 1979 Soviet embargo further contributed to restraint. Finally, the U.S. eventually opted for "blended" rather than intermediate credit (discussed below) because it involved less administrative fuss and no long-term obligations, did not require a commitment to development projects, and placed more emphasis on credit guarantees.

Although the IC program was short-lived, the disagreements were unresolved to the end. The basic problem was developing an agricultural trade order when a powerful exporter used buyer incentives that put its competitors at a disadvantage. The CSD has rules to protect smaller exporters, but the FAO Catalogue does not clearly identify three- to ten-year credits as commercial or concessional. As a result, the United States and its opponents both maintained that the CSD supported their positions and argued their case starting from the desired result; the U.S. wished to avoid CSD procedures, while Canada and other exporters wanted to see them applied. The United States never agreed to place the IC program under FAO procedures, and the inconclusive outcome shows that the agricultural trade regime was poorly equipped to deal with the conflict. The IC program was also far more important than its actual market impact would suggest since it initiated the current series of American export financing measures that pit the United States against the European Community.

In October 1982, the United States introduced another innovative program, referred to as *blended credit*. Since blended credit combined direct credits with credit guarantees, the relationship between these two types of credit should be briefly discussed. For about twenty-five years the CCC provided direct credits only, but credit guarantees have been available since 1979. They are designed to permit countries to purchase U.S. agricultural commodities when guarantees are needed to get private financing. Credit guarantees have become an important U.S. market development instrument because the budget for direct credits has declined in recent years. The short-term *Export Credit Guarantee Program* (referred to as GSM 102) offers importing countries credit from U.S. banks for up to three years at commercial interest rates. This credit, which is guaranteed by the CCC, is used to buy American agricultural products. The 1985 U.S. Food Security Act increased the CCC's export credit guarantee authority with an *Intermediate Export Credit Guarantee Program* (GSM-103) to provide guarantees for three- to ten-year credits. Like the IC program of 1978 (which provided direct credits), GSM-103 occupies a "grey area" between concessional and commercial transactions.[51]

The *Blended Credit Program* combined interest-free direct credits with credit guarantees at commercial interest rates in a one-to-four ratio, with repayment terms of up to three years. The direct credit funding in blended credit could be used flexibly for interest buy-down, export credit sales, or export subsidies to enable U.S. farmers to compete in international trade. The Foreign Agricultural Service (FAS) maintained that the program provided no direct export subsidies. However, there were definite similarities between blended credit and the EC's *crédit-mixte* concept, which relies on export subsidies.[52] The United States overcame its reluctance to use blended credit as its battle against EC export subsidies intensified, surpluses continued to increase, and American farmers were adversely affected by the Soviet grain embargo.

Buyers responded enthusiastically to the Blended Credit Program, and the first $100 million were allocated in less than two months. In January 1983, an additional $250 million in credits and $1 billion in guarantees were authorized. A CSD report on blended credit noted that "some exporters believe it introduces concessionary elements into markets which they consider normal commercial markets." As with intermediate credit, however, the United States insisted that blended-credit transactions "are commercial in nature and therefore outside the scope of . . . the CSD."[53] Furthermore, the FAS indicated that blended credit was "not intended to destabilize commodity markets" but to "reduce the impact on U.S. government outlays over the next few years."[54] Canadian authorities were not reassured, and the CWB expressed "great concerns" over "moves in the United States toward credit subsidies."[55] In addition, a 1985 Canadian government review of export financing noted that U.S. blended credit had "given cause for concern and . . . created disruptions in some markets, particularly those where grains are now paid for in cash."[56] Canada also felt threatened by American moves to regain a foothold in the Soviet market with credit sales, even though the Soviets did not receive blended credit. After the USSR purchased U.S. corn and U.S. and Australian wheat on short-term credit in 1982, the Canadian Wheat Board "found it necessary to offer 180-day-credit to the Soviet Union."[57]

However, Canada's reaction to blended credit was rather subdued compared to its vigorous protests over intermediate credit. While blended credit had concessional features, it was only extended for periods of up to three years. Canadian officials undoubtedly viewed the three- to ten-year intermediate credit transactions as more objectionable because of the precedent they established. Canada was also more reluctant to criticize U.S. blended credit because of its own sales successes in the early 1980s to the USSR, China, Eastern Europe, and the Middle and Far East. Although the Canadian government initially supported the Soviet embargo and exploited the situation less than some other exporters, its wheat sales to the USSR rose from about 2.6 million tonnes in 1979–80 (pre-embargo) to 4.2 million in 1980–81 (embargo), and to 5 million in 1981–82 (post-embargo).[58] Indeed, the U.S. Congress took note of Canada's 1982–83 wheat and barley sales to the Soviets and criticized Canada for expanding its wheat acreage, offering $1 billion credit guarantees to the USSR, and permitting the CWB to borrow at slightly below commercial rates for guaranteed credit lines.[59] Thereafter, the CWB kept a deliberately low profile because of concerns that its sales successes "might be interpreted in the U.S. as good reason for escalating the largely rhetorical trade war of the past year."[60]

Despite its acknowledged success, the Blended Credit Program was suspended in February 1985 for an unexpected reason. In that year, a U.S. court decided that the Cargo Preference Act applied to blended credit. The CCC then discontinued the program because the impact of increased costs for transport in U.S.-registered vessels made it less competitive. Nevertheless, an end to blended credit did not signify that U.S. efforts to increase its credit offerings were abating. Indeed, the 1985 Food Security Act required the CCC to make available no less than $5.5 billion in short- and intermediate-term credit guarantees a year.[61]

As price competition intensified in the 1980s, it became evident that credit programs alone could not prevent the erosion of the U.S. market share. In fact, the CCC was not able to allocate the full $5.5 billion in credit guarantees to importing countries because U.S. agricultural prices were not competitive in the world market. Credit and credit guarantees were also being offered by other exporters, and the CCC would not provide guarantees to some countries that were high credit risks.[62] The United States therefore began to focus its efforts on export subsidies through the Export Enhancement Program. While the EEP does not involve the provision of credit, the two export promotion techniques are interrelated. For example, export credit guarantees have been made available in many of the EEP initiatives, and "the credit guarantee has been extremely important in consummating some EEP sales."[63]

In contrast to the United States, Canada's agricultural export assistance in the 1980s has not thus far led to any significant innovations. The financing facilities of the Credit Grain Sales Program were considered "reasonably adequate" for CWB exports and relied on the private financial sector without calling on the existing authority for government credit guarantees. The EDC could offer mixed credits (concessional loans combined with commercial EDC export credits) from 1981 "to help otherwise competitive Canadian exporters obtain financing that at least matched foreign concessional offers."[64] The Canadian government did create a new agricultural export promotion mechanism in January 1984, the controversial crown corporation Canagrex, but it was described as duplicating other facilities and was dissolved in March 1985. Finally, plans for an "aid-trade facility" were abandoned in early 1986 as a result of budgetary constraints.

CONCLUSIONS

In conclusion, Canada was often able to compete with the United States in providing agricultural export credit. Canada was therefore willing to adopt unilateral strategies and frequently led the way in such areas as extending export credits to the Communist countries, lengthening the time-frame for commercial credits, and linking credit with long-term agreements. Throughout most of the period examined there was a close interrelationship between the two countries' policies in this area. For example, Canada's Expanded Credit program of the early 1970s drew upon some elements of the PL 480 long-term credit program, and the U.S. Intermediate Credit program in turn adopted some of the features of Canada's Expanded Credit. Both countries introduced a number of innovative credit practices, and their competition contributed to changing perceptions of commercial versus concessional credit terms in the global food regime. In this sense Canadian-American interactions were similar to a "surrogate system" in the absence of adequate regime arrangements, as in the case of the duopoly discussed in Chapters 2 and 4. The two countries normally managed their conflicts by exercising restraint in the use of credit practices and by eventually accepting each other's credit innovations over time. International bodies such as the CSD then provided endorsement for the new consensus (e.g., regarding commercial versus concessional credit) established by the U.S., Canada, and other major exporters.

However, in periods when the United States adopted concessional or grey-area methods to dispose of burdensome surpluses, Canada had great difficulty in remaining competitive. For example, Canadian export credits were no match for U.S. tied sales, barter, and Title IV in the 1950s and 1960s. When the United States began to experiment with intermediate and blended credit in the 1970s-80s and to combine credit guarantees with the Export Enhancement Program, Canada was also more inclined to criticize than to emulate these practices. At these times, Canada resorted to multilateral strategies and encouraged the CSD to become more involved with U.S. Title IV and intermediate and blended credit. Beginning in the late 1970s, the United States was showing greater willingness to engage in grey-area transactions to retain its market share, and it became increasingly evident that Canada could not compete on similar terms. In situations such as these, regime regulations provided little guidance regarding the concessional versus commercial nature of U.S. practices. This was certainly the case for CCC credit in the 1960s and for intermediate and blended credit in the late 1970s and 1980s.

As discussed, political-security objectives had mixed effects on Canadian-American relations. The U.S. reluctance to export to China and many Soviet bloc states in the 1950s and 1960s contributed to a division of markets with Canada that was normally a fairly co-operative arrangement. However, the United States had a special interest in Yugoslavia, Poland, and Israel for strategic-security reasons, and it infringed upon Canadian credit markets in these countries. The United States usually did not attempt to exert overt influence on

Canadian credit policies vis-à-vis the Communist states, but when it did try to interfere (as in the case of Canada's credit sales to China in the 1960s), its actions had a negative effect on the bilateral relationship. Finally, when the U.S. trade balance changed to a deficit position, it became willing to extend credit sales to the Soviet Union and China, which presented a new source of competition and conflict in Canadian-American relations.

This chapter provides further confirmation regarding the effects of other variables such as supply in the world market, the U.S. balance of payments, and competition. Thus, conflict over credit practices was most intense during surplus periods, and no major credit innovations were introduced during the 1970s' shortage period. Furthermore, the United States became more aggressive and "innovative" in the use of credit practices as its balance of payment problems and competition with the EC increased. It was in the late 1970s and 1980s that some of the most controversial U.S. credit programs (intermediate and blended credit) were introduced. While Chapters 4 to 6 have focused on American and Canadian efforts to promote their exports, Chapter 7 examines the issues of import barriers and the Canada-U.S. free trade agreement.

7

Agricultural Trade Barriers

Chapters 4 to 6 have focused on American and Canadian efforts to promote their agricultural exports and to pressure other countries to adopt trade liberalization measures. This chapter deals with barriers that the United States and Canada impose on their agricultural imports, particularly on goods moving across their common border. After discussing the issue of agricultural trade barriers in general, some case studies relating to specific commodities—cattle and beef, hogs and pork, and corn—are examined. Some conclusions are then put forward regarding the issue of trade barriers in Canada-U.S. relations. The last part of the chapter deals with American and Canadian attempts to embark on a "new" form of co-operation to deal with growing conflict stemming from bilateral and multilateral trade barriers: the Canada-U.S. free trade agreement.[1]

Canadian-American agricultural trade has alternated historically between cycles of protectionism and liberalization. The commodity groups pressing for protection have changed over time, but the impetus for trade barriers generally increases during periods of economic distress and relatively low farm incomes. One of the major factors associated with low farm incomes is the accumulation of large agricultural surpluses. To understand current U.S.-Canadian trading patterns, it is necessary to provide some background beginning from the 1920s.

In the early 1900s, Canada's policies were affected by close interdependent ties with both the United Kingdom and the United States. For example, the United States responded to falling agricultural prices after World War I with a protectionist Emergency Tariff in 1921. This barrier contributed to a decline in U.S.-Canadian agricultural trade, and Canada therefore sought preferential agreements in the British Empire. A deterioration of economic conditions led to pressures for even greater U.S. protectionism, and Congressional passage of the 1930 Smoot-Hawley bill raised agricultural tariffs to new heights. European states retaliated by increasing their own trade barriers, and Canada also raised its tariffs and signed an agreement with Britain for new agricultural preferences. The resultant breakdown of commercial trade had a disastrous effect that caused the United States to reverse its policies through passage of the Reciprocal Trade Agreements Act in 1934. Canadian-American trade negotiations were authorized under this act, and in November 1935 the two countries concluded an agreement returning tariffs to lower levels.

The 1935 agreement was partly designed to re-establish the co-operative trading relationship that had been damaged by the U.S. Smoot-Hawley tariff and Canada's retaliatory response. The two countries granted each other most-favoured-nation (MFN) status, and Canada extended its entire intermediate tariff (higher than the British Preferential Tariff) to American goods.[2] The United States lowered its tariff rates by 20 to 50 per cent on sixty-three items, including various agricultural products (such as cheese, cream, cattle, and apples), while Canada made concessions on a number of manufactured goods. In 1938, Canada gave up its British imperial preferences for wheat, pears, honey, and salmon and gained easier access to the United States for a number of commodities.[3]

Under the authority of its 1934 trade act, the United States had concluded bilateral trade agreements with twenty-nine foreign countries by the time the GATT was established in 1947, and American tariffs were reduced by over 75 per cent between 1934 and 1962.[4] In general, the GATT was less successful in dealing with agricultural trade than with most other types of commerce. However, from the 1960s the United States and Canada had a shared interest in multilateral trade liberalization in agriculture, and the tariff reductions on farm products moving mainly between the two countries were "one of the few accomplishments of the Kennedy Round of agricultural negotiations."[5] At the GATT Tokyo Round, over $1 billion worth of Canadian agricultural exports benefited from tariff concessions, and the largest gains were made in the U.S. market where concessions of $499 million were obtained. In return, Canada's agricultural concessions to the United States had a trade coverage of $422.6 million.

Largely because of these GATT negotiations, the value of agricultural goods traded between the two countries increased substantially. Thus, American agricultural exports to Canada rose by 146 per cent from 1971–75 (on average) to 1980, and Canadian exports to the United States grew by 152 per cent over the same period.[6] However, the two countries continued to levy significant tariffs for a limited number of agricultural commodities after the Tokyo Round. Canada's tariffs were higher on products that it imported from the United States (such as fruits and vegetables), whereas U.S. tariffs were higher on a number of commodities that were not imported from Canada (such as cucumbers, melons, tomatoes, and soybean products). Tariffs in both countries usually increase with the stage of production. For example, the United States and Canada have zero or low tariffs on imports of oilseeds (soybeans and rapeseed/canola), higher tariffs on crude oil, and the highest tariffs on refined oil.[7] Despite the continuance of tariffs, about 50 per cent of Canadian-American agricultural trade now moves duty free, and the average tariff on the dutiable remainder is about 6 per cent *ad valorem* in both countries.[8]

While tariff rates were declining, however, non-tariff barriers (NTBs) were becoming more important. Non-tariff barriers are "all those restrictions, other than traditional customs duties, which distort international trade."[9] They include an incredibly large number of measures that restrict imports, assist domestic production, and provide direct assistance to exporters. The most important NTBs in Canadian-American agricultural trade are import quotas and licences. For example, both countries impose quotas that limit their imports of dairy products; the Canadian Wheat Board requires import licences for various grain products; Canada has import quotas on turkeys, broilers, and eggs; and both countries have beef quota legislation that is sometimes activated. Besides quotas and licences, other NTBs affecting Canada-U.S. trade include import relief measures such as countervailing and antidumping duties, export-oriented barriers such as subsidies to production and exports, and technical barriers such as restrictions that result from health and sanitary regulations.

Non-tariff barriers can be very damaging to international trade because they often are more restrictive, ill-defined, and inequitable than tariffs. For example, NTBs such as quotas generally keep foreign competition within prescribed limits through precise control over the quantities imported. While some NTBs have clearly demonstrable effects on trade, others (such as sanitary and health regulations) have more subtle effects and tend to be concealed in administrative procedures. Barriers relating to the technical aspects of trade such as labelling, packaging, and grade standards have increased in recent years, partly because of a new awareness of health problems and misleading advertising; but such regulations may also be used to protect farmers from outside competition. Thus, some importers claim that health and sanitary standards are one of the primary means of impeding fluid milk shipments between the American and Canadian markets. Finally, NTBs tend to be more inequitable than tariffs, with some products moving freely between the two markets in one form but not traded at all in another.

Although they frequently infringe on liberal trading principles, NTBs are difficult to reduce through international negotiations. A primary reason for their continuation is that countries tend to view NTBs as adjuncts to their domestic agricultural programs. The "new protectionism" of NTBs involves direct government intervention in the production and marketing processes, and public intervention has become more acceptable in bringing about domestic agricultural adjustment. Other reasons for difficulty in negotiating NTB reductions include the problems in quantifying and measuring their impact and the tendency of each country to view its own NTBs as a response to the barriers imposed by others.

As discussed in Chapter 3, the United States in earlier years frustrated the GATT's efforts to regulate NTBs in agriculture. At American insistence, agriculture was treated as an exception in GATT Article XI on quantitative restrictions and in Section B of GATT Article XVI on export subsidies. Furthermore, in 1955 the U.S. sought and obtained an unusually broad waiver from its GATT Article XI obligations. Canada opposed the U.S. waiver and the GATT exceptions, largely because of its dependence on agricultural exports and its inability to match the export subsidies of larger countries. Indeed, the Canadian delegation to GATT repeatedly raised objections to these policies, maintaining that "it could not agree to permit the United States to exclude imports to any extent considered necessary to protect any programme of the United States Department of Agriculture."[10] Despite Canada's criticisms, it was also becoming more interventionist in agriculture. Policies providing strict control over wheat, oats, barley, and milk imports can be traced to the formation of the Canadian Wheat Board and fluid milk marketing boards in the 1930s. In addition, Canada reacted to low farm incomes with additional subsidies, a more comprehensive stabilization program, and new producer-operated marketing boards.[11]

Although the United States at first tried to limit the GATT's jurisdiction in agriculture, it has generally been committed to liberal trading principles. However, the U.S. balance of trade deficits since 1971 have contributed to rising protectionist sentiments. The United States has a complex array of trade legislation available to domestic industries suffering from foreign competition, and as the competitiveness of some American producers declined, their calls for the use of this legislation increased. The U.S. trade relief laws with the greatest impact on Canada have been countervailing and antidumping duties.[12] Countervailing duties (CVDs) are imposed to offset subsidies which producers receive in the exporting country, and antidumping duties are assessed against sales of foreign goods at prices below those charged in the home or third-country markets.[13]

Many government leaders and scholars often refer to CVD and antidumping laws as "trade remedy" legislation, a term that clearly has positive connotations.[14] Some Canadian analysts, by contrast, describe the U.S. laws in more negative terms as "contingent protection" or "contingency protection" measures. Since trade relief legislation can provide both a remedy for unfair trading practices *and* an excuse for protectionism, I follow the practice of those authors who use more neutral terms. When discussing countervail and antidumping duties, I describe them as "trade laws," "trade relief laws," and "import relief laws."[15]

In the first three decades after World War II, American industries seeking trade relief through countervail and antidumping duties usually lost their cases. As a result, the U.S. Congress responded to pressure from producers by changing the rules and procedures so that import-affected industries could obtain trade relief more easily. The rules were revised in the U.S. Trade Act of 1974 and again in the Trade Agreements Act of 1979.[16] American firms responded to the changed rules in 1974 by filing many more petitions for relief, but they were often disappointed with the outcome of the investigations. After the procedures were altered in the 1979 Act, however, the U.S. petitioners were more successful. The number of CVD investigations initiated by the U.S. Department of Commerce increased from ten in 1980 to forty-three in 1985, and the number of antidumping investigations rose from twenty-six in 1979 to sixty-six in 1985. While the U.S. import relief laws seemed to be fair and objective from an American perspective, Canada and other countries viewed the procedures as being overly susceptible to politics and biased in favour of the complainant. Expert GATT panels have met to establish common standards, but their progress has been limited, and they have not provided adequate guidance in this area.[17]

The increased use of U.S. trade relief legislation had a major effect on Canadian agricultural producers. From 1 January 1980 to 30 June 1986, the U.S. International Trade Commission completed six CVD and six antidumping investigations against Canadian agricultural commodities (including fish products). While several of these investigations ended in negative decisions for the American complainants, duties were eventually imposed on Canadian sugar, raspberries, dried salted codfish, live swine, and groundfish.[18] It is evident, however, that many U.S. producers continue to be dissatisfied. For example, after the Maine potato industry lost an antidumping case against Canadian producers, a representative of the National Potato Council stated that "some things can be done to strengthen trade relief measures in cases of unfair trade practices."[19] Furthermore, producers and their political supporters have on occasion been willing to circumvent U.S. federal law to achieve their objectives. In 1985, for example, five U.S. states imposed a temporary ban on Canadian hog imports over the objections of the U.S. State Department (this issue is discussed below).

Despite its objections to the U.S. trade relief laws, Canada developed its own legislation, and the two countries now have similar regulations in this area. In fact, Canada was the first country to introduce antidumping duties, and its example was widely followed by other major trading nations. The government adopted this innovation in 1904 in response to claims that U.S. manufacturers were selling goods in Canada at prices well below those in the home market.[20] Before 1985, Canada relied on antidumping rather than countervail legislation to protect its domestic producers. Indeed, from 1980 to 1985 Canada completed thirty-one antidumping investigations overall against the United States, and injury was found in twenty-seven of these cases. The United States by contrast completed only ten antidumping cases against Canada and found injury in five cases.[21] Canada adopted CVD regulations patterned after those of the United States when it passed the Special Imports Measures Act in 1984. These regulations were "designed with a distinct procedural bias in favour of domestic complainants."[22] In November 1986 Canada levied a CVD against American grain corn exports, an extremely controversial action which is discussed later in this chapter.

The statistics on trade relief legislation demonstrate that agriculture has become one of the more conflictual issues in Canadian-American relations. While agriculture accounts for only about 4 per cent of total bilateral trade, a majority of the recent CVD and antidumping investigations between the two states have involved agricultural commodities.[23] However, in view of the smaller size of the Canadian economy and its greater dependence on exports, American countervail "can have a severe impact" on Canada, while Canadian countervail is often "little more than another irritant to the United States."[24] Despite the large number of Canadian antidumping investigations involving the United States, most of these cases involved marginal products, and their impact on the U.S. was relatively minor. Canada therefore has a greater stake than the U.S. in limiting the use of import relief measures.

It may seen ironic that U.S. trade relief actions increased in the agricultural area since the United States usually has benefited from positive agricultural trade balances with Canada. However, in 1986 the U.S. had an *overall* trade deficit with Canada that was only exceeded by its deficit with Japan, and this situation has affected American perceptions of the bilateral relationship. Furthermore, the positive U.S. agricultural balance with Canada decreased dramatically from $1.5 billion in 1980 to $600 million in 1986.[25] This decline resulted from a variety of factors, including the relative strength of the American dollar; increased Canadian production of some commodities, such as corn; Canada's search for alternative suppliers of fresh fruit and cotton; and the large Canadian trade surplus with the U.S. in live animals and red meats. Yet another reason for American protectionism is that Canada is the United States' largest supplier of "supplementary" agricultural products. These "are similar to or the same as commodities produced commercially in the importing country," and they compete directly with the importing country's products.[26] In contrast, many American agricultural exports to Canada (such as fruits and vegetables) are either not produced in Canada or are produced during a relatively short growing season.

Disagreements between the United States and Canada over agricultural trade statistics demonstrate that protectionism in both countries can result from starkly different perceptions of the "facts." For example, the American Bureau of the Census reported that the United States became a net agricultural *importer* from Canada for the first time when a small U.S. agricultural trade surplus of $112 million in 1984 became a $272 million deficit in 1985.[27] Statistics Canada agreed that the agricultural trade deficit with the United States was declining, but it reported that Canada still had a *deficit* of $1 billion with the U.S. in 1985.[28] The American publication *FATUS (Foreign Agricultural Trade of the U.S.)* conceded that a substantial part of this discrepancy in statistics was "apparently due to underreporting U.S. export data." Thus, the Census Bureau may have underreported U.S. horticultural exports by $200 million to $550 million. The problem of inaccurate statistics-gathering has increased because of deregulation of the U.S. trucking industry. Many American truckers bringing goods into Canada do not fill out the documents required by statisticians, and Washington therefore does not know the extent of the U.S. exports to Canada until much later.[29] This dispute was revived again a year later. In 1986, U.S. data showed that the United States had an agricultural trade deficit of about $500 million with Canada. Canadian data by contrast indicated that it was *Canada* that had the deficit, in the range of $600 million.[30]

Having described some of the general issues, it is necessary to discuss the problems experienced with trade in specific commodities. An examination of U.S.-Canadian trade in beef, pork, and corn is particularly helpful in illustrating the characteristics of trade barriers between the two states.

BEEF AND BEEF PRODUCTS

In the world beef trade, there is a group of major exporting states and another group of predominantly importing states. The exporters (Australia, New Zealand, Argentina, and Brazil) account for over 60 per cent of global exports, while the importers (the United States, the European Community, Japan, and Canada) account for over 80 per cent of global imports. The United States became a major importer of Australian and New Zealand beef in the late 1950s, and Canada became a significant importer from Oceania in the late 1960s and 1970s. Although both countries are net importers, they also export cattle and beef products, primarily to each other. Canada generally exports manufacturing beef, which is used for U.S. hamburgers and other processed meats, while the United States normally exports higher-quality specialized cuts for Canadian hotels, restaurants, and institutions.

The American beef industry is about ten times larger than the Canadian industry, and there are normally only minimal impediments to beef and cattle trade between the two countries. As a result, Canada's beef production cycles are closely tied to U.S. cycles, and Canadian beef prices are established primarily on the basis of supply and demand in the American market. Canada is extremely dependent on the U.S. market, and 76 per cent of its red meat exports were directed to the United States in 1987. The United States also ships significant amounts of beef and cattle to Canada, but it is far less dependent on the Canadian market. Red meats are the main agricultural item Canada exports to the United States, whereas the main U.S. exports to Canada are fruits and vegetables.

Imported beef and veal accounted for a negligible share of U.S. consumption before the late 1950s, but imports increased to 6.3 per cent of domestic consumption in 1958 and to 9.1 per cent in 1963. As a result, a U.S. Meat Import Law was enacted in 1964 to regulate annual imports. The United States did not impose quotas under this law until 1976 and instead depended on voluntary export restraint (VER) agreements with the major meat-supplying countries. These VER agreements were aimed primarily at Australia and New Zealand, and the U.S. did not press for export restraints with Canada because of their long tradition of cross-border trade in meat and livestock.[31] However, in the 1970s there was a dramatic change in U.S.-Canadian trade relations in this area. At this time, the American beef market experienced serious dislocations, which led to a protective Canadian response involving the imposition of import quotas. When the United States retaliated with its own quotas, the North American livestock and meat market was temporarily divided by a proliferation of trade barriers.

During the 1968-73 period, most meat-importing countries responded to short supplies by liberalizing trade in beef and cattle. In addition, the United States and Canada took actions to combat inflation in 1973 that further encouraged the growth of imports. While the Canadian government suspended tariffs on beef and live cattle, the United States imposed price controls on food products, including a price ceiling on red meat products. Since the U.S. beef price ceiling was to be removed six months later, American producers withheld livestock from the market in anticipation of higher prices. The price freeze did not apply to imports, so this policy stimulated sizeable purchases of Canadian beef and live cattle by U.S. buyers. These purchases exerted strong upward pressures on beef prices in Canada despite its anti-inflation program, and the Canadian government therefore imposed temporary controls on red meat exports, limiting them to historical levels.[32]

In September 1973, the United States removed its beef price ceiling as promised, while Canada removed its export controls and restored its normal tariffs on beef and cattle. When the U.S. price ceiling was lifted, cattle flooded both the American and Canadian markets, and during part of 1973-74 U.S. cattle accounted for about 30 per cent of the total Canadian slaughter. This problem of surpluses was exacerbated by developments in the world market. In the early 1970s almost every beef-producing country had expanded its cattle herds in the expectation of future profitability. When countries began liquidating their herds, beef prices were pushed to exceptionally low levels.[33] The energy crisis of 1973-74, which precipitated a recession in the developed countries, was yet another factor behind the falling beef prices.

Canada took several actions to limit its growing beef imports, especially those coming from the United States. At first it imposed temporary import surtaxes on live cattle and dressed beef, but these were removed in February 1974. Shortly afterwards (in April), Canada established an import certification program to prevent the entry of U.S. meat or animals whose growth had been stimulated by diethystilbestrol (DES), a hormone linked to cancer. The United States, like Canada, had banned the use of DES, but a court judgement had nullified the U.S. ban. Although the Canadian action was presumably taken for health reasons, it effectively blocked American imports and assisted the country's beef industry during a difficult period. In August 1974, the United States and Canada finally agreed upon a DES certification program, and Canadian imports were resumed. However, within two weeks Canada imposed quotas on U.S. cattle and beef imports for a twelve-month period. The United States then retaliated with import quotas on Canadian cattle, hogs, beef, veal, and pork.[34]

The beef trade dispute was not settled until about a year later (in late 1975), when both countries removed their import quotas. However, another major dispute emerged in the late 1970s, this time over differences in American and Canadian meat import legislation. Unlike the United States, Canada had not adopted a Meat Import Law and instead relied on its more general Export and Import Permits Act to restrict imports when necessary. Since Canada did not have a permanent mechanism for limiting imports, Australian and New Zealand beef that could not enter the U.S. market was diverted to Canada where it displaced some Canadian beef. In turn, Canada then exported more live cattle to the United States, thereby circumventing the U.S. Meat Import Law. These events led to dissatisfaction among U.S. producers, who demanded that the law be expanded to cover cattle as well as beef. As a member of Parliament acknowledged in 1976, American producers "are angry at Canada for dumping meat on a run-through from oceanic countries to Canada and then forcing the meat of Canada to be dumped into the United States."[35]

Partly because of the substitution of cheaper Australian and New Zealand manufacturing beef in the Canadian market, Canada's meat exports to the United States in 1976 were exceeding earlier estimates by a considerable margin. In addition, Australia was circumventing its VER agreement with the United States by exporting meat into the Foreign-Trade Zone of Mayaguez, Puerto Rico. To limit beef imports in the face of these pressures, the U.S. imposed a global import quota (under the authority of its 1964 Meat Import Law) in October 1976. The quota was applied to Canada as well as other exporters, with the limit on Canadian shipments established at 80.4 million pounds for the year. Since Canada was accustomed to "exemptionalism" in this area, the assistant deputy minister for International Trade Relations noted that "there was the idea that somehow or other there would be an arrangement between Canada and the United States whereby the United States would not really trigger their law against us."[36] Canada promptly retaliated by establishing a global quota of its own, with the U.S. alloted 4.5 million pounds for the remainder of 1976.

Canada's problems did not end with the U.S. import quota since it had to participate in voluntary export restraint negotiations for beef exports to the United States in 1977. Furthermore, American producers continued to agitate for controls over Canadian cattle imports. In 1977–78 the American Agriculture Movement even blockaded imports at several western border points and stopped Canadian livestock shipments for about a month (see Chapter 2). The revision of the 1964 U.S. Meat Import Law in 1979 was yet another source of contention. The 1964 Law had often reinforced rather than moderated price swings in the cattle cycle. As a result, the revised law included a "countercyclical" provision, under which meat imports were increased as domestic supplies declined and decreased when domestic supplies rose. Exporting countries sought vigorously to circumvent the revised law by sending beef into the unrestricted Canadian market, and Canada in turn escalated its pressure to export to the United States.

Canada was eventually forced to alter its policies because its cattle industry could not afford to be isolated from the American market. In 1979, for example, 91.9 per cent of Canada's beef and veal exports were sent to the United States. To preserve its traditional role as an integral part of the North American livestock economy, Canada developed a Meat Import Act similar to the U.S. legislation to limit off-shore imports. Agriculture Minister Eugene Whelan described the legislation as "broadly parallel with the revised United States Meat Import Law" and explained that "the similarity between these two import control systems will help prevent disruptions in our beef and cattle trade with the U.S."[37] Currently, the impediments to U.S.-Canadian beef trade are minimal, and the Canadian beef and cattle market continues to function as a part of the North American market. For example, Canada announced that it would not restrict beef and veal imports in the early 1980s but that its policy would be reviewed if the United States moved to restrain such imports. When the U.S. unexpectedly asked its principal suppliers (Australia, New Zealand, and Canada) to voluntarily limit their exports for the balance of 1983 in order not to trigger import quotas, Canada also moved to require individual permits for beef and veal imports for the remainder of the year. The agriculture minister explained that this was necessary "to guard against the possibility that the U.S. action may result in diversion with consequent disruption of the Canadian market."[38] In 1984, the minister announced that beef imports would no longer be restricted, but that import action would again be considered "if the U.S. moves to restrain beef and veal imports."[39]

In addition to the major issues discussed above, U.S.-Canadian differences periodically recur over "technical barriers" that also have the effect of limiting supply in the domestic market. For example, in mid-1977 the United States imposed import restrictions on Canadian cattle from Ontario and Quebec because of outbreaks of brucellosis in the northeastern states.[40] Canada's minister of agriculture maintained that this action was merely a pretext for limiting U.S. imports since "the national infection rate in Canada ... [was] lower than the national infection rate in the U.S."[41] Strict U.S. import requirements nevertheless continued for a decade, and they were only eased a year after Ontario and Quebec were declared totally free of bovine brucellosis in 1985-86. As for Canada, it continued to require DES certification for meat animals and products imported from the United States. Although the U.S. introduced a ban on DES use in July 1979, Canada's agriculture minister waited until November 1980 before discontinuing the certification procedure.

To summarize, the beef trade issue provides additional information regarding the independent and dependent variables. Most striking is the much larger size of the American beef industry and the high degree of Canadian vulnerability to U.S. policies. It is not surprising that American beef flooded the Canadian market when the U.S. price ceiling was lifted in September 1973 since changes in U.S. production levels can have a major impact on Canadian producers. Canadian beef producers are also highly dependent on the U.S. market for their exports, and the United States can withstand protracted disputes in this area more easily than Canada. For example, when Canada imposed import quotas in

August 1974, the U.S. clearly demonstrated its ability to retaliate. In contrast, when the United States limited Canadian imports in the late 1970s, Canada eventually had to pattern its beef import legislation after the American law in an effort to resolve the conflict. As discussed, Canadian-American interdependence is partly based on "exemptionalism," and Canada was shocked when it was not exempted from the U.S. global meat import quota in 1976.

Despite this asymmetry, changes in Canadian production and exports can also have some effect on American producers. As a result, the United States at times felt it necessary to limit imports from Canada and to retaliate against Canadian import barriers. This was especially the case when U.S. producers had serious financial problems stemming from an increase in competition and surpluses in the world market. Agriculture Minister Whelan's report of a 1981 discussion with some American farmers is an indication of the difficulties they were experiencing in that period.[42]

> When it was pointed out to them that the sale of live Canadian cattle into their markets, even at the highest point, would not affect one per cent of their market . . . [one of their leaders] said, "If a person is standing in a pool of water and is just barely able to breath, that extra little water in the pool will mean that he or she drowns."

The beef trade issue also strengthens the case that surpluses are conducive to conflict since most of the disputes revolved around the imposition of U.S. and Canadian import barriers to limit supply. In addition, the issue further demonstrates the lack of an adequate agricultural trade regime. Voluntary export restraints and import quotas were regularly used, even though they are frowned upon by the GATT. The decision about which country's beef import legislation would serve as a North American "model" was determined not by international guidelines but by the relative economic size and capacities of the United States and Canada. Finally, the beef trade case reinforces the point stressed throughout this book that bilateral and third-country agricultural trade issues are often closely intertwined. American and Canadian beef import policies vis-à-vis third countries can have a major impact on trade relations between the two North American states.

HOGS AND PORK

Canadian-American trade in hogs and pork was relatively free for many years, and both countries eliminated tariffs on these products as a result of the GATT Tokyo Round. Although some non-tariff barriers related to health regulations have been quite contentious, major disputes did not develop until a Canada-U.S. "hog war" broke out in 1984. After a discussion of bilateral trading patterns in hogs and pork, the circumstances of this conflict are examined.

As in the case of beef, U.S.-Canadian interdependence in the hog/pork sector is highly asymmetrical because of differences in production levels and market size. For example, the American hog slaughter was six times greater than the Canadian in 1984, and Iowa alone produces one and a half times as many hogs as Canada. When American pork exports to Canada were at their peak in 1977, they accounted for only 1 per cent of U.S. production, but for 15 per cent of Canadian consumption. In contrast, Canadian pork exports to the United States in 1984 accounted for 25 per cent of Canadian production, but for only 4 per cent of U.S. consumption. From 1932 to 1950, Britain had been the largest market for Canadian pork exports. This trade declined, however, and the United States and Japan became Canada's major foreign markets.[43] Canada was the prime supplier of pork in the Japanese market in 1982–83, but it then fell back to a poor third place after Denmark and Taiwan. As a result, the Canadian industry now depends primarily on the U.S. market to take its surplus hog and pork production. In 1987, fresh and frozen pork products accounted for 66 per cent of Canada's red meat exports to the United States.

Although Canada has normally been a net exporter of pork to the United States, it became a net importer from 1975 to 1978 because of feedgrain shortages. However, Canadian hog inventories began to recover in 1977, and (partly because of the lower value of the Canadian dollar) Canada returned to its net export position in 1979. After 1979, a surplus of hogs contributed to a deterioration in bilateral relations. American producers had expanded their hog facilities during the 1970s, and they expressed growing concerns as U.S. live hog imports from Canada rose from a monthly average of about thirty-seven thousand in 1983 to one-hundred thousand in early 1984. As a result, the Agriculture Committees of the U.S. Senate and House of Representatives held hearings on the issue. In addition, the Senate Finance Committee asked the U.S. International Trade Commission (ITC) to investigate the competitive position of Canadian hogs and pork in the American market. The purpose of the ITC investigation was merely to gather facts, but before the results were released the National Pork Producers' Council (NPPC) requested that the ITC and Department of Commerce conduct a countervailing duty investigation. The NPPC represents about one hundred thousand pork producers from forty-five member states who account for 90 per cent of U.S. commercial pork production. It alleged that Canadian producers and/or exporters "receive benefits which constitute subsidies . . . and that these imports materially injure or threaten material injury to a U.S. industry."[44]

A countervail case is a rather complicated four-part process involving the International Trade Administration (ITA) of the Department of Commerce and the ITC. The ITA determines the existence and level of subsidies, while the ITC examines claims of material injury. The ITA and ITC generally give more attention to the arguments of domestic producers than to those of foreign suppliers, and they do not consider the subsidies received by U.S. complainants. Furthermore, since the GATT provides only limited guidance regarding the definition and measurement of "subsidies" and "material injury," the ITA and ITC are relatively free to establish their own guidelines. The United States defines "material injury" for CVDs in its 1979 Trade Agreements Act as "harm which is not inconsequential, immaterial or unimportant." In the view of one Canadian analyst

> this is an extremely weak and quite ambiguous definition which is open to wide interpretation. It requires the ITC to demonstrate only a casual relationship between an industry's poor performance and export subsidies in other countries. The subsidies need not in fact be the principal cause of poor performance or, given the various interpretations possible, even a significant cause of it.[45]

However, Canadians were given the opportunity to express their views at the CVD investigation, and they argued that the increased hog/pork exports to the United States were not the result of government subsidies. Other factors were considered responsible, including the weak Canadian dollar; a decrease in U.S. swine production; the rationalization of the American meat-packing industry; the proximity of Canadian production to U.S. meat packers and consumers; and the production of leaner, high-quality Canadian products. On the other hand, the U.S. National Pork Producers' Council has argued that

> since 1980–1981 . . . pork production has increased consistently above the level of Canadian consumption, primarily as a result of the production incentives created by the Canadian subsidy program. . . . [Canada's] surplus exportation dramatically depressed prices of U.S. hog and pork products. American producers receive no protection from government programs and must fend for themselves in an artificially-distorted market.[46]

After the pork producers filed their CVD petition, the ITA first judged (in November 1984) that there was evidence of foreign subsidies. In fact, the ITA "has little leeway to refuse to investigate an allegation that a given foreign government practice could conceivably be a subsidy . . . as long as the claim is supported by *some* evidence."[47] The ITC then ruled unanimously (in December 1984) that there was a "reasonable indication or threat" of material injury to the U.S. industry resulting from Canadian hog/pork exports. (At this stage the ITC did not have to *prove* material injury.) After the ITC's affirmative ruling, the case returned to the ITA, which had to determine whether Canadian hog/pork imports benefited from a net subsidy. In March 1985, the ITA made a preliminary ruling that various federal and provincial programs providing funds to Canadian producers were countervailable, and preliminary duties of about 5.3 cents per pound for pork and 3.8 cents per pound for live hogs were imposed. The funds collected were placed in an escrow account and would be returned if the case was terminated by a negative decision.[48]

The losses to Canadian producers because of the preliminary CVDs were exacerbated by the decision of five states (Iowa, Nebraska, South Dakota, Minnesota, and Wisconsin) to ban Canadian hog imports during 1985. The ban was justified on the basis that Canadian producers were using the antibiotic chloramphenicol, which can cause a serious blood disorder. However, the ban was also partly retaliatory since U.S. producers feel that Canada's thirty-day quarantine on live hog imports is an import barrier. The quarantine exists because of concerns about the disease pseudorabies, but American producers argue that this "imposes a virtual embargo on U.S. hog exports" to Canada.[49] The action of the five states also resulted partly from frustration with the fact that the preliminary CVDs had not produced immediate reductions in hog imports. The U.S. government maintained that the states did not have authority to restrict imports because international trade is a federal responsibility, and the State Department even seemed to encourage Canada to challenge the ban. In addition, some midwest states did not join the ban on imports, probably because of fears that doing so would jeopardize trade liberalization efforts. Nevertheless, the five states succeeded in blocking Canadian imports temporarily, and Canada decided to cease using chloramphenicol.[50]

The ITA's final decision in June 1985 upheld the view that CVDs should be applied and increased the rates to about 5.5 cents per pound for pork and 4.4 cents per pound for live hogs. The last step in the process was the final ruling by the ITC on injury to the domestic industry. In a widely split vote, the ITC overturned its earlier ruling and removed CVDs on Canadian pork exports, but it refused to change the duty on live hogs. Canadian officials were disturbed that the ITC labelled hog stabilization plans as subsidies since this raised questions regarding Canada's entire agricultural stabilization system. Nevertheless, the industry was pleased that the CVD on pork was not upheld.

While Canada was forced to cut live hog exports as a result of the CVD, it was able to increase its shipments of high-margin, labour-intensive items such as ham, sausage, and bacon. Indeed, Canada's pork shipments to the U.S. rose by about 10 per cent in 1986 and 1987, and on a value basis pork was its leading export to the United States. A government document reporting on the change noted with irony that "meat sales have soared at the expense of live animal exports. The U.S. countervail duty on imports of live hogs from Canada was largely responsible for the structural change."[51]

The National Pork Producers' Council was angered by this sequence of events, and (along with six American packers) it wanted the CVD extended to Canadian pork products. In January 1989, the U.S. pork industry filed a new CVD petition, claiming that Canadian pork producers benefited from numerous subsidies. The new petition was aided by changes in 1988 in American trade law, which presume that subsidies in one phase of an industry (e.g., live hogs) automatically flow through to benefit later, value-added phases (e.g., pork products).

In contrast to the earlier countervail case, the ITA and ITC made final determinations (in summer 1989) that Canadian pork imports benefited from "illegal" subsidies and posed a threat to American producers. There are interesting similarities between the Canadian-U.S. disputes involving pork products and softwood lumber. In both cases, producer petitions for CVDs were initially turned down by U.S. regulatory agencies, and later approved as a result of new U.S. legislation and/or new interpretations of existing rules. Following the ITA's final ruling, international trade minister John Crosbie announced that Canada was formally requesting a panel review under Chapter 19 of the Canada-U.S. free trade agreement, and also indicated that Canada might initiate dispute settlement procedures in the GATT.[52] It was evident that the dispute over hogs and pork was threatening to escalate into a major trade conflict.

In summary, as in the case of beef, the market size and production levels in the hogs/pork sector are much greater in the United States than in Canada. Canada is extremely dependent on exporting to the American market, and given "the high percentage of Canadian production exported to the United States, Canadian policies to head off unemployment through subsidizing production might often appear in American eyes to be export subsidies, and be answered as such."[53]

Despite the difference in size of the two countries' agricultural economies, U.S. producers of specific commodities such as pork can be extremely sensitive to changes in their agricultural trade balance with Canada. When American producers are adversely affected by surpluses and by competitive conditions in third-country markets (e.g., for pork exports to Japan), increased imports from Canada can evoke a strong U.S. response. Finally, the pork case provides further evidence of problems with the agricultural trade regime. The GATT has provided little guidance in U.S.-Canadian disputes regarding definitions of "subsidy" and "material injury" or the implementation of trade relief legislation. In this context, the hog case is interesting to consider along with the corn trade dispute, where Canada rather than the United States imposed the countervailing duty.

CORN

Canadian-American trade in feed grains is relatively free from restrictions, and the United States has traditionally exported corn to the deficit eastern Canadian market. The difference in output levels is striking, with the U.S. producing 200.6 million tonnes of corn in 1986–87 and Canada producing only 5.9 million tonnes. However, American corn exports have gradually declined, partly because of substantial increases in Canadian production. In 1986, the United States planned to ship about 20 million bushels of corn to Canada, even though Ontario farmers had so much corn in storage that they were selling it at 40 cents per bushel below cost. American corn accounted for only 4.5 per cent of the Canadian market in 1986 compared with about 20 per cent six years earlier, but the lower-priced U.S. corn was setting the price levels because the border was virtually open. Canadian producers complained that U.S. farm legislation was forcing corn prices down at the same time that price supports insulated American growers from the effects of the low prices. Although corn-growing costs in both countries were about $2.50 per bushel, Canadian growers had to compete with an import price of $1.40. While the Canadian growers were losing more than $1 per bushel, under the 1985 farm bill American farmers were guaranteed a price of $3.03. Canadian farmers were also facing their greatest financial crisis since the Depression, largely because the U.S.-EC trade war had pushed prices to extremely low levels. As a result, the Ontario Corn Producers' Association became the first farm group ever to begin a countervailing duty case against imports of subsidized U.S. produce.

Before 1985, Canada had relied on antidumping rather than countervail legislation to protect domestic producers. However, the number of CVD cases increased significantly in 1986, partly because of the passage of Canada's Special Import Measures Act in December 1984. Canadian CVD actions also increased in response to the U.S.-EC agricultural trade war. Thus, two of the four CVD cases begun in 1986 involved EC agricultural products, and one was the corn case against U.S. producers.[54] In accordance with Canadian procedures, the Ontario producers lodged a formal complaint with Revenue Canada, asking it to conduct an investigation of American corn exports. They claimed that U.S. subsidies were depressing market prices and permitting increased corn sales to

Canada. While the corn producers' association felt that the U.S. subsidies were aimed at the European Community, it maintained that Canadian farmers were nevertheless suffering injury. The U.S. secretary of agriculture described the request for a CVD case as "ridiculous" and vowed that the government would support American producers against the Canadian action.[55]

In November 1986, Canada's Department of National Revenue ruled that five federal and state programs were countervailable subsidies and levied a stiff preliminary CVD of about $ 1.05 US for each bushel of American corn, or about 67 per cent of the corn's value.[56] Collection of the duty was to begin immediately, but it was subject to refund after the review process was completed. The American producers were furious with the decision, and an executive with the National Corn Growers' Association said that they intended "to pursue every available legal recourse to obtain a reversal."[57] He argued that Revenue Canada's preliminary decision ignored several facts: Canadian corn production had risen by 22 per cent and U.S. corn exports to Canada had fallen by 78 per cent from 1980 to 1985; Canada was increasing its corn exports to the United States; U.S. farm subsidies supported world corn prices at Washington's expense; and American programs encouraged rather than injured Canadian corn production.

The effect of Revenue Canada's preliminary decision on American producers was limited since only about 1 per cent of U.S. corn exports is sent to Canada. However, the decision had major implications that extended far beyond the U.S. corn industry. This was the first time that American subsidies were found in contravention of the GATT and the first time that a foreign country levied CVDs in an effort to neutralize them. The corn duties came at an especially embarrassing time for the Reagan administration since it was criticizing other countries for paying subsidies. American officials denied that an export subsidy existed, and the agriculture secretary argued that the CVD decision was inconsistent with efforts to bring about freer bilateral trade. Indeed, the Canadian action came five days before Canada and the United States were scheduled to resume talks to liberalize their trading relationship. However, the U.S. secretary did not refer to the 15 per cent American duty that had been imposed against Canadian softwood lumber exports three weeks earlier. A Washington lawyer examining the psychological impact of the Canadian countervail decision stated that

> this is a tremendously significant step because, until now, Congress has acted as if the United States was invulnerable. One of the reasons why countervailing duty cases are the United States' chosen weapon is that no one ever used that weapon against the United States. . . .
>
> There is a clear perception within the U.S. government (both Congress

and the administration) that the United States is pure and the rest of the world is unfair. It makes foreign companies dealing in the United States absolutely livid.[58]

The *New York Times* gave the countervail case fairly extensive coverage, and a *Times* editorial acknowledged that U.S. corn farmers were heavily subsidized and that Canada was correct in its decision. However, the editorial also cautioned that the indirect effect of the decision could be substantial because "other American commodities are subsidized in the same way, and Canada's action could serve as a precedent for other governments".[59]

The case next moved to the second stage of the CVD procedure, in which Revenue Canada took a closer look at the U.S. subsidies and the Import Tribunal held public hearings to decide whether Canadian farmers had suffered material injury. In February 1987, Revenue Canada upheld its earlier decision that American corn producers were subsidized but reduced the import duty from $1.05 (U.S.) per bushel to 85 cents. The Canadian Import Tribunal made its final decision in March 1987, deciding that subsidized U.S. corn imports were injuring Canadian producers and upholding the 85-cent duty. The majority found that a major objective of the 1985 U.S. farm bill was to lower corn prices in an effort to recover lost export markets, while giving U.S. farmers deficiency payments to protect their incomes. It was felt that the lower prices had a major adverse effect on Canadian producers.[60]

The U.S. National Corn Growers' Association reacted strongly to the CVD decision and asked the administration to retaliate by blocking imports of Canadian fructose (a sweetener made from corn). Furthermore, the U.S. Senate voted 99 to 0 to ask the U.S. trade representative to determine whether or not the tariff violated the GATT. In April 1987, the deputy trade representative announced that the U.S. government was appealing the corn duty decision to GATT. The United States contended that Canada violated the GATT subsidy code by imposing countervailing duties without adequate proof of material injury to Canadian producers. However, a former Canadian finance minister indicated that the Ontario corn producers' CVD action exposed "United States subsidy practices . . . [and] the inconsistency of United States officials . . . who have condemned the Canadian tribunal for doing precisely what the U.S. has been attempting to do to Canada and to others."[61]

It is of interest that a number of Canadian industry associations argued against the imposition of countervailing duties. These included the Industrial Corn Users' Group, the Association of Canadian Distillers, the Canadian Feed Industry Association, the Brewers' Association of Canada, the Canadian Pork Council, the Maritime Farmers' Council, and various Alberta marketing boards.

In February 1988, the minister of state for finance announced that the CVD on corn would be lowered to 46 cents a bushel since farmers were not receiving the full benefit of the larger duty, and "it was causing a problem for other users." The minister was reportedly "motivated partly by evidence that the higher duty left industrial users uncertain about what premium they would have to pay above the U.S. price."[62] The U.S. National Corn Growers' Association and four Ontario-based industrial corn users also launched (separate) appeals to the Canadian Federal Court of Appeal, maintaining that the CVD on U.S. corn was not justified. However, on 30 December 1988, the Court of Appeal upheld the finding of the Canadian Import Tribunal that the 1986 CVD was necessary to prevent a flood of cheap U.S. corn into Canada.[63]

Before discussing the Canada-U.S. free trade agreement, it is useful to draw some conclusions here regarding linkages between the variables and the issue of trade barriers. Both the general discussion of trade barriers and the examination of the beef, pork, and corn sectors show that there is a close correlation between the existence of surpluses and the rise of protectionism. Increased protectionism in turn often leads to retaliation and conflict and to interference with both countries' agricultural export objectives. These findings reinforce the view that

> surplus capacity erodes liberal trade and investment policies. Demands by workers and companies for profits and jobs, worries of government technocrats about retaining a role for domestic firms in a key world market, and the force of more general political bargains . . . coalesce to induce more government intervention in a particular sector.[64]

Canadian producers often turn to protectionism to avoid being inundated by surpluses from across the border. Thus, Table 7–1 demonstrates that the U.S. agricultural economy is much larger than the Canadian for the three commodities examined. On the other hand, U.S. producers may be concerned about an increase of imports in their particular sectors. For example, Table 7–1 shows that the United States had a negative trade balance for pork in 1986 of 470,000 tonnes. American producers in a particular sector and region of the country may also feel that the macro-statistics are of little relevance to them personally. A statement by the chairman of a Congressional subcommittee summarizing the testimony of Idaho potato growers clearly illustrates this view:

> You say the Canadian view is that with the U.S. fall crop over 300 million their exports of one to two percent are not a factor. And then you say let me show what's really happening to Idaho using the 1982 crop year in just

TABLE 7–1

PRODUCTION AND TRADE IN BEEF, PORK, AND CORN, 1986*

(thousand tonnes)

	United States	Canada
Beef and veal		
production	11,292	1,040
exports	239	105
imports	978	112
Pork		
production	6,379	908
exports	39	215
imports	509	14
Corn		
production	200,600	5,900
exports	38,200	100
imports	0	600

* The figures for corn are for 1986-87.
Source: Adapted from Mary Anne Normile and Carol A. Goodloe, *U.S.-Canadian Agricultural Trade Issues: Implications for the Bilateral Trade Agreement* (Washington, D.C.: USDA, Economic Research Service, Agriculture and Trade Analysis Division, March 1988), pp. 5, 7.

three markets. In Boston we're down 35 percent in 1983, down 16 percent in 1984 from the 1982 year.[65]

However, surplus capacity alone is not sufficient to explain the rise in protectionism in recent years since agricultural surpluses have been a common occurrence in the postwar period. Additional factors include the deterioration in the U.S. balance of payments and the increase in both competition and conflict in the agricultural trade regime. Furthermore, the positive U.S. balance of trade in agriculture has been eroded in recent years, which has caused American farm groups in various sectors to demand more aggressive government action to promote "fair trade." To achieve fair trade, non-tariff barriers and/or trade relief legislation are sometimes considered to be necessary.

Canada and other countries have been disturbed by U.S. criteria for defining subsidies and imposing countervailing duties, but the United States is obviously not the only source of this problem. The GATT developed a new Subsidies Code as part of the Tokyo Round, with the goals of reducing or eliminating the trade-distorting effects of subsidies and of bringing them under more effective international discipline. However, this code did not resolve the major agricultural subsidy issues in dispute. While Article 9 of the code prohibits export subsidies, agricultural products continue to be treated as an exception. Furthermore, the European Community indicated at the Tokyo Round that the basic elements of its Common Agricultural Policy were not negotiable. Not surprisingly, the main lawsuits brought to enforce the Subsidies Code (cases involving EC export subsidies on wheat, flour, and pasta) ended in an impasse. The GATT was clearly ill-equipped to develop a consensus on subsidies in agricultural trade, and its failure to do so has contributed to conflict in Canadian-American relations:

> the hog and corn countervailing duty cases show that practically any government program can be considered a subsidy. The United States determined that Canadian Federal and Provincial stabilization programs for hogs constituted subsidies, while Canadian officials determined that the U.S. feed grain program—commodity loans, deficiency payments, diversion payments, Commodity Credit Corporation (CCC) expenses—conferred subsidies upon producers.[66]

The beef and hog cases also demonstrate the problems with providing regime guidance in regard to technical standards such as health and sanitary regulations. The United States and Canada sometimes have widely divergent rules in this area, and it is often difficult to assess their justifiability. Thus, Canada imposed a ban on U.S. beef with diethylstilbestrol at a time when American beef was inundating its market, and some U.S. states banned Canadian hogs treated with chloramphenicol during a period or rising imports from Canada. In both cases there were potential health risks, but the timing of the import restrictions is certainly of interest.

Finally, this section on trade barriers provides additional information about the effects of Canadian-American interdependence. Because the two countries are highly interdependent in the beef, pork, and corn trade, these three cases demonstrate that trade interdependence can under some conditions contribute to conflict:

> Commodities that have been the center of U.S.-Canadian trade disputes have not always been those where border protection—that is, tariffs, quotas, licenses—has been the most restrictive. Rather, complaints have tended to focus on domestic programs that effectively alter the production function, terms of trade, or comparative advantage for one country's com-

modity(ies) over the other's. . . . Disputes have arisen over corn and hogs because trade is relatively unhindered by restrictions and the products flow to the best return.[67]

Canadian-American interdependence is of course highly asymmetrical, and Canada is extremely dependent on exporting to the much larger U.S. market. Thus, even in cases where U.S. trade barriers are directed primarily at others (e.g., in beef trade), Canada's agricultural export objectives can be seriously affected. The strong reaction of American corn producers to Canada's countervail action demonstrates that U.S. producers in particular sectors can also rely somewhat on exports to the Canadian market. However, only about 1 per cent of American corn exports are normally sent to Canada, and the U.S. government was *primarily* concerned with the establishment of a precedent for other countries and other commodities. Another indication of asymmetrical interdependence was Canada's adoption of a Meat Import Act patterned after the U.S. legislation in efforts to prevent disruptions in its vital beef and cattle trade with the United States. The corn case demonstrates that Canada as well as the U.S. sometimes takes unilateral action to impose import barriers and/or trade relief legislation. However, if trade is seriously disrupted (as it was in the beef trade dispute), Canada can suffer from such interruptions more than the United States. It was primarily because U.S. protectionism was posing an increasing threat to Canada's exports that the Canadian government sought the free trade agreement, and it is to this agreement that I now turn.

TRADE BARRIERS AND BILATERAL FREE TRADE

At the "Shamrock Summit" in March 1985, President Reagan and Prime Minister Mulroney asked their trade officials to explore ways of reducing and eliminating trade barriers between the United States and Canada. This opening was followed by Mr. Mulroney's formal request that the two countries examine the possibilities for negotiating a bilateral free trade (BFT) agreement. The free trade negotiations began when the U.S. Senate Finance Committee narrowly endorsed "fast-track" procedures in April 1986.[68] After many months of bargaining, the president and prime minister signed the final text of a free trade agreement on 2 January 1988. The U.S. House of Representatives and Senate endorsed the agreement, but final approval in Canada awaited the outcome of a contentious election in November 1988. With the re-election of a Conservative majority government, the free trade accord came into effect on 1 January 1989.

There are close linkages between the BFT accord and Canadian-American trade barriers since the agreement was concluded largely to counteract rising protectionist forces in bilateral and multilateral trade. Canada was especially concerned about gaining more secure access to the American market, and this objective acquired greater urgency as pressures for U.S. protectionism increased. The United States also had concerns related to its negative trade balance with Canada and to its perception of Canada's "unfair" trade practices involving subsidies and import barriers. Nevertheless, in view of their asymmetrical relationship, the U.S. interest in a BFT agreement stemmed primarily from its multilateral objectives.[69] American government officials felt that a BFT accord would provide a model to be emulated at the GATT Uruguay Round and an instrument for pressuring GATT members to agree to certain policies in such areas as services and agriculture.

The provisions relating to agriculture in the BFT agreement are rather limited since various programs to support and stabilize farm incomes and prices are (at present) not affected. Nevertheless, the agricultural provisions "provoked some of the loudest debate, the most exaggerated claims of hurt and benefit and the most sweeping generalizations of any section of the deal."[70] The controversy stemmed from the fact that the United States, Canada, and other major trading nations commonly have viewed agriculture as a special or exceptional case. Before examining the linkages between the BFT accord and agricultural trade barriers, it is necessary to provide some historical background on the role of agriculture in Canada-U.S. free trade negotiations.

A HISTORICAL OVERVIEW OF FREE TRADE NEGOTIATIONS

A noted political historian has observed that there is one economic issue in Canada which "comes close to rivalling the linguistic and race question for both longevity and vehemence, and this is, of course, the question of free trade with the United States."[71] Canadian attitudes regarding bilateral free trade are a prime example of "the politics of attraction and distance."[72] Although Canada has often felt the need for a free trade agreement to ensure it of access to the large U.S. market, it has also feared that such an accord would further increase its dependence on (and hence its vulnerability to) the United States.

Bilateral free trade negotiations in earlier years always included agricultural commodities. In 1854, the United States and Canada concluded a Reciprocity Treaty that was limited in scope to natural products and provided for free admission of grain, livestock, meat, dairy products and fish. The treaty was to continue for ten years and could be ended on one year's notice thereafter by either country. British North America strongly supported the Reciprocity Treaty since it opened the huge American market to Canada's agricultural exports. However, the United States abrogated it in 1866, largely because of its dissatisfaction with the bilateral trade balance, the increased Canadian duties on U.S. manufactures, and the British role in the American Civil War.

In the years after 1866, Canada made a number of attempts to renew reciprocity.[73] It was particularly interested in the free admission of natural products—including agricultural commodities—to the United States. However, the U.S. government never seriously considered these proposals. The Conservative government in Canada therefore instituted the protectionist National Policy in 1879, and after 1891 Canadian enthusiasm for reciprocity declined. It was not until a U.S.-Canadian tariff war became a distinct possibility that the two countries again tried to renew reciprocity in 1911. The 1911 accord provided for free trade in a large number of natural products and, in fact, "seemed designed for the agricultural community."[74] Canadian producers were to have almost free access to the U.S. market for their agricultural exports, and the Americans would gain major concessions on farm machinery exports. However, Canadian manufacturers feared that reciprocity would weaken their tariff protection under the National Policy. They therefore joined with other opponents to defeat the Liberal government of Prime Minister Wilfrid Laurier, and reciprocity, in the 1911 election.

The objective of a bilateral free trade accord did not disappear after 1911, but the prospects were thwarted by a rise in protectionism following World War I. To repair the damage caused by this protectionism, the United States and Canada signed trade agreements in 1935 and 1938. Although these agreements lowered tariffs (including agricultural tariffs), they were not free trade accords. They therefore did "not carry the emotional baggage" of the 1911 reciprocity treaty, which had led to fears of "selling out Canada to the Americans."[75]

After World War II, the United States and Canada made their first serious attempt to devise a free trade arrangement since 1911. A plan developed in March 1948 called for the removal of all duties by both countries. While agricultural products were to be included, the United States would have the right to maintain import quotas on wheat and flour, and Canada would be able to impose seasonal quotas on fresh fruits and vegetables. In the end, Prime Minister Mackenzie King refused to approve the plan, largely because of his concerns about political opposition, and free trade negotiations were not revived until the 1980s.

In summary, the United States and Canada sometimes responded to increased protectionism by seeking bilateral trade liberalization or free trade (for example, in 1911 and 1935). In view of their interdependence, the two countries demonstrated a willingness to seek new forms of co-operation to resolve their differences. On the other hand, Canada was fearful of establishing overly close ties with the U.S., and this wariness contributed to the breakdown of free trade negotiations in 1911 and 1948. Earlier free trade proposals all included agriculture, but in the 1948 plan the two countries were beginning to view certain agricultural commodities as exceptions.

THE ISSUE OF INCLUDING AGRICULTURE IN THE BFT AGREEMENT

Despite the inclusion of agriculture in earlier free trade proposals, the establishment of complex domestic support programs in the postwar period contributed to the view of many analysts that agriculture should be treated differently. For example, the Canadian-American Committee was highly sceptical regarding the inclusion of agriculture in a free trade agreement. A 1963 study published by the committee indicated that "agriculture promises to be the principal obstacle to the all-inclusive approach" to bilateral free trade because policies in this area "are politically sensitive to change."[76] In addition, a 1965 committee report on a possible free trade plan called for "the initial exemption of an agreed-upon list of agricultural products for which the Plan's provisions are 'clearly inapplicable'."[77] It should be mentioned that not all analysts in the 1960s viewed agriculture as an exception. For example, one co-authored study concluded that the harmonization of U.S. and Canadian agricultural policies "would not seem to be a major economic problem." Furthermore, a major conference during this period focused on the possibilities for the economic integration of North American agriculture.[78]

In the 1970s, most studies on trade liberalization and free trade (governmental as well as non-governmental) continued to view agriculture as an exception. For example, the Economic Council of Canada (ECC) issued a report recommending that the government explore the possibility of establishing free trade with other countries. While the ECC recommended that agricultural trade be liberalized, it determined that "it would be difficult to include agriculture fully within the ambit of a free trade arrangement."[79] Canada's Standing Senate Committee on Foreign Affairs also recommended further study of a Canada-U.S. free trade agreement, but it indicated that food and agricultural issues would not even be considered.[80]

Interest in free trade gradually increased in the late 1970s and 1980s but in the tradition of earlier years, agriculture usually was either ignored or viewed as a special area. The 1974 U.S. Trade Act had permitted the president "to initiate negotiations for a trade agreement with Canada to establish a free trade area." In the 1979 U.S. Trade Agreements Act, this position was broadened to include the possibility of agreements "with countries in the northern part of the western hemisphere."[81] Congressional hearings were subsequently held on establishing a "North American accord," but they stemmed primarily from a growing concern with establishing a secure U.S. supply of energy and other resources. Thus, agricultural trade with Canada was not even mentioned in the hearings.[82]

In 1982, a report of the Canadian Senate Committee on Foreign Affairs endorsed the idea of a comprehensive free trade accord, but it stated that "the most notable exception in a Canada-U.S. agreement would be agriculture."[83] Canada's External Affairs Department expressed a preference for a sectoral rather than a comprehensive approach to free trade, but agriculture was not one of the sectors considered.[84] In 1985, the Royal Commission on the Economic Union and Development Prospects for Canada endorsed the Canadian Senate's idea of a comprehensive BFT agreement, but it concluded that "potential problems may justify deferring free trade for agricultural products to which import quotas currently apply."[85]

During the negotiations for the BFT agreement, Canadian farming groups were sharply divided in their views. The Canadian Federation of Agriculture (CFA), the largest national farmer organization, voiced reservations about the accord. However, the National Farmers' Union (NFU), the smaller and more militant of the two general farm groups in Canada, expressed much stronger opposition. In its submission to the Senate committee hearings on free trade, the NFU even stated that "Bill C-130 merely represents the legislative surgery required to fit this nation into an economic mould that will firmly fuse and integrate it into a U.S.-dominated North American economy."[86] A number of commodity groups (discussed below) shared some of the reservations of the general farm organizations. However, Canadian beef and hog producers were very interested in an agreement since they are quite competitive, have only modest protection, and export primarily to the United States. Major regional differences also existed, with the Ontario and Quebec agricultural industries more inclined to be protectionist. Their farmers are extremely dependent on supply management, stabilization, and import control policies. Many farmers in the Prairie provinces also had concerns about the BFT accord, but they were more inclined to favour free trade. It was felt that western products such as grains, oilseeds, beef, and hogs would be competitive with U.S. production.

American farming groups initially gave little attention to the BFT negotiations, but later they also expressed a diversity of views. For example, the National Association of Wheat Growers and various soybean organizations took a cautious approach, and they were later critical. On the other hand, meat organizations in the United States were generally supportive of an agreement. Some of the general U.S. farm organizations were opposed to the BFT accord. For example, the National Farmers' Union (NFU) stated that "the most ill-advised and damaging provision occurs in Article 70(1)," in which the parties agree to work toward eliminating all subsidies on a global basis that distort agricultural trade. The NFU was concerned that "subsidies" would be interpreted too broadly and would further threaten the family farm.[87] The National Farmers' Organization (NFO) was also concerned that the BFT accord would affect U.S. price supports and subsidies, and it recommended that "this agreement should not be approved as submitted to Congress."[88] However, the largest U.S. general farm organization, the American Farm Bureau Federation (AFBF), was generally supportive of the accord. In a letter to the U.S. Senate, the Farm Bureau urged "ratification by Congress as an important step toward reducing trade-distorting practices in agriculture between our two countries."[89] This endorsement marked a contrast to the Farm Bureau's Canadian counterpart, the Canadian Federation of Agriculture, which voiced increasingly strong reservations over time and eventually stated that "CFA cannot support the implementation of the FTA in its current form."[90]

Since most analyses of bilateral free trade either ignored agriculture or viewed it as a special case and farmers were sharply divided on the issue, the question arises as to why agriculture was included in the agreement. The two governments supported the BFT agricultural provisions, not only to liberalize bilateral trade but also to influence the Uruguay Round of GATT negotiations. As discussed, the United States and Canada have common concerns about European and Japanese trade barriers and about European export subsidies (U.S. export subsidies are also a major concern to Canada). Thus, a U.S. Department of Agriculture official has stated that "If our two nations—both of which have highly developed systems, and both of which have a big stake in freer and fairer agricultural trade—cannot resolve the issues that trouble our trade, what chance for success will there be for the Uruguay Round?"[91]

Agriculture may also have been included because of GATT Article XXIV-8-b, which states that in free trade areas "duties and other restrictive regulations of commerce" are to be "eliminated on substantially all the trade between the constituent territories." The General Agreement does not provide a definition of "substantially all trade," and the European Free Trade Association (formed in 1960) largely exempted agricultural products from its free trade arrangement. Nevertheless, excluding large economic sectors such as agriculture in a free trade arrangement today might be judged to be incompatible with Article XXIV. The United States and Canada would probably be granted a waiver, but such an exception could damage the prospects for agricultural trade liberalization in the GATT Uruguay Round.[92]

A third reason for including agriculture related to U.S. concerns regarding its declining agricultural trade surplus with Canada. The U.S. ambassador expressed dissatisfaction with this situation when he suggested that "Canada has placed quotas on more categories of imports than has the U.S., particularly in agricultural products."[93] American officials felt that the BFT accord would deal (in part) with Canada's "unfair" advantages, resulting from its grain transportation subsidies, its import barriers on U.S. poultry products and eggs, its health quarantine on U.S. live hogs, and its tariffs on U.S. horticultural products.

A fourth reason for the inclusion of agriculture was that both countries were aware of their interdependence in this area and of the need to harmonize policies. The interdependence is of course asymmetrical, and in beef trade, for example, "harmonization" meant that Canada patterned its meat import act after the U.S. legislation. Finally, agriculture was included to avoid a situation where the food and beverage sectors of manufacturing would have to be excluded. Canadian manufacturers in these sectors argued that they would not be competitive if their U.S. counterparts benefited from cheaper agricultural inputs. Canadian food processors in fact continue to be unhappy with the agreement since it does not affect various marketing boards that contribute to higher agricultural prices.

Although agriculture is included in the BFT accord, domestic agricultural interests remain strong and are often in conflict with liberal trading principles. Furthermore, farmers and their representatives on both sides of the border have concerns about the fairness or equity of specific provisions in the agreement. The following discussion focuses on the agricultural provisions and the varied reactions to them.

AGRICULTURAL PROVISIONS IN THE BILATERAL FREE TRADE AGREEMENT[94]

The stated objectives of the BFT agreement (in Article 102) are to eliminate trade barriers between the two states, to facilitate fair competition, to liberalize conditions for investment, to establish procedures for the resolution of disputes, and to provide a foundation for further bilateral and multilateral cooperation. Bilateral tariffs, including agricultural tariffs, are to be phased out over a ten-year period beginning on 1 January 1989. Chapter 7 of the accord contains provisions specific to agriculture, and Chapter 19 on binational dispute settlement is also relevant to this study.[95]

Grains and Oilseeds

The United States and Canada normally produce wheat and other grains in excess of domestic demand, and some of these products move across their common border. In 1986, Canada exported about Cdn $225 million of grains and oilseeds to the United States, primarily consisting of wheat, barley, flaxseed, soybeans, and canola (and their products). American exports to Canada in 1986 were valued at Cdn $425 million and consisted mainly of corn and soybeans.[96] The United States limits its grain imports with some tariffs and has legislation in place to impose quantitative restrictions on imports, while Canada depends on tariffs and licensing requirements. The Canadian Wheat Board (CWB) issues import licences for wheat, oats, and barley only when it determines that domestic supplies are inadequate. Furthermore, Canada provides transportation subsidies for moving grains to ports for export, and the United States utilizes export subsidies.

In accordance with Article 705 of the BFT agreement, the United States can no longer use Section 22 of the Agricultural Adjustment Act to limit Canadian grain imports.[97] Canada will also eliminate its import licences for wheat, oats, and barley as soon as support levels or subsidies by both governments are judged to be "equivalent." Thus, import restrictions will still apply to American wheat, which is subsidized by about $50 a tonne more than in Canada. Canada has had a two-price system where a premium is paid for grain sold in the domestic market, and the price of exported grain is established according to world levels. Since import controls will eventually be removed, it will no longer be possible for the Wheat Board to maintain this system. Both countries reserve the right to reimpose restrictions if imports increase "significantly" as a result of "substantial" changes in support programs.[98]

Article 701 prohibits export subsidies on agricultural trade between the two states. In addition, Canada is to eliminate its rail subsidies on exports to the United States shipped through west coast ports. Thus, Canadian millfeeds, canola meal, and corn distilled byproducts moving into the U.S. Pacific northwest will not qualify for the thirty-dollar per tonne subsidized freight rates under the 1983 Western Grain Transportation Act. Finally, the two states agree to take account of each other's interests when using export subsidies in sales to third-country markets.

Canadian grain producers have been divided in their views of the BFT provisions. For example, delegates to the United Grain Growers' annual meeting in November 1987 strongly endorsed the UGG's stance in favour of free trade. However, the majority of Saskatchewan Wheat Pool delegates voted against the preliminary BFT accord in early December 1987.[99] Some of their main concerns relate to how much authority the Wheat Board will lose and how much income they will lose when Canada's two-price wheat system is dropped. The loss of income is a particularly salient issue since farmers are already suffering from a steep decline in world wheat prices. The federal government has pledged to compensate Canadian farmers for their income losses when the two-price system is abandoned, but there are uncertainties regarding the amount of the subsidies and the length of time they would be provided.

Spokesmen for the Liberal and New Democratic Parties, as well as various farm groups, feel that the federal government has broken its promise to protect the Canadian Wheat Board. Their concerns were heightened when the government decided to remove the oats trade from the control of the board shortly after the BFT agreement was approved. Indeed, the largest Prairie farm group, the 130,000-member Prairie Pools, Inc., stated that the government might have a "hidden agenda" to sacrifice the CWB as part of the free trade deal.[100] Farmers were deeply divided on the decision regarding oats, with some groups calling for the resignation of the grains minister and others supporting him. However, it is significant that the Advisory Committee of the Wheat Board (a producer-elected body) voted seven to four against the removal of oats from CWB control.

Some critics of the accord also feel that the government was misguided in agreeing to remove the rail subsidies on grain shipped through Canada's west coast ports. In their view, it remains to be proven that the transportation payments are a trade-distorting subsidy. Furthermore, Canada is at a major disadvantage with regard to oilseed exports since its transportation subsidy was removed immediately after the BFT agreement came into effect. This quick action contrasts with American tariffs on Canadian canola oil and meal, which will only be removed over a ten-year period. Finally, there are fears that Canada's entire grain transportation subsidy program could be attacked in the GATT Uruguay Round as a result of the bilateral agreement.[101]

Another contentious issue relates to the two governments' agreement to take account of each other's interests when using export subsidies on sales to third countries. According to the U.S. trade representative,

> the Canadians wanted very badly to get the right of prior consultation on all of our export enhancement program decisions. This is a concession that we were not willing to make. . . .
>
> Both the U.S. and Canada . . . agreed to take the export interests of the other country into effect in using export subsidies on agricultural goods shipped to third-country markets. This doesn't mean that we can't use export subsidies in markets in which the Canadians are present. But it does mean that we recognize the negative effects that such subsidies may have on other exporters.[102]

Critics in Canada maintain that the United States is not taking this provision seriously since it is continuing to subsidize grain exports to Canadian markets. There is obviously no way to enforce this provision in the BFT agreement because the United States is not likely to scale down its export subsidies without similar concessions from the European Community.

On the American side, there has also been dissatisfaction with the provisions on grains and oilseeds. In the 1986 crop year, Canada exported 645,800 tonnes of wheat, oats, and barley to the United States, but U.S. exports of these commodities were barred by Canada's licensing system. Under the BFT agreement, Canada will be able to increase its wheat exports to the United States, but it will also continue to ban U.S. wheat until subsidies by both governments are judged to be "equivalent."[103] The fifty-thousand-member National Association of Wheat Growers (NAWG) has complained that the subsidies will never be considered equal because the Canadian Wheat Board has hidden subsidies and the method of measuring subsidies (through the use of "Producer Subsidy Equivalents") is methodologically flawed. The NAWG is also dissatisfied that transportation subsidies will be removed only for grains moving through Canada's west coast ports. American soybean organizations have joined the NAWG in criticizing this aspect of the agreement since most oilseeds are shipped to the United States through Canada's eastern ports.[104] Finally, the NAWG has criticized the fact that Canada will be permitted to bar imports of inferior grades of American wheat.[105]

Despite the Reagan administration's objections, the NAWG voted to oppose the agreement at its annual meeting in January 1988. The association also threatened that the United States would retaliate against increased Canadian wheat shipments with a countervail case, a boycott of Canadian products, or some other action.[106] The American wheat growers had some important allies because a number of other natural resource producers shared their concerns. Indeed, on 23 February 1988, twenty senators called on President Reagan to provide guarantees that Canada would end subsidies to its natural resource producers as American tariffs were lowered under the BFT pact. These senators were mostly from western states that produce wheat, nonferrous metals, coal, plywood, and natural gas.[107] However, the natural resource producers did not have sufficient influence to block the free trade accord in the U.S. Congress.

American criticisms of Canadian grain-marketing practices stem largely from the view that the Wheat Board is a form of "state trading" that gives Canada unfair advantages. For example, a former U.S. policymaker stated "the Canadian and Australian Wheat Boards have continued to expand exports instead of building stocks" and that the United States should recognize "the immense effects of state buying and selling practices" on its current export problems.[108] In a "Statement of Administrative Action" regarding implementation of the BFT agreement, the U.S. government therefore indicated that it

> intends to pursue consultations with Canada regarding the price setting policy of the CWB as it affects goods exported to the United States. These consultations will be directed toward establishing a method to determine the price at which the CWB is selling agricultural goods to the United States and the CWB's acquisition price for those goods. The ideal method would be a public price setting mechanism transparent to the U.S. Government, producers and processors.[109]

The U.S. Statement of Administrative Action sparked a strong reaction from Canadian producers. In fact, the Advisory Committee to the Canadian Wheat Board stated that:

> after careful review of the . . . "Statement of Administrative Action," The Advisory Committee considers the proposed Free Trade Agreement will . . . undermine the ability of the Canadian Wheat Board to be an effective marketing agent on behalf of Canadian grain producers.[110]

The Saskatchewan Wheat Pool, the Canadian Federation of Agriculture, and the National Farmers' Union joined the advisory committee in criticizing the U.S. "statement." The remarks of a Canadian agricultural economist illustrate the philosophical gulf that separates many Canadians and Americans on this issue:

> I don't know why the Wheat Board remains a mysterious agency to some Americans. Take pricing, for example: the Board does not disclose selling price information. But . . . Cargill and other similar firms do not tell you folks how much money they make from wheat and their selling prices in the international marketplace either. It's a trade secret for the Wheat Board just as it is in any private company, so why do we have the perception that the Board distorts trade and the private sector does not?[111]

Finally, in the view of some Canadians the U.S. is in no position to criticize the CWB since the American government itself is heavily involved in the wheat trade through support programs and export decisions made on a political basis. Until international organizations such as the GATT provide clearer guidelines on what is permissible in terms of subsidies, support programs, and government involvement in agriculture, it is likely that Canadian-American differences over institutions such as the Wheat Board will persist.

Poultry and Eggs

The United States has a very favourable trade balance with Canada in poultry and eggs. In fiscal year 1986, American exports of poultry meat to Canada were valued at US $31.5 million, while Canadian exports to the U.S. amounted to only $3.7 million. The trade in eggs was not as unbalanced, with American exports to Canada valued at $13.9 million, and Canadian exports to the U.S. valued at $9 million.[112] Both countries impose tariffs on poultry products and maintain inspection procedures to meet health and processing standards. Canada also imposes import quotas, and the poultry industry is one of the most highly protected in Canadian agriculture. The United States is far less protectionist for these products and imposes no major non-tariff barriers on poultry product imports. Article 706 of the BFT agreement calls for a small increase of Canadian global import quotas for chickens, turkeys, and eggs to reflect the increase in imports from the U.S. in recent years (i.e., when demand for these products in Canada exceeded domestic supply.)

Canada's import quotas on poultry, eggs, and dairy products are closely linked with supply management plans. National and provincial boards administer marketing schemes for these products, with domestic producers allocated production quotas. The marketing boards are designed to provide adequate and stable incomes for producers, partly by imposing limitations on the entry of lower-priced imports. This type of protection has sometimes provoked a strong reaction from the United States. For example, in 1975 the U.S. government sought a GATT ruling regarding the legality of Canadian import quotas designed to facilitate the establishment of a national egg marketing board.[113] However, Canadian producers feel that the marketing boards protect them from U.S. competitors, who have economies of scale advantages since they produce for a much larger domestic market. The feeling exists that, without protection, American producers could capture the Canadian market with lower prices.[114]

Despite the small increase in Canadian import quotas, the external affairs minister has provided assurances that Canada's farm marketing boards are part of "the distinct fabric of the country" and will not be affected by free trade.[115] The Canadian government's synopsis of the free trade accord also carefully states that "marketing systems, farm income stabilization and price support programs remain unimpaired by the Agreement."[116]

Many Canadian farmers, however, are not convinced that marketing boards will remain intact after the BFT accord is implemented. Their suspicions are understandable in view of the considerable opposition to the boards in both the U.S. and Canada. Indeed, the U.S. trade representative stated that "in the course of the FTA negotiations we sought to have Canada's supply management scheme for poultry and eggs eliminated, but the Canadians were unwilling to go beyond a quota increase."[117] Canadian consumer groups also felt that the BFT accord should have dealt with the problems of marketing boards since consumers are paying a cost for them through higher prices. Marketing boards have the power not only to protect Canadian producers from foreign competition but also to prevent effective competition between Canadian provinces. Some boards simply facilitate the common marketing of commodities, but others raise prices and augment farm incomes by restricting foreign and domestic supplies. Thus, a study of egg, turkey, and chicken marketing found that "the substantial widening in Canada-United States price differentials alone confirms the substantial and increasing consumer costs" of Canada's supply management programs.[118] Canadian food processors are also dissatisfied with the exclusion of marketing boards from the BFT accord since they must use the higher-priced Canadian commodities as raw materials. To compete with their U.S. counterparts, Canadian processors argue that they must be able to obtain these products at North American equivalent prices.

Despite the domestic as well as foreign opposition to some Canadian marketing boards, they are permissible under current GATT regulations since they are linked with supply management schemes.[119] As in the case of the Wheat Board, then, bilateral disputes between the United States and Canada are closely linked with regulations (or the lack thereof) in the agricultural trade regime.

Meat Products

The United States and Canada both have countercyclical beef import laws that limit imports when domestic supplies are adequate and permit increased imports when domestic supplies are low. Under Article 704 of the BFT accord, the United States and Canada will exempt each other from these laws, thus ensuring bilateral free trade in beef and veal. Many Canadian beef producers strongly support this article since they are quite competitive and could increase exports to the U.S. Pacific Northwest. Canadian producers have also experienced problems with U.S. trade relief measures, and they want to have security of access to the American market.[120] However, the BFT accord does not deal with the countervailing duty on Canadian live hog exports to the United States or with the CVD on U.S. grain corn exports to Canada. These issues will have to be resolved as trade rules are rewritten and as both sides determine what constitutes a countervailable subsidy.

Despite expressing some reservations, the U.S. National Cattlemen's Association agreed with its Canadian counterpart that the BFT agreement is "a step

in the right direction to improve . . . trade relations between our two countries."
The U.S. National Pork Producers' Council was also "generally supportive" of
the BFT's "effort to eliminate trade barriers." However, the NPPC expressed
dissatisfaction with the thirty-day Canadian quarantine on live hogs and with
"the failure to eliminate Canadian federal and provincial subsidies [which] will
need to be resolved in the current multilateral trade negotiations."[121]

While Article 704 establishes free trade in meat products, Section 2 of the
article adds an important qualification:

> If a Party imposes any quantitative import restrictions on meat goods from
> all third countries, or negotiates agreements limiting exports from third
> countries, and the other Party does not take equivalent action, then the first
> Party may impose quantitative import restrictions on meat goods originat-
> ing in the territory of the other Party.

This section is designed to avoid bilateral conflict over the diversion of meat
exports as occurred in the 1970s. The BFT accord seeks to ensure that the two
countries will take "equivalent action," which in essence means that Canada's
actions will be patterned after those of the United States.

Fresh Fruits and Vegetables

The United States has climatic advantages in producing a number of agricultural products, including citrus fruits and all other fruits and vegetables when
they are not in season in Canada. As a result, about 41 per cent of American
agricultural exports to Canada are horticultural products, and U.S. cross-border
exports of these products are about five times greater than its imports. Fresh
fruits and vegetables are a prime example of the greater size and diversity of
the American agricultural economy since there are no agricultural products
where Canada has a comparable "natural" advantage. To protect its growers,
Canada imposes seasonal tariffs on U.S. produce for periods extending from
eight to forty weeks, depending on the crop. The tariffs are applied automatically when the produce becomes available in Canada and are removed when the
crop is finished. The United States also imposes seasonal tariffs on imported
fresh vegetables to protect its domestic producers. However, Canada's tariffs
are higher and are imposed for longer periods, primarily because of the shorter
Canadian growing season.

Under the BFT accord, Canada and the United States have agreed to remove
their seasonal tariffs on each other's fresh fruits and vegetables. However, they
can temporarily restore tariffs on these products for a twenty-year period when

prices are depressed (Article 702). This provision applies only if the average acreage under cultivation for the product is constant or declining. Even though both countries can restore tariffs on a temporary basis, many Canadian horticultural producers are not reassured about the survival of their industry. The Canadian Federation of Agriculture maintains that there has been "an apparent sacrifice of certain sectors of the horticultural industry" in the BFT agreement. It has argued that "unless some offsetting action is taken" as tariffs are removed, "there will be a very adverse effect on the more climatically sensitive productions." More specifically, the Canadian Horticultural Council has asked the government to monitor the needs of producers for adjustment assistance for a twelve-year period.[122]

Not surprisingly, the U.S. United Fresh Fruit and Vegetable Association has taken a very different position, stating that it "supports and encourages the . . . free trade agreement, provided that growers of horticultural products in both countries can market their product in an open and fair environment."[123] However, for horticultural products where Canada is more competitive, the attitudes of producers in the two countries are sometimes reversed. For example, the United States had a positive trade balance in fresh potatoes with Canada during the 1970s, but since crop year 1980–81 the U.S. balance has been negative in most years. The National Potato Council has warned that the BFT agreement "could have a devastating impact on the U.S. potato industry if it permits the elimination of U.S. duties . . . and does not resolve the Canadian tariff, subsidies and nontariff barriers."[124] In contrast, the Prince Edward Island Potato Marketing Board supports the agreement as a means of gaining "freer access to the 62-million population base in New England."[125]

The potato issue is an interesting example where the producers in the eastern United States and Canada have very different problems from their western compatriots. On the east coast, the Maine potato industry filed an antidumping petition against Canada, but the ITC ruled that it could not determine if Maine was injured by Canadian imports. On the west coast, the British Columbia potato industry won an antidumping case against the United States in 1986–87. A congressman from Washington State pointed to the fact that the trade concerns of agricultural producers are regionally as well as commodity-oriented, whereas their federal governments have a very different perspective:

We have distinct regional differences, in that British Columbia potato growers would like to keep Washington State and Oregon potatoes out of that neck of the woods, while the opposite is true in the northeastern United States. The northeastern United States potato growers would like to protect from the invasion of their area by Canadian potatoes.

And a concern that we have is that national figures could be used to establish agreements that had regional implications on the movement of these products under some of the provisions for fruits and vegetables.[126]

Sugar-containing Products

Under Article 707, the United States has agreed to exempt Canadian products containing 10 per cent or less sugar by dry weight from future U.S. quotas on sugar-containing products. This is an interesting case where American political-security objectives emerged during Congressional hearings on the free trade agreement. The U.S. trade representative indicated that Canada must certify that it is not exporting Cuban sugar to the United States, and he added that

> Canada ought to stop importing Cuban sugar, period. Whether it comes to us or not, it seems to me they do not contribute to the cause of the Western world by importing Cuban sugar at all, and we have told them that with regularity.[127]

However, major U.S.-Canadian differences on American sugar import policies are based on economic rather than political-security issues.

Technical Regulations and Standards

Article 708 is designed to reduce regulatory barriers and to harmonize the two countries' health and sanitary regulations for trade in food and agricultural products. To implement this article, working groups are being established for animal and plant health, meat and poultry inspection, veterinary drugs, pesticides, and so forth. While technical regulations and standards are often maintained for legitimate reasons, they may also be used as an excuse for imposing import barriers. Countries frequently disagree on the necessity for particular regulations, and conflict therefore results. For example, I previously discussed disputes over a Canadian ban related to the use of the hormone diethylstilbestrol and over a U.S. ban in response to the use of the antibiotic chloramphenicol. These disputes may be lessened by Annex 708.1 of the BFT accord, in which the two countries agree to "make equivalent . . . health and safety regulatory requirements" with respect to veterinary drugs. Annex 708.1 also commits the two states to "work toward the eradication of . . . diseases." The United States and Canada both have extended embargoes for health reasons for lengthy periods, and this provision should be useful in resolving disputes.

Binational Dispute Settlement

Chapter 19 of the BFT accord deals with binational dispute settlement, which is relevant to agriculture because of the large number of trade relief cases involving agricultural products. Canada viewed dispute settlement as the single most important negotiating issue since it wanted more assured access to the U.S. market. While Canada wanted a binding arbitration panel to resolve all trade complaints, it did not achieve this objective. Instead, trade complaints are to proceed through normal domestic procedures in each country, with access to a binational dispute panel only after the domestic process has been completed.

The binational dispute-settlement panels will examine the trade rules in each country and determine whether or not the country in question has made a decision in accordance with its own laws. The panels will consist of five members, with each government choosing two panelists and both jointly choosing the fifth; findings of the panels are to be binding on both governments. The panel system will exist for five to seven years, during which time the United States and Canada will try to develop a new set of joint rules for the use of antidumping and countervailing duties. If no agreement is reached after the seven years, either country can terminate the BFT accord on six months' notice. In the interim, the U.S. and Canada may continue to bring trade relief cases against each other's imports under current domestic laws. Canadian critics have argued that the binational dispute-settlement mechanism does not provide assured access to the U.S. market, but it is clear that a stronger provision would have raised serious constitutional questions in the U.S. Congress. Indeed, a former senior official in the U.S. Department of Agriculture stated that "it seems rather far-fetched for Canada to think that it might be inoculated against retaliation by the U.S. in response to real and imaginary threats to U.S. farm interests."[128]

CONCLUSIONS

Conclusions were discussed above regarding agricultural trade barriers, and these comments focus primarily on efforts to break down trade barriers through the BFT agreement. The most important variable affecting the BFT negotiating process in agriculture was the lack of regime norms and rules. Thus, a former U.S. agricultural policy-maker has stated that

> agriculture is different . . . because the rules for agriculture, in essence, now say that any policy instruments are allowed as long as the outcome is agreeable to the contracting parties. Thus, GATT disputes over nonagri-

cultural issues have hinged on whether a particular policy instrument is compatible with the GATT, whereas agricultural disputes have been largely over whether the use of the instruments has been "fair." Since fairness, like beauty, is in the eye of the beholder, major contracting parties have been dissatisfied with the GATT's agricultural rules.[129]

An examination of attitudes toward the BFT provisions demonstrates that many agricultural producers on both sides of the border are dissatisfied with the agreement. There are numerous examples of charges and countercharges that the other side is using "unfair" trading practices to expand exports and limit imports. Part of the problem stems from the fact that it "is the fate of negotiators, to achieve . . . far less than the Congressional, commodity, and sectoral constituencies thought would have been fair."[130] However, another major part of the problem derives from the fact that the trade regime has done little to help define what is permissible in agriculture. The question arises whether the BFT accord will help in establishing a set of norms and rules that will facilitate the breaking down of U.S. and Canadian agricultural trade barriers with each other and with third countries.

As has been shown, agricultural trade provisions in the accord are limited, and they were included largely in the hopes that they would provide a stimulus to multilateral reform. However, bilateralism that emphasizes discrimination and retaliation against outsiders will not achieve significant agricultural trade liberalization. The Canada-U.S. free trade agreement could be viewed as a reversion from the multilateral GATT system that will contribute to a regionalization of the globe into bilateral and plurilateral trading blocs. The planned consolidation of the European Community in 1992 could be viewed as yet another step in this regionalization process. However, another interpretation is that the Canada-U.S. accord will facilitate a move toward wider trade liberalization through an opening of the bilateral agreement to other countries and/or through a consideration of similar issues in the GATT.

In the BFT talks, the two countries have discussed a number of issues relevant to agriculture that are also being addressed at the multilateral trade negotiations. These include efforts to stem the increase of agricultural trade barriers and to phase out the barriers that now exist; to clarify what subsidies are trade-distorting and therefore countervailable; to develop a consensus on measuring and comparing subsidy practices in different countries; to freeze trade-distorting agricultural subsidies at their present levels and then decrease them over time; to harmonize the differences in technical regulations, standards, and certification procedures regarding health and product safety that hinder trade; and to improve dispute-settlement processes.[131]

In certain respects, the BFT accord is more ambitious than a multilateral agreement is likely to be. For example, there is no consensus on the multilateral use of binding arbitration in dispute settlement, and the bilateral arrangements go further than anything feasible in the GATT in this area. Nevertheless, the most important agricultural commodities that the United States and Canada export—grains and oilseeds—are sent primarily to third countries. Fundamental agricultural trade issues, including the use of agricultural subsidies, therefore must be dealt with in multilateral fora where major competitors such as the European Community are included. The United States and Canada are simply unwilling to make substantial concessions to each other in these areas before third countries have also offered concessions.

Another important variable affecting the BFT issue is the interdependence between the United States and Canada which led the two countries to seek this means of confronting some of their bilateral and multilateral trade problems. However, many of the variables contributing to bilateral trade protectionism, such as the U.S. balance of trade problems and the increase in competition and surpluses, were factors in limiting the scope of the BFT agricultural provisions. These factors have also contributed to producer dissatisfaction with the provisions included in the accord. Political-security objectives played a minor role in regard to the BFT issue, but even here some differences emerged in discussion of the provision on U.S. sugar imports.

Two other important variables are the relative size of the two countries' economies overall and of their agricultural economies. Regarding the former variable, the National Farmers' Union expressed the concerns of some Canadians that Canada would be integrated into a North American economy dominated by the United States. Regarding the latter variable, Canadian producers of some commodities have feared "the potential of their large trading partner to drown them in a sea of production surpluses."[132] However, the hog/pork and potato disputes demonstrate that American producers in particular regions can also feel threatened by their Canadian counterparts. Producer groups are obviously going to define success in achieving their agricultural trade objectives in more commodity-specific and regional terms than their national leaders. The U.S. trade representative described the BFT accord as a "win-win Agreement," and he criticized those "who will seek to identify winners and losers" as taking a narrow approach.[133] Nevertheless, it is certainly understandable why producer groups in both countries would be concerned with their own immediate gains and losses arising from the free trade agreement.

8

Conclusion

International relations and foreign policy specialists have written numerous studies on the Canadian-American relationship. However, they have devoted surprisingly little attention to interactions between the two countries in the food and agricultural area. This book is designed to fill a gap in the literature by focusing on U.S.-Canadian agricultural trade relations from the perspective of international politics. Since many agricultural trade issues cannot be examined solely in bilateral terms, primary emphasis has been placed on issues involving third countries, such as pricing, export subsidies, surplus disposal, and export credits. Nevertheless, I have also discussed some major issues which are strictly bilateral, including agricultural trade barriers and the bilateral free trade agreement. Most of this book deals with Canadian-American relations from the 1950s to the 1980s, but earlier periods were discussed in some chapters to provide historical background. The analytical framework draws upon several theoretical approaches, and a number of independent and dependent variables are examined (see Table 8-1). This chapter provides some conclusions regarding the combined as well as individual effects of the independent variables and the interactions among the four dependent variables. Finally, suggestions are offered for further areas of study.

CONFLICT AND CO-OPERATION IN THE BILATERAL RELATIONSHIP

The first two dependent variables, *Canadian-American co-operation and conflict*, are discussed together because there are often such close linkages between them. *Supply in the world market* is one of the independent variables that has had a major effect on the level of co-operation and conflict. This variable is

TABLE 8- I

CANADIAN-AMERICAN AGRICULTURAL TRADE RELATIONS: VARIABLES

Independent Variables

Environmental
U.S. balance of payments
Political-security objectives
Relative economic size
Bilateral interdependence

Agricultural
Supply in world market
Relative size of agricultural economies
Conflict in agricultural trade
Competition in agricultural trade
Strength of the agricultural trade regime

Dependent Variables

Bilateral conflict
Bilateral co-operation
Strategies to achieve agricultural trade objectives
Ability to achieve agricultural trade objectives

---

cyclical in nature, although surpluses in relation to effective demand (or demand backed by purchasing power) were far more common than shortages during the period of study. Indeed, surplus capacity has been a chronic problem in U.S. and Canadian agriculture. It stems from a variety of factors, including the increase in output resulting from technological advances, the slow rate of growth of per capita consumption of farm products, the immobility of human and physical resources involved with agriculture, and the unpredictable and often uncontrollable changes in supply and demand for farm products.[1] Most theoretical studies on surplus capacity have focused on manufacturing industries, but my findings confirm the views of these studies that conflict is more likely during surplus periods.[2] This was clearly the case in Canadian-American agricultural trade relations in the 1950s and 1960s and in the late 1970s and 1980s. American surplus disposal and export subsidy programs and U.S. and Canadian export credit innovations were normally developed during surplus periods, and they were often a source of contention in the bilateral relationship. Surpluses also contributed to pressures for trade protectionism in both countries, which frequently led to retaliation and conflict.

The early to mid-1970s was the only major shortage period, and it was a time of relatively low conflict in bilateral agricultural trade relations. Thus, export credit was not a contentious issue during this period, and the United States suspended its controversial export subsidies, tied sales, and barter agreements since they were no longer needed.[3] The tensions that did occur at this time tended to result from American efforts to benefit from the shortage situation by expanding its market share. However, U.S. aggressiveness during the shortage period can be explained by the operation of two other independent variables: *competition in agricultural trade* and the U.S. *balance of payments*. Competition increased in the late 1960s, and it contributed to the breakdown of the 1967 International Grains Arrangement (IGA). France played an important role in undercutting the IGA's minimum prices, and the European Community's protectionist Common Agricultural Policy (which came into effect for grains in July 1967) was a source of growing tension. The U.S. balance of payments situation was also worsening in the 1970s, and the country had its first balance of trade deficit in the twentieth century in 1971. President Richard Nixon imposed a 10 per cent import surcharge to deal with these problems, and Canada responded with its Third Option policy (see Chapter 1). Under the circumstances, it is remarkable that there were so few disputes in bilateral *agricultural* trade at this time, and a major reason for the lack of conflict was the existence of foodgrain shortages.[4]

However, when surpluses re-emerged in the late 1970s, the increase in competition and the U.S. balance of payments problems had a far more drastic effect. The tensions developing from the late 1970s resulted not only from surpluses *per se*, but also from the instability in supply, exports, and world prices. Thus, Robert Paarlberg has noted that "boom and bust global macroeconomic instability has been a fact of life since 1971 when the 'Bretton Woods' system of fixed international currency exchange rates finally collapsed" and that "farm markets . . . have borne much of the burden of this collapse."[5] During the 1970s shortage period, a number of American grain farmers had invested heavily in land and equipment in the expectation that agricultural prices would remain high. When surpluses re-emerged, competition was greater than it had been in the 1960s, and many of these farmers faced financial hardship. One result was the establishment of the American Agriculture Movement (AAM). The AAM was the strongest U.S. farm protest group in recent years, and it blockaded Canadian livestock shipments to the western United States for about one month.[6]

As the surpluses persisted in the 1980s, American antidumping and countervailing duty (CVD) cases in agriculture increased, the Export Enhancement Program was established, and the stage was set for a U.S.-EC agricultural trade war. Protectionism in Canada also increased during this period as a number of antidumping duties (and one countervailing duty) were imposed on American agricultural products. The Canadian duties, however, were levied primarily on commodities that were of marginal importance to the United States. Furthermore, American protectionism had far more serious implications for Canada than Canadian protectionism had for the United States. This was primarily the result of the effects of the independent variables involving relative size.

Relative economic size and *the relative size of the two countries' agricultural economies* are variables that frequently contributed to conflict in the bilateral relationship. The size and diversity of the American agricultural economy have often been a source of massive surpluses, and the overall size and capacity of the U.S. economy provided the means to dispose of those surpluses. In the 1950s and 1960s, the United States engaged in a wide array of surplus disposal activities, including agricultural barter and tied sales. Canada simply lacked the resources to emulate these practices and repeatedly maintained that the United States was infringing on its commercial markets. As U.S. balance of payments problems increased in the 1960s, it focused more on surplus disposal activities that provided hard currency benefits (see Chapters 2 and 5). The PL 480 program therefore shifted its focus to more affluent LDCs (less-developed countries) that were also targets for Canadian commercial sales, which merely heightened the tensions in the bilateral relationship.

When surpluses re-emerged in the late 1970s, the United States adopted a succession of export practices that were beyond the reach of the Canadian treasury. Since the U.S. balance of payments situation had worsened, these were more in the realm of "grey-area" transactions than the PL 480 sales of the 1950s and 1960s, and they were therefore more threatening to Canada. After developing intermediate and blended credit programs, the United States turned to the Export Enhancement Program (EEP) in 1985. The EEP was aimed at a competitor of comparable economic size, the European Community, but Canada (along with other smaller countries in the Cairns Group) felt that it suffered most from this "contest between giants."

The variables pertaining to relative economic size also contributed to conflict in cross-border trade. The United States was a much larger producer than Canada of many agricultural commodities, such as beef, pork, and corn (discussed in Chapter 7). Canadian producers were therefore often fearful of being flooded by American imports, even in cases when they (temporarily) had a balance of trade surplus. The disparity in output was greatest in the case of corn, with the United States producing thirty-four times as much as Canada in 1986 (see Table 7-1). Corn was also one of the products benefiting from the Export Enhancement Program, and it is no accident that Canada's first countervail action against the United States involved this commodity.[7] The Canadian market in fact was relatively insignificant for American corn producers, and the intense U.S. reaction to the corn CVD resulted primarily from third-country issues. Thus, the U.S. government was extremely concerned that other larger competitors (particularly the European Community) might follow the Canadian example and launch their own CVD cases against the United States.

The strength of the agricultural trade regime is a variable that changed little during the period of study. For example, GATT rules on import restrictions (Article XI) and export subsidies (Article XVI) treated agriculture as an exception in the 1950s, and agriculture was still considered to be different in the late 1980s. Many bilateral conflicts developed over "grey-area" transactions that were neither fully commercial nor fully concessional, and the regime norms and rules provided little guidance in this area. For example, the United States maintained that its CCC credit (in the 1960s) and its intermediate and blended credit (in the 1970s and 1980s) were commercial, but Canada argued that they were concessional. On the other hand, the U.S. was sceptical of Canada's claims that its own practices (such as credit sales to the Communist countries) were fully commercial. Bilateral disputes also arose over the legality of certain practices (such as U.S. tied sales), the definition and measurement of terms (such as a trade-distorting subsidy), and the ideological preferences of each country (such as the U.S. opposition to "state trading" by the Canadian Wheat Board). In each of these cases, the regime was of little assistance in resolving the differences. While the agricultural trade regime changed little, the problems with it became more apparent as the U.S. balance of payments deficit increased, competition and conflict escalated, and surpluses re-emerged in the late 1970s and 1980s. The marked rise in the number of trade relief cases, the increase in protectionism, and the U.S.-EC export subsidy contest all pointed to the fact that regime norms and rules for dispute settlement and for agricultural import and export practices were inadequate in resolving bilateral and multilateral conflicts.[8]

Political-security objectives was a variable that had mixed and complex effects. In the 1950s and 1960s, the United States normally did not sell grain to the People's Republic of China (PRC), the USSR, and some other Soviet bloc states, primarily for political-security reasons.[9] This policy actually contributed to Canadian-American co-operation during a time when PL 480 sales were infringing on Canadian markets in Western Europe and the LDCs. There was a tacit division of markets, with Canada's increased sales to the Communist states partly compensating for its losses to the United States elsewhere. However, there were some less significant cases where the United States became actively involved in exporting to certain countries for political-security reasons, and in these markets competition with Canada increased. For example, Yugoslavia, Israel, and Poland were major recipients of PL 480 food aid in the 1950s and 1960s, and in each case there were important strategic-security reasons.[10] Canada had been extending credit grain sales to all three of these countries, but it simply could not compete with the more generous PL 480 terms (see Chapter 6). Nevertheless, the Communist countries that were *not* importing grain from the United States in the 1950s and 1960s were far more important and numerous, and the primary effect of the East-West factor on Canadian-American relations during this period was positive.

In the 1970s, the Americans began to sell to the major Communist countries largely for *economic* reasons. Thus, the Soviet Union became eligible for CCC export credits in 1971 (the same year as the first U.S. balance of trade deficit), and China was offered CCC credit beginning in February 1972. As an American agricultural economist has stated,

> The environment of U.S. foreign policy has changed dramatically in the last decade or two. As a consequence the focus of U.S. foreign policy has shifted from political and military goals toward economic goals, which are no longer being sacrificed as readily to the other two. The reasons for the greater importance of economic goals are found in the fact that the United States is no longer the single dominant economic power in the world. The United States has as well moved from trade surplus to deficit and from being the world's largest creditor to its largest debtor nation. Economic goals become far more important when you get into this much economic trouble.[11]

The convergence of American and Canadian markets contributed to a heightening of competition and, when surpluses re-emerged in the late 1970s, to greater possibilities for conflict. For example, Canada vigorously opposed the extension of the Export Enhancement Program to the Soviet Union, but the United States declared the USSR eligible for the program in August 1986 (see Chapter 4). The United States, of course, continues to attach more importance than Canada to East-West issues. The U.S. position is demonstrated by such actions as the embargo in response to the Soviet invasion of Afghanistan, the delay in negotiating a new U.S.-USSR grains agreement in response to the imposition of martial law in Poland, and the delay in extending the EEP to the Soviet Union and China. Indeed, in November 1986 an official with the Continental Grain Company maintained that

> each of our last four Presidents, including the incumbent, has found a way

to embargo grain shipments to the Soviet Union . . . to use shipments of food as a tool of foreign policy. We in the grain trade obviously disagree. Our friends in Argentina and France and Canada and Australia disagree.[12]

Nevertheless, the United States is no longer willing to remove itself from the major Communist markets on a longer-term basis, and this change has provided a new source of competition and conflict in Canadian-American agricultural trade relations. A clear example of the intent to limit the influence of political-security factors is the Congressional actions taken after the 1980 U.S. embargo against the Soviet Union. The Agriculture and Food Act of 1981 makes the imposition of a selective embargo (i.e., an embargo that does not affect all commodities exported to a country) an expensive process since farmers must receive high levels of compensation. Several statutes are also designed to protect the sanctity of contracts signed before an embargo is established. Furthermore, the 1985 Food Security Act states that agricultural embargoes should be imposed only in periods of national emergency and that even in these cases pre-existing contracts should not be tampered with.[13]

There is yet another issue to consider in regard to the political-security variable. When the United States applied political-security goals to itself alone, it often contributed to bilateral co-operation; but when it expected Canada to adhere to these objectives, conflict sometimes resulted. Canada is far more dependent on trade than the United States, and exports accounted for about 27.3 per cent of its gross domestic product in 1986 (compared with 6.7 per cent for the U.S.). Thus, economic objectives were always more important in Canadian trade policy, and Canada sometimes reacted harshly when the U.S. pressured it to emphasize political-security concerns. For example, in the early 1960s, the United States (through its Trading with the Enemy Act and Foreign Assets Control legislation) interfered with Canadian purchases in the U.S. and Canada that were needed for the shipment of wheat flour to China. The Canadian government responded by protesting against the extraterritorial application of American law. There is also evidence that the Canada-U.S. quarterly meetings were suspended (in 1963) partly because of U.S. objections to Canada's pricing of wheat sales to the Soviet Union and China. Almost two decades later, Canada complied (more or less) with American calls for a Soviet embargo in response to the 1979 invasion of Afghanistan. However, bilateral tensions eventually developed over U.S. efforts to recoup its losses with increased sales to China and over Canada's decision to end participation in the embargo in late 1980 (see Chapters 2 and 6). Instances of conflict resulting from American efforts to impose its political-security objectives on Canada were, nevertheless, infrequent. In the 1950s and 1960s, there was usually co-operation based on a division of markets, but this co-operative framework broke down for the economic reasons mentioned above.

While a number of the independent variables have been discussed, I have not yet referred to one that has significant effects on the others: *the interdependence between the two states*. As with political-security objectives, interdependence had mixed and complex effects. In Chapter 1, evidence was presented that Canadian-American interdependence in trade (and a number of other areas) steadily increased during the period of study. Raymond Hopkins and Donald Puchala maintain that when interdependence increases, states become more vulnerable to "disrupting events" and are pressured to respond in some manner. This response can be either defensive and conflictual or co-operative in nature.[14]

In some instances, interdependence contributed to Canadian-American conflict in the agricultural trade area. For example, I examined three cases in Chapter 7, related to trade in beef and cattle, hogs and pork, and corn. These commodities were selected because Canadian-American disputes involving them were particularly salient. However, these were also commodities in which there was a high degree of interdependence in trade. This strengthens the thesis of some authors that U.S.-Canadian agricultural trade disputes sometimes arise "because trade is relatively unhindered by restrictions and the products flow to the best return."[15] In each of the three cases examined, producers in Canada or the United States felt vulnerable to cross-border imports, and their complaints led to the erection of trade barriers and/or to a countervailing duty case. Conflict resulted because producers in the other country reacted strongly to this attempt to limit their exports.

The asymmetrical nature of Canadian-American interdependence was an additional factor that sometimes contributed to conflict. As discussed, the United States adopted a number of policies to promote its exports, extending from PL 480 practices in the 1950s and 1960s to intermediate credit, blended credit, and the Export Enhancement Program in the late 1970s and 1980s. In most cases, these programs were not aimed specifically at Canada, and in some instances (e.g., the EEP) they were clearly directed against the European Community. Nevertheless, Canada is highly vulnerable to American agricultural trade policies toward third countries, and U.S. programs such as the EEP threatened Canadian markets and contributed to bilateral tensions and/or conflict. In strictly bilateral trade, the asymmetry in Canadian-American interdependence contributed to the "politics of attraction and distance." While Canada often sought the economic gains associated with closer ties with the United States, it also was concerned about its high degree of dependence and vulnerability vis-à-vis its larger neighbour. These concerns were frequently associated with the rise of Canadian nationalism and with the heightening of conflict in the bilateral relationship.[16]

Although conflict sometimes results from interdependence, in the Canadian-American relationship interdependence has normally been more important as a source of co-operation. Indeed, I hypothesized earlier that conflict may induce interdependent states to seek new forms of consultation and co-operation to resolve their differences, and there is considerable evidence that such developments occurred in the agricultural trade area. In this sense, I have viewed *conflict* as an independent variable and co-operation as a dependent variable.[17] Many of the Canadian-American groupings discussed in Chapter 3, for example, were originally formed (at least in part) to deal with bilateral conflict. These included the Ministerial Committee on Trade and Economic Affairs, the Consultative Committee on Grain Marketing, the Quarterly Meetings on Wheat and Related Matters, and the Interparliamentary Group. In every case, these groups also eventually served as fora for discussing joint policies and co-operative ventures. Thus, the quarterly meetings were established to resolve problems arising out of U.S. surplus disposal activities, but they also became a forum for exchanging views and co-ordinating policies on the GATT, the World Food Program, the International Wheat Agreements, and the European Community's Common Agricultural Policy.

Interdependence was a factor in American and Canadian efforts to seek co-operative solutions not only to bilateral conflict but also to conflict in the multilateral trading system. For example, the Canadian-American duopoly was a "surrogate system" designed to compensate for the weakness of norms and regulations in the agricultural trade regime.[18] The duopoly played a major role in limiting conflict in the international wheat trade by regulating supply, stabilizing prices, and promoting food security. The success of the duopoly depended upon American and Canadian co-operation in controlling domestic production, maintaining stocks, and supporting the International Wheat Agreements (see Chapter 4). Export credit was another area where the United States and Canada repeatedly sought co-operative solutions to competition and conflict in the absence of adequate regime norms and rules. Thus, in the 1950s and 1960s, both countries eventually accepted each other's credit innovations as legitimate, which contributed to a degree of consensus on definitions of commercial versus concessional credit in the global food regime (see Chapter 6).

Finally, there were numerous instances where interdependence had a moderating effect on American and Canadian actions and helped to prevent serious disputes from arising. For example, the United States altered some of its PL 480 barter and tied sales techniques in response to Canadian complaints, and it often provided assurances that U.S. programs were not aimed at Canada and would not interfere with Canadian export markets.[19] While Canada extended credit sales to China in the 1960s, it was somewhat responsive to American views regarding the terms on which credit was offered, and it deferred to the United States on the issue of political recognition. Furthermore, Canada was often more reticent than other countries—such as Australia—to strongly criticize the U.S. in multilateral and plurilateral groupings such as the Cairns Group. This difference can be explained by the fact that the Canadian-American relationship is more interdependent than the relationship between Australia and the United States.[20]

However, the effect of interdependence in promoting co-operation in the agricultural trade area should not be overestimated. Indeed, countries are normally reluctant to recognize their interdependence when they are pressured to alter their domestic agricultural programs. The difference in attitudes toward agricultural and nonagricultural trade issues is clearly illustrated by the responses to the Canada-U.S. free trade (BFT) agreement.

The BFT accord was generally designed to expand economic ties between the two states and to promote co-operative means of dealing with both bilateral and multilateral conflicts. Since Canadian-American interdependence has increased substantially over the years, the leaders in both countries were prepared to take this major step. Their support for it contrasted with the Canadian decisions in 1911 and 1948 to eschew free trade. The agricultural provisions in the BFT agreement, however, are extremely limited, and even these are controversial. As discussed in Chapter 7, many agricultural producers on both sides of the border were opposed to the agreement. In 1983, Dale Hathaway wrote that "no sovereign country is willing to put its domestic food and fiber policy forward as a candidate for outside negotiation and determination," and this attitude (though it had changed *somewhat* in the late 1980s) inevitably affected the negotiators.[21] However, the agricultural provisions in the BFT accord are also limited because the most important issues (such as export subsidies) involve third countries. It was hoped that the decision to include agriculture in the accord would contribute to progress in the GATT Uruguay Round, but it is evident that countries are still reluctant "to alter national programs to make international agreements function."[22]

In conclusion, a number of the independent variables have contributed to increased Canadian-American conflict in agricultural trade: the American balance of payments and trade problems, the surpluses in many products traded, the declining role of U.S. political-security objectives, the disparity in size of the two countries' economies (agricultural and overall), and the weak agricultural trade regime. However, Canadian-American economic interdependence has continued to increase, and there are costly effects (especially to Canada) when the relationship is disrupted. Furthermore, the most important Canadian-U.S. agricultural trade issues involve third countries. The United States and Canada are aware that they *both* can lose from surpluses overhanging the world market, from increased competition and conflict with important actors such as the European Community, and from the weakness of the agricultural trade regime. Thus, Canadian-American interdependence has often served to promote co-operation between the two states. Bilateral co-operation is, nevertheless, no longer as effective in dealing with agricultural trade conflicts as it was in the days of the Canada-U.S. duopoly. It is therefore necessary to discuss the strategies the United States and Canada use and the capabilities of the two countries in pursuing their agricultural trade objectives.

STRATEGIES TO ACHIEVE AGRICULTURAL TRADE OBJECTIVES

Four major objectives related to agricultural trade have been examined in this study: *to restore, maintain, or increase market share; to export commodities at remunerative prices; to maintain or achieve a more favourable agricultural trade balance*; and *to limit imports of supplementary agricultural products*. States are particularly interested in controlling imports of supplementary commodities since they are directly competitive with those produced domestically. However, imports may also be regulated more generally for balance of payments reasons. This study has provided evidence that the United States and Canada sometimes attach different priorities to these four objectives and that the priorities of both countries have changed over time. The issue of priorities is discussed when I assess the ability of each country to achieve its objectives.

The United States and Canada may employ unilateral, bilateral, plurilateral, and multilateral strategies to achieve their agricultural trade objectives.[23] Critical variables affecting the strategies adopted in the 1950s and 1960s were *relative economic size, the relative size of the two countries' agricultural economies, the weakness of the agricultural trade regime*, and *supply in the world market*. The United States often chose to, and was able to, adopt unilateral strategies to promote its agricultural export objectives during the 1950s and 1960s. As the leading country in terms of gross national product, grain exports, and overall food exports, it often adopted policies for largely domestic reasons and neither sought nor felt the need for collaboration with others. Indeed, the United States played a major role in limiting GATT regulations with regard to agricultural import restrictions and export subsidies, primarily because it would not permit regime interference with its price support, export subsidy, and surplus disposal measures. The United States also obtained an unusually broad waiver from its GATT obligations in 1955, which further undercut the organization's role in regulating agricultural trade. These early U.S. policies contributed to the weakness of the agricultural trade regime and thus provided legitimacy to unilateral actions by others—such as the European Community—in subsequent years. To export its surpluses in the 1950s and 1960s the United States (primarily under its PL 480 program) introduced a series of unilateral innovations, such as local currency loans, long-term dollar credits, tied sales, and agricultural barter.

In view of its smaller economic size and capacities (both generally and in agriculture), Canada could not consider emulating many of the American PL 480 practices. Such measures as tied sales and agricultural barter represented a threat to Canadian agricultural export objectives in the 1950s and 1960s, and Canada resorted to multilateral and plurilateral strategies to express its grievances. Canada preferred to convey its views in organizations such as the GATT and the FAO's Consultative Subcommittee on Surplus Disposal (CSD), where it could seek allies and thus more effectively pressure the United States to alter its policies. As a result, Canada wanted these organizations to function effectively, and it criticized the GATT exceptions for agriculture and the U.S. waiver from its GATT obligations. Canada also was a strong supporter of CSD discussions and reports on tied sales and barter in the 1950s and 1960s since they focused multilateral attention on American export practices. For example, in 1963 Canada and the Netherlands suggested that the CSD should form a consensus on the legitimacy of tied sales, and this proposal led to the creation of a working group on the subject. After the first tied sales report was completed, Canada supported the creation of a second working group to continue examining the issue. In addition, Canada supported the establishment of a CSD working group on agricultural barter.

The CSD has less legal authority and is less demanding than the GATT (see Chapter 3), and the United States was willing to co-operate to some extent with the subcommittee. The *interdependence* variable certainly played a role here, and the United States often tried to accommodate the demands of Canada and other CSD members. For example, while the U.S. had serious reservations about the CSD working group on tied sales, it agreed to provide the group with a substantial amount of information on its practices. However, the U.S. was reluctant to have multilateral bodies closely scrutinize its agricultural trade policies. Thus, it prevented the CSD from setting up a second working group on tied sales, and it refused to provide the subcommittee with detailed information on its barter transactions.

Since international organizations could not deal adequately with Canada's concerns about U.S. surplus disposal practices, Canada resorted to bilateral as well as multilateral strategies. Bilateral strategies were also consistent with

Canada's tendency to seek exemptions from U.S. economic measures that had a detrimental effect on other states. For example, in the 1950s and 1960s, Canada proposed that the bilateral Ministerial Committee on Trade and Economic Affairs be established to deal with U.S. protectionism; that the Consultative Committee on Grain Marketing and the Quarterly Meetings be created to discuss U.S. surplus disposal policies; and that an Interparliamentary Group be formed to sensitize the U.S. Congress to Canadian concerns. It is significant that the United States agreed to the establishment of these bilateral groupings largely because of the interdependence between the two states. The United States clearly felt that its close ties with Canada necessitated the maintenance of a co-operative relationship.

Although the United States was more inclined than Canada to adopt unilateral strategies, under certain conditions Canada also resorted to unilateral actions. Despite its protests over the 1955 U.S. GATT waiver, Canada acted unilaterally (as did other countries) in limiting agricultural imports, and both the U.S. and Canada contributed to the agricultural import barriers that were erected between them. In its export trade, Canada adopted multilateral and bilateral strategies in areas (such as surplus disposal and export subsidies) where it could not compete with the United States. However, in areas where it was more competitive, Canada was not averse to unilateralism. For example, Canada was often competitive with the United States in providing agricultural export credits and credit guarantees since less funding was normally required. The Canadian government therefore introduced the three-year "Polish credit terms" in the 1950s, took the initiative in providing credit to a number of Communist markets, and introduced three- to ten-year Expanded Credit in the late 1960s (see Chapter 6). Nevertheless, Canada could not compete over the long term with U.S. credit programs that involved grey-area or concessional transactions, and in these cases (as in the case of U.S. surplus disposal) Canada turned to multilateralism. In the 1960s, for example, Canada criticized U.S. Title IV long-term credit in the CSD, and it encouraged the United States to subject its CCC credit sales to CSD procedures. As a smaller country that is extremely dependent on exports, Canada *usually* felt that its agricultural trade objectives could best be achieved through multilateral and bilateral strategies.

While Canada turned to unilateralism under certain circumstances, there were also conditions under which the United States expressed a preference for bilateralism and multilateralism. Thus, the United States was willing to join with Canada in pursuing common objectives vis-à-vis third countries when such joint efforts seemed to be in U.S. interests. A prime example of this co-operation was the Canadian-American duopoly, which sometimes took a plurilateral form when Australia and Argentina participated. As the largest wheat exporters, the U.S. and Canada had a common interest in controlling surpluses and stabilizing commercial prices. They therefore agreed to keep large wheat reserves off the commercial market, and they endorsed a series of international wheat agreements with pricing provisions. The United States and Canada also had common interests vis-à-vis the European Community, which contributed to their support for multilateralism in agriculture. While the United States was largely responsible for the GATT's ineffectiveness in agriculture in the 1950s, the emergence of the EC as a major competitor demonstrated to the U.S. that unilateral strategies could be dangerous when employed by others. The U.S. and Canada therefore insisted that agriculture be included in the GATT Kennedy and Tokyo Rounds and supported a decrease of EC agricultural trade protectionism.

However, as the largest agricultural exporter, the United States continued to feel that unilateral strategies were often in its self-interest. For example, in the 1960s several variables came into play that led to American dissatisfaction with the duopoly. These were the *U.S. balance of payments* and *competition and conflict in agricultural trade*. Under the duopoly, the United States was the residual supplier in the commercial wheat market (see Chapter 4), but it became less willing to assume this role as its balance of payments problems increased. Intensified competition in the late 1960s further contributed to U.S. dissatisfaction with the duopoly and to its eventual demise. When grain surpluses re-emerged in the late 1970s, Canada felt that the wheat exporting states should consider establishing an exporters' pricing agreement, which would be similar *in some respects* to the old duopoly.[24] However, the United States was less committed than Canada to this plurilateral strategy, and a pricing agreement was not concluded. There were a number of reasons for this difference in attitude, but the disparity in size of the American and Canadian economies (and agricultural economies) was a major factor. The United States was less dependent on the maintenance of international prices because of its large domestic market and its income and price supports, wheat was less important to the U.S. since it was also a leading exporter of coarse grains and oilseeds, and U.S. government officials felt that a wheat cartel supported by higher American prices would permit other exporters to undercut those prices.

The United States was also more enthusiastic about applying multilateral regulations to the European Community's and Japan's agricultural policies than to its own. For example, the U.S. began two lawsuits in the mid-1970s, claiming that EC agricultural trade measures were in violation of GATT obligations. The United States had refused to relinquish its waiver *from those same obligations*, but it "defended its arguably two-faced legal posture by claiming that, if the EC wanted the same legal freedoms as the United States, it too should seek a waiver."[25] The American attitude towards the CSD as well as the GATT in the 1970s could be characterized as ambivalent. When Canada insisted that the U.S. Intermediate Credit Program should be under CSD auspices, with provisions made for establishing usual marketing requirements (UMRs), the United States would not agree to apply the CSD procedures. Instead, the U.S. tried to shift discussion of its intermediate credit from the CSD to the Organization for Economic Cooperation and Development (OECD). However, the OECD has less demanding requirements than the CSD and has no procedure for establishing UMRs. Canada therefore opposed the U.S. proposal and felt that nothing should be done to undermine the authority of the CSD (see Chapter 6). One could, of course, argue that it has always been easier for Canada to support multilateral scrutiny of national programs because (unlike the case of the U.S.) Canadian programs are rarely the main focus of multilateral attention.

In the late 1970s and 1980s, the United States also demonstrated a decided preference for unilateralism in its agricultural import policies. Increased protectionism and trade relief actions resulted from a wide variety of factors, including the overall U.S. trade deficit, the increased competition in agricultural trade, the high value of the U.S. dollar, the problems of U.S. farmers stemming from the re-emergence of surpluses, and perceptions of unfair trading practices by other exporters. While Canadian protectionist actions also increased during this period, Canada was more dependent on the U.S. market and thus was more willing to contemplate bilateral solutions. For example, Canada responded to U.S. restrictions on meat imports by developing a Meat Import Act patterned after the American legislation. It hoped that "the similarity between these two import control systems" would "help prevent disruptions" in U.S.-Canadian beef and cattle trade.[26] However, Canada's most important bilateral strategy in the 1980s was its support for the bilateral free trade (BFT) agreement. As American protectionism increased, Canadian officials felt that this would be the best means of gaining more assured access to the U.S. market. While the U.S. government was also supportive of the BFT accord, it did not share Canada's preference for a strong binational dispute settlement mechanism. The United States was insistent on maintaining its unilateral prerogatives to retaliate, and a stronger dispute settlement provision would have raised major constitutional questions in the U.S. Congress.

Both the United States and Canada supported an expanded GATT role in liberalizing agricultural trade in the 1980s, as was evident in the Uruguay Round. Thus, in July 1987 the U.S. government proposed that all trade-distorting farm subsidies be eliminated by the end of the century, and the Canadian government was generally supportive of this proposal. As the costs of their agricultural policies escalated in response to heightened competition and growing surpluses, the two countries felt that a downgrading of subsidies would ease their balance of payments problems and permit them to benefit from their natural advantages in agriculture. The global interdependence in agriculture had also become more evident, and it was felt that a co-operative solution had to be found to the serious conflicts in this area. Agriculture was included in the BFT accord largely to set a bilateral example that it was hoped the multilateral system would emulate. Nevertheless, the United States also relied on unilateralism to achieve its multilateral objectives and tried to force the European Community to the bargaining table with its Export Enhancement Program. As usual, Canada opted instead for a group strategy and joined with other members of the Cairns Group in seeking a middle path between the extreme positions of the EC and the United States.

In conclusion, some interesting parallels can be drawn between the dependent variable *strategies to achieve agricultural trade objectives* and the *conflict and co-operation* variables. Agriculture is by nature an interdependence issue (see Chapter 1), but the increased competition and conflict in agricultural trade in recent years has made this fact more evident. While conflict increased, so did the attempts to develop new forms of co-operation. Thus, the Uruguay round marked the first time that *serious* consideration was given to strengthening the agricultural trade regime. The increase in conflict, on the one hand, and the more urgent search for co-operative arrangements, on the other, were reflected in the strategies adopted by the United States and Canada. Never before had the U.S. employed such a broad range of unilateral, bilateral, and multilateral strategies so vigorously. For example, the unilateral Export Enhancement Program, the bilateral free trade accord, and the multilateral proposal on trade-distorting agricultural subsidies were all elements of American policy aimed at achieving U.S. agricultural trade objectives. Because of its smaller economic size and capacities, Canada was less inclined than the U.S. to try unilateralism. Yet, Canada was also employing a wide variety of strategies, involving the BFT accord, the Cairns Group, and the GATT. The multiple strategies adopted in the late 1980s were a reflection of the crisis situation in agricultural trade and the urgent search for a resolution of outstanding problems.

ABILITY TO ACHIEVE AGRICULTURAL TRADE OBJECTIVES

The discussion of this dependent variable is extremely complex because the United States and Canada attach different priorities to the four agricultural trade objectives and because each country's priorities change over time.[27] A state's ability to achieve agricultural trade objectives can also be affected by the relative importance it attaches to these objectives vis-à-vis other goals (domestic as well as foreign). As discussed, an in-depth examination of domestic issues is beyond the scope of this study, and the independent variables examined are primarily systemic in nature.

In earlier years, American agricultural trade objectives often took second place to other objectives. When the United States enacted the 1933 and 1938 Agricultural Adjustment Acts, creating price supports and supply controls, it basically "forfeited its export markets for price supported commodities." At this time, "domestic farm policy behavior dictated that there be no concern for international trade in these commodities."[28] In refusing to trade with the major Communist states during the 1950s and 1960s, the United States also showed a willingness to subsume its agricultural export objectives to *political-security objectives*. Since agricultural trade was given a lower priority at this time, the United States did little to strengthen regime norms and rules in this area. Indeed, it was largely through U.S. pressure that agriculture was treated as an exception in the GATT, and in 1955 the United States was granted a major waiver from its GATT obligations. As for priorities among its agricultural export objectives, the U.S. had an interest in maintaining commercial wheat prices. However, it was willing to provide large amounts of concessional exports in the 1950s and 1960s to stabilize the commercial market, and market share was given a higher priority than the price of its wheat exports.

The American policies at this time had both negative and positive effects on Canada's ability to achieve its own objectives. As a smaller country highly dependent on commercial exports, Canada complained that the PL 480 program was undercutting its prices in some markets. The United States was somewhat constrained in the use of PL 480 in view of its *interdependence* with Canada (and other competitors), and it altered some of its more objectionable surplus disposal practices. However, the U.S. continued to employ such methods as tied sales and barter over Canadian objections until the shortage period of the 1970s. Canadian export objectives were also threatened by *the weakness of the agricultural trade regime*. For example, in 1953–54, the United States induced Canada to limit its cross-border exports of oats (under threat of a U.S. quota) and imposed quantitative import restrictions on Canadian rye. While the minister of trade and commerce viewed these measures as "contradictory of the principles upon which trade has been developed between Canada and the United States," there was little that Canada could do about the matter.[29]

Nevertheless, in a number of respects Canadian agricultural export objectives were furthered by American policies. From the 1950s to the early 1960s, the United States accounted for about 40 per cent of global wheat exports. However, the U.S. was not an aggressive competitor for *commercial* markets at this time, and Canada was therefore not seriously affected by the *relative size* variables.[30] High U.S. support prices bolstered the prices Canada received for its exports, and PL 480 also strengthened commercial prices since it moved the massive U.S. surpluses largely through concessional channels. Since the United States was the largest grain exporter, its price supports became guidelines for Canada and other competitors in setting their own export prices. American farmers forfeited their stocks to the Commodity Credit Corporation when export prices fell below the support price, and Canada could therefore gain a competitive advantage by setting its own export prices just below the U.S. support level. Canada also benefited from the U.S. preoccupation with political-security objectives, and it was able to consolidate its markets in a number of Communist countries through a combination of export credits, credit guarantees, and long-term supply agreements.

Despite their divergent interests during the 1950s and 1960s, the United States and Canada also had a common interest in controlling agricultural surpluses and stabilizing commercial prices. As the two largest wheat exporters, they were quite successful in achieving these objectives through their duopolistic arrangement and the International Wheat Agreements. However, the duopoly depended primarily on American goodwill, and Canada (and other states) could do little to prevent the breakdown of the duopoly when the United States became dissatisfied with it. As *U.S. balance of payments problems* increased in the 1960s, it began to give more attention to the price of its exports as well as to its market share. The United States therefore enacted a number of measures in the 1960s to reduce agricultural expenditures and promote commercial exports. In "embracing export market development as the key to agricultural development," U.S. objectives became more similar to Canada's.[31] However, in view of their disparity in economic size, Canada had far more to fear from the entrance of the United States into its commercial markets. While American political-security objectives continued to be a positive factor for Canada throughout the 1960s, the Communist markets were inherently unstable. In fact, Canada became a net agricultural importer (for one year) in 1969 when the Soviet Union entered the commercial market as a wheat exporter.

In the late 1960s, the United States as well as Canada had concerns about maintaining market share as *competition increased*, and the breakdown of the 1967 International Grains Agreement raised concerns about stabilizing prices. With the onset of shortages in the 1970s, however, the two countries achieved their export pricing objectives in the absence of an effective agreement, and costly export promotion programs became less necessary. Nevertheless, the U.S. became preoccupied with *increasing* its market share during this period, which obviously represented a threat to Canadian objectives. Since the United States had a negative trade balance almost every year after 1971, it decided to build aggressively on its natural advantages in agriculture. This was also the period when the U.S. downgraded its political-security objectives (to some extent) and concluded several large export agreements with the major Communist markets. Although demand was strong during this period, Canada was understandably concerned about its future ability to promote its exports. Indeed, from 1970–71 to 1975–76, the American market share of global wheat exports increased from 36.5 to 47.4 per cent, while the Canadian share declined from 21.4 to 18.2 per cent.

With the re-emergence of *surpluses* in the late 1970s and 1980s, it became far more difficult for *both* the United States and Canada to achieve their market share and pricing objectives. Moreover, the United States now placed a much higher priority on these objectives because its dependence on agricultural exports had increased. While agricultural exports had accounted for about 13 per cent of total U.S. farm income in the 1960s, this figure rose to well over 25 per cent in the 1980s. The major problems for the United States and Canada in the 1980s stemmed from the instability of prices, declining markets, and increased competition.

The instability of grain prices resulted from a variety of factors, including macroeconomic instability following the collapse of the Bretton Woods system, the lack of co-operation among the major exporters, and the marked increase in the share of wheat exports going to the centrally planned economies and LDCs. The decline in markets resulted from large production increases in the European Community, China, and India and from problems the indebted LDCs had in paying for food imports. The increase in competition resulted primarily from the growing importance of the European Community, and there were few regime norms and rules to regulate its highly protectionist Common Agricultural Policy. The United States also had special problems stemming from its strong dollar and its high domestic support prices.

In contrast to the days of the duopoly, the United States and Canada were no longer able (or willing) to act as a surrogate system to limit surpluses and stabilize prices. The United States therefore resorted to unilateral measures to restore what it viewed as its fair market share. In pursuing this objective, the U.S. could depend on the massive size of its agricultural economy; and Canada, with its smaller agricultural resources, was clearly at a disadvantage. For example, "U.S. negotiators were apparently able to use U.S. domination in the corn market as leverage to increase the amounts of U.S. wheat the Soviets agreed to purchase" in 1983 U.S.-USSR long-term agreement. That they were able to do so was not surprising since the Soviet Union had depended on U.S. corn to maintain its livestock production since the early 1970s.[32] The United States also decided that its export objectives could best be achieved by directly confronting the European Community with its own export subsidy programs. In establishing the Export Enhancement Program, the United States decided to give priority to regaining its market share over export pricing objectives. Despite its balance of payments problems, the U.S. put aside its pricing objectives for the moment, on the assumption that the EC would eventually agree to alter its policies.

Unlike the PL 480 program in the 1950s and 1960s, the U.S. and EC export promotion programs in the 1980s were aimed directly at the commercial market, and the inevitable effect was a rapid decline in prices. Indeed, global wheat prices fell by about 45 per cent from 1981 to 1987, and export subsidies were a major factor.[33] As a smaller country, Canada was always more dependent than the United States (and the EC) on the price of its grain exports, and the U.S.-EC export subsidy war had serious consequences for the Canadian agricultural economy. Furthermore, the U.S. and EC were competing for exports to the major Communist markets, and U.S. political-security objectives no longer precluded its participation in these markets. Although Canadian exports to the USSR benefited from the U.S. embargo in response to the Afghanistan invasion, President Reagan clearly indicated that embargoes of this nature would not be repeated. Indeed, it is evident that the Afghanistan experience interfered with U.S. agricultural export objectives, and yet the embargo did not do significant harm to the Soviet Union.[34] The U.S. delay in extending the EEP to the Soviet Union resulted partly from political-security factors, but the eventual extension of the program was an indication that economic considerations now took priority. Canadian-American interdependence was still a factor, with the United States assuring Canada that its EEP was aimed only at the European Community and the U.S. and Canada jointly pressuring for agricultural trade reform at the GATT Uruguay Round. Yet, in the area of grain exports, U.S. interdependence with the EC had become more important than its interdependence with Canada, and any significant changes in American policy relied first and foremost on the actions of the Community. Canada attempted to affect U.S. and EC policies as a member of the Cairns Group, but there was uncertainty as to how much influence this group would exert over the long term.

American agricultural import as well as export objectives were more difficult to achieve in the late 1970s and 1980s, which inevitably affected the country's policies. U.S. producers of various commodities (non-agricultural as well as agricultural) had experienced growing trade problems, and they were a factor in the revision of the country's trade relief legislation. Thus, the rules and procedures were revised in the 1974 U.S. Trade Act and the 1979 Trade Agreements Act to permit producers to obtain trade relief more easily. American producers responded to these changes by filing many more antidumping and countervailing duty (CVD) petitions, and a large number of the petitions aimed at Canada involved agricultural commodities. These CVD cases are not surprising since the United States had become increasingly dissatisfied with its cross-border agricultural trade.

While the United States normally had a positive agricultural trade balance with Canada, it had a large trade deficit overall, which had a major influence on perceptions. Furthermore, the U.S. agricultural balance with Canada decreased from $1.5 billion in 1980 to $600 million in 1986. This decline stemmed from a number of factors, including the strength of the American dollar, the increase of Canadian imports from non-U.S. suppliers, the large Canadian trade surplus with the United States in live animals and meats, and the increase in Canadian production of supplementary products such as corn. Since the United States and Canada export a number of agricultural commodities almost exclusively to each other, it is not surprising that the complaints of many American producers were focused on their Canadian counterparts. Moreover, Canada is the largest supplier of supplementary agricultural exports to the United States, and the volume of some of these exports (such as pork) had increased substantially in recent years.

The increase in protectionism was, of course, not solely one-sided, and Canada concluded a number of trade relief cases against U.S. agricultural imports. Many Canadian producers were fearful of being flooded by imports from the much larger U.S. agricultural economy, and this concern was certainly a major factor in Canada's corn CVD case. However, Canada was also more dependent on exporting to the larger U.S. market, and the increase in American protectionism seriously threatened Canadian producers. As with the case of third-country exports, the norms and rules of the agricultural trade regime did little to insulate Canada from the rise in U.S. protectionism. Furthermore, the share of Canada's total exports going to the United States had increased from 65.7 per cent in 1971 to 75.2 per cent in 1985, and it was clear that a major change in policy was necessary. As discussed, the primary reason the Canadian government wanted the BFT agreement was to gain assured access to the American market. This expectation was in the tradition of "exemptionalism" in Canadian-American relations (see Chapter 1). However, some Canadian policy-makers were rather naive since the United States would not relinquish the right to retaliate with trade relief actions and other measures that it might consider necessary. As a result, there was considerable dissatisfaction on both sides of the border with the agricultural provisions of the BFT accord. They were actually quite limited, partly because the most serious problems regarding agriculture involve third countries and can only be dealt with in the GATT.

However, the controversy over the provisions that were included demonstrates that the task of reforming world agriculture in the GATT is formidable.

In conclusion, both the United States and Canada found it increasingly difficult to achieve their agricultural trade objectives in the 1980s. Most of the variables examined also point to increased conflict in the agricultural trade area, bilaterally as well as multilaterally. Furthermore, I discussed the fact that the United States and (to a lesser extent) Canada were employing a wider variety of strategies to achieve their agricultural trade objectives. Many writers feel that there is currently a crisis in agricultural trade, and the United States and Canada are clearly feeling the effects.[35] While agriculture has always been an interdependence issue, the crisis situation demonstrated to many countries, as never before, that there was an urgent need for new forms of co-operation to resolve their differences. The United States and Canada responded to this challenge by including agriculture in the Canada-U.S. free trade agreement and by calling for major agricultural reform in the GATT. As this study has outlined, however, the resistance to agricultural reform in the major trading nations (including the U.S. and Canada) is great, the problems involved in reform extremely complex, and the possibilities for a resolution of major conflicts uncertain.

DIRECTIONS FOR FUTURE RESEARCH

This book has dealt with an aspect of Canadian-American relations that has thus far received little attention from an international relations perspective. There were so many major topics to discuss that it was beyond the scope of this study to examine the relationship between relevant systemic and domestic variables. While primary emphasis was placed on systemic variables, some preliminary findings and suggestions are now offered for further research on the interaction between systemic and domestic issues. These suggestions are not designed to be comprehensive; that is, I only offer some examples of themes that should be examined further.

Robert Keohane and Joseph Nye attributed Canada's success rate in conflicts with the United States partly to "the intensity and coherence of the smaller state's bargaining position."[36] My preliminary findings indicate that, under certain conditions, intensity and coherence worked to Canada's advantage for some third-country issues. Canada strongly protested against various PL 480 surplus disposal programs, the U.S. Intermediate Credit Program, and the Export Enhancement Program, and there was little evidence of significant Canadian divisions on these issues. On the other hand, there were divisions in the United States on all of these policies, and the *initial or short-term* outcomes of bilateral conflicts were sometimes closer to the Canadian objectives. For example, Canada opposed PL 480 Title IV long-term credit sales and U.S. agricultural barter. In the 1950s there were domestic cleavages within the Eisenhower administration, and between the administration and the Congress, on these programs. As a result, the programs either were not implemented (Title IV) or were not expanded (barter) during this period. There were also domestic U.S. divisions on intermediate credit and on extending the EEP to the Soviet Union. The Intermediate Credit program, in fact, never took hold, and the EEP (in accordance with the wishes of Canada and other exporters) was not initially extended to the Soviet Union. However, there is evidence that Canada was more successful in delaying U.S. actions than in preventing them. For example, when John F. Kennedy became president there were more common objectives between the administration and the Democratic Congress, and Title IV was implemented and U.S. agricultural barter transactions increased. Furthermore, the United States eventually extended the EEP to the Soviet Union in 1986, and there was nothing that Canada could do to prevent it.

A historical view of Canadian-American agricultural trade relations in regard to third-country issues therefore demonstrates that many conflicts were more protracted than Keohane and Nye imply and that short-, medium-, and long-term outcomes must all be examined. For example, these authors briefly discussed a Canadian-American "conflict over wheat sales to third countries, 1954–64." They noted that "Canada repeatedly requested that U.S. restrict dumping of surplus wheat" and concluded that the outcome of this conflict was closer to Canadian objectives.[38] Nevertheless, U.S. "dumping of surplus wheat" did not end in 1964, and it still continues under the Export Enhancement Program in the 1980s. Numerous systemic variables (such as supply conditions, U.S. balance of payments, and others discussed in this study) must be examined in conjunction with domestic variables (such as intensity and coherence of each country's bargaining position) to explain the short-, medium-, and long-term outcomes of disputes. One hypothesis to examine would be that Canada is sometimes more successful in conflicts with the United States over the short term because of such variables as intensity and coherence. However, in protracted conflicts, the United States is likely to be more successful because of the disparity in the size and capacities of the two countries' economies (in agriculture and overall). Many agricultural trade conflicts over third-country issues have changed in form (e.g., from emphasis on surplus disposal programs to export subsidies) but persisted in substance, and Canada seems to be experiencing less success over the long term (for a variety of reasons discussed in this study).

It is even more difficult to generalize about the effects of intensity and coherence in regard to strictly bilateral agricultural trade issues since so many commodities and regional actors are involved. For example, I found evidence of wide divisions and fragmentation within *Canada* on such issues as the Canadian countervailing duty on corn, protectionism in the potato trade, the failure to include marketing boards in the bilateral free trade agreement, and the acceptability of the agricultural provisions in the BFT accord. While divisions also existed in the United States on a variety of cross-border issues, it is certainly not self-evident that U.S. fragmentation was greater than Canadian. Furthermore, commodity groups on both sides of the border held extremely strong positions on such issues as subsidies and trade relief decisions, and there was no clearcut evidence that the views of Canadian producers (e.g., wheat producers) were more intense than those of their American counterparts. American agricultural producers were initially less informed and less interested in the bilateral free trade agreement than the Canadians. However, once the U.S. producers received information on the agreement, many of them held extremely intense views about it. There are so many different groups with diverse interests in both countries that a more detailed study of domestic actors is required to assess the applicability of Keohane and Nye's hypothesis regarding the intensity and coherence of the smaller state's bargaining position to cross-border agricultural trade.

My findings also suggest that there are numerous possibilities for transnational and transgovernmental linkages between Canada and the United States. For example, these linkages clearly developed among groups committed to an exporters' pricing agreement during the 1979 negotiations for a new International Wheat Agreement.[37] However, further study is necessary to determine the extent to which such linkages actually occurred in a number of specific instances. Thus, there were indications that Canada was encouraged by various U.S. interests to oppose the five-state ban on Canadian hog exports. Canada also had common interests with American actors who opposed various U.S. export promotion programs and the extreme actions taken by the American Agriculture Movement. On the other hand, the United States had common interests with a variety of Canadian groups opposed to the countervailing duty on corn and to Canadian marketing boards. However, further research is needed to identify the cases in which cross-border collusion actually developed and to describe the most common forms of collusion. It is the wide diversity of agricultural interests and views in the United States and Canada that will make a study combining international *and* domestic variables very challenging, but this subject is certainly worthy of further study.

Notes

NOTES TO CHAPTER ONE

1 Report of the Special Joint Committee of the Senate and House of Commons on Canada's International Relations, *Independence and Internationalism* (Ottawa: Queen's Printer, 1986), pp. 1, 115.

2 This statement does not do justice to economists such as J. Clayton Gilson, D. Gale Johnson, Don Paarlberg, T. K. Warley, and others who have been highly attuned to political issues.

3 International relations scholars have examined certain aspects of this subject, such as U.S.-Canadian co-operation in maintaining wheat prices. For example, see Jon McLin, "Surrogate International Organization and the Case of World Food Security, 1949–1969," *International Organization* 33-1 (Winter 1979): 35–55; Theodore Cohn, "The 1978–9 Negotiations for an International Wheat Agreement: An Opportunity Lost?" *International Journal* 35-1 (Winter 1979–80): 132–49; and various articles in Raymond F. Hopkins and Donald Puchala, *The Global Political Economy of Food*, special issue of *International Organization* 32-3 (Summer 1978).

4 Charles Doran, *Forgotten Partnership: U.S.-Canada Relations Today* (Baltimore: Johns Hopkins University Press, 1984), p. 29.

5 For example, see ibid.; Peter Morici, *The Global Competitive Struggle: Challenges to the United States and Canada* (Toronto: C. D. Howe Institute, 1984), chapter 8; William T. R. Fox, *A Continent Apart: The United States and Canada in World Politics* (Toronto: University of Toronto Press, 1985); John Whalley, "Canada-United States Relations and the Global Trading System," in *Southern Exposure: Canadian Perspectives on the United States*, eds. D. H. Flaherty and W. R. McKercher (Toronto: McGraw-Hill Ryerson, 1986), pp. 83–94; the articles in *The North American Political Economy*, special issue of *International Journal* 42 (Winter 1986–87); William Diebold, Jr., ed., *Bilateralism, Multilateralism and Canada in U.S. Trade Policy* (Cambridge, MA: Ballinger, 1988); and Lauren McKinsey and Kim Richard Nossal, eds., *America's Alliances and Canadian-American Relations* (Toronto: Summerhill, 1988).

6 For a broader focus on North American trade issues, see Theodore Cohn, "Canadian and Mexican Trade Policies towards the United States: A Perspective from Canada," in John Curtis and David Haglund, eds., *Canada and International Trade*, vol. 1 (Montreal: Institute for Research on Public Policy, 1985), pp. 3–61.

7 Stephen D. Krasner, "Structural Causes and Regime Consequences: Regimes as Intervening Variables," *International Organization* 36 (Spring 1982): 186.

8 Michael J. Carey, "Introduction: The Political Economy of Food—The Regional Approach," in

Food Politics: The Regional Conflict, eds. David N. Balaam and Michael J. Carey (Totowa: Allanheld, Osmun, 1981), p. 4.

9 For a regime approach to global food issues, see the articles in Hopkins and Puchala, *The Global Political Economy of Food*. Other relevant writings by these two authors include "The Failure of Regime Transformation: A Reply," *International Organization* 34-2 (Spring 1980): 303-5, and "International Regimes: Lessons from Inductive Analysis," *International Organization* 36-2 (Spring 1982): 245-75. See also Helge Ole Bergeson, "A New Food Regime: Necessary but Impossible," *International Organization* 34-2 (Spring 1980): 285-302.

10 Richard Shaffner, Frank J. Quinn, and John E. Carroll, "Other Replenishable Resources," in *Natural Resources in U.S.-Canadian Relations*, vol. 2, eds. Carl E. Beigie and Alfred O. Hero, Jr. (Boulder: Westview, 1980), pp. 542-44; Canadian Wheat Board, *Annual Report 1985-86* (Winnipeg: Canadian Wheat Board).

11 The ten largest food importers in 1985, with their shares of global imports, were the U.S. (12%), Federal Republic of Germany (9.5%), Japan (9.0%), USSR (8.5%), Britain (6.5%), Italy (6.5%), Netherlands (6.0%), Belgium-Luxembourg (3.5%), and Canada (2%). The top ten importers accounted for almost 64 per cent of all global food imports in 1985, while the top ten exporters accounted for 54 per cent of global food exports.

12 T. K. Warley, "Canadian Agriculture in a Global Context: An Overview," in *Canadian Agriculture in a Global Context: Opportunities and Obligations*, eds. Irene Sage Knell and John R. English (Waterloo: University of Waterloo Press, 1986), p. 19.

13 Gerry Vogel was the World Food Program's executive director until his death in 1981; Eugene Whelan, the World Food Council president; Noel O'Connell, the International Wheat Council chairman; Gerry Trant, the executive director of the World Food Council; and Glen Flaten, the president of the International Federation of Agricultural Producers.

14 McLin, "Surrogate International Organization."

15 The Group of Seven countries are the United States, Japan, West Germany, France, Britain, Italy, and Canada. The Cairns Group first met in August 1986 and includes Argentina, Australia, Brazil, Canada, Chile, Colombia, Fiji, Hungary, Indonesia, Malaysia, New Zealand, The Philippines, Thailand, and Uruguay.

16 Robert O. Keohane and Joseph S. Nye, Jr., *Power and Interdependence: World Politics in Transition* (Boston: Little, Brown, 1977), pp. 8-13; David A. Baldwin, "Interdependence and Power: A Conceptual Analysis," *International Organization* 34 (Autumn 1980): 489-92.

17 "The Food and Agriculture Organization," *External Affairs* 6 (July 1954): 230.

18 See Raymond F. Hopkins and Donald Puchala, *Global Food Interdependence—Challenge to American Foreign Policy* (New York: Columbia University Press, 1980), and William P. Browne and Don F. Hadwiger, eds., *World Food Policies: Towards Agricultural Interdependence* (Boulder: Lynne Rienner, 1986).

19 James N. Rosenau, "Capabilities and Control in an Interdependent World," *International Security* 1 (Fall 1976): 40-43.

20 Thomas L. Brewer, *American Foreign Policy* (Englewood Cliffs, NJ: Prentice-Hall, 1980), p. 15.

21 T. K. Warley, "Western Trade in Agriculture Products," *Politics and Trade*, vol. 1, in *International Economic Relations of the Western World 1959-1971*, ed. Andrew Shonfield (London: Oxford University Press, 1976), pp. 293-94.

22 Daniel G. Amstutz, "International Impact of U.S. Domestic Farm Policy," *American Journal of Agricultural Economics* 66 (December 1984): 728-30.

23 I. M. Destler, "United States Food Policy 1972-1976: Reconciling Domestic and International Objectives," *International Organization* 32-3 (Summer 1978): 652.

24 Dale Hathaway, "Agricultural Trade Policy for the 1980s," in *Trade Policy in the 1980s*, ed. William R. Cline (Washington, D.C.: Institute for International Economics, 1983), pp. 443-44.

25 Keohane and Nye, *Power and Interdependence*, p. 199. These two authors include data on third-country issues in their empirical examination of bilateral interdependence. For example, see their tables 7.9 and 7.13 on "conflicts involving relations with third countries."

26 Canada, Agriculture Canada, Communications Branch, *Canada's Trade in Agricultural Products, 1984, 1985, 1986* (Ottawa: Ministry of Supply and Services, 1986), pp. 15, 17.

27 James P. Houck, *The Tokyo/Geneva Round: Its Relation to U.S. Agriculture—2*, Prepared for the U.S. Subcommittee on International Trade, Committee on Finance, U.S. Senate, June 1979,

p. 29; B. Wilkinson and M. Shabany Ghazvini, "Agriculture in a Free Trade Agreement," in *Canada among Nations—1985*, eds. Maureen Appel Molot and Brian Tomlin (Toronto: Lorimer, 1986), p. 199.

28 Andrew Schmitz, "Canada's Agricultural Trade and Growth Potential," in *Transforming Western Canada's Food Industry in the 80's and 90's*, ed. Barry Sadler (Banff: Banff Centre School of Management, 1984), p. 83.

29 Shaffner, Quinn, and Carroll, "Other Replenishable Resources," pp. 541-42.

30 U.S., President's Export Council, *The Export Imperative*, vol. 2, Report to the President (Washington, D.C.: U.S. Department of Commerce, December 1980), p. 50.

31 "Introduction," in *International Conflict and Conflict Management*, eds. Robert O. Matthews, Arthur G. Rubinoff, and Janice Gross Stein (Scarborough: Prentice-Hall, 1984), p. 2.

32 Hopkins and Puchala, "The Failure of Regime Transformation," pp. 304-5. See also Bergesen, "A New Food Regime," pp. 285-302.

33 The linkage between conflict and subsequent efforts to seek new forms of co-operation is examined in more detail when I discuss the independent variables.

34 Keohane and Nye, *Power and Interdependence*, p. 188.

35 Elmer L. Menzie and Barry E. Prentice, *Barriers to Trade in Agricultural Products between Canada and the United States* (Washington, D.C.: USDA, Economic Research Service, International Economics Division, April 1983), p. 9.

36 Richard Gilmore, *A Poor Harvest: The Clash of Policies and Interests in the Grain Trade* (New York: Longman, 1982), pp. 146-50. When Japan responded to the U.S. embargo by turning to Canada for more rapeseed, the Canadian government imposed its own export controls.

37 I. M. Destler, *Making Foreign Economic Policy* (Washington, D.C.: Brookings Institution, 1980), p. 52. The United States also placed embargoes on certain grain exports to the USSR in 1974 and 1975 because of fears that supplies were limited. The 1980 U.S. embargo imposed in response to the Soviet invasion of Afghanistan was obviously different, and it is discussed under political-security objectives.

38 My definition of plurilateral strategies is adapted from the discussion in Harold K. Jacobson, *Networks of Interdependence* (New York: Knopf, 1979), p. 13; and from William Diebold, Jr., "The History and the Issues," in *Bilateralism, Multilateralism and Canada in U.S. Trade Policy*, ed. William Diebold, Jr. (Cambridge, MA: Ballinger, 1988), p. 2.

39 Keohane and Nye, *Power and Interdependence*, p. 200.

40 Ibid., p. 188.

41 For a discussion of environmental variables affecting Canada's export trade in general, see Michael C. Webb and Mark W. Zacher, "Canadian Export Trade in a Changing International Environment," in *Canada and the International Political/Economic Environment*, Royal Commission on the Economic Union and Development Prospects for Canada, vol. 28, research co-ordinators, Denis Stairs and Gilbert R. Winham (Toronto: University of Toronto Press, 1985), pp. 85-150.

42 Caroline Pestieau, *A Balance of Payments Handbook* (Montreal: C. D. Howe Research Institute, 1974), pp. 3-5; David Crane, *A Dictionary of Canadian Economics* (Edmonton: Hurtig, 1980), p. 17.

43 Joan Edelman Spero, *The Politics of International Economic Relations*, 3rd ed. (New York: St. Martin's, 1985), pp. 42-53; David H. Blake and Robert S. Walters, *The Politics of Global Economic Relations*, 3rd ed. (Englewood Cliffs, N.J.: Prentice-Hall, 1987), pp. 65-67.

44 Spero, *International Economic Relations*, p. 102; Judith Goldstein, "Ideas, Institutions, and American Trade Policy," *International Organization* 42 (Winter 1988): 179. It is not the purpose of this study to assess the diversity of attitudes regarding the decline of U.S. hegemony or leadership. For competing views on this subject, see John J. Kirton, "America's Hegemonic Decline and the Reagan Revival," in *Southern Exposure: Canadian Perspectives on the United States*, eds. D. H. Flaherty and W. R. McKercher (Toronto: McGraw-Hill Ryerson, 1986), pp. 42-61; Robert Gilpin with Jean M. Gilpin, *The Political Economy of International Relations* (Princeton: Princeton University Press, 1987); Bruce Russett, "The Mysterious Case of Vanishing Hegemony; or, Is Mark Twain Really Dead?" *International Organization* 39 (Spring 1985): 207-31; and Susan Strange, "The Persistent Myth of Lost Hegemony," *International Organization* 41 (Autumn 1987): 551-74.

45 John Whalley, "Canada-United States Relations and the Global Trading System," in *Southern Exposure: Canadian Perspectives on the United States*, eds. D. H. Flaherty and W. R. McKercher (Toronto: McGraw-Hill Ryerson, 1986), p. 93.

46 IMF, *Direction of Trade Statistics Yearbooks* (Washington, D.C.: IMF). In many years Canada's current account balance was unfavourable because its positive trade balance was more than offset by a negative balance on invisibles. Furthermore, Canadian officials argued that the United States benefited more from the *composition* of their bilateral trade. While Canada had a trade surplus of $1.2 billion (Canadian) with the U.S. in 1981, its end product deficit with the U.S. exceeded $15 billion. (See Cohn, "Canadian and Mexican Trade Policies," p. 20).

47 Paul R. Viotti and Mark V. Kauppi, *International Relations Theory: Realism, Pluralism, Globalism* (New York: Macmillan, 1987), p. 33.

48 See Theodore Cohn, *Canadian Food Aid: Domestic and Foreign Policy Implications* (Denver: University of Denver Graduate School of International Studies, 1979), pp. 95–107, and *The Politics of Food Aid—A Comparison of American and Canadian Policies* (Montreal: McGill University Studies in International Development no. 36, January 1985).

49 Crane, *A Dictionary of Canadian Economics*, p. 154.

50 The GNP figures are in constant (1980) prices. The data in this section are taken from International Monetary Fund, *International Financial Statistics* (Washington, D.C.: IMF, 1987, 1988).

51 The GDP is the total final output of goods and services produced by an economy—by residents and nonresidents—regardless of the allocation to domestic and foreign claims.

52 Keohane and Nye, *Power and Interdependence*, p. 50.

53 Richard Rosecrance, Alan Alexandroff, Wallace Koehler, John Kroll, Shlomit Lacqueur, and John Stocker, "Whither Interdependence?" in *Globalism versus Realism*, eds. Ray Maghroori and Bennett Ramberg (Boulder: Westview, 1982), p. 135; Keohane and Nye, *Power and Interdependence*, p. 165.

54 Keohane and Nye, *Power and Interdependence*, pp. 168–69.

55 Ibid., table 7.18, p. 208.

56 James T. Bonnen, "Institutions, Instruments, and Driving Forces behind U.S. National Agricultural Policies," in *U.S.-Canadian Agricultural Trade Challenges: Developing Common Approaches*, eds. Kristen Allen and Katie Macmillan (Washington, D.C.: Resources for the Future, 1988), p. 29.

57 H. Garth Coffin, "Driving Forces, Instruments, and Institutions in Canadian Agricultural Policies," in ibid., p. 61. It is interesting to note that Keohane and Nye also do not examine domestic structures and political processes in detail. They therefore state that "we do not claim . . . to have developed a general theory of world politics under conditions of complex interdependence. Our systemic models would need to be supplemented by analysis of the interplay between international interdependence and domestic politics before such a theory could be constructed" (*Power and Interdependence*, p. 224).

58 Hopkins and Puchala, "Failure of Regime Transformation," pp. 304–5.

59 Maureen Appel Molot, "Canada-U.S. Relations: The Politics of Attraction and Distance," *Jerusalem Journal of International Relations* 6-2 (1982): 88–89.

60 Keohane and Nye, *Power and Interdependence*, pp. 198–202.

61 David Baldwin defines "vulnerability interdependence" as the opportunity costs involved in altering or disrupting a relationship ("Interdependence and Power," pp. 471–506).

62 Keohane and Nye, *Power and Interdependence*, p. 209.

63 Doran, *Forgotten Partnership*, pp. 21–22.

64 Molot, "Canada-U.S. Relations," p. 94. This can be viewed as "one period" because the issues in the 1980s were similar (in heightened form) to those in the 1970s, and the same prime minister (Pierre Trudeau) was in office.

65 Carl E. Beigie and James K. Stewart, *New Pressures, Old Constraints: Canada-United States Relations in the 1980s*, issue of *Behind the Headlines*, 40-6 (1983): 5.

66 Mitchell Sharp, secretary of state for external affairs, "Canada-U.S. Relations: Options for the Future," *International Perspectives*, special issue (Autumn 1972).

67 It is beyond the scope of this study to provide more detail here. For further discussion of the 1970s-80s period, see Stephen Clarkson, *Canada and the Reagan Challenge: Crisis and Adjustment, 1981-85* (Toronto: Lorimer, 1985); and Theodore Cohn and Inge Bailey, "Newspaper

Coverage of Canadian-U.S. Economic Relations: 1972 and 1982," *Canadian Journal of Communication* 13 (Summer, 1988): 1–15.

68 Canada, Department of External Affairs, *A Review of Canadian Trade Policy* (Ottawa: Minister of Supply and Services, 1983), p. 239.

69 Brian W. Tomlin and Maureen Appel Molot, eds., *Canada among Nations—1986: Talking Trade* (Toronto: Lorimer, 1987), p. 10.

70 Susan Strange, "The Management of Surplus Capacity: Or, How Does Theory Stand Up to Protectionism 1970s Style?" *International Organization* 33 (Summer 1979): 308.

71 Peter F. Cowhey and Edward Long, "Testing Theories of Regime Change: Hegemonic Decline or Surplus Capacity?" *International Organization* 37 (Spring 1983): 162.

72 See Theodore Cohn, "Food Surpluses and Canadian Food Aid," *Canadian Public Policy* 3 (Spring 1977): 141–54, and "Canadian Aid and Trade in Skim Milk Powder: Some Recent Issues," *Canadian Public Policy* 4 (Spring 1978): 213–26.

73 Susan Strange and Roger Tooze, "States and Markets in Depression: Managing Surplus Industrial Capacity in the 1970s," in *The International Politics of Surplus Capacity*, eds. Susan Strange and Roger Tooze (London: Allen and Unwin, 1981), p. 13.

74 *American Heritage Dictionary*.

75 Lynden Moore, *The Growth and Structure of International Trade Since the Second World War* (Sussex: Wheatsheaf, 1985), p. 242.

76 Ibid., p. 265.

77 Robert L. Paarlberg, *Fixing Farm Trade: Policy Options for the United States* (Cambridge, MA: Ballinger, 1988), p. 10.

78 International regimes were defined above as "sets of implicit or explicit principles, norms, rules, and decision-making procedures around which actors' expectations converge in a given area of international relations" (Krasner, "Structural Causes and Regime Consequences," p. 186).

79 Examples of studies with a largely domestic focus include Willard W. Cochrane and Mary E. Ryan, *American Farm Policy, 1948-1973* (Minneapolis: University of Minnesota Press, 1976); Don Paarlberg, *Farm and Food Policy* (Lincoln: University of Nebraska Press, 1980); Ronald D. Knutson, J. B. Penn, and William T. Boehm, *Agricultural and Food Policy* (Englewood Cliffs, N.J.: Prentice-Hall, 1983); J. D. Forbes, R. D. Hughes, and T. K. Warley, *Economic Intervention and Regulation in Canadian Agriculture*, (Ottawa: Minister of Supply and Services, 1982); J. D. Forbes, *Institutions and Influence Groups in Canadian Farm Policy*, Monograph No. 10, (Toronto: Institute of Public Administration of Canada, 1985); and Grace Skogstad, *The Politics of Agricultural Policy-Making in Canada* (Toronto: University of Toronto Press, 1987).

80 Bonnen, "U.S. National Agricultural Policies," p. 29.

81 Coffin, "Canadian Agricultural Policies," p. 49.

82 A future study will be devoted to the interaction between domestic and systemic variables.

NOTES TO CHAPTER TWO

1 Rostow identifies "trend periods" of abundance and scarcity of foodstuffs on the international market from 1870 to 1980. See Walt W. Rostow, *The World Economy—History and Prospect* (Austin: University of Texas Press, 1978), pp. 103–304.

2 The relevant legislation included the 1933 and 1938 U.S. Agricultural Adjustment Acts. Nonrecourse loans are discussed later in this chapter.

3 A concessional sale "involves price or credit terms that contain substantial . . . government subsidies." See Knutson, Penn, and Boehm, *Agricultural and Food Policy*.

4 In January 1989, the federal grains minister announced that the Wheat Board would no longer export oats starting from 1 August 1989 (the next crop year). Some critics maintain that there are linkages between the controversial decision to deregulate the oats market and the Canada-U.S. free trade agreement. The issue is discussed in Chapter 7.

5 T. K. Warley, *Agriculture in an Interdependent World: U.S. and Canadian Perspectives* (Washington, D.C.: Canadian-American Committee, C. D. Howe Institute, 1977), pp. 13–14.

6 W. E. Hamilton and W. M. Drummond, *Wheat Surpluses and Their Impact on Canada-U.S. Relations* (Washington, D.C.: Canadian-American Committee, January 1959), p. 2. Trade data

suggest that PL 480 did in fact interfere with some Canadian commercial exports. For example, see Jerome M. Stam, "The Effects of Public Law 480 on Canadian Wheat Exports," *Journal of Farm Economics* 46 (November 1964): 805.

7 USDA, Foreign Agricultural Service, "Competitive Position of U.S. Farm Products Abroad, 1956," (Washington, D.C., March 1956), pp. 99-100.
8 Stam, "Effects of Public Law 480," p. 806.
9 Frank Shefrin, "World Agricultural Production and Trade," in *Conference on International Trade and Canadian Agriculture*, Economic Council of Canada and Agricultural Economics Research Council of Canada, Banff, Alberta, 10-12 January 1966 (Ottawa: Queens Printer, 1966), p. 47.
10 Confidential source.
11 Rt. Hon. J. G. Diefenbaker, Canada, House of Commons, *Debates*, 17 April 1959, p. 2788. In a December 1957 meeting of the North Atlantic Treaty Organization, Mr. Diefenbaker had proposed the creation of a food bank that was similar in some respects to the Eisenhower plan. (See Rt. Hon. J. G. Diefenbaker, Canada, House of Commons, *Debates*, 14 April 1959, p. 2655.)
12 Don Paarlberg quoted in Trudy Huskamp Peterson, *Agricultural Exports, Farm Income, and the Eisenhower Administration* (Lincoln: University of Nebraska Press, 1979), p. xii.
13 J. Price Gittinger, *North American Agriculture in a New World* (Washington, D.C.: Canadian-American Committee, March 1970), pp. 48-55.
14 Stam, "Effects of Public Law 480," p. 817.
15 Even with direct payments, market prices tended to rest on support levels before 1972; thus, sizable export subsidies were required during most of the 1960s. See Knutson, Penn, and Boehm, *Agricultural and Food Policy*, p. 220.
16 Warley, *Agriculture in an Interdependent World*, p. 14.
17 Canadian Agriculture Congress position paper, "Wheat, Feed Grains, and Oilseeds," n.d., p. 4.
18 The USSR imported 10.4 million tonnes of grain in 1963, including 8 million from Canada and 1.8 million from the United States. See "U.S.-Soviet Grain Sales Agreement," *U.S. Department of State Bulletin* 82-2067 (October 1982), p. 41.
19 Omero Sabatini, *Canada's Export Market Development for Agricultural Products* (Washington, D.C.: USDA, Economic Research Service, Foreign Agricultural Economic Report no. 107, May 1975), p. viii.
20 Cohn, *Canadian Food Aid*, p. 26.
21 Sabatini, *Canada's Export Market Development*, p. 1. The American and Canadian actions were somewhat surprising, since data on agricultural prices, production and consumption show that the supply-demand balance had been gradually tightening from as early as the mid-1960s. See Knutson, Penn and Boehm, *Agricultural and Food Policy*, p. 20.
22 Earl Butz, "U.S. Food Policy in a Changing World," *Economic Planning* 11 (November-December 1975): 3.
23 Luther G. Tweeten, "Agricultural Policy: A Review of Legislation, Programs, and Policy," in *Food and Agricultural Policy* (Washington, D.C.: American Enterprise Institute for Public Policy Research, 1977), p. 41.
24 Quoted in Charles M. Benjamin and Charles A. Powell, "Negotiating the 1988 U.S.-U.S.S.R. Long Term Agreement on Grain Purchases," A case study sponsored by the PEW Initiative in Diplomatic Training, Center for International Studies, University of Southern California, n.d.
25 James T. Hill, "Changes in United States Agriculture Policy and the Implications for Canada," *Agriculture Abroad* 32 (December 1977): 30.
26 The Two-Price Wheat Act was also passed in May 1975, in which a premium was paid for wheat sold in the domestic market. For a detailed discussion of Canada's price and income stabilization programs, see Skogstad, *The Politics of Agricultural Policy-Making*, pp. 53-83.
27 Don Paarlberg, "On Sleeping with an Elephant," J. S. McLean Memorial Lecture, University of Guelph, 13 October 1977, p. 2.
28 Sabatini, *Canada's Export Market Development*, p. vii. See also Andrew Cooper, "Subnational Activity and Foreign Economic Policy-Making in Canada and the U.S.: Perspectives on Agriculture," *International Journal* 41-3 (Summer 1986): 663.
29 Organization for Economic Cooperation and Development, *Recent Developments in United States Agricultural Policies* (Paris: OECD, 1976), p. 45.
30 President Carter originally proposed only modest increases in target prices for wheat and

corn, but lobbyists and congressmen pressed for much higher prices. Although the president raised his target figures, the Congressional bill contained even higher targets than he had agreed to. See D. Paarlberg, *Farm and Food Policy*, p. 49.

31 The "parity price" is the price that today gives a unit of a commodity the same purchasing power as it had in 1910 to 1914. A 100 per cent parity situation was achieved only twice in this century: in 1910–14 and during World War II.

32 The AAM's style of confrontation bore some results, but it could not be sustained on a regular basis. After the movement was formed in Colorado and replicated in many states during 1977–78, it became far less effective by 1979. See John Kramer, "Agriculture's Role in Government Decisions," in *Consensus and Conflict in U.S. Agriculture—Perceptions from the National Farm Summit*, eds. Bruce L. Gardner and James W. Richardson (Texas: Texas A&M University Press, 1979), p. 213.

33 OECD, Joint Working Party of the Committee for Agriculture and the Trade Committee, "The United States Agricultural Trade Act of 1978" (Paris: *OECD*, AGR/TC/WP(79)2, 14 August 1979).

34 Robert L. Paarlberg, "Lessons of the Grain Embargo," *Foreign Affairs* 59–1 (Fall 1980): 144–52.

35 Lenard J. Cohen and Paul Marantz, "Soviet-Canadian Trade: The Politics of Inter-Vulnerability," in *Canada and International Trade*, vol. 1, eds. John Curtis and David Haglund (Montreal: Institute for Research on Public Policy, 1985), p. 90. American officials noted that they were merely placing the U.S. in the same position as Canada and Australia, which already had long-term grain agreements with China. (See U.S., GAO, *Long-Term Bilateral Grain Agreements with the Soviet Union and China* [GAO/NSIAD-89-63, March 1989], p. 2).

36 Fred H. Sanderson, "U.S. Farm Policy in Perspective," *Food Policy* 8–1 (February 1983): 4–11.

37 J. B. Penn, "Agricultural Structural Issues and Policy Alternatives for the Late 1980s," *American Journal of Agricultural Economics* 66 (December 1984): 572.

38 Barbara Insel, "A World Awash in Grain," *Foreign Affairs* 63 (Spring 1985): 892–95.

39 USDA, Economic Research Service, *Embargoes, Surplus Disposal, and U.S. Agriculture*, Agricultural Econ. Report No. 564 (December 1986): 3–15.

40 United States, GAO, *U.S. Food/Agriculture in a Volatile World Economy* (Washington, D.C.: GAO/RCED-86-3BR, November 1985), pp. 26–31; U.S., GAO, "Agricultural Competitiveness—An Overview of the Challenge to Enhance Exports" (Washington, D.C.: GAO/RCED-87-100, May 1987), pp. 14–21.

41 U.S., GAO, *U.S. Food/Agriculture*, p. 32.

42 U.S., GAO, "Implementation of the Agricultural Export Enhancement Program" (Washington, D.C.: GAO/NSIAD-87-74 BR, March 1978), p. 16.

43 U.S., GAO, "Agricultural Competitiveness," p. 24.

44 Wheat Rivals Assail U.S., E.C. Subsidies," *Globe and Mail*, 26 August 1986, sec. B, p. 3.

45 Robert E. Hudec, "Dispute Settlement in Agricultural Trade Matters: The Lessons of the GATT Experience," in *U.S.-Canadian Agricultural Trade Challenges: Developing Common Approaches*, eds. Kristen Allen and Katie Macmillan (Washington, D.C.: Resources for the Future, 1988), p. 149.

NOTES TO CHAPTER THREE

1 See Harold K. Jacobson, *Networks of Interdependence* (New York: Knopf, 1979), pp. 251–82, and Jock A. Finlayson and Mark W. Zacher, "The GATT and the Regulation of Trade Barriers: Regime Dynamics and Functions," *International Organization* 35–4 (Autumn 1981): 561–602. The MFN principle stipulates that when one GATT member grants a trade concession to another, the same concession is to be extended to other GATT signatories.

2 See Kal J. Holsti and Thomas Allan Levy, "Bilateral Institutions and Transgovernmental Relations between Canada and the United States," in *Canada and the United States—Transnational and Transgovernmental Relations*, eds. Annette Baker Fox, Alfred O. Hero, Jr., and Joseph S. Nye, Jr. (New York: Columbia University Press, 1980), p. 283.

3 A 1976 U.S. Senate report on American organizational activities in global food affairs lists eighty-nine intergovernmental bodies, and it is not the purpose of this study to examine such a wide range of organizations. See Hopkins and Puchala, *Global Food Interdependence*, p. 127.

4 References to the GATT Articles are taken from the General Agreement on Tariffs and Trade, *Text of the General Agreement* (Geneva: GATT, July 1986). There are a number of important sources recently written on the GATT and agricultural trade. These include Frank Stone, *Canada, the GATT, and the International Trading System* (Montreal: Institute for Research on Public Policy, 1984), chapter 13; Dale E. Hathaway, *Agriculture and the GATT: Rewriting the Rules* (Washington, D.C.: Institute for International Economics, September 1987); Geoff Miller, *The Political Economy of International Agricultural Policy Reform* (Canberra: Australian Government Publishing Service, 1987); R. Paarlberg, *Fixing Farm Trade*; and William E. Miner and Dale E. Hathaway, eds., *World Agricultural Trade: Building a Consensus* (Halifax: Institute for Research on Public Policy and Institute of International Economics, 1988).

5 Warley, "Western Trade in Agricultural Products," pp. 345–50.

6 D. Gale Johnson, "Domestic Agricultural Policy in an International Environment: Effects of Other Countries' Policies on the United States," *American Journal of Agricultural Economics* 66 (December 1984): 737.

7 Gilbert R. Winham, *International Trade and the Tokyo Round Negotiation* (Princeton: Princeton University Press, 1986), p. 156.

8 Stone, *Canada, the GATT, and the International Trading System*, pp. 162–63.

9 Hathaway, "Agricultural Trade Policy," p. 453.

10 T. K. Warley, "Issues Facing Agriculture in the GATT Negotiations" (Guelph: Department of Agricultural Economics and Business, University of Guelph, n.d.), pp. 3–4.

11 "Yeutter Warns U.S. May Quit GATT Talks Over Services," *Globe and Mail*, 8 September 1986, sec. A, p. 10.

12 "U.S. Seeks End to Farm Subsidies," *Vancouver Sun*, 6 July 1987, sec. A, p. 1.

13 U.S., GAO, *Current Issues in U.S. Participation in the Multilateral Trading System* (Washington, D.C.: GAO/NSIAD-85-118, 23 September 1985), p. 11.

14 Warley, "Issues Facing Agriculture," pp. 5–12.

15 Warley, "Western Trade," pp. 359–72; U.S., GAO, *Current Issues*, p. 7. See OECD, "Gentleman's Agreement on Exports of Whole Milk Powder—Revised Understanding" (Paris: OECD, 31 August 1973).

16 Robert Bard, *Food Aid and International Agricultural Trade* (Lexington, MA: Heath, 1972), p. 242.

17 FAO, *FAO Principles of Surplus Disposal and Cumulative Obligations of Member Nations*, 2d ed. (Rome: FAO, 1980), p. 2.

18 Erik Mortensen, "Impact and Implications of Foreign Surplus Disposal on Developed Economies and Foreign Competitors: The Competitor's Perspective," *Journal of Farm Economics* 42–5 (December 1960): 1052.

19 The GATT and the FAO Committee on Commodity Problems generally deal with surplus disposal activities that do not involve significant amounts of food aid.

20 FAO, *FAO Principles*, pp. 68–70.

21 Warley, "Western Trade," pp. 357–58.

22 William Willoughby, *The Joint Organizations of Canada and the United States* (Toronto: University of Toronto Press, 1979), p. 14.

23 Roger Frank Swanson, *Intergovernmental Perspectives on the Canada-U.S. Relationship* (New York: New York University Press, 1978), pp. 146–60.

24 Canada, Standing Senate Committee on Foreign Affairs, *Canada-U.S. Relations*, vol. 1, *The Institutional Framework for the Relationship* (Ottawa: Queen's Printer, December 1975), p. 22.

25 Charles F. Wilson, *C. D. Howe: An Optimist's Response to a Surfeit of Grain* (Ottawa: Grains Group, October 1980), p. 340.

26 Willoughby, *Joint Organizations*, pp. 197–202.

27 C. F. Wilson, *C. D. Howe*, p. 403.

28 Confidential source.

29 Swanson, *Intergovernmental Perspectives*, pp. 181–82; Willoughby, *Joint Organizations*, pp. 202–3.

30 Agriculture Canada, "U.S., Canada to Set Twice Yearly Agricultural Trade Meetings," *Agriculture Canada—This Month* 17 (September/October 1984).

31 Quoted in Matthew J. Abrams, *The Canada-United States Interparliamentary Group* (Toronto: Canadian Institute of International Affairs, 1973), p. 3.

32 Willoughby, *Joint Organizations*, pp. 215–17.

33 Abrams, *Canada-United States Interparliamentary Group*, p. 82.

34 See "Ad Hoc Meetings of the Canada-United States Interparliamentary Group to Discuss International Wheat Marketing, 26 July 1980 and 24 October 1981," Report by the U.S. Delegation Pursuant to Public Law 42, 86th Cong., January 1981 and March 1982 (Washington, D.C.: Government Printing Office, 1981 and 1982).

35 For example, see "Twenty-ninth meeting of the Canada-United States Interparliamentary Group, 5–9 May 1988," Report by the Chairman of the House of Representatives Delegation Pursuant to Public Law 42, 86th Cong., June 1988 (Washington, D.C.: Government Printing Office, 1988).

36 Standing Senate Committee, *Canada-U.S. Relations*, Vol. I, p. 49.

37 Hamilton and Drummond, *Wheat Surpluses*, p. vii.

38 The first Canadian sponsor was the Private Planning Association, but in 1973 the C. D. Howe Institute was established by the merger of the C. D. Howe Memorial Foundation and the Private Planning Association.

39 Hamilton and Drummond, *Wheat Surpluses*, p. vii.

40 Keohane and Nye, *Power and Interdependence*, p. 200.

41 Hamilton and Drummond, *Wheat Surpluses*, p. vii.

NOTES TO CHAPTER FOUR

1 C. F. Wilson, *C. D. Howe*, pp. 328–29.

2 Ibid., pp. 24–25.

3 Ibid., p. 328.

4 International Wheat Council, "International Wheat Agreements: A Historical and Critical Background," EX (74/75) 2/2, 14 August 1974, p. 3.

5 Ibid, p. 9.

6 McLin, "Surrogate International Organization," pp. 44–46.

7 An Advisory Committee on Price Equivalents set up by the IWA monitored price equivalents, and the IWC Executive Committee settled disputes in this area.

8 Later in this chapter I briefly discuss alternative models of the world wheat market as a duopoly (where the actions of any one of two sellers affect price); an oligopoly (where the actions of any one of a small number of sellers affect price); an oligopsony (where the actions of any one of a small number of purchasers can affect price); or as none of the above.

9 Alex F. McCalla, "Implications for Canada of U.S. Farm Policies," *Journal of Farm Economics* 49 (1967): 1044; Alex F. McCalla, "A Duopoly Model of World Wheat Pricing," *Journal of Farm Economics* 48-3 (August 1966): 713–20.

10 McLin, "Surrogate International Organization," pp. 54–55.

11 Quoted in Thomas B. Curtis and John Robert Vastine, Jr., *The Kennedy Round and the Future of American Trade* (New York: Praeger, 1971), p. 55.

12 Charles W. Gibbings, "A Canadian Looks at Some Wheat Questions," *Requested Papers* vol. 8 (Washington, D.C.: National Advisory Commission on Food and Fiber, August 1967), p. 74.

13 Hedlin Menzies and Associates Ltd., *The Wheat and Oilseeds Economy in Canada* (Winnipeg: Federal Task Force on Agriculture, August 1968), p. 104. Maximum and minimum prices were determined more precisely in the 1967 Wheat Trade Convention since quality differentials were negotiated for fourteen different wheats and each of these wheats had its own price range.

14 Curtis and Vastine, *The Kennedy Round*, p. 63.

15 Gibbings, "Some Wheat Questions," p. 82; John H. E. Taplin, "Demand in the World Wheat Market and the Export Policies of the United States, Canada and Australia," Ph.D. diss., Cornell University, 1969, p. 51.

16 G. E. Brandow, "Conflicts and Consistencies in the Agricultural Policies of the United States and Canada," *American Journal of Agricultural Economics* (December 1973): 782.

17 Chris M. Alaouze, A. S. Watson, and N. H. Sturgess, "Oligopoly Pricing in the World Wheat Market," *American Journal of Agricultural Economics* 60 (May 1978): 173–85.

18 Cohn, *Canadian Food Aid*, pp. 25–26; D. Paarlberg, "On Sleeping With an Elephant," p. 4; R. K. Sahi and W. J. Craddock, "Establishing the Effects of Operation LIFT on 1970 Prairie Land Utilization," *Canadian Farm Economics* 6 (December 1971): 2–6.

19 IWC, "International Wheat Agreements," p. 26.

20 R. Paarlberg, *Fixing Farm Trade*, p. 14.

21 Liaquat Ali, "The World Wheat Market and International Agreements," *Journal of World Trade Law* 16–1 (January-February 1982): 68–69.

22 William M. Miner speaking as witness, "Problems of International Cooperation in the Marketing of Grains and Other Agricultural Products," in Canada, *Proceedings of the Standing Senate Committee on Agriculture*, 28 February 1979, 2:16.

23 Cohn, "The 1978–9 Negotiations for an International Wheat Agreement," pp. 132–49.

24 "Collapse of Grain Talks: The Reasons Why," *International Development Review* 21–2 (1979): 21. The influence of the United States, Canada, the EC, and Japan is also reflected in the International Wheat Council's voting structure. Exporters and importers have equal numbers of votes, and council decisions (with specified exceptions) are taken by a majority of exporter votes and a majority of importer votes, counted separately. As of 30 June 1982, a majority of the exporters' 1,000 votes were held by Canada (284) and the United States (284); the EC (324) and Japan (199) held a majority of the importers' 1,000 votes. (The EC also has exporter votes.)

25 Robert O. Keohane and Joseph S. Nye, Jr., "Introduction: The Complex Politics of Canadian-American Interdependence," in *Canada and the United States: Transnational and Transgovernmental Relations*, eds., Annette Baker Fox, Alfred O. Hero, Jr., and Joseph S. Nye, Jr. (New York: Columbia University Press, 1976), p. 4.

26 Miner, "Problems of International Cooperation," 2:11.

27 Clarence Fairbairn, "Hope of Achieving IWA Still High, Despite Setbacks," *Western Producer*, 3 August 1978, p. 8. When wheat prices fell in the late 1970s and early 1980s, U.S. agricultural interests associated with the American Agriculture Movement and National Farmers' Union suggested the formation of an Organization of Wheat Exporting Countries (OWEC) patterned after the Organization of Petroleum Exporting Countries (OPEC).

28 United States, Senate, *Congressional Record*, 95th Cong., 2d sess., 17 July 1978, pp. s 10936–37.

29 Ibid., p. s 10934.

30 Ibid., p. s 10937.

31 For a comparison of Canadian and U.S. views of producer associations, see Alan R. Winberg, *Raw Material Producer Associations and Canadian Policy*, issue of *Behind the Headlines* 34–4 (1976).

32 Canada, Senate, *Debates*, 29 November 1978, p. 286.

33 Barry Wilson, "Meeting Sees No Use in Price War," *Western Producer*, 17 May 1979, pp. 1, 3.

34 Adrian Ewins, "1979 Grain Meeting Had Similar Views," *Western Producer*, 5 June 1986, p. 30; Maggie McNeil, "Wheat Meet Finds No Solution," *Western Producer*, 26 February 1987, sec. A, p. 4.

35 For a more detailed discussion of the concept of "food power" applied to both the United States and Canada, see Cohn, *Canadian Food Aid*, chapter 7, and *Politics of Food Aid*.

36 Thomas Grennes and Paul R. Johnson, "Import Tariffs and Price Formation in the World Wheat Market: Comment," *American Journal of Agricultural Economics* 62–4 (November 1980): 821; Colin Carter and Andrew Schmitz, "Import Tariffs and Price Formation in the World Wheat Market," *American Journal of Agricultural Economics* 61 (August 1979): 517–22.

37 Vernon L. Sorenson and George E. Rossmiller, "Future Options for U.S. Agricultural Trade Policy," *American Journal of Agricultural Economics* (December 1983): 897. For a detailed examination of cartels, see Andrew Schmitz, Alex F. McCalla, Donald O. Mitchell, and Colin Carter, *Grain Export Cartels* (Cambridge, MA: Ballinger, 1981).

38 David Blandford and Nancy E. Schwartz, "Is the Variability of World Wheat Prices Increasing?" *Food Policy* (November 1983): 306–11.

39 The U.S. Cabinet-level interagency Economic Policy Council in its May 1985 discussions indicated that EEP sales were not to compete directly with sales made by major debtor nations such as Argentina, Brazil, and Mexico. The council did *not* specifically refer to Canada and Australia, but in practice the EEP sales were also not to compete directly with Canadian and

Australian sales. See U.S., GAO, *Implementation of the Agricultural Export Enhancement Program* (Washington, D.C.: GAO/NSIAD-87-74BR, March 1987).

40 U.S., GAO, *The Export Enhancement Program, U.S. Foreign Agricultural Market Development Programs, Commodity Credit Corporation Export Credit Guarantee Programs, and Long-Term Bilateral Grain Agreements and Countertrade*, statement of Allan I. Mendelowitz before the Subcommittee on Department Operations, Research and Foreign Agriculture, House Committee on Agriculture (Washington, D.C.: 30 September 1986), p. 12.

41 Alexander M. Haig, Jr., *Caveat: Realism, Reagan, and Foreign Policy* (New York: Macmillan, 1984), p. 111.

42 Ibid., p. 112.

43 U.S., GAO, *The Export Enhancement Program*, pp. 2-6. Soviet trade representatives mentioned price considerations and problems with U.S. grain quality as the main factors.

44 U.S., GAO, *Long-Term Bilateral Agreements with the Soviet Union and China*, p. 33.

45 "U.S. Farm, Foreign Policy Makers at Odds," *Globe and Mail*, 14 August 1986, sec. B, p. 9.

46 Adrian Ewins, "U.S. Feels Justified Using Subsidies as Sales Tactic," *Western Producer*, 5 February 1987, sec. B, p. 1.

47 U.S., GAO, *Long-Term Bilateral Agreements with the Soviet Union and China*, p. 6.

48 U.S., GAO, *The Export Enhancement Program*, p. 17.

49 Hathaway, "Agricultural Trade Policy," p. 447.

50 The American proposal was developed by the U.S. Department of Agriculture and the Office of the U.S. Trade Representative. See U.S., GAO, *Agricultural Trade Negotiations—Initial Phase of the Uruguay Round* (Washington, D.C.: GAO/NSIAD-88-144BR, May 1988), 2.

51 "U.S. Seeks End to Farm Subsidies," *Vancouver Sun*, 6 July 1987, sec. A, p. 1.

52 Jennifer Lewington, "Reagan Proposes Global Elimination of Farm Subsidies," *Globe and Mail*, 7 June 1987, p. 1; Greg McCune, "Farm Group Seen Hurdle to Ending Global Subsidies," *Globe and Mail*, 17 September 1987, sec. B, p. 7; Barry Wilson, "Trade Talks Have Farmers Fearing the Worst," *Western Producer*, 13 August 1987, p. 15.

53 Barry Wilson, "Wise Wants Canadian Support for U.S. Subsidy Fight," *Western Producer*, 10 September 1987, p. 3; Gatt, The Uruguay Round, "Proposal by Canada Regarding the Multinational Trade Negotiations in Agriculture," MTN.GNG/NG5/W/19, 20 October 1987, p. 3.

54 See Uruguay Round Trade Negotiations Committee, "Chairman's Texts on Agriculture, Trade-Related Aspects of Intellectual Property Rights, Textiles and Clothing and Safeguards," agreed in Geneva, 8 April 1989.

55 Keohane and Nye, *Power and Interdependence*, pp. 165-218.

56 Canada, External Affairs, *The Canada-U.S. Free Trade Agreement* (Ottawa: External Affairs, 10 December 1987), p. 79.

57 Report of the Special Joint Committee of the Senate and House of Commons on Canada's International Relations, *Independence and Internationalism* (Ottawa: Queen's Printer, 1986), p. 115.

NOTES TO CHAPTER FIVE

1 Canadian-American Committee, *Towards a Solution of Our Surplus Wheat Problems* (n.p.: National Planning Association and Private Planning Association of Canada, October 1959), p. 2.

2 Ibid.

3 "Howe Sees Little Loan Demand," *Winnipeg Free Press*, 28 November 1955, pp. 1, 4.

4 GATT Information Service, European Office of the United Nations, Geneva, 12th Session of the Contracting Parties, "Disposal of Surplus Agricultural Products: Discussion in Plenary Session," press release, GATT/378, 25 November 1957, p. 12.

5 The UMR figure is somewhat arbitrary because it is virtually impossible to know how much a country would have imported commercially in the absence of food aid. UMR requirements normally are stated in terms of volume rather than value of a commodity.

6 The United States defined friendly countries as those from the "free world."

7 FAO, "CSD Report on Tied Sales," CCP 69/13/3, 17 July 1969, pp. 4-5. As discussed in Chapter 3, the Consultative Subcommittee on Surplus Disposal is a subcommittee of the FAO Committee on Commodity Problems (CCP).

8 Statement by the U.S. representative at the 189th Meeting of the CSD, "Offset Purchase Requirement," 11 April 1973, in FAO, "Second CSD Report on Tied Sales," CCP 73/19, September 1973, p. 38.

9 Statement by the delegate for Canada at the 189th meeting of the CSD, "Canadian Objection to Practice of 'Tied Sales' in Food Aid Transactions," 10 April 1973, in ibid., p. 35.

10 Some of the discussion in this chapter is based on confidential sources.

11 Hamilton and Drummond, *Wheat Surpluses*, p. 26.

12 There were still some linkages between tied UMRs and wheat sales after 1959. For example, PL 480 wheat sales to Poland in 1964 were linked with requirements that Poland purchase 200,000 tonnes of feedgrains on commercial terms from the United States. Technically, the U.S. abided by its commitment not to employ tying for wheat since the tied UMR was for Polish feedgrain purchases.

13 Canadian-American Committee, *Towards a Solution*, pp. 5–6.

14 Canada Treaty Series 1971, no. 26, "Wheat Trade and Food Aid Conventions 1971," pp. 15–16.

15 FAO, "CSD Report on Tied Sales," p. 1.

16 Ibid., pp. 6–9.

17 U.S. statement on "tied sales" delivered at the 12 September 1972 CSD meeting, 14 February 1973, in FAO, "Second CSD Report on Tied Sales," p. 27.

18 FAO, "CSD Report on Tied Sales," p. 2.

19 Ibid., p. 9.

20 U.S. statement on "Tied Sales," "Second CSD Report on Tied Sales," p. 26.

21 Section 103 (n) of PL 480, as amended, stated that "the President shall . . . take maximum precautions to assure that sales for dollars on credit terms under this Act shall not displace any sales of United States agricultural commodities which would otherwise be made for cash dollars" (emphasis added).

22 Statement by Delegate for Canada, in "Second CSD Report on Tied Sales," p. 36.

23 FAO, *FAO Principles*, p. 43.

24 Some U.S. tied offset purchasing requirements may have been of the unrestricted variety. See Bard, *Food Aid*, ch. 9.

25 U.S., GAO, *Uses and Limitations of Countertrade*, statement of Allan I. Mendelowitz before the Subcommittees on International Economic Policy and Trade, and Arms Control, International Security and Science Committee on Foreign Affairs, House of Representatives (Washington, D.C.: GAO-T-NSIAD-87-39, 1 July 1987), pp. 2–3; Pompiliu Verzariu, *Countertrade, Barter and Offsets* (New York: McGraw Hill, 1985), p. 24.

26 USDA, Office of the General Sales Manager, statement of Francis A. Woodling, deputy assistant sales manager, before the House Committee on Armed Services, Subcommittee on Seapower and Strategic Critical Materials, (Washington, D.C.: n.d.), pp. 1–2.

27 Glenn H. Snyder, *Stockpiling Strategic Materials: Politics and National Defense* (San Francisco: Chandler, 1966), p. 218.

28 USDA, press release 1378-61, "USDA Eases Barter Rules for Federal Procurements," 1 May 1961.

29 For example, barter was more common during the 1930s Depression era when normal means of payment broke down. In one agreement, a private U.S. company and the Brazilian government exchanged 25 million bushels of wheat for 1.3 million sacks of coffee.

30 USDA, press release 1761-61, "Barter Program Task Force Meets," 5 June 1961; press release issued by the White House, 25 September 1962; USDA, press release 494-63, "USDA Announces Revisions in Barter Program," 13 February 1963.

31 Selected issues of *Foreign Agricultural Trade of the United States (FATUS)*.

32 Canadian-American Committee, *Wheat Surpluses and the U.S. Barter Program* (n.p.: National Planning Association and Private Planning Association of Canada, March 1960), p. 12.

33 USDA, Office of the General Sales Manager, Woodling, appendix, p. 1.

34 G. W. Green, "The Agricultural Barter Issue in the United States," *Agriculture Abroad* 34 (1984): 46.

35 U.S., Public Law 99-198, 99th Cong., *Food Security Act of 1985*, 23 December 1985.

36 U.S., GAO, *Long-Term Bilateral Grain Agreements and Grain Countertrade* (Washington, D.C.: GAO/NSIAD-89-91, April 1989), pp. 24–30; Gustavo del Castillo and Rosario Barajas

de Vega, "U.S.-Mexican Agricultural Relations: The Upper Limits of Linkage Formation," in *World Food Policies: Toward Agricultural Interdependence*, eds. William P. Browne and Don F. Hadwiger (Boulder: Lynne Rienner, 1986), p. 166.

37 The ad hoc working group established in 1981 by the U.S. Defense Department had difficulty in identifying countries willing to barter strategic materials for U.S. dairy products. Nigeria and China were the only countries identified with a potential interest, but the working group felt that they would probably be reluctant to negotiate barter agreements. See U.S., Senate, Comptroller General, report to chairman, Subcommittee on Preparedness, Committee on Armed Services, *Conditions That Limit Using Barter and Exchange to Acquire National Defense Stockpile Materials*, 19 October 1983, appendix 2, pp. 9–10.

38 U.S., GAO, *Long-Term Bilateral Grain Agreements and Grain Countertrade*, pp. 24–30.

39 "Howe Sees Little Loan Demand."

40 FAO, "Twenty-Sixth Report of the CSD to the Committee on Commodity Problems," CCP/CSD/76/184, 27 September 1976, p. 5. See Chapter 3 for a discussion of the Quarterly Meetings.

41 Theodore Cohn with Inge Bailey, "Canadian-American Relations and Agricultural Surpluses: The Case of Barter," in *Canadian Agriculture in a Global Context: Opportunities and Obligations*, eds. Irene Sage Knell and John R. English, (Waterloo: University of Waterloo Press, 1986), pp. 186–91.

42 U.S., Department of State, *Foreign Relations of the United States, 1952-1954* (Washington, D.C.: U.S. Government Printing Office, 1983), 1:195.

43 Elmer L. Menzie and Robert G. Crouch, *Political Interests in Agricultural Export Surplus Disposal through Public Law 480* (Tucson: University of Arizona Press, Agricultural Experiment Station Technical Bulletin 161, September 1964), p. 40.

44 USDA, Office of the General Sales Manager, Woodling, appendix. South Africa was the largest supplier, India was third, and Jamaica was fourth.

45 Hamilton and Drummond, *Wheat Surpluses*, pp. 3–4.

46 Confidential source.

NOTES TO CHAPTER SIX

1 Gary Clyde Hufbauer, "Subsidy Issues after the Tokyo Round," in *Trade Policy in the 1980s*, ed. William R. Cline (Washington, D.C.: Institute for International Economics, 1983), p. 342; Knutson, Penn, and Boehm, *Agricultural and Food Policy*, p. 123.

2 Bruce Fitzgerald and Terry Monson, "Export Credit and Insurance for Export Promotion," *Finance and Development* 25 (December, 1988): 53.

3 See "List of Transactions," types 10 and 11, in FAO, *FAO Principles*, appendix F, p. 69.

4 See *Interim Report on Work of "Grey Area" Panel*, approved by CSD for submission to 38th sess. of FAO Committee on Commodity Problems, CCP 65/7 Suppl. 1, 20 April 1965; Bard, *Food Aid*, pp. 158–61.

5 Confidential source. Canada considered some U.S. credit sales to be concessional because CCC interest rates were lower than prevailing bank rates. However, the U.S. argued that these sales were commercial because private-sector trade channels were utilized.

6 C. F. Wilson, *C. D. Howe*, pp. 450–51.

7 USDA, Foreign Agricultural Service, *Canadian Agriculture—Competitive Position* (Washington, D.C.: Foreign Agricultural Report no. 110, July 1958), p. 58.

8 C. F. Wilson, *C. D. Howe*, p. 451.

9 Peterson, *Agricultural Exports*, pp. 127–28.

10 Poland later became the second largest beneficiary (after South Korea) of American CCC credit exports, receiving over one-seventh of the $7 billion total spent from March 1956 to September 1978. See U.S., GAO, Comptroller General of the U.S., *Stronger Emphasis on Market Development Needed in Agriculture's Export Credit Sales Program* (Washington, D.C.: ID-80–01, 26 October 1979), pp. 60–61.

11 C. F. Wilson, *C. D. Howe*, pp. 405–8. I discuss the Consultative Committee on Grain Marketing and the other bilateral committees in Chapter 3.

12 Ibid., p. 464.

13 I. Moravcik, "Prospects for Soviet and East European Purchases of Canadian Wheat," *Canadian Slavonic Papers* 7 (1965): 161.
14 S. C. Hudson, *Future Market Outlets for Canadian Wheat and Other Grains* (Ottawa: Economic Council of Canada, Queen's Printer, 1970), pp. 43, 190; Peterson, *Agricultural Exports*, pp. 60, 83.
15 Mitchel Wallerstein refers to U.S. PL 480 aid to Yugoslavia during this period as "political enticement" (see *Food for War—Food for Peace* [Cambridge, MA: MIT Press, 1980], pp. 122–25).
16 Carl H. McMillan, *Canada's Postwar Economic Relations with the USSR: An Appraisal* (Ottawa: Carleton University, Institute of Soviet and East European Studies, 1980), pp. 11–12.
17 Peterson, *Agricultural Exports*, pp. 93–94.
18 Confidential source.
19 FAO, Committee on Commodity Problems, "Report of the Ad Hoc Working Group on Public Law 480, Title IV, Government-to-Private Trade Agreements," 41st sess. (Rome: CCP 67/18/2, 25 January 1967).
20 Peter A. Toma, with Frederick A. Schoenfeld, *The Politics of Food Aid: Executive-Legislative Interaction* (Tucson: University of Arizona Press, 1967), pp. 51–2.
21 M. M. Kostecki, "Canada's Grain Trade with the Soviet Union and China," *Canadian Journal of Agriculture Economics* 30–2 (July 1982): 233.
22 Francis Conrad Raabe, "The China Issue in Canada: Politics and Foreign Policy," Ph.D. diss., Pennsylvania State University, 1970, pp. 298–308.
23 Bill Miner, "Canada's Trade in Grains and the China Market," paper presented at conference, "Canadian Agriculture in a Global Context: Opportunities and Obligations," Centre on Foreign Policy and Federalism, University of Waterloo, Waterloo, Ontario, 21–23 May 1985, p. 17.
24 The U.S. State Department supported the Canadian government and eventually prevailed over the Treasury Department, which sought to impede the deliveries. See Raabe, "The China Issue," pp. 295, 312.
25 James I. W. Corcoran, "The Trading with the Enemy Act and the Controlled Canadian Corporation," *McGill Law Journal* 14–2 (1968): 187–201; I. A. Litvak and C. J. Maule, "Conflict Resolution and Extraterritoriality," *Journal of Conflict Resolution* 13–3 (September 1969): 309–14.
26 Tong P. Chen, "Legal Aspects of Canadian Trade with the People's Republic of China," *Law and Contemporary Problems* 38–2 (Summer-Autumn 1973): 211.
27 Confidential source.
28 Ibid.
29 Cochrane and Ryan, *American Farm Policy*, p. 274. Most of the data in this section are from the USDA, Economic Research Service, *FATUS*, and *FATUS Supplements* (Washington, D.C.).
30 U.S., GAO, Comptroller General, *Stronger Emphasis*, p. 19.
31 Canada, House of Commons, Standing Committee on Agriculture, 28th Parliament, 4th sess., 27 June 1972, p. 37. For China's reticence to use U.S. credit, see Kasimierz Grzybowski, "Control of U.S. Trade with China: An Overview," *Law and Contemporary Problems* 38–2 (Summer-Autumn 1973): 181.
32 James Trager, *The Great Grain Robbery* (Toronto: Ballantine, 1975), pp. 20–21; I. A. Litvak and C. H. McMillan, "A New United States Policy on East-West Trade—Some Implications for Canada," *International Journal* 28–2 (Spring 1973): 302–6.
33 Canada, Report of the Federal Task Force on Agriculture, *Canadian Agriculture in the Seventies* (Ottawa: December 1969), pp. 87–88.
34 Sabatini, *Canada's Export Market Development*, p. 31.
35 Canada, Report of the Federal Task Force on Agriculture, p. 58.
36 Canada, Government of Canada, *Export Financing: Consultative Paper* (Ottawa: Ministry of Supply and Services, January 1985).
37 Sabatini, *Canada's Export Market Development*, p. 41.
38 Hudson, *Future Market Outlets*, pp. 179–84.
39 Confidential source.
40 Hudson, *Future Market Outlets*, p. 186.
41 Confidential source.

42 Frank Shefrin, director, International Liaison Service, Agriculture Canada, paper presented to the Provincial Marketing Seminar on International Trade, Hespeler, Ontario, 1972, p. 4.

43 Sabatini, *Canada's Export Market Development*, p. 21.

44 OECD, *Recent Developments in United States Agricultural Policies* (Paris: OECD, 1976), p. 25. By Spring 1977, however, wheat and other grains again appeared on the eligibility lists for CCC credit. See USDA, "USDA Announces Commodities Eligible for CCC Credit in April: Program Status," *News*, 4 April 1977.

45 "CCC Intermediate Credit Export Sales Program for Foreign Market Development Facilities," *Federal Register* 45–153, 6 August 1980, p. 52343.

46 Howard W.Hjort, "U.S. and Canadian Food and Agricultural Policies: Goals and Objectives, Conflicts and Cooperation," *American Journal of Agricultural Economics* 60 (1978): 787.

47 FAO, *Twenty-Eighth Report of the CSD to the Committee on Commodity Problems* (Rome: CCP/CSD/81/120, 2 July 1981), p. 9.

48 Ibid. Even before the IC legislation was passed, Canada had lobbied vigorously against it. A June 1978 letter from the Canadian embassy in Washington had set forth the concerns that Canada later expressed after the program was enacted. See U.S. Congress, House of Representatives, Committee on International Relations, *Agricultural Exports and U.S. Foreign Economic Policy: Hearings before the Committee on International Relations*, 95th Cong., 2d sess., 18 April-9 August 1978, appendix 12, pp. 327–28.

49 In 1969, an OECD agreement covered downpayments, maximum length of credits, and interest rates applicable to exports of ships. In 1978, an "Arrangement on Guidelines for Officially Supported Export Credits" was signed by all OECD countries except Iceland and Turkey. Additional OECD agreements on export credits have been negotiated in the 1980s. (See T. M. Burns, "The Trade Jungle of Export Credits," *International Perspectives* [January-February] 1983: 23.)

50 Confidential source.

51 U.S., GAO, *The Export Enhancement Program*, pp. 31–35.

52 The *crédit-mixte* concept blends aid funds with regular official export credits to produce a highly concessional rate of interest overall. The French terminology is normally used because France first developed this practice. However, other countries—including Canada—have adopted variations of this technique. See Burns, "Trade Jungle," p. 23; and "Fact File: The Blended Credit Program," *Foreign Agriculture* (March 1983): 7–8.

53 FAO, *Twenty-Ninth Report of the Consultative Sub-Committee on Surplus Disposal to the Committee on Commodity Problems* (Rome: CCP/CSD/83/187, 11 July 1983).

54 "Fact File," p. 7.

55 Canadian Wheat Board, *Annual Report 1981-82*, p. 5.

56 Canada, Government of Canada, *Export Financing*.

57 Canadian Wheat Board, *Annual Report 1981-82*, p. 5.

58 Ibid., tables 13, 14.

59 U.S., *Congressional Record*, 24 May 1983, pp. 57381–82.

60 Edward Greenspan, "Grain Sales, Crop Outlook Are Both Winners," *Financial Post*, 6 August 1983, p. 1.

61 U.S., GAO, *Commodity Credit Corporation's Export Credit Guarantee Programs* (Washington, D.C.: GAO/NSIAD-88-194, June 1988), p. 10.

62 Ibid.

63 U.S., GAO, *The Export Enhancement Program*, p. 18. In fiscal years 1986 and 1987, the U.S. provided $967.2 million in export credit guarantees in conjunction with the EEP to ten countries (see U.S., GAO, *Commodity Credit Corporation's Export Credit Guarantee Programs*, p. 19).

64 Canada, Government of Canada, *Export Financing*, pp. 17, 23.

NOTES TO CHAPTER SEVEN

1 The word "new" is put in quotations because the United States and Canada had a trade reciprocity treaty from 1854 to 1866 providing for free trade in natural products, and the idea of bilateral free trade periodically was revived after 1866. Nevertheless, the agreement signed

on 2 January 1988 marked the first time in the twentieth century that the two countries were prepared to implement the idea of free trade.

2 For a good historical discussion of Canada's 3-column tariff structure, see John H. Young, *Canadian Commercial Policy* (Ottawa: Royal Commission on Canada's Economic Prospects, November 1957), pp. 101-17.

3 J. L. Granatstein, "Free Trade between Canada and the United States," in *The Politics of Canada's Economic Relationship with the United States*, vol. 29, eds. Denis Stairs and Gilbert R. Winham (Toronto: University of Toronto Press with the Royal Commission on the Economic Union and Development Prospects for Canada, 1985), p. 33. See also Edelgard E. Mahant and Graeme S. Mount, *An Introduction to Canadian-American Relations* (Toronto: Methuen, 1984), p. 135.

4 49th Parallel Institute for Canadian-American Relations, *U.S.-Canada Free Trade: A Western Regional Perspective* (Bozeman: 49th Parallel Institute, August 1988), p. 139

5 Warley, "Western Trade in Agricultural Products," p. 324.

6 Menzie and Prentice, *Barriers to Trade*, pp. 2-6, 60.

7 Mary Anne Normile and Carol A. Goodloe, *U.S.-Canadian Agricultural Trade Issues: Implications for the Bilateral Trade Agreement* (Washington, D.C.: Economic Research Service, Agriculture and Trade Analysis Division, March 1988), pp. 15-16.

8 Michael N. Gifford, "A Briefing by the Canadian Agricultural Negotiator," in *U.S.-Canadian Agricultural Trade Challenges: Developing Common Approaches*, eds. Kristen Allen and Katie Macmillan (Washington, D.C.: Resources for the Future, 1988), p. 10. Later in this chapter I discuss the fact that agricultural tariffs are to be phased out over a ten-year period under the Canada-U.S. free trade agreement.

9 Jimmye S. Hillman, *Nontariff Agricultural Trade Barriers* (Lincoln: University of Nebraska Press, 1978), p. 14.

10 GATT Contracting Parties, 9th Session, "Summary Record of the 44th Meeting," Geneva, SR.9/44, 15 March 1955, p. 10.

11 Menzie and Prentice, *Barriers to Trade*, pp. 4-5.

12 Other major types of U.S. trade relief laws include "escape clause" actions (Section 201 of the 1974 Trade Act) and tariff suspension and import restriction provisions (Section 301). The trade legislation for antidumping and countervailing duties is discussed below. See I. M. Destler, *American Trade Politics: System under Stress* (Washington, D.C.: Institute for International Economics, 1986).

13 If no other comparative market exists, antidumping duties can be imposed against sales at below the cost of production. (Kristen Allen and Murray Smith, "An Overview of Agricultural Issues in the U.S.-Canadian Free Trade Agreement, in *U.S.-Canadian Agricultural Trade Challenges: Developing Common Approaches*, eds. Kirsten Allen and Katie Macmillan [Washington, D.C.: Resources for the Future, 1988], p. 6.)

14 The first two definitions of "remedy" in the *American Heritage Dictionary* are "something, such as medicine or therapy, that relieves pain, cures disease, or corrects a disorder" and "something that corrects any evil, fault, or error."

15 This terminology is used in Murray G. Smith, "Negotiating Trade Laws: Possible Approaches," in *Bridging the Gap: Trade Laws in the Canadian-U.S. Negotiations*, by Murray G. Smith, with C. Michael Aho and Gary N. Horlick (Toronto: Canadian-American Committee, January 1987), p. 5. The terms "contingent" and "contingency protection" measures are used in Rodney de C. Grey, *Trade Policy in the 1980s: An Agenda for Canadian-U.S. Relations* (Montreal: C. D. Howe Institute, 1981), and in Fred Lazar, *The New Protectionism: Non-Tariff Barriers and Their Effects on Canada* (Toronto: Lorimer, 1981), pp. 27-45.

16 The U.S. rules were also revised for other reasons (e.g., to accord with the GATT regulations in some respects), but a detailed examination of the changes is beyond the scope of this book. The CVD authority is contained in Section 701 of the 1979 Trade Agreements Act (an amended version of Section 303 of the 1974 Act). The U.S. Anti-Dumping Act of 1921, as amended by the 1974 and 1979 Trade Acts, is the principal statute governing dumping cases. Additional changes in the trade relief procedures are contained in the U.S. Trade and Tariff Act of 1984. For a more detailed discussion of U.S. and Canadian trade relief rules see Lazar, *The New Protectionism*, pp. 27-45; Rodney de C. Grey, *United States Trade Policy Legisla-*

tion: A Canadian View (Montreal: Institute for Research on Public Policy, 1982); Destler, *American Trade Politics*, pp. 111–42; and Smith, with Aho and Horlick, *Bridging the Gap*.
17 Destler, *American Trade Politics*, pp. 111–27.
18 U.S., GAO, *International Trade Commission's Agricultural Unfair Trade Investigations* (Washington, D.C.: NSIAD-88-58BR, December 1987), pp. 10–12.
19 Hearing before the Subcommittee on Monetary and Fiscal Policy of the Joint Economic Committee, U.S. Congress, *The Canadian Agricultural Import Problem*, 99th Cong., 2d sess., 2 July 1986 (Washington, D.C.: Government Printing Office, 1987), p. 12.
20 As early as 1859, the Canadian tariff provided for an undervaluation duty. See Young, *Canadian Commercial Policy*, p. 135; and G. A. Elliott, *Tariff Procedures and Trade Barriers* (Toronto: University of Toronto Press, 1955), p. 180.
21 Smith, "Negotiating Trade Laws," p. 7; Shelly P. Battram and Peter L. Glossop, "Dispute Resolution under a Canada/United States Free Trade Agreement," American Bar Association National Institute on Resolution of International Commercial Disputes, Miami, 5–6 November 1987, pp. 6, 13.
22 Debra P. Steger, "Recent Canadian Experience with Countervailing Duties: The Case of Agriculture," *Canada-U.S. Trade in Agriculture: Managing the Disputes*, ed. University of Guelph and Ontario Ministry of Agriculture and Food (Guelph: University of Guelph, October 1987, AEB/87/6), p. 16.
23 Debra P. Steger, "Canadian-U.S. Agricultural Trade: A Proposal for Resolving Disputes," in *U.S.-Canadian Agricultural Trade Challenges: Developing Common Approaches*, eds. Kristen Allen and Katie Macmillan (Washington, D.C.: Resources for the Future, 1988), p. 161.
24 Grey, *Trade Policy in the 1980s*, pp. 56–57.
25 Normile and Goodloe, *Agricultural Trade Issues*, p. 10.
26 Menzie and Prentice, *Barriers to Trade*, p. 9; Leo V. Mayer, "A Briefing by the U.S. Agricultural Negotiator," in *U.S.-Canadian Agricultural Trade Challenges: Developing Common Approaches*, eds. Kristen Allen and Katie Macmillan (Washington, D.C.: Resources for the Future, 1988), p. 18.
27 "U.S.-Canadian Agricultural Trade Balance Reverses Direction," *FATUS* (March-April 1986): 139.
28 Canada, Agriculture Canada, International Trade Policy Division, *Canada's Trade in Agricultural Products 1983, 1984 and 1985* (Ottawa: Ministry of Supply and Services, 1986), p. 18.
29 "U.S.-Canadian Agricultural Trade Balance Reverses Direction," p. 139.
30 Normile and Goodloe, *Agricultural Trade Issues*, p. 10.
31 James T. Hill, "The U.S. Meat Import Law," *Agriculture Abroad* 32 (February 1977): 42–43.
32 W. J. Anderson, "North American Food and Agricultural Policies: Conflict and Cooperation—Trade Interdependencies," *American Journal of Agricultural Economics* (December 1978): 797–98.
33 There were various reasons why herds were liquidated in the early 1970s. For example, the dramatic increase in grain prices threatened Canadian feedlot operations with widespread bankruptcy.
34 Canada, Senate, Standing Committee on Agriculture, *Recognizing the Realities: A Beef Import Policy for Canada* (Ottawa: Queen's Printer, October 1977), pp. 15–28. The Canadian government established global quotas to be controlled through the Export and Import Permits Act. The U.S. measures were effective retroactively from August 1974. They were taken under Section 252 of the 1962 Trade Expansion Act, which allowed the administration to retaliate when a country unjustifiably denied access to U.S. products.
35 Canada, House of Commons, *Debates*, 28 October 1976, p. 544.
36 Canada, Senate, Standing Committee on Agriculture, *Proceedings*, 16 February 1977, 4:13.
37 "Meat Import Legislation Tabled," *Agriculture Canada—News* E-69, 24 November 1980, p. 1. Canada's Import Control Act does not trigger automatically when imports reach a certain level as the American act does. In Canada, the government must make a decision to invoke the act when imports exceed a limit set by international treaty (Barry Wilson, "Flood of Beef Imports has Cattlemen Concerned," *Western Producer*, 13 October 1988, p. 5).
38 "Beef and Veal Imports," Government of Canada, News Release, 19 August 1983, p. 2.
39 "1984 Imports of Beef and Veal," Government of Canada, News Realease, 2 February 1984, p. 2.

40 Bovine brucellosis is a contagious disease that causes abortion and production losses in cattle and can also cause undulant fever in humans.

41 "U.S. Imposes Import Restrictions," *Agriculture Canada—News* B-45, 18 July 1977, p. 2.

42 Canada, House of Commons, *Debates*, 10 April 1981, p. 9166.

43 M. H. Hawkins, R. K. Bennett, and A. M. Boswell, *North American Hog/Pork Study*, A Summary Report Prepared by Canada Department of Agriculture, Economics Branch (Ottawa: n.d.), p. 12.

44 J. Clayton Gilson, "The U.S.-Canadian Hog War," *Western Economic Review* 4–3 (Fall 1985): 2.

45 Lazar, *The New Protectionism*, p. 31.

46 "Testimony of the National Pork Producers Council," in *Data and Material Related to the United States-Canada Free Trade Negotiations*, written comments received by the Committee on Finance, U.S. Senate, September 1987, p. 254.

47 Gary N. Horlick and Kathleen Chagnon, "Dealing with U.S. Trade Laws: Before, During and After," in *Canada-U.S. Trade in Agriculture: Managing the Disputes*, ed. University of Guelph and Ontario Ministry of Agriculture and Food (Guelph: University of Guelph, October 1987, AEB/87/6), p. 9.

48 Carol A. Goodloe, "U.S. Producers and the Countervailing Duty Case against Canadian Pork and Hogs," *Western Economic Review* 4–3 (Fall 1985): 17–19.

49 "Testimony of the National Pork Producers Council," p. 256.

50 Andrew Cooper, "Subnational Activity and Foreign Economic Policy-Making in Canada and the U.S.: Perspectives on Agriculture," *International Journal* 41–3 (Summer 1986): 661–69.

51 D. L. Aube, *Canada's Trade in Agricultural Products 1984, 1985 and 1986*, Agriculture Canada, International Trade Policy Division, August 1987, p. 17.

52 Minister for international trade, news release no. 194, "Canada Requests Panel Review for Pork under Chapter 19 of the Canada-U.S. Free Trade Agreement," 22 August 1989; Barry Wilson, "Pork Duty Could Hurt Free Trade Says Mazankowski," *Western Producer*, 1 June 1989; " Pork and Beefs," *Globe and Mail*, 31 August 1989.

53 Quoted in Smith, "Negotiating Trade Laws," p. 6.

54 Steger, "Recent Canadian Experience with Countervailing Duties," p. 16.

55 Randy Burton, "Corn Growers Sift Lyng's Words," *Western Producer*, 31 July 1986, p. 18.

56 The CVDs applied to imports of grain corn in all forms except seed corn, sweet corn, and popping corn, originating in or exported from the United States.

57 Oliver Bertin, "U.S. Government, Corn Producers Set for Battle over Canadian Tariff," *Globe and Mail*, II November 1986, sec. B, p. 10.

58 Gary N. Horlick, "Comments," in *Bridging the Gap: Trade Laws in Canadian-U.S. Negotiations*, by Murray G. Smith, with C. Michael Aho and Gary N. Horlick (Toronto: Canadian-American Committee, 1987), pp. 49–50.

59 "Read between the Lines: Trade War," *New York Times*, 11 November 1986, p. 22.

60 Steger, "Recent Canadian Experience with Countervailing Duties," p. 23.

61 Hon. Donald S. MacDonald, "The Need for Bilateral and Multilateral Agreements Concerning Agriculture," in *Canada-U.S. Trade in Agriculture: Managing the Disputes*, ed. University of Guelph and Ontario Ministry of Agriculture and Food (Guelph: University of Guelph, October 1987, AEB/86/6), p. 5.

62 Barry Wilson, "Corn Duty Chopped to 46 Cents," *Western Producer*, 11 February 1988, p. 9.

63 "Appeal Court Says Duty on U.S. Corn is Justified," *Globe and Mail*, 31 December 1988, p. A4.

64 Peter F. Cowhey and Edward Long, "Testing Theories of Regime Change: Hegemonic Decline or Surplus Capacity?" *International Organization* 37 (Spring 1983): 162.

65 Statement by Senator Steven D. Symms, hearing before the Subcommitte on Monetary and Fiscal Policy of the Joint Economic Committee, U.S. Congress, "The Canadian Agricultural Import Problem," p. 16.

66 Bob H. Robinson, Mary Anne Normile, Carol A. Goodloe, and Robert M. House, "U.S.-Canadian Trade Liberalization: Key Issues," and Hudec, "Dispute Settlement in Agricultural Trade Matters," in *U.S.-Canadian Agricultural Trade Challenges: Developing Common Approaches*, eds. Kristen Allen and Katie Macmillan (Washington, D.C.: Resources for the Future, 1988), pp. 69, 152.

67 Robinson et al., "U.S.-Canadian Trade Liberalization," p. 69.

68 Section 102 of the 1974 U.S. Trade Act authorizes the president to enter into bilateral free trade agreements and to have Congress approve them on a "fast-track" basis. For a bilateral agreement to qualify for fast-track consideration, one condition is that the negotiation must be requested by the foreign country—in this case Canada. (See U.S., House of Representatives, hearings before the Subcommittee on Trade of the Committee of Ways and Means, 100th Cong. 2d sess., *United States-Canada Free Trade Agreement*, 9, 26, and 29 February and 1, 11, and 25 March 1988, p. 19.)

69 Canada also had multilateral objectives, particularly in agriculture.

70 Barry Wilson, "Farming Gets the Free Trade Spotlight," *Western Producer*, 4 February 1988, p. 12.

71 Granatstein, "Free Trade," p. 11.

72 Molot, "Canada-U.S. Relations," p. 89.

73 I am using the historical definition of "reciprocity" here, namely "an agreement for U.S.-Canadian free trade, covering at least a sizable share of trade." See Paul Wonnacott, *The United States and Canada: The Quest for Free Trade*, Policy Analyses in International Economics Series 16 (Washington, D.C.: Institute for International Economics, 1987), p. 11.

74 Granatstein, "Free Trade," p. 21.

75 Ibid., p. 33. See also Mahant and Mount, *Introduction to Canadian-American Relations*, p. 135.

76 Sperry Lea, *A Canada-U.S. Free Trade Arrangement* (Washington, D.C.: Canadian-American Committee, October 1963), p. 30.

77 Canadian-American Committee, *A Possible Plan for a Canada-U.S. Free Trade Area: A Staff Report* (Washington, D.C.: National Planning Association and Private Planning Association of Canada, February 1965), p. 30.

78 Harry G. Johnson, Paul Wonnacott, and Hirofumi Shibata, *Harmonization of National Economic Policies under Free Trade* (Toronto: University of Toronto Press for the Private Planning Association of Canada, 1968), p. 30; *A North American Common Market* (Ames: Iowa State University Press, 1969).

79 Economic Council of Canada, *Looking Outward: A New Trade Strategy for Canada—1975* (Ottawa: Minister of Supply and Services, 1976), p. 151. Chapter 9 of this report focuses on the United States.

80 Canada, Senate, Standing Committee on Foreign Affairs, *Canada-United States Relations*, vol. 2, *Canada's Trade Relations with the United States* (Ottawa: Queen's Printer, 1978), p. 2.

81 The U.S. proposals were remarkably unspecific regarding the form such an agreement would take, and the terms "common market," "accord," and "free-trade area" were often used interchangeably. For further discussion of this issue, see Cohn, "Canadian and Mexican Trade Policies," pp. 11–17; and Alicia Puyana, "La Idea del Mercado Común de América del Norte y las Implicaciones para México," in *México-Estados Unidos 1982*, compilador, Lorenzo Meyer, (México, D. F.: El Colegio de México, 1982), pp. 131–64.

82 The Congressional hearings did examine U.S.-Mexican trade in certain agricultural commodities, such as tomatoes. See U.S., Senate, hearings before the Subcommittee on International Trade of the Committee on Finance, 96th Cong., 1st sess., *North American Economic Interdependence*, 6 June and 1 October 1979; U.S. House of Representatives, hearings before the Subcommittee on Inter-American Affairs of the Committee on Foreign Affairs, 96th Cong., 2d sess., *Update: United States-Canadian/Mexican Relations*, 17 and 26 June 1980.

83 Canada, Senate, Standing Committee on Foreign Affairs, *Canada-United States Relations*, vol. 3, *Canada's Trade Relations with the United States* (Ottawa: Minister of Supply and Services, 1982), p. 93.

84 Canada, External Affairs, *A Review of Canadian Trade Policy* (Ottawa: Minister of Supply and Services, 1983), 212. This report was released while Pierre Trudeau was prime minister.

85 Royal Commission on the Economic Union and Development Prospects for Canada, *Report*, vol. 1 (Ottawa: Minister of Supply and Services, 1985), p. 308.

86 National Farmers' Union, submission to the Select Standing Committee on Bill C-130, *An Act to Implement the Free Trade Agreement between Canada and the United States of America*, 28 July 1988, p. 1. See also Canadian Federation of Agriculture, submission to the Standing Senate Committee on Foreign Affairs, *Examination of a Free Trade Agreement between Canada and the United States*, 8 August 1988.

87 "Priorities in U.S. Trade Legislation," recommendations of the National Farmers' Union, in

U.S., House of Representatives, hearing before the Committee on Agriculture, *United States-Canadian Free Trade Agreement*, 100th Cong., 2d sess., 25 February 1988, p. 155.

88 Letter from Charles L. Frazier, director, Washington Office, National Farmers' Organization, to chairman, Committee on Agriculture, in ibid., p. 161.

89 Letter from John Datt, executive director, American Farm Bureau Federation, to the Honorable Lloyd Bentsen, U.S. Senate, 7 April 1988, p. 2. For the American Farm Bureau Federation's position on free trade, see *U.S.-Canadian Trade Agreement, Farm Bureau Analysis and Assessment* (n.p. :n.d.). While the Farm Bureau's stance on the BFT agreement was consistent with its traditional preference for free enterprise, agricultural commodity groups have had some success in forcing the AFBF to change its free-market philosophy. (See Bonnen, "Institutions, Instruments, and Driving Forces," p. 31).

90 *Statement by the Canadian Federation of Agriculture on Free Trade Legislation* (n.p.: n.d.).

91 Leo V. Mayer, "U.S.-Canadian Negotiations and the GATT Round: U.S. Perspectives, in *Canada-U.S. Trade in Agriculture: Managing the Disputes*, eds. University of Guelph and Ontario Ministry of Agriculture and Food (Guelph: University of Guelph, October 1987, AEB/87/6), p. 40.

92 John S. Lambrinidis, *The Structure, Function, and Law of a Free Trade Area: The European Free Trade Association* (New York: Frederick A. Praeger, 1965), pp. 256–59. Andreas F. Lowenfeld, "What GATT Says (Or Does Not Say)," in *Bilateralism, Multilateralism and Canada in U.S. Trade Policy*, ed. William Diebold, Jr. (Cambridge, MA: Ballinger, 1988), pp. 55–68.

93 Wilkinson and Ghazvini, "Agriculture in a Free Trade Agreement," p. 197.

94 See Canada, External Affairs, *The Canada-U.S. Free Trade Agreement* (Ottawa: External Affairs, 10 December 1987).

95 I do not deal with the provisions on wine and distilled spirits, which are in a different part of the agreement from agriculture.

96 Barry D. Mehr, "Canada-U.S. Agricultural Trade: Market Realities and Opportunities," in *U.S.-Canadian Agricultural Trade Challenges: Developing Common Approaches*, eds. Kristen Allen and Katie Macmillan (Washington, D.C.: Resources for the Future, 1988), p. 77.

97 The United States has not in fact imposed Section 22 import restrictions on wheat since 1974.

98 The Saskatchewan Wheat Pool has warned that the words "significantly" and "substantial" are not defined or quantified and could create disputes (*Saskatchewan Wheat Pool Submission to the Legislative Committee on Bill C-130, An Act to Implement the Free Trade Agreement*, July 1988, p. 5).

99 While over 50 per cent of the delegates voted to oppose the agreement, a two-thirds majority is required to pass a resolution at the Saskatchewan Wheat Pool's annual meeting. Thus, the Wheat Pool did not adopt a formal position on the BFT accord at this meeting. See testimony by Garf Stevenson, Prairie Pools, Inc., in Canada, House of Commons, *Minutes of Proceedings and Evidence of the Standing Committee on External Affairs and International Trade*, 26 November 1987, 49:10.

100 Geoffrey York, "Wheat Board Action Revives Trade Fears," *Globe and Mail*, 25 January 1989, p. A8.

101 See testimony of Stevenson, *Minutes of Proceedings and Evidence*, 49:11.

102 Letter from the U.S. Trade Representative Clayton Yeutter to the Honorable Charles W. Stenholm in U.S., House of Representatives, hearing before the Committee on Agriculture, 25 February 1988, p. 19.

103 The method of calculating the level of government support for wheat, oats, and barley is set out in Annex 705.4 of the agreement.

104 The transportation subsidy was removed on shipments through west coast ports because these ports are conditioned upon export. Thus, the transport subsidy through the western ports is also considered to be an export subsidy. In contrast, the transportation subsidy for shipment through Thunder Bay in the east is generally available; that is, it is used for products shipped to Ontario as well as for those that are exported. The BFT accord does not deal with generally available subsidies. A U.S. example would be the waterway subsidy, which is not affected by the agreement.

105 See Statement of Carl F. Schwensen, National Association of Wheat Growers in U.S., House of Representatives, hearing before the Committee on Agriculture, 25 February 1988, pp. 143–46.

106 "Farm Lobby Group Votes to Reject Free Trade Deal," *Globe and Mail*, 25 January 1988, sec. B, p. 3.

107 Clyde H. Farnsworth, "20 Senators Ask for Guarantees on Canada Pact," *New York Times*, 24 February 1988, p. 33.

108 Hathaway, "Agricultural Trade Policy for the 1980s," pp. 446–47.

109 The United States-Canada Free Trade Agreement Implementation Act, *Statement of Administrative Action*, draft, 17 June 1988, p. 4.

110 Press release, Advisory Committee to the Canadian Wheat Board, "Advisory Committee Issues Statement on Major Farm Issues," 2 August 1988, p. 1.

111 Andrew Schmitz, "Summing Up: The Canadian Perspective," in *U.S.-Canadian Agricultural Trade Challenges*, pp. 194–95.

112 Susan B. Epstein, *Agriculture in the U.S.-Canadian Free Trade Agreement* (Washington, D.C.: Congressional Research Service Report for Congress, 87-985 ENR, 22 December 1987), pp. 16–17.

113 Richard R. Barichello and T. K. Warley, *Agriculture and Negotiation of a Free Trade Area: Issues in Policy Harmonization* (Vancouver: University of British Columbia, 1985), p. 5.

114 Debra P. Steger, *A Concise Guide to the Canada-United States Free Trade Agreement* (Toronto: Carswell, 1988), p. 22.

115 Geoffrey York, "Political Hay Seen in Possible Threat to the Wheat Board," *Globe and Mail*, 7 October 1987, p. A 10.

116 Canada, External Affairs, *The Canada-U.S. Free Trade Agreement—Synopsis* (Ottawa: External Affairs, 10 December 1987), p. 28.

117 U.S., House of Representatives, hearing before the Committee on Agriculture, 25 February 1988, p. 29.

118 Menzie and Prentice, *Barriers to Trade*, p. 61–62.

119 GATT, *Text of the General Agreement* (Geneva: GATT, July 1986), Article XI.

120 See testimony by the Canadian Cattlemen's Association, the Canadian Pork Council, and the Canadian Meat Council, in *Minutes of the Standing Committee on External Affairs and International Trade*, 17, 24, and 27 November, 1987.

121 Testimony by Tom Cook, director industry affairs, National Cattlemen's Association, and by Tom Miller, president, National Pork Producers' Council, in U.S., House of Representatives, hearing before the Committee on Agriculture, 25 February 1988, pp. 135, 153.

122 Canadian Federation of Agriculture, submission to the Standing Senate Committee on Foreign Affairs, 8 August 1988, pp. 5–8.

123 "Comments on U.S.-Canada Free Trade Area," presented by the United Fresh Fruit and Vegetable Association, in *Data and Materials Related to United States-Canada Free Trade Negotiations*, September 1987, p. 355. The United Fresh Fruit and Vegetable Association is the national trade association for the U.S. fresh fruit and vegetable industry.

124 "Statement of the National Potato Council on the U.S.-Canada Free Trade Area Negotiations," in ibid., p. 259.

125 Testimony by Leslie MacKay, chairman, Prince Edward Island Potato Marketing Board, in *Minutes of the Standing Committee on External Affairs and International Trade*, 2 December 1987, 57:44.

126 Hon. Sid Morrison, in U.S., House of Representatives, hearing before the Committee on Agriculture, 25 February 1988, p. 60.

127 Ambassador Clayton Yeutter, ibid., p. 15.

128 John A. Schnittker, "Agricultural Issues in a Comprehensive Canada-U.S. Trade Agreement—An American Perspective," in U.S., House of Representatives, hearings before a Subcommittee of the Committee on Government Operations, *U.S. Agricultural Exports: Does Administration Effort Match Potential?* 100th Cong., 1st sess., 5, 10, 18, and 24 February, 18 and 25 March, and 19 and 20 May 1987, p. 71.

129 Dale E. Hathaway, "Discussion: Linkages between Bilateral and Multilateral Negotiations in Agriculture," in *U.S.-Canadian Agricultural Trade Challenges: Developing Common Approaches*, eds. Kristen Allen and Katie Macmillan (Washington, D.C.: Resources for the Future, 1988), p. 179.

130 Schnittker, "Agricultural Issues," p. 72.

131 T. K. Warley, "Linkages between Bilateral and Multilateral Negotiations in Agriculture," in

U.S.-Canadian Agricultural Trade Challenges: Developing Common Approaches, eds. Kristen Allen and Katie Macmillan (Washington, D.C.: Resources for the Future, 1988), pp. 169–78.

132 Barry E. Prentice and Elmer L. Menzie, "Formal and Informal Nontariff Barriers to Agricultural Trade between the United States and Canada," in *U.S.-Canadian Agricultural Trade Challenges: Developing Common Approaches*, eds. Kristen Allen and Katie Macmillan (Washington, D.C.: Resources for the Future, 1988), p. 136.

133 Testimony of Ambassador Clayton Yeutter, in U.S., House of Representatives, hearing before the Committee on Agriculture, 25 February 1988, p. 72.

NOTES TO CHAPTER EIGHT

1 Warley, "Western Trade in Agricultural Products," pp. 293–94.

2 Analyses of the effects of surplus capacity in non-agricultural areas include Strange, "Management of Surplus Capacity," pp. 303–34; Strange and Tooze, *The International Politics of Surplus Capacity*; and Cowhey and Long, "Testing Theories of Regime Change," pp. 157–88.

3 The suspension of the Commodity Credit Corporation's export subsidy programs in 1973 also resulted from the criticism of subsidized U.S. grain sales to the Soviet Union at a time when world prices were increasing. The export subsidy programs were reinstated in 1983.

4 For evidence that Canada's Third Option policy was less relevant to agricultural issues, see Theodore Cohn, "Canada and the European Economic Community's Common Agricultural Policy: The Issue of Trade in Cheese," *Journal of European Integration* 1 (January 1978): 125–42.

5 R. Paarlberg, *Fixing Farm Trade*, p. 14. The demise of the Bretton Woods system was, of course, related to the U.S. balance of payments and trade problems.

6 The AAM is far less effective today, but it continues to express highly protectionist views. For example, in February 1987 the movement's national director stated that the AAM was "tired of having people talk about free trade" and that "the only free trade that exists in the world is coming into the United States for imports." See "Statement of David Senter, American Agriculture Movement," in U.S., House of Representatives, *U.S. Agricultural Exports*, pp. 35–36.

7 As discussed, two of the four Canadian CVD cases begun in 1986 involved the European Community, and one involved the United States. The U.S.-EC export subsidy contest clearly was a factor in these cases, even though the U.S. Export Enhancement Program has not been used for products exported to Canada. (See "Statement of Ann Veneman, associate administrator, Foreign Agriculture Service, USDA," in U.S., House of Representatives, hearings before the Subcommittee on Trade of the Committee on Ways and Means, *United States-Canada Free Trade Agreement*, 100th Cong., 2d sess., 9, 26, 29 February, 1, 11, 25 March 1988, 475).

8 The agricultural trade regime is discussed in more detail below.

9 In 1963, the U.S. exported 1.8 million tonnes of grain to the Soviet Union, but this was an unusual situation. (See Chapters 2 and 6).

10 Agricultural commodities under PL 480 were sent to Yugoslavia from 1954, to Israel from 1955, and to Poland from 1957.

11 Bonnen, "Institutions, Instruments, and Driving Forces," p. 37.

12 M. R. Laserson, Continental Grain Company, "The Soviet Union and COMECON Countries as International Grain Buyers," in U.S., House of Representatives, *U.S. Agricultural Exports*, p. 574.

13 U.S., GAO, *Long-Term Bilateral Grain Agreements with the Soviet Union and China*, p. 21.

14 Hopkins and Puchala, "The Failure of Regime Transformation," pp. 303–5.

15 Robinson et al., "U.S.-Canadian Trade Liberalization," p. 69.

16 See Molot, "Canada-U.S. Relations," pp. 88–107; and Keohane and Nye, *Power and Interdependence*, pp. 198–202.

17 Conflict is a dependent variable in relation to the other independent variables in the study. (See Chapter 1).

18 See McLin, "Surrogate International Organization," pp. 35–55.

19 Some U.S. assurances—as in the case of the Export Enhancement Program—were inconsistent with its actions.

20 See Keohane and Nye, *Power and Interdependence*, chapter 7, for a comparison of Canadian and Australian interdependence with the United States.

21 Hathaway, "Agricultural Trade Policy for the 1980s," p. 443.

22 Ibid., p. 451.

23 Plurilateralism involves more countries than bilateralism but fewer than multilateralism (see Chapter 1).

24 The proposal for an exporters' pricing agreement was to be implemented if the negotiations for a new international wheat agreement ended in failure (see Chapter 4). In this respect, the duopoly was different since it was partly designed to strengthen the international wheat agreements.

25 Hudec, "Dispute Settlement in Agricultural Trade Matters," p. 150.

26 "Meat Import Legislation Tabled," *Agriculture Canada—News* E-69, 24 November 1980, p. 1.

27 As stated, the four objectives are to restore, maintain, or increase market share; to export commodities at remunerative prices; to maintain or achieve a more favourable agricultural trade balance; and to limit imports of supplementary agricultural products.

28 Bonnen, "Institutions, Instruments, and Driving Forces," p. 24.

29 Quoted in C. F. Wilson, *C. D. Howe*, p. 336.

30 The two variables in question are *relative economic size* and *relative size of the two countries' agricultural economies*.

31 Warley, *Agriculture in an Interdependent World*, p. 14.

32 U.S., GAO, *Long-Term Bilateral Grain Agreements with the Soviet Union and China*, p. 5.

33 R. Paarlberg, *Fixing Farm Trade*, p. 4.

34 The Economic Research Service of the U.S. Department of Agriculture estimated that the gross cost of the embargo to the United States was over $2 billion. The embargo also hurt the U.S. reputation as a reliable supplier (see *Long-Term Bilateral Grain Agreements*, p. 4).

35 For examples of those referring to the "crisis" in agricultural trade, see R. Paarlberg, *Fixing Farm Trade*; Institute for International Economics and the Institute for Research on Public Policy, *Reforming World Agricultural Trade* (Washington, D.C.: Institute for International Economics, May 1988); Hathaway, *Agriculture and the GATT*; Miller, *The Political Economy of International Agricultural Policy Reform*; Miner and Hathaway, *World Agricultural Trade*; and Michael Franklin, *Rich Man's Farming: The Crisis in Agriculture* (London: Routledge, 1988).

36 Keohane and Nye, *Power and Interdependence*, p. 206.

37 Ibid., p. 191.

38 See Cohn, "The 1978-9 Negotiations for an International Wheat Agreement," pp. 132-49.

Selected Bibliography

BOOKS AND MONOGRAPHS

Abrams, Matthew J. *The Canada-United States Interparliamentary Group*. Toronto: Canadian Institute of International Affairs, 1973

Allen, Kristen, and Murray Smith. "An Overview of Agricultural Issues in the U.S.-Canadian Free Trade Agreement." In *U.S.-Canadian Agricultural Trade Challenges: Developing Common Approaches*, eds. Kristen Allen and Katie Macmillan, pp. 1–8. Washington, D.C.: Resources for the Future, 1988

Anderson, James E., David W. Brady, and Charles Bullock. *Public Policy in America*. North Scituate, MA: Duxbury Press, 1978

Anderson, Walton J. *Canadian Wheat in Relation to the World's Food Production and Distribution*. Saskatoon: Modern Press, 1964

Asher, Robert E. *Grants, Loans, and Local Currencies: Their Role in Foreign Aid*. Washington, D.C.: Brookings Institution, 1966

Balaam, David N., and Michael J. Carey, eds. *Food Politics: The Regional Conflict*, Totowa: Allanheld, Osmun, 1981

Barber, Clarence. "The Impact of United States Farm Policy on Canadian Agriculture." In *The American Economic Impact on Canada*, ed. H. G. J. Aitken, pp. 69–87. Durham, N.C.: Duke University Press, 1959

Bard, Robert. *Food Aid and International Agricultural Trade*. Lexington, MA: Heath, 1972

Barichello, Richard R., and T. K. Warley. *Agriculture and Negotiation of a Free Trade Area: Issues in Policy Harmonization*. Vancouver: University of British Columbia, December 1985

Baxter, Ian F. G., and Ivan R. Feltham, eds. *Export Practice*. Commercial Law Series, no. 1. Toronto: Osgoode Hall Law School, 1964

Beigie, Carl E., and James K. Stewart. *New Pressures, Old Constraints: Canada-United States Relations in the 1980s*. Issue of *Behind the Headlines* 40-6 (August 1983)

Benedict, Murray R., and Elizabeth K. Bauer. *Farm Surpluses—U.S. Burden or World Asset?* Berkeley: University of California, Division of Agricultural Sciences, 1960

Blake, David H., and Robert S. Walters. *The Politics of Global Economic Relations*. 3rd ed. Englewood Cliffs, N.J.: Prentice-Hall, 1987

Bonnen, James T. "Institutions, Instruments, and Driving Forces behind U.S. National Agricultural Policies." In *U.S.-Canadian Agricultural Trade Challenges: Developing Common Approaches*, eds. Kristen Allen and Katie Macmillan, pp. 21-39. Washington, D.C.: Resources for the Future, 1988

Bray, C. E., P. L. Paarlberg, and F. D. Holland. *The Implications of Establishing a U.S. Wheat Board*. Washington, D.C.: USDA, Economics and Statistics Service, Foreign Agricultural Report no. 163, April 1981

Brewer, Thomas L. *American Foreign Policy*. Englewood Cliffs, N.J.: Prentice-Hall, 1980

Browne, William P., and Don F. Hadwiger, eds. *World Food Policies: Toward Agricultural Interdependence*. Boulder: Lynne Rienner, 1986

Canadian-American Committee. *A Possible Plan for a Canada-U.S. Free Trade Area: A Staff Report*. Washington, D.C.: National Planning Association and Private Planning Association of Canada, February 1965

—. *Towards a Solution of Our Surplus Wheat Problems*. Montreal: National Planning Association and Private Planning Association of Canada, October 1959

—. *Wheat Surpluses and the U.S. Barter Program*. Montreal: National Planning Association and Private Planning Association of Canada, March 1960

Carey, Michael J. "Introduction: The Political Economy of Food—The Regional Approach." In *Food Politics: The Regional Conflict*, eds. David N. Balaam and Michael J. Carey, pp. 1-8. Totowa: Allanheld, Osmun, 1981

Castillo, Gustavo del, and Rosario Barajas de Vega. "U.S.-Mexican Agricultural Relations: The Upper Limits of Linkage Formation." In *World Food Policies: Toward Agricultural Interdependence*, eds. William P. Browne and Don F. Hadwiger, pp. 153-70. Boulder: Lynne Rienner, 1986

Cathie, John. *The Political Economy of Food Aid*. Aldershot: Gower, 1982

Clabough, Samuel F., and Edwin J. Feulner, Jr. *Trading with the Communists: A Research Manual*. Washington, D.C.: Center for Strategic Studies, Georgetown University, 1968

Clarkson, Stephen. *Canada and the Reagan Challenge*. Toronto: Lorimer, 1985

Cochrane, Willard W., and Mary E. Ryan. *American Farm Policy, 1948-1973*. Minneapolis, University of Minnesota Press, 1976

Cohen, Lenard J., and Paul Marantz. "Soviet-Canadian Trade: The Politics of Intervulnerability." In *Canada and International Trade*, Vol. 1, eds. John Curtis and David Haglund, pp. 63-117. Montreal: Institute for Research on Public Policy, 1985

Cohn, Theodore. "Canadian and Mexican Trade Policies towards the United States." In *Canada and International Trade*, Vol. 1, eds. John Curtis and David Haglund, pp. 3-61. Montreal: Institute for Research on Public Policy, 1985

—. *Canadian Food Aid: Domestic and Foreign Policy Implications*. Denver: University of Denver, Graduate School of International Studies, 1979

—. *The Politics of Food Aid—A Comparison of American and Canadian Policies*. Montreal: McGill University Studies in International Development, no. 36, January 1985

—, with Inge Bailey. "Canadian-American Relations and Agriculture Surpluses: The Case of Barter." In *Canadian Agriculture in a Global Context: Opportunities and Obligations*, eds. Irene Sage Knell and John R. English, pp. 175-98. Waterloo: University of Waterloo Press, 1986

Crane, David. *A Dictionary of Canadian Economics*. Edmonton: Hurtig, 1980

Curtis, Thomas B., and John Robert Vastine, Jr. *The Kennedy Round and the Future of American Trade*. New York: Praeger, 1971

Dam, Kenneth W. *The GATT—Law and International Economic Organization*. Chicago: University of Chicago Press, 1970

Destler, I.M. *American Trade Politics: System under Stress*. Washington, D.C.: Institute for International Economics, 1986

—. *Making Foreign Economic Policy*. Washington, D.C.: Brookings Institution, 1980

Diebold, William, Jr. "The History and the Issues." In *Bilateralism, Multilateralism and Canada in U.S. Trade Policy*, ed. William Diebold, Jr., pp. 1-36. Cambridge, MA: Ballinger, 1988

—, ed. *Bilateralism, Multilateralism and Canada in U.S. Trade Policy*. Cambridge, MA: Ballinger, 1988

Doran, Charles F. *Forgotten Partnership: U.S.-Canada Relations Today*. Baltimore: Johns Hopkins University Press, 1984

Drummond, Ian M. *Canada's Trade with the Communist Countries of Eastern Europe*. Montreal: Private Planning Association of Canada, 1966

Eicher, Carl, and Lawrence Witt, eds. *Agriculture in Economic Development*. Toronto: McGraw-Hill, 1964

Bibliography

Elliott, G. A. *Tariff Procedures and Trade Barriers*. Toronto: University of Toronto Press, 1955

Fairbairn, Jerry Lawrence. *Will the Bounty End? The Uncertain Future of Canada's Food Supply*. Saskatoon: Western Producer Prairie Books, 1984

Farnsworth, Helen C. *Multiple Pricing of American Wheat: Present System and Two-Price Plan*. Stanford: Food Research Institute, Stanford University, 1958

Ferguson, Elizabeth S., ed. *U.S. Trade Policy and Agricultural Exports*. Ames: Iowa State University Press, 1973

Forbes, J. D. *Institutions and Influence Groups in Canadian Farm Policy*, Monograph No. 10. Toronto: Institute of Public Administration of Canada, 1985

—, R. D. Hughes, and T. K. Warley. *Economic Intervention and Regulation in Canadian Agriculture*. Ottawa: Minister of Supply and Services, 1982

49th Parallel Institute for Canadian-American Relations. *U.S.—Canada Free Trade: A Western Regional Perspective*. Bozeman: 49th Parallel Institute, August 1988

Fox, William T. R. *A Continent Apart: The United States and Canada in World Politics*. Toronto: University of Toronto Press, 1985

Franklin, Michael. *Rich Man's Farming: The Crisis in Agriculture*. London: Routledge, 1988

Gifford, Michael N. "A Briefing by the Canadian Agricultural Negotiator." In *U.S.-Canadian Agricultural Trade Challenges: Developing Common Approaches*, eds. Kristen Allen and Katie Macmillan, pp. 9–13. Washington, D.C.: Resources for the Future, 1988

—. "The Canada/USA Negotiations and the GATT Round: Canadian Agricultural Perspective." In *Canada-U.S. Trade in Agriculture: Managing the Disputes*, pp. 42–46. Guelph: University of Guelph and Ontario Ministry of Agriculture and Food, October 1987, AEB/87/6

Gilmore, Richard. *A Poor Harvest: The Clash of Policies and Interests in the Grain Trade*. New York: Longman, 1982

Gilpin, Robert, with Jean Gilpin. *The Political Economy of International Relations*. Princeton: Princeton University Press, 1987

Gilson, J. Clayton. "Canadian Agricultural Export Capabilities." In *Canadian Agriculture in a Global Context: Opportunities and Obligations*, eds. Irene Sage Knell and John R. English, pp. 33–52. Waterloo: University of Waterloo Press, 1986

Gittinger, J. Price. *North American Agriculture in a New World*. Washington, D.C.: Canadian-American Committee, March 1970.

Granatstein, J. L. "Free Trade between Canada and the United States." In *The Politics of Canada's Economic Relationship with the United States*, Vol. 29, eds. Dennis Stairs and Gilbert R. Winham, pp. 11–54. Royal Commission on the Economic Union and Development Prospect for Canada. Toronto: University of Toronto Press, 1985

Grey, Rodney de C. *Trade Policy in the 1980s: An Agenda for Canadian-U.S. Relations*. Montreal: C. D. Howe Institute, 1981

—. *United States Trade Policy Legislation: A Canadian View*. Montreal: Institute for Research on Public Policy, 1982

Haig, Alexander M., Jr. *Caveat: Realism, Reagan, and Foreign Policy*. New York: Macmillan, 1984

Hamilton, W. E., and W. M. Drummond, *Wheat Surpluses and Their Impact on Canada-United States Relations*. Washington, D.C.: Canadian-American Committee, 1959

Hathaway, Dale E. *Agriculture and the GATT: Rewriting the Rules*. Washington, D.C.: Institute for International Economics, 1987

—. "Agricultural Trade Policy for the 1980s." In *Trade Policy in the 1980s*, ed. William R. Cline, pp. 435–53. Washington, D.C.: Institute for International Economics, 1983

—. "Discussion: Linkages between Bilateral and Multilateral Negotiations in Agriculture." In *U.S.-Canadian Agricultural Trade Challenges: Developing Common Approaches*, eds. Kristen Allen and Katie Macmillan, pp. 179–82. Washington, D.C.: Resources for the Future, 1988

Hedlin Menzies and Associates Ltd. *The Wheat and Oilseeds Economy in Canada*. Winnipeg: Federal Task Force on Agriculture, August 1968

Hillman, Jimmye S. *Nontariff Agricultural Trade Barriers*. Lincoln: University of Nebraska Press, 1987

Ho, Samuel P. S., and Ralph W. Huenemann. *Canada's Trade with China: Patterns and Prospects*. Montreal: Canadian Economic Policy Committee and Private Planning Association of Canada, 1972

Holsti, Kal J., and Thomas Allen Levy. "Bilateral Institutions and Transgovernmental Relations between Canada and the United States." In *Canada and the United States—Transnational and Transgovernmental Relations*, eds. Annette Baker Fox, Alfred O. Hero, Jr., and Joseph S. Nye, Jr., pp. 283–309. New York: Columbia University Press, 1976

Hopkins, Raymond, and Donald Puchala. *Global Food Interdependence—Challenge to American Foreign Policy*. New York: Columbia University Press, 1980

—, eds. *The Global Political Economy of Food*. Special issue of *International Organization* 32–3 (Summer 1978)

Horlick, Gary N. "Comments." In *Bridging the Gap: Trade Laws in the Canada-*

U.S. Negotiations, by Murray G. Smith, with C. Michael Aho and Gary N. Horlick, pp. 49–55. Toronto: Canadian-American Committee, January 1987

—, and Kathleen Chagnon. "Dealing with U.S. Trade Laws: Before, During and After." In *Canada-U.S. Trade in Agriculture: Managing the Disputes*, pp. 6–15. Guelph: University of Guelph and Ontario Ministry of Agriculture and Food, October 1987, AEB/87/6

Hudec, Robert E. "Dispute Settlement in Agricultural Trade Matters: The Lessons of the GATT Experience." In *Canadian-U.S. Agricultural Trade Challenges: Developing Common Approaches*, eds. Kristen Allen and Katie Macmillan, pp. 145–53. Washington, D.C.: Resources for the Future, 1988

Hudson, S. C. *Future Market Outlets for Canadian Wheat and Other Grains*. Ottawa: Economic Council of Canada, Queen's Printer, 1970

Hufbrauer, Gary Clyde. "Subsidy Issues after the Tokyo Round." In *Trade Policy in the 1980s*, ed. William R. Cline, pp. 327–61. Washington, D.C.: Institute for International Economics, 1983

Institute for International Economics and the Institute for Research on Public Policy. *Reforming World Agricultural Trade*. Washington, D.C.: Institute for International Economics, May 1988

Jacobson, Harold K. *Networks of Interdependence*. New York: Knopf, 1979

Johnson, D. Gale. *The Soviet Impact on World Grain Trade*. Washington, D.C.: British-North American Committee, 1977

—, and John Schnittker, eds. *U.S. Agriculture in a World Context: Policies and Approaches for the Next Decade*. New York: Praeger, 1974

Johnson, Harry G., Paul Wonnacott, and Hirofumi Shibata. *Harmonization of National Economic Policies under Free Trade*. Toronto: University of Toronto Press for the Private Planning Association of Canada, 1968

Kaufman, Burton I. *Trade and Aid: Eisenhower's Foreign Economic Policy, 1953-1961*. Baltimore: Johns Hopkins University Press, 1982

Keohane, Robert O., and Joseph Nye, Jr. "Introduction: The Complex Politics of Canadian-American Interdependence." In *Canada and the United States— Transnational and Transgovernmental Relations*, eds. Annette Baker Fox, Alfred O. Hero, Jr., and Joseph S. Nye, Jr., pp. 3–15. New York: Columbia University Press, 1976

—. *Power and Interdependence: World Politics in Transition*. Boston: Little, Brown, 1977

Kirton, John J. "America's Hegemonic Decline and the Reagan Revival." In *Southern Exposure: Canadian Perspectives on the United States*, eds. D. H. Flaherty and W. R. McKercher, pp. 42–61. Toronto: McGraw-Hill Ryerson, 1986

Knutson, Ronald D., J. B. Penn, and William T. Boehm. *Agricultural and Food Policy*. Englewood Cliffs, N.J.: Prentice-Hall, 1983

Kock, Karin. *International Trade Policy and the GATT, 1947-1967*. Stockholm: Almqvist and Wiksell, 1969

Kramer, John. "Agriculture's Role in Government Decisions." In *Consensus and Conflict in U.S. Agriculture—Perceptions from the National Farm Summit*, eds. Bruce L. Gardner and James W. Richardson, pp. 204-41. Texas: Texas A&M University Press, 1979

Krasner, Stephen D., ed., *International Regimes*, special issue of *International Organization* 36-2. Spring 1982

Lambrinidis, John S., *The Structure, Function, and Law of a Free Trade Area: The European Free Trade Association*. New York: Praeger, 1965

Lazar, Fred. *The New Protectionism: Non-Tariff Barriers and Their Effects on Canada*. Toronto: Lorimer, 1981

Lea, Sperry. *A Canada-U.S. Free Trade Arrangement*. Washington, D.C.: Canadian-American Committee, October 1963

Lowenfeld, Andreas F. "What GATT Says (or Does Not Say)." In *Bilateralism, Multilateralism and Canada in U.S. Trade Policy*, ed. William Diebold, Jr., pp. 55-68. Cambridge, MA.: Ballinger, 1988

Lyon, Peyton V. *Canada in World Affairs, 1961-1963*. Toronto: Oxford University Press, 1968

McCalla, Alex F., and Timothy E. Josling, eds. *Imperfect Markets in Agricultural Trade*. Montclair, NJ: Allanheld, Osmun, 1981

MacDonald, Hon. Donald S. "The Need for Bilateral and Multilateral Agreements Concerning Agriculture." In *Canada-U.S. Trade in Agriculture: Managing the Disputes*, pp. 1-5. Guelph: University of Guelph and Ontario Ministry of Agriculture and Food, October 1987, AEB/87/6

McKinsey, Lauren, and Kim Richard Nossal, eds. *America's Alliances and Canadian-American Relations*. Toronto: Summerhill, 1988

McMillan, Carl H. *Canada's Postwar Economic Relations with the USSR: An Appraisal*. Ottawa: Carleton University, Institute of Soviet and East European Studies, 1980

Maghroori, Ray, and Bennett Ramberg, eds. *Globalism versus Realism: International Relations' Third Debate*. Boulder, CO: Westview, 1982

Magil, Norman. "The Role of Two Price Systems in Canada." In *Policy Review and Outlook 1975: Restructuring the Incentive System*, ed. Judith Maxwell, pp. 103-33. Toronto: C. D. Howe Research Institute, 1975

Mahant, Edelgard E., and Graeme S. Mount. *An Introduction to Canadian-American Relations*. Toronto: Methuen, 1984

Martin, Lawrence. *The Presidents and the Prime Ministers*. Toronto: Double-day, 1982

Matthews, Robert O., Arthur G. Rubinoff, and Janice Gross Stein, eds. *International Conflict and Conflict Management*. Scarborough: Prentice-Hall, 1984

Mayer, Leo V. "A Briefing by the U.S. Agricultural Negotiator." In *U.S.-Canadian Agricultural Trade Challenges: Developing Common Approaches*, eds. Kristen Allen and Katie Macmillan, pp. 15–20. Washington, D.C.: Resources for the Future, 1988

—. "U.S.-Canadian Negotiations and the GATT Round: U.S. Perspectives." In *Canada-U.S. Trade in Agriculture: Managing the Disputes*, pp. 36–41. Guelph: University of Guelph and Ontario Ministry of Agriculture and Food, October 1987, AEB/87/6

Mehr, Barry D. "Canada-U.S. Agricultural Trade: Market Realities and Opportunities." In *U.S.-Canadian Agricultural Trade Challenges: Developing Common Approaches*, eds. Kristen Allen and Katie Macmillan, pp. 75–79. Washington, D.C.: Resources for the Future, 1988

Menzie, Elmer L., and Robert G. Crouch. *Political Interests in Agricultural Export Surplus Disposal through Public Law 480*. Tucson: University of Arizona Agriculture Experiment Station, Technical Bulletin 161, September 1964

Mikesell, Raymond F. *Agriculture Surpluses and Export Policy*. Washington, D.C.: American Enterprise Association, February 1958

Miller, Geoff. *The Political Economy of International Agricultural Policy Reform*. Canberra: Australian Government Publishing Service, 1987

Miner, William E., and Dale E. Hathaway. *World Agricultural Trade: Building a Consensus*. Halifax: Institute for Research on Public Policy and Institute of International Economics, 1988

Moore, Lynden. *The Growth and Structure of International Trade since the Second World War*. Sussex: Wheatsheaf, 1985

Morgan, Dan. *The Merchants of Grain*. New York: Viking, 1979

Morici, Peter. *The Global Competitive Struggle: Challenges to the United States and Canada*. Toronto: Canadian-American Committee, C. D. Howe Institute, 1984

Molot, Maureen Appel. "Canada's Relations with China since 1968." In *Foremost Nation*, eds. Norman Hillmer and Garth Stevenson, pp. 230–67. Toronto: McClelland and Stewart, 1977

A North American Common Market. Iowa State University Center for Agricultural and Economic Development. Ames: Iowa State University Press, 1969

The North American Political Economy. Special issue of *International Journal* 42 (Winter 1986–87)

Paarlberg, Don. *Farm and Food Policy—Issues of the 1980s*. Lincoln: University of Nebraska Press, 1980

Paarlberg, Robert L. *Fixing Farm Trade*. Cambridge, MA: Ballinger, 1988

Pestieau, Caroline. *A Balance of Payments Handbook*. Montreal: C. D. Howe Research Institute, 1974

Peterson, Trudy Huskamp. *Agricultural Exports, Farm Income, and the Eisenhower Administration*. Lincoln: University of Nebraska Press, 1979

Prentice, Barry E., and Elmer L. Menzie. "Formal and Informal Nontariff Barriers to Agricultural Trade between the United States and Canada." In *U.S.-Canadian Agricultural Trade Challenges: Developing Common Approaches*, eds. Kristen Allen and Katie Macmillan, pp. 123–28. Washington, D.C.: Resources for the Future, 1988

Puyana, Alicia. "La Idea del Mercado Común de América del Norte y las Implicaciones para México." In *México-Estados Unidos 1982*, compilador, Lorenzo Meyer, pp. 131–64. México, D.F.: El Colegio de México, 1982

Robinson, Bob H., Mary Anne Normile, Carol A. Goodloe, and Robert M. House. "U.S.-Canadian Trade Liberalization: Key Issues." In *U.S.-Canadian Agricultural Trade Challenges: Developing Common Approaches*, eds. Kristen Allen and Katie Macmillan, pp. 65–74. Washington, D.C.: Resources for the Future, 1988

Rosecrance, Richard, Alan Alexandroff, Wallace Koehler, John Kroll, Shlomit Lacquer, and John Stocker. "Whither Interdependence?" In *Globalism versus Realism*, eds. Ray Maghroori and Bennett Ramberg, pp. 125–69. Boulder: Westview, 1982

Rostow, Walt W. *The World Economy—History and Prospect*. Austin: University of Texas Press, 1978

Schmitz, Andrew. "Canada's Agricultural Trade and Growth Potential." In *Transforming Western Canada's Food Industry in the 80s and 90s*, ed. Barry Sadler, pp. 75–101. Banff: Banff Centre School of Management, 1984

—. "Summing Up: The Canadian Perspective." In *U.S.-Canadian Agricultural Trade Challenges: Developing Common Approaches*, eds. Kristen Allen and Katie Macmillan, pp. 193–95. Washington, D.C.: Resources for the Future, 1988

—, Alex F. McCalla, Donald O. Mitchell, and Colin Carter. *Grain Export Cartels*. Cambridge, MA: Ballinger, 1981

Shaffner, Richard, Frank J. Quinn, and John E. Carroll. "Other Replenishable Resources." In *Natural Resources in U.S.-Canadian Relations*, Vol. 2, eds. Carl E. Beigie and Alfred O. Hero, Jr., pp. 541–73. Boulder, CO: Westview, 1980

Sharp, Mitchell. *Canada-U.S. Relations: Options for the Future*. Special issue of *International Perspectives* (Autumn 1972)

Shefrin, Frank. "World Agricultural Production and Trade." In *Conference on International Trade and Canadian Agriculture*, pp. 33–75. Sponsored by Economic Council of Canada and Agricultural Economic Research Council of Canada. Ottawa: Queen's Printer, 1966

Skogstad, Grace. *The Politics of Agricultural Policy-Making in Canada*. Toronto: University of Toronto Press, 1987

Smith, Murray G. "Negotiating Trade Laws: Possible Approaches." In *Bridging the Gap: Trade Laws in the Canadian-U.S. Negotiations*, by Murray G. Smith, with C. Michael Aho and Gary N. Horlick, pp. 1–39. Toronto: Canadian-American Committee, January 1987

Snyder, Glenn H. *Stockpiling Strategic Materials: Politics and National Defense*. San Francisco: Chandler, 1966

Spero, Joan Edelman. *The Politics of International Economic Relations*. 3rd ed. New York: St. Martin's, 1985

Spicer, Keith. *A Samaritan State?* Toronto: University of Toronto Press, 1966

Stanley, Robert G. *Food for Peace: Hope and Reality of U.S. Food Aid*. New York: Gordon and Breach, 1973

Steger, Debra P. *A Concise Guide to the Canada-United States Free Trade Agreement*. Toronto: Carswell, 1988

—. "Canadian-U.S. Agricultural Trade: A Proposal for Resolving Disputes." In *U.S.-Canadian Agricultural Trade Challenges: Developing Common Approaches*, eds. Kristen Allen and Katie Macmillan, pp. 161–67. Washington, D.C.: Resources for the Future, 1988

—. "Recent Canadian Experience with Countervailing Duties: The Case of Agriculture." In *Canada-U.S. Trade in Agriculture: Managing the Disputes*, pp. 16–25. Guelph: University of Guelph and Ontario Ministry of Agriculture and Food, October 1987, AEB/87/6

Stone, Frank. *Canada, the GATT, and the International Trading System*. Montreal: Institute for Research on Public Policy, 1984

Strange, Susan, and Roger Tooze. "States and Markets in Depression: Managing Surplus Industrial Capacity in the 1970s." In *The International Politics of Surplus Capacity*, eds. Susan Strange and Roger Tooze, pp. 3–21. London: Allen and Unwin, 1981

Swanson, Roger Frank. *Intergovernmental Perspectives on the Canada-U.S. Relationship*. New York: New York University Press, 1978

Toma, Peter A., with Frederick A. Schoenfeld. *The Politics of Food Aid: Executive-Legislative Interaction*. Tucson: University of Arizona Press, 1967

Tomlin, Brian W., and Maureen Appel Molot. "Talking Trade: Perils of the

North American Option." In *Canada Among Nations*, eds. Brian W. Tomlin and Maureen Appel Molot, pp. 3-13. Toronto: Lorimer 1987

Tracy, Michael. *Agriculture in Western Europe—Challenge and Response 1880-1980*. 2d ed. London: Granada, 1982

Trager, James. *The Great Grain Robbery*. Toronto: Ballantine, 1975

Tucker, Michael. *Canadian Foreign Policy: Contemporary Issues and Themes*. Toronto: McGraw-Hill Ryerson, 1980

Tweeten, Luther G. "Agricultural Policy: A Review of Legislation, Programs, and Policy." In *Food and Agricultural Policy*, American Enterprise Institute for Public Policy Research, pp. 29-58. Washington, D.C.: AEI, 1977

Uren, Philip E., ed. *East-West Trade: A Symposium*. Toronto: Canadian Institute of International Affairs, 1966

Veeman, Terry, and Michele Veeman. *The Future of Grain: Canada's Prospects for Grains, Oilseeds and Related Industries*. Canadian Institute for Economic Policy Series. Toronto: Lorimer, 1984

Verzariu, Pompiliu. *Countertrade, Barter, and Offsets*. New York: McGraw-Hill, 1985

Viotti, Paul R., and Mark V. Kauppi. *International Relations Theory*. New York: Macmillan, 1987

Wallerstein, Mitchel B. *Food for War—Food for Peace*. Cambridge, MA: MIT Press, 1980

Waltz, Kenneth N. *Theory of International Politics*. Reading, MA: Addison-Wesley, 1979

Warley, T. K. *Agriculture in an Interdependent World: U.S. and Canadian Perspectives*. Washington, D.C.: Canadian-American Committee, C. D. Howe Institute, 1977

—. "Canadian Agriculture in a Global Context: An Overview." In *Canadian Agriculture in a Global Context: Opportunities and Obligations*, eds. Irene Sage Knell and John R. English, pp. 17-31. Waterloo: University of Waterloo Press, 1986

—. "Linkages between Bilateral and Multilateral Negotiations in Agriculture." In *U.S.-Canadian Agricultural Trade Challenges: Developing Common Approaches*, eds. Kristen Allen and Katie Macmillan, pp. 169-78. Washington, D.C.: Resources for the Future, 1988

—. "Western Trade in Agriculture Products." In *International Economic Relations of the Western World 1959-1971*, Vol. 1, *Politics and Trade*, ed. Andrew Shonfield, pp. 287-402. London: Oxford University Press, 1976

Webb, Michael C., and Zacher, Mark W. "Canadian Export Trade in a Changing International Environment." In *Canada and the International Political/Economic Environment*, Royal Commission on the Economic Union and Development Prospects for Canada, Vol. 28, research co-ordinators Denis Stairs and Gilbert R. Winham, pp. 85–150. Toronto: University of Toronto Press, 1985

Weintraub, Sidney, ed. *Economic Coercion and U.S. Foreign Policy*. Boulder: Westview, 1982

Whalley, John. "Canada-United States Relations and the Global Trading System." In *Southern Exposure: Canadian Perspectives on the United States*, eds. D. H. Flaherty and W. R. McKercher, pp. 83–94. Toronto: McGraw-Hill Ryerson, 1986

Wilkinson, Bruce W., and M. Shabany Ghazvini. "Agriculture in a Free Trade Agreement." In *Canada Among Nations—1985*, eds. Maureen Appel Molot and Brian Tomlin, pp. 196–214. Toronto: Lorimer, 1986

Willoughby, William. *The Joint Organizations of Canada and the United States*. Toronto: University of Toronto Press, 1979

Wilson, Charles F. *C. D. Howe: An Optimist's Response to a Surfeit of Grain*. Ottawa: Grains Group, October 1980

—. *Grain Marketing in Canada*. Winnipeg: Canadian International Grains Institute, 1979

Winberg, Alan R. *Raw Material Producer Associations and Canadian Policy*. Issue of *Behind the Headlines* 34-4 (1976)

Winham, Gilbert R. *International Trade and the Tokyo Round Negotiation*. Princeton: Princeton University Press, 1986

Wonnacott, Paul. *The United States and Canada: The Quest for Free Trade*. Policy Analyses in International Economics Series 16. Washington, D.C.: Institute for International Economics, 1987

Wyse, Peter. *Canadian Foreign Aid in the 1970's: An Organizational Audit*. Monograph No. 16. Montreal: Centre for Developing Studies, McGill University, 1983

Young, John H. *Canadian Commercial Policy*. Ottawa: Royal Commission on Canada's Economic Prospects, November 1957

GOVERNMENT DOCUMENTS

International

Allen, G. R., and R. G. Smethurst. *The Impact of Food Aid on Donor and Other Food-Exporting Countries*. Rome: FAO, 1965

Commonwealth Secretariat. *Grain Crops: A Review*. London: HMSO, 1969

General Agreement on Tariffs and Trade. Contracting Parties, 9th Session.

"Summary Record of the 44th Meeting." Geneva, SR. 9/44, 15 March 1955, p. 10.

—. Information Service, European Office of the United Nations, Geneva, 12th Session of the Contracting Parties. "Disposal of Surplus Agricultural Products: Discussion in Plenary Session." Press Release GATT/378, 25 November 1957

—. *International Trade.* Geneva: GATT, selected years

—. *Text of the General Agreement.* Geneva: GATT, July 1986

—. Uruguay Round. "Proposal by Canada Regarding the Multinational Trade Negotiations in Agriculture." MTN.GNG/NG5/W/19, 20 October 1987

—. Uruguay Round Table Negotiations Committee. "Chairman's Texts on Agriculture, Trade-Related Aspects of Intellectual Property Rights, Textiles and Clothing and Safeguards." Agreed in Geneva, 8 April 1989

International Monetary Fund. *Direction of Trade Statistics Yearbooks.* Washington, D.C.: IMF

—. *International Financial Statistics.* Washington, D.C.: IMF, 1987, 1988

International Wheat Council. *Review of the World Grain Situation.* London: International Wheat Council, 1966–70

—. *Review of the World Wheat Situation.* London: International Wheat Council, 1960–83

Organization for Economic Co-operation and Development. *Agricultural Policy in Canada.* Paris: OECD, 1973

—. *Development Cooperation, 1981 Review.* Paris: OECD, 1981

—. "Gentleman's Agreement on Exports of Whole Milk Powder—Revised Understanding." Paris: OECD, 31 August 1973

—. *Recent Developments in Canadian Agricultural Policy.* Paris: OECD, 1978

—. *Recent Developments in United States Agricultural Policies.* Paris: OECD, 1976

—. *Review of Agriculture Policies in OECD Member Countries, 1974-1976.* Paris: OECD, 1977

—. Joint Working Papers of the Agriculture and the Trade Committee. "The United States Agricultural Trade Food Act of 1978." Paris: OECD. AGR/TC/WP(79)2, 14 August 1979

United Nations. Food and Agriculture Organization. "Changing Attitudes toward Agricultural Surpluses." CCP/CSD/63/27, 12 April 1963

—. "CSD: Adaptation to Changing Conditions." CCP/CSD/74/102, 31 July 1974

—. "CSD Report on Tied Sales." CCP 69/13/3, 17 July 1969

—. "Second CSD Report on Tied Sales." CCP 73/19, September 1973

—. *FAO Principles of Surplus Disposal and Consultative Obligations of Member Nations.* 2d ed. Rome: FAO, 1980
—. *Interim Report on Work of "Grey Area" Panel.* Approved by CSD for Submission to 38th Sess. of FAO Committee on Commodity Problems, CCP 65/7 Suppl. 1, 20 April 1965
—. "Reports of the Consultative Sub-Committee on Surplus Disposal to the Committee on Commodity Problems." Rome: FAO. Various issues, 1954–85
—. Committee on Commodity Problems. "Report of the Ad Hoc Working Group on Public Law 480, Title IV, Government-to-Private Trade Agreements." 41st Session. Rome: CCP 67/18/2, 25 January 1967

United States

"Ad Hoc Meetings of the Canada-United States Interparliamentary Group to Discuss International Wheat Marketing, 26 July 1980 and 24 October 1981." Report by the U.S. Delegation Pursuant to Public Law 42, 86th Congress, January 1981 and March 1982. Washington, D.C.: Government Printing Office, 1981, 1982
Epstein, Susan B. *Agriculture in the U.S.-Canadian Free Trade Agreement.* Washington, D.C.: Congressional Research Service Report for Congress, 87–985 ENR, 22 December 1987
Gibbings, Charles W. "A Canadian Looks at Some Wheat Questions." In *Requested Papers*, Vol. 8. Washington, D.C.: National Commission on Food and Fiber, August 1967
Houck, James P. *The Tokyo/Geneva Round: Its Relation to U.S. Agriculture—2.* Prepared for the Subcommittee on International Trade, Committee on Finance, U.S. Senate, June 1979
Menzie, Elmer L., and Barry E. Prentice. *Barriers to Trade in Agricultural Products between Canada and the United States.* Washington, D.C.: USDA, Economic Research Service, April 1983
Normile, Mary Anne, and Carol A. Goodloe. *U.S.-Canadian Agricultural Trade Issues: Implications for the Bilateral Trade Agreement.* Washington, D.C.: USDA, Economic Research Service, Agriculture and Trade Analysis Division, March 1988
President's Export Council. *The Export Imperative*, Vol. 2. Report to the President. Washington, D.C.: Department of Commerce, December 1980
Public Law 99–198. 99th Cong. *Food Security Act of 1985.* 23 December 1985
Sabatini, Omero. *Canada's Export Market Development for Agricultural Products.* Washington, D.C.: USDA, Economic Research Institute, Foreign Agricultural Economic Report 107, May 1975

Bibliography

"Twenty-Ninth Meeting of the Canada-United States Interparliamentary Group, 5–9 May 1988." Report by the Chairman of the House of Representatives Delegation Pursuant to Public Law 42, 86th Congress, June 1988. Washington, D.C.: Government Printing Office, 1988

United States. *Federal Register*. Various issues

U.S. Congress. Congressional Budget Office. *Public Policy and Changing Structure of American Agriculture*. Washington, D.C.: Superintendent of Documents, September 1978

—. *Congressional Record*. 1978 and 1983

—. Hearing before the Subcommittee on Monetary and Fiscal Policy of the Joint Economic Committee. *The Canadian Agricultural Import Problem*. 99th Cong., 2d sess., 2 July 1986

—. House. Committee on International Relations. *Agricultural Exports and U.S. Foreign Economic Policy: Hearing before the Committee on International Relations*. 95th Cong., 2d sess., 18 April-9 August 1978

—. House. Hearings before the Committee on Agriculture. *United States-Canadian Free Trade Agreement*. 100th Cong., 2d sess., 25 February 1988

—. House. Hearings before a Subcommittee of the Committee on Government Operations. *U.S. Agricultural Exports: Does Administration Effort Match Potential?* 100th Cong., 1st sess., 5, 10, 18, 24 February, 18, 25 March, 19, 20 May 1987

—. House. Hearings before the Subcommittee on Inter-American Affairs of the Committee on Foreign Affairs. *Update: United States-Canadian/Mexican Relations*. 96th Cong., 2d sess., 17 and 26 June 1980

—. House. Hearings before the Subcommittee on Trade of the Committee on Ways and Means. *United States-Canada Free Trade Agreement*. 100th Cong., 2d sess., 9, 26, 29 February, 1, 11, 25 March 1988

— Senate. Committee on Foreign Relations. *Treaty Document 97-9—Two Protocols for the Extension of the International Wheat Agreement*. 97th Cong., 1st sess., 24 November 1981

—. Senate. Comptroller General. Report to Chairman, Subcommittee on Preparedness, Committee on Armed Services. *Conditions That Limit Using Barter and Exchange to Acquire National Defense Stockpile Materials*, appendix 2, 19 October 1983

—. Senate. *Data and Material Related to the United States-Canada Free Trade Negotiations, Written Comments Received by the Committee on Finance*, September 1987

—. Senate. Hearing before the Subcommittee on International Finance of the Committee on Banking, Housing, and Urban Affairs. *Export Policy*. 95th Cong., 2d sess., 30 March 1978

—. Senate. Hearings before the Subcommittee on International Trade of the Committee on Finance. *North American Economic Interdependence*. 96th Cong., 1st sess., 6 June and 1 October 1979

—. *U.S.S.R. and Grain: A Staff Report Prepared for the Use of the Subcommittee on Multinational Corporations of the Committee on Foreign Relations. United States Senate*. Prepared by Richard Gilmore. Washington, D.C.: Government Printing Office, 1976

U.S. Department of Agriculture. "Competitive Position of U.S. Farm Products Abroad, 1956." Washington, D.C., March 1956, pp. 99–100

—. Economic Research Service. *Agricultural Policies in the Western Hemisphere*. Washington, D.C.: Foreign Agricultural Economic Report no. 36, October 1967

—. Economic Research Service. *Embargoes, Surplus Disposal, and U.S. Agriculture*. Washington, D.C.: Agricultural Economic Report no. 564, December 1986

—. Economic Research Service. *Foreign Agricultural Trade of the United States (FATUS)*. "U.S.-Canadian Agricultural Trade Balance Reverses Direction." Washington, D.C.: March-April 1986, pp. 139–42

—. Economic Research Service. *FATUS* and *FATUS, Supplement*. Various issues

—. Foreign Agricultural Service. "Canadian Agriculture—Competitive Position." Washington, D.C.: Foreign Agricultural Report no. 110, July 1958, pp. 56–73

—. Office of the General Sales Manager. Statement of Francis A. Woodling, deputy assistant sales manager, before the House Committee on Armed Services, Subcommittee on Seapower and Strategic and Critical Materials. Washington, D.C.: n.d.

—. Press releases, 1961–63

U.S. Department of State. *Foreign Relations of the United States, 1952-1954*. Washington, D.C., 1983

—. *The Trade Debate*. Department of State Publication 8943, Office of Public Communication, Bureau of Public Affairs. Washington, D.C.: U.S. Government Printing Office, May 1978

—. "U.S. Soviet Grain Sales Agreement." *U.S. Department of State Bulletin* 82-2067, October 1982, pp. 40–42

U.S. General Accounting Office. *Agricultural Competitiveness—An Overview of the Challenge to Enhance Exports*. Washington, D.C.: GAO/RCED-87-100, May 1987

—. *Agricultural Trade Negotiations—Initial Phase of the Uruguay Round*. Washington, D.C.: GAO/NSIAD-88-144BR, May 1988

—. *Agriculture's Implementation of GAO's Wheat Export Subsidy Recommendations and Related Matters*. Washington, D.C.: ID-76-39, March 1976

—. *Alternative Practices for International Grain Trade*. Washington, D.C.: GAO/NSIAD-87-90BR, March 1987

—. *Changing Character and Structure of American Agriculture: An Overview*. Washington, D.C.: CED-78-178, 26 September 1978

—. *Commodity Credit Corporation's Export Credit Guarantee Programs*. Washington, D.C.: GAO/NSIAD-88-194, June 1988

—. *Conditions that Limit Using Barter and Exchange to Acquire National Defense Stockpile Materials*. Washington, D.C.: GAO/RCED-84-24, 19 October 1983

—. *Current Issues in U.S. Participation in the Multilateral Trading System*. Washington, D.C.: GAO/NSIAD-85-118, 23 September 1985

—. *The Export Enhancement Program, U.S. Foreign Agricultural Market Development Programs, Commodity Credit Corporation Export Credit Guarantee Programs, and Long-Term Bilateral Grain Agreements and Countertrade*. Statement of Allan I. Mendelowitz before the Subcommittee on Department Operations, Research and Foreign Agriculture, House Committee on Agriculture, Washington, D.C.: 30 September 1986

—. *Implementation of the Agricultural Export Enhancement Program*. Washington, D.C.: GAO/NSIAD-87-74-BR, March 1987

—. *International Trade Commission's Agricultural Unfair Trade Investigations*. Washington, D.C.: NSIAD-88-58BR, December 1987

—. *Lessons to Be Learned from Offsetting the Impact of the Soviet Grain Sales Suspension*. Washington, D.C.: CED-81-110, 27 July 1981

—. *Long-Term Bilateral Grain Agreements and Grain Countertrade*. Washington, D.C.: GAO/NSIAD-89-91, April 1989

—. *Long-Term Bilateral Grain Agreements with the Soviet Union and China*. Washington, D.C.: GAO/NSIAD-89-63, March 1989

—. *Stronger Emphasis on Market Development Needed in Agriculture's Export Credit Sales Program*. Washington, D.C.: ID-80-01, 26 October 1979

—. *U.S. Food/Agriculture in a Volatile World Economy*. Washington, D.C.: GAO/RCED-86-3BR, November 1985

—. *Uses and Limitations of Countertrade*. Statement of Allen I. Mendelowitz before the Subcommittee on International Economic Policy and Trade, and Arms Control, International Security and Science Committee on Foreign Affairs, House of Representatives. Washington, D.C.: GAO-T-NSIAD-87, 39, 1 July 1987

United States-Canada Free Trade Agreement Implementation Act, The. *Statement of Administrative Action*. Draft, 17 June 1988

Canada

Canada. Agriculture Canada, International Trade Policy Division. *Canada's Trade in Agricultural Products*. Ottawa: Minister of Supply and Services. 1967–87
—. Marketing Service, Economics Division. *Canada Trade in Agricultural Products with the United Kingdom, the United States and all Countries*. Ottawa: Canada Department of Agriculture, 1955–66
—. News, 1977–80
—. *Orientation of Canadian Agriculture: A Task Force Report*. Ottawa: Canada Department of Agriculture, Vols 1–4, 1977
Canada. Agriculture Canada and Industry, Trade and Commerce. *Agricultural and Food Products Market Development Assistance Program*. Ottawa: Department of Agriculture, Information Services, 1977
Canada. *Conference on International Trade and Canadian Agriculture*. Sponsored by Economic Council of Canada and the Agriculture Economic Research Council of Canada. Banff, Alberta, 10–12 January 1966. Ottawa: Queen's Printer, 1966
Canada. Department of External Affairs. *A Review of Canadian Trade Policy*. Ottawa: Minister of Supply and Services, 1983
—. *The Canada-U.S. Free Trade Agreement*. Ottawa: External Affairs, 10 December 1987
—. *The Canada-U.S. Free Trade Agreement Synopsis*. Ottawa: External Affairs, 10 December 1987
Canada. Economic Council of Canada. *Looking Outward: A New Trade Strategy for Canada—1975*. Ottawa: Minister of Supply and Services, 1976
Canada. Government of Canada. *Export Financing: Consultative Paper*. Ottawa: Ministry of Supply and Services, January 1985
—. News Releases. 1983–84
Canada. House of Commons. *Debates*. 1976 and 1981
—. *Minutes of Proceedings and Evidence of the Standing Committee on Agriculture*. 1977
—. *Minutes of Proceedings and Evidence of the Standing Committee on External Affairs and International Trade*. October to December 1987
Canada. *The Report of the Canadian Grain Marketing Review Committee*. Submitted to the Canadian Wheat Board. Winnipeg, 12 January 1971

Canada. Report of the Federal Task Force on Agriculture. *Canadian Agriculture in the Seventies*. Ottawa: December 1969

Canada. Report of the Special Joint Committee of the Senate and House of Commons on Canada's International Relations. *Independence and Internationalism*. Ottawa: 1986

Canada. Senate. *Debates*. 1978

—. Standing Committee on Agriculture. *Recognizing the Realities: A Beef Import Policy for Canada*. Ottawa: Queen's Printer for Canada, October 1977

—. Standing Committee on Foreign Affairs. *Canada-U.S. Relations*. Vol. 1, *The Institutional Framework for the Relationship*. Ottawa: Queen's Printer, December 1975

—. Standing Committee on Foreign Affairs. *Canada-U.S. Relations*. Vol. 2, *Canada's Trade Relations with the United States*. Ottawa: Queen's Printer for Canada, 1978

—. Standing Committee on Foreign Affairs. *Canada-U.S. Relations*. Vol. 3, *Canada's Trade Relations with the United States*. Ottawa: Minister of Supply and Services, 1982

Canada Treaty Series 1971, no. 26. "Wheat Trade and Food Aid Conventions 1971." n.p.

Canadian Wheat Board. *Annual Reports*. Winnipeg: The Canadian Wheat Board, 1964–87

Eastman, H. C. "International Trade Policy for Agricultural Products." *Federal Task Force on Agriculture*. Project no. 12. Ottawa, n.d.

Hawkins, M. H., R. K. Bennett, and A. M. Boswell. *North American Hog/Pork Study*. A Summary Report Prepared by Canada Department of Agriculture, Economics Branch. Ottawa: n.d.

Royal Commission on the Economic Union and Development Prospects for Canada. *Report*. Vol. 1. Ottawa: Minister of Supply and Services, 1985

PERIODICALS

"Agriculture in the U.S." *Barclay's Bank Review* 43 (November 1968): 71–75

Alaouze, Chris M., A. S. Watson, and N. H. Sturgess. "Oligopoly Pricing in the World Wheat Market." *American Journal of Agricultural Economics* 60 (May 1978): 173–85

Ali, Liaquat. "The World Wheat Market and International Agreements." *Journal of World Trade Law* 16–1 (January-February 1982): 59–80

Amstutz, Daniel G. "International Impact of U.S. Domestic Farm Policy," *American Journal of Agricultural Economics* 66 (December 1984): 728–34

Anderson, W. J. "North American Food and Agricultural Policies: Conflict and

Cooperation—Trade Interdependencies." *American Journal of Agricultural Economics* 60 (1970): 797–99

Baldwin, David A. "Interdependence and Power: A Conceptual Analysis." *International Organization* 34-4 (Autumn 1980): 471-506

Bergesen, Helge Ole. "A New Food Regime: Necessary but Impossible." *International Organization* 34-2 (Spring 1980): 285-305

Blandford, David, and Nancy E. Schwartz. "Is the Variability of World Wheat Prices Increasing?" *Food Policy* (November 1980): 305-12

Brandow, G. E. "Conflicts and Consistencies in the Agricultural Policies of the United States and Canada." *American Journal of Agricultural Economics* (December 1973): 778-84

Britnell, G. E. "The Implications of United States Policy for the Canadian Wheat Economy." *Canadian Journal of Economics and Political Science* 22-1 (February 1956): 1-16

Burns, T. M. "The Trade Jungle of Export Credits." *International Perspectives* (January/February 1983): 22-24

Butz, Earl. "U.S. Food Policy in a Changing World." *Economic Planning* 11 (November-December 1975): 3-5

Caldwell, C. D. "The American Agriculture Movement." *Agriculture Abroad* 33-2 (April 1978): 49-53

—. "United States Agricultural Legislation in the 95th Congress." *Agriculture Abroad* 34 (February 1979): 38-47

"The Canadian Beef Industry." *Agriculture Abroad* 31-4 (August 1976): 31-34

"Canadian—not U.S.—Banks Will Handle Financing of Wheat Deal with Soviets." *Business Week* (28 September 1963): 128

Carmichael, J. S. "Canadian Wheat Flour Situation." *Canadian Farm Economics* 12 (February 1977): 14-19

Carter, Colin A. "International Trade Opportunities for Canadian Agriculture." *Canadian Journal of Agricultural Economics and Farm Management* 32 (July 1985): 1-17

—, and Andrew Schmitz. "Import Tariffs and Price Formation in the World Wheat Market." *American Journal of Agricultural Economics* 61 (August 1979): 517-22

Cathie, John. "U.S. and EEC Agricultural Trade Policies." *Food Policy* (February 1985): 14-28

Chen, Tong P. "Legal Aspects of Canadian Trade with the People's Republic of China." *Law and Contemporary Problems* 38-2 (Summer-Autumn 1973): 201-29

Cohn, Theodore. "Canada and the European Economic Community's Common

Agricultural Policy: The Issue of Trade in Cheese." *Journal of European Integration* (January 1978): 125-42

—. "Canadian Aid and Trade in Skim Milk Powder: Some Recent Issues." *Canadian Public Policy* 4 (Spring 1978): 213-26

—. "Food Surpluses and Canadian Food Aid." *Canadian Public Policy* 3 (Spring 1977): 141-54

—. "The 1978-9 Negotiations for an International Wheat Agreement: An Opportunity Lost?" *International Journal* 35-1 (Winter 1979-80): 132-49

—, and Inge Bailey. "Newspaper Coverage of Canadian-U.S. Economic Relations: 1972 and 1982." *Canadian Journal of Communication* 13-3 and 13-4 (Summer 1988): 1-15

"Collapse of the Grain Talks: The Reasons Why." *International Development Review* 21-2 (1979): 20-22

Cooper, Andrew. "Subnational Activity and Foreign Economic Policy-Making in Canada and the U.S.: Perspectives on Agriculture." *International Journal* 41-3 (Summer 1986): 655-73

Corcoran, James I. W. "The Trading with the Enemy Act and the Controlled Canadian Corporation." *McGill Law Journal* 14-2 (1968): 174-208

—. "The Trading with the Enemy Act: The Impact of the Amended Foreign Assets Control Regulations on Canadian Corporations Owned by Americans." *McGill Law Journal* 16-3 (1970): 460-87

Cowhey, Peter F., and Edward Long. "Testing Theories of Regime Change: Hegemonic Decline or Surplus Capacity?" *International Organization* 37 (Spring 1983): 157-88

Danielson, R. "Canadian Agricultural Trade Highlights, 1978." *Agriculture Abroad* 34-3 (June 1979): 46-51

Davenport, Charles R. "Trading Farm Products through Barter." USDA-FAS, *Foreign Agriculture* 19-12 (December 1955): 240-41

Davidson, R. "U.S. Beef and Veal Industry." *Agriculture Abroad* (December 1980): 41-53

Denny, David L., and Daniel D. Stein. "Recent Developments in Trade between the U.S. and the People's Republic of China: A Legal and Economic Perspective." *Law and Contemporary Problems* 38-2 (Summer/Autumn): 260-73

Destler, I. M. "United States Food Policy 1972-1976: Reconciling Domestic and International Objectives." *International Organization* 32-3 (Summer 1978): 617-53

"Developments in Canadian Agriculture." *Agriculture Abroad* 31-4 (August 1976): 31-34

Dobou, G. J., and M. N. Gifford. "International Trade, the GATT and Canadian Agriculture." *Canadian Farm Economics* 6-6 (February 1972): 1-5

Bibliography

"Fact File: The Blended Credit Program." *Foreign Agriculture* (March 1983): 7–8

Fan, Liang-shing. "The Economy and Foreign Trade of China." *Law and Contemporary Problems* 38-2 (Summer/Autumn 1973): 249–59

Farnsworth, Helen C. "The Problem of Multiplying Effects of Special Wheat Programs." *American Economic Review* 51-2 (May 1961): 353–70

Finlayson, Jock A., and Mark W. Zacher. "The GATT and the Regulation of Trade Barriers: Regime Dynamics and Functions." *International Organization* 35-4 (Autumn 1981): 561–602

Fitzgerald, Bruce, and Terry Monson. "Export Credit and Insurance for Export Promotion." *Finance and Development* 25 (December 1988): 53–55

"The Food and Agriculture Organization." *External Affairs* 6 (July 1954): 230–34

Fulton, C. V. "U.S. Farm Programs for Wheat and Feed Grains." *Canadian Farm Economics* 16-1 (1981): 12–23

Gifford, M. N. "A Net Importer in 1969: Canada's Agricultural Trade in Perspective." *Canadian Farm Economics* 5-4 (October 1970): 1–10

Gilson, J. Clayton. "A Canadian View of Conflicts and Consistencies in the Agricultural Policies of Canada and the United States." *American Journal of Agricultural Economics* (December 1973): 785–90

—. "The U.S.-Canadian Hog War." *Western Economic Review* 4-3 (Fall 1985): 2–14

Goldstein, Judith. "Ideas, Institutions, and American Trade Policy." *International Organization* 42-1 (Winter 1988): 179–217

Goodloe, Carol A. "U.S. Producers and the Countervailing Duty Case against Canadian Pork and Hogs." *Western Economic Review* 4-3 (Fall 1985): 15–23

Green, G. W. "The Agricultural Barter Issue in the United States." *Agriculture Abroad* 34-1 (1984): 46–52

Grennes, Thomas, and Paul R. Johnson. "Import Tariffs and Price Formation in the World Wheat Market: Comment." *American Journal of Agricultural Economics* 62-4 (November 1980): 819–22

Grzybowski, Kasimierz. "Control of U.S. Trade with China: An Overview." *Law and Contemporary Problems* 38-2 (Summer/Autumn 1973): 175–81

Halcrow, Harold G. "Discussion: Canadian and U.S. Agricultural Price Policies." *Journal of Farm Economics* 49 (1967): 1051–53

Hallett, Graham. "Trading Blocs and Canadian Agriculture." *Canadian Journal of Agricultural Economics* 2 (1963): 40–48

Hayward, T. E. "U.S. Food and Agriculture Act of 1981." *Agriculture Abroad* 37-2 (April 1982): 29–40

Hill, James T. "Changes in United States Agriculture Policy and the Implications for Canada." *Agriculture Abroad* 32 (December 1977): 29–33

—. "Current Status of United States Farm and Food Policy Legislation." *Agriculture Abroad* 32 (April 1977): 23–30

—. "United States Agriculture Policy—A General Overview." *Agriculture Abroad* 36–4 (August 1981): 28–33

—. "The U.S. Meat Import Law." *Agriculture Abroad* 32 (February 1977): 42–45

Hiscocks, G. A. "The Role of the Federal Government in Export Market Development." *Canadian Farm Economics* 8–6 (December 1973): 6–10

Hjort, Howard W. "U.S. and Canadian Food and Agricultural Policies: Goals and Objectives, Conflicts and Cooperation." *American Journal of Agricultural Economics* 60 (1978): 785–88

Holsti, Kal J. "A New International Politics? Diplomacy in Complex Interdependence." *International Organization* 32–2 (Spring 1978): 513–30

Hopkins, Raymond F., and Donald Puchala "Perspectives on the International Relations of Food." *International Organization* 32–3 (Summer 1978): 581–616

—. "The Failure of Regime Transformation: A Reply." *International Organization* 34–2 (Spring 1980): 303–5

Hudson, S. C., and Randolph Gherson. "Competition in International Trade with Particular Reference to Agricultural Commodities." *Journal of Farm Economics* 40–5 (December 1958): 1717–28

Huff, H. Bruce. "Canada's Future Role in the World Wheat Market." *Canadian Journal of Agricultural Economics* 17 (February 1969): 1–13

Insel, Barbara. "A World Awash in Grain." *Foreign Affairs* 63 (Spring 1985): 892–912

Johnson, D. Gale. "Domestic Agricultural Policy in an International Environment: Effects of Other Countries' Policies on the United States." *American Journal of Agricultural Economics* 66 (December 1984): 735–44

—. "National Agriculture Policies and Market Relations." *American Journal of Agricultural Economics* 60 (1978): 789–92

Karmen, Bradley. "Exporters Use Diverse Strategies for Marketing Wheat." *Foreign Agriculture* (May 1983): 19–20

Kostecki, M. M. "Canada's Grain Trade with the Soviet Union and China." *Canadian Journal of Agricultural Economics* 30–2 (July 1982): 223–38

Krasner, Stephen D. "Structural Causes and Regime Consequences: Regimes as Intervening Variables." *International Organization* 36–2 (Spring 1982): 185–205

Kristjanson, R. L. "Discussion: Impact of Surplus Disposal on Foreign Competitors and the International Perspective on Surplus Disposal." *Journal of Farm Economics* 42 (December 1960): 1081–83

Leyton-Brown, David. "Extraterritoriality in Canadian-American Relations." *International Journal* 36-1 (Winter 1980–81): 185–207

—. "The Multinational Enterprise and Conflict in Canadian-American Relations." *International Organization* 28-4 (Autumn 1974): 733–54

Lin, Sol, and Gail Labrosse. "Canada's Agricultural and Food Trade in the 1970s." *Canadian Farm Economics* 15-4 (August 1980): 1–8

Litvak, I. A., and C. J. Maule. "Conflict Resolution and Extraterritoriality." *Journal of Conflict Resolution* 13-3 (September 1969): 305–19

Litvak, I. A., and C. H. McMillan, "A New United States Policy on East-West Trade: Some Implications for Canada." *International Journal* 28-2 (Spring 1973): 297–314

Lohoar, J. S. "The Multilateral Trade Negotiations and Canadian Agriculture." *Canadian Farm Economics* 14-5 (October 1979): 1–8

McCalla, Alex F. "A Duopoly Model of World Wheat Pricing." *Journal of Farm Economics* 48-3 (August 1966): 711–27

—. "Implications for Canada of U.S. Farm Policies." *Journal of Farm Economics* 49 (1967): 1038–51

—. "North American Food and Agricultural Policy: Conflict and Cooperation— A General Introduction." *American Journal of Agricultural Economics* 60 (1978): 782–84

—, Andrew Schmitz, and Gary G. Storey. "Australia, Canada and the United States: Trade Partners or Competitors." *American Journal of Agricultural Economics* 61-5 (December 1979): 1022–29

McClatchy, D., and M. Cluff. "Developments in the Canadian Beef and Cattle Market during 1984." *Canadian Farm Economics* 20-1 (1986): 19–27

MacFarlane, David L. "Discussion: Canadian and U.S. Agricultural Price Policies." *Journal of Farm Economics* 49 (1967): 1053–56

McLin, Jon. "Surrogate International Organization and the Case of World Food Security, 1949–1969." *International Organization* 33-1 (Winter 1979): 35–55

Martellaro, Joseph A. "Normalization and Subsequent Sino-American Economic Relations." *Asian Profile* 13-4 (August 1985): 289–306

Menzie, E. L. "Developments in Canadian Agricultural Policy 1929–1979." *Canadian Farm Economics* 15-2 (April 1980): 15–19

Molot, Maureen Appel. "Canada-U.S. Relations: The Politics of Attraction and Distance." *Jerusalem Journal of International Relations* 6-2 (1982): 88–107

Moravcik, I. "Prospects for Soviet and East European Purchases of Canadian Wheat." *Canadian Slavonic Papers* 7 (1965): 159–72

Mortensen, Erik. "Impact and Implications of Foreign Surplus Disposal on Developed Economies and Foreign Competitors: the Competitor's Perspective." *Journal of Farm Economics* 42-5 (December 1960): 1052-62

Murray, Kenneth L. "Credit and the Communist Countries." *Foreign Agriculture* (July 1982): 17

—. "Export Credits Build Markets in Developing Countries." *Foreign Agriculture* (July 1982): 16-17

Paarlberg, Robert L. "Lessons of the Grain Embargo." *Foreign Affairs* 59-1 (Fall 1980): 144-62

Penn, J. B. "Agricultural Structural Issues and Policy Alternatives for the Late 1980s." *American Journal of Agricultural Economics* 66 (December 1984): 572-76

Puchala, Donald, and Raymond Hopkins. "International Regimes: Lessons from Inductive Analysis." *International Organization* 36-2 (Spring 1982): 245-75

Richardson, B. T. "Canada and the Wheat Agreement." *International Journal* (Autumn 1953): 274-83

Rosenau, James N. "Capabilities and Control in an Interdependent World." *International Security* 1 (Fall 1976): 32-49

Rosenfeld, Stephen S. "The Politics of Food." *Foreign Policy* 14 (Spring 1974): 17-29

Rower, Jack. "Credit Competition Intensifies in the World Markets." *Foreign Agriculture* (July 1982): 9

Russett, Bruce. "The Mysterious Case of Vanishing Hegemony: or, Is Mark Twain Really Dead?" *International Organization* 39 (Spring 1985): 207-31

Sahi, R. K., and W. J. Craddock. "Establishing the Effects of Operation LIFT on 1970 Prairie Land Utilization." *Canadian Farm Economics* 6 (December 1971): 2-6

Sanderson, Fred H. "U.S. Farm Policy in Perspective." *Food Policy* 8-1 (February 1983): 3-12

Schnittker, John A. "Action Proposal: Grain Reserves Now." *Foreign Policy* 20 (Fall 1975): 225-31

Schruben, Leonard W. "Grain Marketing Methods in the U.S.A.—The Theory, Assumptions and Approaches." *American Journal of Agricultural Economics* 55-5 (1973): 800-4

Severin, R. Keith. "How Canada Markets Wheat: Government Is in Charge." *Foreign Agriculture* (December 1983): 10-12

Shefrin, Frank. "Prospects for Canadian Agriculture in International Trade." *Agricultural Institute Review* 21 (1966): 54-58

Sorenson, Vernon L., and George E. Rossmiller. "Future Options for U.S.

Agricultural Trade Policy." *American Journal of Agricultural Economics* (December 1983): 893–900

"Soviet-Canadian Deal Stirs a Wheat Tempest." *Business Week*, 21 September 1963, p. 28

Stam, Jerome M. "The Effects of Public Law 480 on Canadian Wheat Exports." *Journal of Farm Economics* 46 (November 1964): 805–19

Stone, P. "Canadian Agricultural Trade 1976." *Agriculture Abroad* 32 (August 1977): 44–49

Strange, Susan. "The Management of Surplus Capacity: Or, How Does Theory Stand Up to Protectionism 1970s Style?" *International Organization* 33 (Summer 1979): 303–34

—. "The Persistent Myth of Lost Hegemony." *International Organization* 41 (Autumn 1987): 551–74

Tracy, T. "Credit Programs Crucial to U.S. Exports." *Foreign Agriculture* (July 1982): 4–5

Trant, G. I. "Presidential Address: 'Adjustment Problems and Policies within a Framework of Political Economy'." *American Journal of Agricultural Economics* 55–5 (1973): 888–91

—. "World Trade and Canadian Agriculture." *Agriculture Abroad* 31 (April 1976): 27–31

"U.S. Agricultural Exports under Government-Financed Programs." *Agriculture Abroad* 31 (December 1976): 40–41

U.S. Department of Agriculture. Foreign Agricultural Service. *Foreign Agriculture* 23–4 (April 1959): 5–20

"United States Export Development Programs." Excerpts from a report prepared by the USDA for the Senate Committee on Agriculture, Nutrition and Forestry. *Agriculture Abroad* 36–4 (August 1981): 33–41

"U.S. Farm Prices and Income." *Agriculture Abroad* 32–6 (December 1977): 40–42

Wallerstein, Mitchel B. "Dynamics of Food Policy Formulation in the USA." *Food Policy* 7–3 (August 1982): 229–39

—. "Foreign-Domestic Intersections in U.S. Food Policy." *Food Policy* 5–2 (May 1980): 83–96

Warley, T. K. "Issues Facing Agriculture in the GATT Negotiations." Guelph: Department of Agricultural Economics and Business, University of Guelph, n.d., pp. 3–4

West, Quentin M. "The Developing Nations and U.S. Agricultural Trade." *Foreign Agriculture* 8–14 (4 April 1970): 2–7

Whelan, Eugene. "Canada's Interest in World Agriculture." Notes for an address at the 19th Session of the FAO Conference in Rome, 16 November 1977. *Agriculture Abroad* 32-6 (December 1977): 21-25

Wilcox, Walter W. "Implications of Recent Changes in United States Farm Price Support Policies." *Journal of Farm Economics* 49 (1967): 1032-37

Wong, John. "China's Wheat Import Programme." *Food Policy* 5-2 (May 1980): 117-31

Zeman, Zybuek. "Economic Planning of Eastern Europe and the USSR: The Role of Agriculture." *Food Policy* (May 1975): 127-35

UNPUBLISHED MATERIALS

Battram, Shelly P., and Peter L. Glossop. "Dispute Resolution under a Canada/ United States Free Trade Agreement." American Bar Association National Institute on Resolution of International Commercial Disputes. Miami, 5-6 November 1987

Benjamin, Charles M., and Charles A. Powell. "Negotiating the 1988 U.S.-U.S.S.R. Long Term Agreement on Grain Purchases." Case study sponsored by the PEW Initiative in Diplomatic Training. Los Angeles: Center for International Studies, University of Southern California, n.d.

Canadian Federation of Agriculture. Submission to the Standing Senate Committee on Foreign Affairs. Examination of a Free Trade Agreement between Canada and the United States, 8 August 1988

Letter from John Datt, executive director, American Farm Bureau Federation, to the Honorable Lloyd Bentsen, U.S. Senate, 7 April 1988, p. 2

Miner, Bill. "Canada's Trade in Grains and the China Market." Paper presented at Conference, "Canadian Agriculture in a Global Context: Opportunities and Obligations." Centre on Foreign Policy and Federalism, University of Waterloo, 21-23 May 1985

National Corn Growers' Association. "Issue: U.S.-Canadian Free Trade Agreement"

National Farmers' Union (Canada). Submission to the Select Standing Committee on Bill C-130. *An Act to Implement the Free Trade Agreement between Canada and the United States of America*, 28 July 1988

Paarlberg, Don. "On Sleeping with an Elephant." J. S. McLean Memorial Lecture. University of Guelph, 13 October 1977

Press Release. Advisory Committee to the Canadian Wheat Board. "Advisory Committee Issues Statement on Major Farm Issues." 2 August 1988

Raabe, Francis Conrad. "The China Issue in Canada: Politics and Foreign Policy." Ph.D. diss., Pennsylvania State University, 1970

Saskatchewan Wheat Pool Submission to the Legislative Committee on Bill C-130, An Act to Implement the Free Trade Agreement, July 1988

Shefrin, Frank, director, International Liaison Service, Agriculture Canada. Paper presented to the Provincial Marketing Seminar on International Trade. Hespeler, Ontario, 1972

Statement by the Canadian Federation of Agriculture on Free Trade Legislation

Taplin, John H. E. "Demand in the World Wheat Market and the Export Policies of the United States, Canada and Australia." Ph.D. diss., Cornell University, 1969

U.S.-Canadian Trade Agreement. Farm Bureau Analysis and Assessment

Warley, T. K. "Canadian Agriculture in a Global Context: An Overview." Presented at Conference, "Canadian Agriculture in a Global Context: Opportunities and Obligations." Centre on Foreign Policy and Federalism, University of Waterloo, 21–23 May 1985

—, and R. R. Barichello. "Agricultural Issues in a Comprehensive Canada-USA Trade Agreement: A Canadian Perspective"

"Wheat, Feed Grains, and Oilseeds." Canadian Agriculture Congress Position Paper. A-102–4

Acronyms and Abbreviations

AAA	Agricultural Adjustment Act
AAM	American Agriculture Movement
AFBF	American Farm Bureau Federation
ASA	Agricultural Stabilization Act
BFT	Bilateral Free Trade
CAP	Common Agricultural Policy
CCC	Commodity Credit Corporation
CCP	Committee on Commodity Problems
CFA	Canadian Federation of Agriculture
CSD	Consultative Subcommittee on Surplus Disposal
CTA	Committee on Trade in Agriculture
CVD	Countervailing duty
CWB	Canadian Wheat Board
DES	Diethylstilbestrol
EC	European Community
ECC	Economic Council of Canada
ECIC	Export Credit Insurance Corporation
EDC	Export Development Corporation
EEP	Export Enhancement Program
FAC	Food Aid Convention
FAO	Food and Agriculture Organization
FAS	Foreign Agricultural Service
FIRA	Foreign Investment Review Agency
GAO	General Accounting Office
GATT	General Agreement on Tariffs and Trade
GDP	Gross Domestic Product
GNP	Gross National Product

IC	Intermediate Credit
IGA	International Grains Arrangement
ITA	International Trade Administration
ITC	International Trade Commission
ITO	International Trade Organization
IWA	International Wheat Agreement
IWC	International Wheat Council
LDC	Less-developed country
LIFT	Lower Inventory for Tomorrow
LTA	Long-term agreement
MFN	Most-favoured nation
MTM	Ministerial Trade Mandate
NAWG	National Association of Wheat Growers
NEP	National Energy Program
NFO	National Farmers' Organization
NFU	National Farmers' Union
NPPC	National Pork Producers' Council
NTB	Non-tariff barrier
OECD	Organization for Economic Co-operation and Development
OEEC	Organization for European Economic Co-operation
OPEC	Organization of Petroleum Exporting Countries
PIK	Payment in Kind
PTE	Private Trade Entity
TNC	Transnational Corporation
UGG	United Grain Growers
UMR	Usual marketing requirement
USDA	United States Department of Agriculture
VER	Voluntary export restraint
WTC	Wheat Trade Convention
WUC	Wheat Utilization Committee

Index